The Perils of Belonging

The Perils of Belonging

Autochthony, Citizenship, and Exclusion in Africa and Europe

PETER GESCHIERE

THE UNIVERSITY OF CHICAGO PRESS   CHICAGO AND LONDON

The University of Chicago Press, Chicago 60637
The University of Chicago Press, Ltd., London
© 2009 by The University of Chicago
All rights reserved. Published 2009.
Printed in the United States of America
20 19 18 17 16 15 14 13 12 11   3 4 5 6 7

ISBN-13: 978-0-226-28964-9 (cloth)
ISBN-13: 978-0-226-28965-6 (paper)
ISBN-10: 0-226-28964-8 (cloth)
ISBN-10: 0-226-28965-6 (paper)

Library of Congress Cataloging-in-Publication Data

Geschiere, Peter.
    The perils of belonging : autochthony, citizenship, and exclusion in Africa and Europe /
Peter Geschiere.
        p. cm.
    Includes bibliographical references and index.
    ISBN-13: 978-0-226-28964-9 (cloth : alk. paper)
    ISBN-13: 978-0-226-28965-6 (pbk. : alk. paper)
    ISBN-10: 0-226-28964-8 (cloth : alk. paper)
    ISBN-10: 0-226-28965-6 (pbk. : alk. paper) 1. Group identity—Cameroon.
2. Group identity—Netherlands. 3. Ethnicity—Cameroon. 4. Ethnicity—
Netherlands. 5. Cosmopolitanism—Cameroon. 6. Cosmopolitanism—
Netherlands. I. Title.
    HM753.G47   2009
    305.80096711—dc22   2008032270

♾ This paper meets the requirements of ANSI/NISO z39.48-1992
(Permanence of Paper).

Contents

Preface and Acknowledgments

One of my most inspiring commentators suggested that this book should have the title *For the Migrant*.[1] He certainly had good reasons. This book is about the surprising obsession in our globalizing world with belonging—notably in its most localizing variant, "autochthony." Therefore it is also about the migrant as the antipode of all this belonging. However, in my case that title would risk being presumptuous. I was born less than three miles from where I came to live thirty-five years ago now. So I can hardly claim to be a migrant. I may have traveled a lot, but so far I have always come back to where I seem to belong. Dedicating this book to the migrant might therefore be a bit out of place for me; belonging seems to be more my style.

Still, it is the aim of this book to show that migration is part and parcel of the order of things—anywhere, both in time and in space. Working in Africa, but also as a citizen of the Netherlands, I have become increasingly intrigued—not to say shocked—by how easily, over the last few decades, migration has been depicted as something exceptional, outside the normal order. In Cameroon, for instance, Beti and Bulu people now proudly proclaim to be *autochtones*—"born from the soil"—of the forest area in the south of the country. Yet the same Beti/Bulu may clinch arguments over to whom the forest "really" belongs with the simple statement "La forêt est à nous puisqu'on l'a conquise" (the forest is ours because we conquered it), referring to their epic immigration from the savannah southward into

the forest 150 to 200 years ago. These past migrations seem to be forgotten whenever they position themselves in contrast to others, mainly
Bamileke from the west of the country, who came later and can therefore be branded as *allogènes* or "strangers." The Dutch used to be proud
of their country as the place where people from all over contributed to
a Golden Age. Among many of my friends, genealogy has become a favorite pastime, leading often to the proud discovery of some Huguenot
ancestor who entered the country fleeing French "Papists" in the sev-
enteenth century. Despite these roots, today many Dutch identify themselves as *autochtonen*—though they seem to be at a loss to give more substance to this notion that, here again, may appear to be self-evident but in
practice is always highly elusive and slippery.

Such intriguing shifts made me decide to pursue the notion of autochthony and its appeal in very different corners of the world. Its strength is
apparently its self-evident, naturalizing appearance: being rooted in the
soil would seem to be the most primordial kind of belonging. Yet tracing
it turned out to be an adventurous journey, not only because such diverse
thinkers as Heidegger, Lévi-Strauss, and Derrida were at some time inspired by it but also because it crops up at the most unexpected moments
in time and space. Its history goes back as far as classical Athens of the
fifth century BC. In many respects this classical locus already expressed,
in a most condensed form, all the paradoxes and ambiguities that beset
this notion, in all its variable manifestations, up until today.

Clearly, claims to "belong" and therefore to have special rights to resources, both locally and at national and global levels, are not new. But it
might be worthwhile to explore why they have emerged with such force
in highly different parts of the globe at precisely this moment. Even more
challenging might be to try to understand autochthony's vanishing quality,
which may be its most intriguing aspect: self-evident and primordial as a
claim to autochthony may seem, in practice it rapidly dissolves into basic
uncertainties as soon as it must materialize. The main aim of this book
is, therefore, to show that it pays to give autochthony—and belonging in
general—back to history.

*   *   *

I owe special thanks to my "first-line" commentators, Jean-François Bayart, Birgit Meyer, and Gyanendra Pandey, for all their encouragement
and inspiration. For the chapters on Cameroon I greatly profited from the

long-term collaboration with my former PhD students from that country—Cyprian and Grace Fisiy, Margaret Niger-Thomas, Antoine Socpa, Timothée Tabappsi, Ibrahim Mouiche, Basile Ndjio, and Robert Akoko—and also with Francis Nyamnjoh and Paul Nkwi. Equally inspiring were contacts with Cameroonologists from elsewhere: Piet Konings, Janet Roitman, Mitzi Goheen, Dominique Malaquais, Michael Rowlands, Jane Guyer, Phil Burnham, Alec Leonhardt, Robert Moise, and Jose van Santen. For the chapter on the Netherlands, Frank Bovenkerk was very generous in helping me to find my way in unknown territory; so were Hans van Amersfoort, Bambi Ceuppens, Jan-Willem Duyvendak, Wasif Shadid, Jeroen Doomernik, Mark Leijen, and Oskar Verkaaik. For the short passages on classical Athens, Diederik Burgersdijk gave solid advice. Moreover, special thanks to the two still anonymous readers for University of Chicago Press for their very kind but also really challenging reports.

For the theme in general, it was a real boost to work with what I like to call the former SSRC autochthony quartet in New York—Stephen Jackson, Seteney Shami, Ron Kassimir, and Alcinda Honwana—which led to most lively discussions during subsequent workshops on the topic with Marcial Godoy, Anna Tsing, Rosanna Regillio, Loren Landau, Jesse Ribot, Kathy Boone, Peter Sahlins, and many others.

More broadly, Achille Mbembe, Arjun Appadurai, and Jean and John Comaroff were true fountains of inspiration, also for this book; so were Veena Das, Jim Ferguson, Ruby Lal, Liisa Malkki, Charles Piot, Daniel Smith, Karel Arnaut, Armando Cutolo, and Mick Taussig. Equally stimulating were my ongoing exchanges with colleagues in Amsterdam and Leiden—Francio Guadeloupe, Mattijs van de Port, Rafael Sanchez, Patricia Spyer, Karin Willemse, Jan Jansen, Peter Pels, Gerd Bauman, Heather Sutherland, Reimar Schefold, Mineke Schipper, and Niko Besnier—and encounters in Johannesburg with Isak Niehaus, Carolyn Hamilton, Graeme Reid, and Deborah Posel. Special mention must be made of the two "youngsters" in this global company, Ruth Marshall and Juan Obarrio, who keep showing me that science can be fun. Many thanks also to Ivan Mettrop for helping me out with the index and especially to Ruth Goring from University of Chicago Press for all her patience and creativity in polishing my English.

But my deepest gratitude must go to two people who have become family in Cameroon, Meke Blaise and Peter Geschiere me-Meti, for showing me the deeper meanings of belonging in changing circumstances.

CHAPTER ONE

Introduction

Autochthony—the Flip Side of Globalization?

This book addresses the "return of the local" in a world that believes it is globalizing. The New World Order so proudly announced by George H. W. Bush in 1989 upon the fall of the Berlin Wall and the end of the cold war seemed to evoke a world of free-floating cosmopolitans. Yet since then, cosmopolitanism and globalization have followed quite surprising trajectories. The world in which the earlier Bush's son plays such a central role is marked by entrenched forms of communalism, celebrating difference and exclusion, both in the North and in the South. Rather surprisingly, the trend toward a growing cosmopolitanism has been overshadowed by what Tania Murray Li (2000) aptly calls "a global conjuncture of belonging."[1] Religion plays a front-stage role in this quest for belonging. But in many contexts there seems to be also an inherent link between globalization and a return of the local in unexpected forms and with equally unexpected force. This "local" is of course deeply marked by ever intensifying processes of globalization, summarized well by Roland Robertson (1992) in his notion of "glocalization"—maybe a less elegant term, but then this return of the local often takes less elegant forms.

This book tries to address the return of the local not only as some sort of screen for ongoing globalization—although it is true that even the harshest forms of localist thinking often turn out to express struggles to gain or retain access to the global. My purpose is rather to take localist thinking seriously and try to trace its complex implications, often hidden behind apparent self-evidence, by following its different expressions. I focus on a particularly pregnant expression of the local: the idea of *autochthony*—"to be born from the soil"[2]—and its highly variable manifestations which proved to have such mobilizing force in very different corners of our globe. To Anglophone readers this notion may appear somewhat exotic and even quaint. It does figure in the *Oxford English Dictionary*, but it is certainly not a familiar term.[3] Yet there are two reasons why it is of special importance. First of all, it seems to represent the most authentic form of belonging: "born from the earth itself"—how could one belong more? This means that the notion not only condenses the essence of the idea of belonging but also highlights in a particularly pregnant form its inherent ambiguities. A second reason to study it is its impressively wide but fragmented spread: it turns up at highly different moments and places, without a clear link, yet assuming everywhere the same aura of self-evidence.

A Primordial yet Global Form of Belonging?

The claim to be autochthonous is certainly not the only kind of belonging that people tend to stress in the present-day context of globalization. As noted, religious belonging has become, also quite surprisingly, at least as important in our modern world. Yet, certainly to its protagonists, autochthony—the special link with the soil—seems to have some sort of primordial quality. In a seminal article, Jean and John Comaroff, following up on the botanical connotations the term *autochthonous* seems to have in English (see note 3 above), emphasized its "naturalizing capacity," which makes it "the most 'authentic,' the most essential of all modes of connection" (Comaroff and Comaroff 2001:658–59). Precisely its natural appearance, with the soil as a powerful referent, turns the claim of autochthony into a kind of *ur*-belonging. All the more reason to emphasize that underneath this self-evidence it hides basic inconsistencies that seem to beset most other claims to belonging as well—ambiguities that acquire particular impact in this most essentialist claim to belong.

Autochthony's global spread, noted above, is equally remarkable. Precisely because the upsurge of this notion seems to be linked to specific local factors, it is all the more important to emphasize that lately it has become a truly global phenomenon—even though autochthony explosions in different parts of the world do not seem to be related. For some time the notion was especially associated with Francophone Africa, as various countries there became the scene of violent struggles between self-styled "autochthons" and strangers (often citizen of the same nation-state). The brutal exclusion in Ivory Coast[4] of *allogènes* (or *allochtons*)—the "Other" for the self-defined autochthon—splitting the nation in two and leading to the economic implosion of this once so successful country, became world news. A particularly blatant example of where preoccupations with autochthony can lead was the Opération Nationale d'Identification launched by Laurent Gbagbo shortly after he became Ivory Coast's new president.

. . . .

In 2002—in a situation of growing hatred and violence between southern *autochtones* and northern immigrants (who come from both the northern parts of the country and neighboring states)—the Gbagbo regime, pushing the autochthony idea to its very limits, announced its intention to oblige all Ivorians to return to their village "of origin" in order to be registered there as citizens. Abidjan, the country's megapolis, was not to be considered a "village of origin" except for the Ebrié, "historical autochthons." All persons who could not claim a village of origin within the country were to be considered as immigrants and would therefore lose their citizenship.

Thus, the Ivorian National Identification Campaign became a most pregnant example of the trend, everywhere in the continent, that the preoccupation with belonging—the fear of becoming someone "without bearings"—brings a *retour en force* of "the" village. As Mr. Séry Wayoro, "director of identification" in this *opération*, explained: "Whoever claims to be Ivorian must have a village. Someone who has done everything to forget the name of his village or who is incapable of showing he belongs to a village is a person without bearings and is so dangerous that we must ask him where he comes from" (quoted in Marshall 2006:28).

Ruth Marshall (2006:26) describes the rage of the northern "rebels" at their roadblocks when people present IDs with the new marks—how they violently tear up these papers that threaten to rob them of their very citizenship. For the time being this *opération* has been executed in only mitigated form [see chap. 4 below], but the basic idea is still very much around. It is clearly at the heart of the frightening violence that in subsequent years has marked everyday life, especially in the southwestern parts of the country.

. . . .

In Ivory Coast the defense of autochthony may have taken on especially violent forms under the inspired leadership of Gbagbo and his wife,
with the Jeunes Patriotes as their storm troopers. But similar struggles over
the exclusion of "strangers" (often citizens of the same country) plague
Cameroon, the two Congos, and Senegal—to mention just a few examples.

It is small wonder that the term *autochthonous* gained special currency
in Francophone Africa, since it is an inherent part of the French colonial
heritage: the term was introduced to the continent around 1900 by French
empire builders—often at the same time administrators and ethnograph-
ers—in a determined effort to gain control over the kaleidoscopic jumble
of groups and communities that confronted them in the newly conquered
territories (see below). But recently it has been spreading into Anglophone parts of the continent as well. Moreover, although I propose to focus first of all on areas where the term itself is cropping up, it is clear that
similar issues of belonging have become highly explosive in other parts
of the continent as well. Issues like the xenophobic reaction in present-
day South Africa against the *Makwere-kwere* ("strangers" from across the
Limpopo; see Landau 2006 and chap. 4 below) or the ways in which questions of belonging affected political competition in Zambia and Malawi
play on similar registers as the autochthony craze in Francophone Africa.

However, it may be even more important to emphasize that such confrontations are not unique to the African continent—indeed, this is one of
the main aims of this book. Since the 1970s, the Dutch and the Flemings
adopted a similar terminology of *autochtonen* versus *allochtonen* in their
efforts to deal with ever more pressing immigration issues. Other protagonists of the New Right in Europe play with the same notions. These
notions are now very present also in the Pacific and have a longer history
in Canada, though with quite a different meaning. It is striking—and this
is a central theme of this book—that the same notions seem to apply in
such varying situations. Even more remarkable is that they can have such
strong emotional appeal and mobilizing force in highly different settings.

Indeed, this book is born from a coincidence that did surprise me. In
spring 1996, I returned from Cameroon quite impressed by the vivid images
on Cameroon TV of the large demonstrations of the Sawa ("sea people")
in Douala, the country's main port and economic hub. The local Sawa
people were clearly enraged that in the municipal elections—the first since
democratization and the reinstatement of a multiparty system—Bamileke
immigrants had been elected as mayors in four of the five municipalities
of the city. The demonstrators' language—in their songs, slogans, and post-
ers—was clear: they were the *autochtones*; these "strangers" (*allogènes*)

should go back home and vote there, and not try to rule in the land of their hosts. Clearly the new style of democratic elections had created a true panic among the small coastal groups, the Douala (the original inhabitants of the city) and other "Sawa": they had foreseen that they would be outvoted in their own hometown by the much more numerous immigrants from the interior, and this was indeed what happened in this city, as in many other cities in the continent. Thus, the democratization wave of the early 1990s had the unexpected effect in Cameroon and in many other African countries of triggering fierce autochthony movements and often quite violent efforts to exclude "strangers" (who are often citizens of the same nation-state).

Back home, I switched on the radio and—this was the surprise—suddenly realized that I was hearing exactly the same slogans, but now in good Dutch. It was a program on the Vlaams Blok, a New Right party in Belgium (Flanders) that recently had had striking electoral successes.[5] Its main leader, Filip de Winter—often described as looking like "the ideal son-in-law"—explained the aims of the party in terms that seemed to come straight from the autochthony demonstrators in Cameroon: *Eigen volk eerst* (your own people first); the need to protect the "ancestral heritage" that risked being "soiled" by "strangers." Even the central term was the same: in Dutch/Flemish, the term *autochtoon* has become a rallying point, initially for the New Right but in recent years also for middle-of-the-road parties, now that concerns over how to address the issue of new immigrants and their "integration" have become ever more general.

Striking in all this is that even though the Cameroonian and the Flemish/Dutch contexts are completely different, the autochthony discourse seems to come across as self-evident, almost "natural," in both situations. Precisely this self-evidence seems to give it considerable mobilizing impact.[6] This panacea quality and its apparent capacity to emerge at completely different points in our globalizing world makes autochthony a fascinating notion for understanding present-day preoccupations with belonging. Since we are seeking to understand its impressively wide applicability, it would be counterproductive to work from a strict definition of this quite enigmatic notion. My intention is rather to try to follow what meanings and associations people in strongly different situations attach to it, and how it can retain its apparent self-evidence and thus its plausibility in such different contexts.

Clearly the sudden upsurge of notions of autochthony in highly different parts of the globe has to be placed in a broader context: the "global conjuncture of belonging" mentioned before. I borrow this expression from the Canadian anthropologist Tania Murray Li, who launched it in her studies of conflicts over "indigeneity" in Southeast Asia (Li 2000). Her notion of "conjuncture" is especially apposite since she shows how all sorts of apparently unrelated trends converge into turning *belonging* into a pressing issue. Her studies focus on the global attention to "indigenous peoples" and "disappearing cultures," but also global concern over loss of biodiversity and ecological knowledge, as major trends in making people obsessed with the question of who "really" belongs (and even more so, who does not). Elsewhere other tendencies may promote such preoccupations: in Africa, democratization and decentralization, the two main issues on the neoliberal agenda, have the paradoxical effect of triggering an obsession with belonging (hardly in line with what one would expect from earlier versions of liberalism); in Europe, meanwhile, it is popular dissatisfaction over increasing immigration and the idea that the second generation of immigrants refuses to "integrate" that triggers similar concerns (see chap. 5).

Strikingly, discourses of belonging seem to be able to gloss over such crucial variations, turning questions like *who belongs?* and *how one can prove belonging?* into truly worldwide concerns. Autochthony's capacity to crop up in quite dispersed moments and places across the globe makes for an intriguing difference with the parallel notion of *indigenous*, which made a similar comeback in recent decades (see Ceuppens and Geschiere 2005). While *indigenous* became increasingly centered in its meaning— roughly referring to the "tribal other"—*autochthonous* became employed in much more variable ways. Its use is no longer restricted to marginal areas, since even majority groupings within the West came to defend their position in the name of their "autochthony." It is the free-floating profile of this term, combining apparent self-evidence with great ambiguity and variation in its meaning, that makes it of particular interest for unraveling the general conundrum of belonging in our globalizing world. A brief digression into history can highlight the ambivalences in autochthony discourse underneath its show of authenticity.

Autochthony's Genealogy: Some Elements

Two crucial moments in autochthony's long and tortuous history may be of particular interest here. Both highlight certain inherent inconsistencies in this apparently so self-evident a notion. So what may seem here to be an overly long detour through history will help to outline key dimensions for analyzing the issue of autochthony and belonging in present times.

While I was working on this book, the complex historical vicissitudes of the notion became ever more intriguing to me. As noted, I started to dig into autochthony because I was struck by the coincidence that the same jargon quite abruptly became highly politically charged in such different contexts as Cameroon and the Netherlands. However, following the central notion of autochthony turned out to be quite an adventurous journey. I had certainly not expected that it would take me to widely different spots in the world and in history: it was like a magical bird, turning up in unexpected places. Leading thinkers have used it and still do so, though in quite different ways. Claude Lévi-Strauss (1958:238) gave it a central place in his analysis of the Oedipus figure.[7] Martin Heidegger (1934–35/1989) proposed the heavy term *Bodenständigkeit* as a translation of *autochthony* and used it to defend a more communitarian form of nationalism for Germany, in contrast to Anglo-Saxon and French versions of an all too individualistic nationalism (unfortunately, but probably not accidentally, this was also in the days that he made overtures to the Nazis). Derrida (1997:95, orig. 1994), on the other hand, criticized autochthony as a mark of a too limited (even "phallic") form of democracy that we urgently need to surpass for a more universalistic version.[8]

Classical Athens: The Cradle of Autochthony

The presence of the autochthony notion in the work of these leading thinkers highlights its long historical pedigree, since all three drew their inspiration—albeit with highly different purport—from the central role the idea of *autochthonia* played in classical Athens. Apparently, Athenian citizens of the fifth century BC—the city's Golden Age, the time of Pericles, Euripides, and Plato—were prone to boast of their "autochthony" as proof that their city was exceptional among all the Greek *poleis*. All other cities had histories of having been founded by immigrants; only the Athenians were truly autochthonous—that is, born from the land where they lived. This was also the reason that Athenians would have a special propensity for *demokratia*. The classical texts—Euripides, Plato, Demosthenes—are surprisingly forceful on this point. To the present-day reader, it might come as a shock to read in the text of these venerated classics the same language of autochthony that is now so brutally propagated by Europe's prophets of the New Right. And indeed the correspondence has not gone unnoticed by these prophets themselves, as may be clear from an incident in France.

On May 2, 1990, a member of Parliament in the French National Assembly, a certain Marie-France Stirbois, member for Jean-Marie Le Pen's National Front—still the most right-wing party in France—surprised her colleagues by delivering a passionate speech about classical Athens and the way in which Euripides, Plato, and even Socrates himself defended autochthony. Apparently her colleague *deputés* were somewhat surprised, since until then Mme Stirbois's interventions had not betrayed such an in-depth interest in the classics (or for that matter in any academic subject). Clearly another sympathizer of the National Front—probably a professor at the Sorbonne—had written her speech for her.

The incident had its pathetic overtones, but the good thing was that it inspired two leading French classicists, Nicole Loraux (a good friend of Derrida) and Marcel Detienne, to look into the issue of Athenian autochthony. Both authors have since shown with impressive eloquence that it pays off to take the old authors seriously, since these classical voices highlight quite sharply—though maybe inadvertently—the tensions inherent to the autochthony notion as such.

At first sight the Athenian claim to autochthony seems to be as natural and as unequivocal as, for instance, President Laurent Gbagbo's claims that one needs to distinguish *Ivoiriens "de souche"* (literally "from the trunk of the tree") from later immigrants (Le Pen uses similar terms in France). The Athenian declarations appear as emotional and sincere as the furious protests, cited above, of the Sawa (sea people) in Douala against being dominated by immigrants in their own area.[9] However, Loraux and Detienne's visionary analysis shows that it may indeed be worthwhile to take a closer look at Athenian language on autochthony. This will require a de-tour in time, and the lively imaginary of Greek mythology may put to the test the reader's patience. Yet such a return to the classical locus of the autochthony notion is rewarding, since here the tensions and inconsisten-cies of this apparently unequivocal notion come to the fore in particularly striking ways. The following examples testify to both the vigor and the complexities of autochthony in Athenian thinking.

· · · · · · · · · · · · · ·

In Erechtheus, one of Euripides' most popular tragedies,[10] the playwright has Praxithea, King Erechteus's wife, offer her own daughter for sacrifice in order to save the city: "I, then, shall give my daughter to be killed. I take many things into account, and first of all, that I could not find any city better than this. To begin with, we are an autochthonous people, not introduced from elsewhere; other communities, founded as it were through board-game moves, are imported, different ones from different places. Now someone who settles in one city from another is like a peg ill-fitted in a piece of wood—a citizen in name, but not in his actions."

Heavy language under heavy circumstances. In the play, Athens is threatened with destruction by Eumolpus and his Thracians invading Attica. The Delphi oracle has prophesied that King Erechtheus can save the city only by sacrificing one of his own offspring. He seems to hesitate, but his wife gives him a lesson regarding what autochthony means in practice: "This girl, not mine in fact except through birth, I shall give to be sacrificed in defense of our land. If the city is captured, what share in my children have I then? Shall not the whole then be saved, so far as is in my power?" (Euripides 1995:159–60; cf. also Detienne 2003:36-39).

• • • • • • • • • • • • • •

Euripides' tragedy was based on a myth, placed in a mythical time (Erechtheus is supposed to have been mentioned already by Homer), but it was clearly very topical to Athens's situation of 422 BC, when the play was first performed: the city was at the height of its naval power but was locked in mortal combat with its archrival, Sparta. There was, indeed, some reason for celebrating Athenian uniqueness at the time. In other respects as well, Praxithea's words must have seemed highly to the point for the audience. Her scorn comparison of people "who settle in one city from another" to "a peg ill-fitted in a piece of wood" no doubt had special meaning in a city where in its heyday the majority of the population were seen as foreign immigrants (*metoikoi*), among whom quite a few were much richer than many a true citizen by descent.

With Plato, Athenian *autochthonia* seems to be equally self-evident.

• • • • • • • • • • • • • •

Plato makes Socrates—when instructing young Menexenes on how to deliver a funeral oration for fallen soldiers (a major occasion in fifth-century Athens)[11]—celebrate Athenian uniqueness in no uncertain terms: "The forefathers of these men were not of immigrant stock, nor were these their sons declared by their origin to be strangers in the land sprung from immigrants, but natives sprung from the soil living and dwelling in their own true fatherland."

As the next step in his didactic model for a funeral speech, Plato, still speaking through Socrates' mouth, makes his famous equation of *autochthonia* and *demokratia*:

> For whereas all other States are composed of a heterogeneous collection of all sorts of people, so that their polities also are heterogeneous, tyrannies as well as oligarchies, some of them regarding one another as slaves, others as masters; we and our people, on the contrary, being all born of one mother, claim to be neither the slaves of one another nor the masters; rather does our natural birth-equality drive us to seek lawfully legal equality. (Plato, *Menexenus*, in 2005:343–47)

· · · · · · · · · · · · · ·

As in Africa (see below), funerals, and particularly funeral orations, must have been high points in the expression of Athenian autochthony.[12] In general, autochthony in Greece—again, as elsewhere—must have been linked to heavy ritual and symbols that verged on the burlesque.

· · · · · · · · · · · · · ·

In Euripides' tragedy, Eurechtheus is punished for his dearly bought victory over the Thracians by Poseidon, who is still furious that the Athenians preferred the goddess Athena to him as the city's protector. With his terrible trident Poseidon makes a deep cleft right through the Akropolis (Athens's main mountain), and Erechteus disappears in the chasm, to remain literally "locked in the earth"—an appropriate position in view of his emphatic chtonic character, invariably repeated whenever he is mentioned.[13] But finally Athena, the city's chosen goddess, appears to redeem the situation. In honor of the king-locked-in-the-earth, she ordains the consecration of a small temple, the Erechteion, to be situated on the Akropolis and made the focal point for celebrating Athenian autochthony.

Burlesque as some of the founding myths of this Athenian particularity may seem now, it is clear that this heavy symbolism had a powerful appeal. The reference to the soil is affirmed by a king-locked-in-the-earth and the rhetoric of the funeral orations in particularly graphic ways. All this confirmed an idea of Athenian autochthony as a long-standing trait of this particular city—Homer had already mentioned Erechtheus as an archchtonian—which was later also accepted by many modern classicists (cf. Rosivach 1987:294).

. . . .

Yet recently several historians have raised doubts about this shiny image of classical Athenian autochthony—problems that must have worried contemporaries as well. There is a clear tension with the study of history as it was practiced already at the time. Striking is that the two most prominent historians of those days do not make special mention of Athens being exceptional in regard to the origin of its citizens. Herodotus mentions a wide array of autochtonous groupings—some more autochthonous than others—but he does not relate autochthony to Athens (Detienne 2003:49). And Thucydides seems determined to avoid the very word *autochthoon*, probably because he distrusted its rhetorical use. He explains Athens's preeminence instead in reference to its success in attracting immigrants (the *metoikoi* mentioned before) from all over Greece, even allowing at least some of them "to become citizens" (Loraux 1996:94).

Vincent Rosivach (1987) goes even further, trying to show that the term *autochthoon* must have been of a much later coinage, probably in the fifth century BC, when Athens was emerging as the major power among the Greek cities. He proposes to distinguish an "indigenous" and a "chtonic" use of the term. It is certainly true that already Homer mentions, for instance, Erechtheus from Attic as a chtonic figure. But in Rosivach's view this is in a different sense, as some sort of primal, serpentlike figure (a monster?) closely tied to the earth. Only during Athens's upsurge was Erechtheus linked to the Athenians' desire to prove their exceptional indigeneity, giving the chtonic component in *autochthoon* a quite different implication. Rosivach's line of argumentation may be quite hypothetical.[14] Yet his insistence on the reverse meaning of attributing a chtonic origin— primitivizing a being or a group as some kind of primal phenomenon—is very relevant for other situations as well. Throughout this book this double meaning will come up time and again: the autochthon as prestigious first-comer but also as primitive or even prehuman.

Along the same lines as Rosivach, Marcel Detienne (2003) emphasizes that in general Greek claims to autochthony must have been somewhat ahistorical since they denied by definition the great era of Greek colonization of the seventh and sixth centuries BC, when new *poleis* were founded all over the eastern Mediterranean in an adventurous expansion process. Athens itself was very much a city in formation up to the fifth century. It is striking, that the laws on citizenship promulgated in 509 by Cleisthenes, Athens's great legislator during the city's ascendance, were much more open and inclusive than was Pericles' law of 451 BC, during the city's heyday. Although Pericles' law came only a little over fifty years later, it brought incisive changes, reserving Athenian citizenship only for those who could claim that both parents were Athenian (Detienne 2003:53).[15]

Nicole Loraux (1996) problematizes Athenian autochthony, and hence autochthony in general, at an even deeper level. For her, an insistence on having remained on the same spot is a basic denial of history, which always implies movement. It is a kind of negative history that always needs an Other—movement in any form—in order to define itself (see notably 1996:82, 99). At a very practical level, this implied for Athenians a guilty denial of memories of earlier migrations, especially for the city's aristocratic families, who used to be proud of their founding history, often referring to their provenance from elsewhere, as some sort of mythical charter. Loraux signals that in other classic texts on autochthony as well, history and movement are a kind of hidden subtext undermining autochthony's rigid memory.

A stark expression of this is to be found in one of Euripides' most famous tragedies, *Ion*—probably the most outspoken celebration of autochthony he left us. For modern readers (and viewers), the force of the play lies mostly in Euripides' beautiful verses in which he allows the actors to express their rage—contained by deep respect—against the gods and the careless way they handle mortals. But another possible reading of the text, one that takes into account the Athenians' preoccupation with autochthony, suggests that a concern with origins must have been at least as important. Consider Ion's statement when his "father" (who later turns out not to be his real father) tries to take him to Athens, while Ion still believes he himself is a stranger to the city:[16] "They say that the famous Athenians, born from the soil, are no immigrant race. I would be suffering from two disabilities if I were cast there, both the foreignness of my father and my own bastardy. . . . For if a foreigner, even though nominally a citizen, comes into that pure-bred city, his tongue is enslaved and he has no freedom of speech" (Euripides 1999:397, 403). This is vintage autochthony thinking!

However, in the unfolding of the tragedy this theme leads to so many complications that the drama can also be read as a sort of carnival of auto-

chthony: Ion has to be crowned in the end as Athens's truly autochthonous king, though he is Apollon's son and has been adopted by a father who himself is a stranger (the latter is even led to believe that he is
Ion's "real" father)—and so forth, and so forth. As Detienne puts it so
aptly, "nothing is impossible in autochthony" (2003:59). There is a clear
reflection here of the deep unrest in autochthony thinking, which Loraux
brings out well by insisting on the sheer impossibility of excluding history. Persons are not what they seem to be. If a foreigner like Ion can
turn out to be an autochthon, the reverse can be true also. Indeed, the
obsession with having traitors "inside" and needing urgently to unmask
them, which was evident in the preceding examples from Ivory Coast and
Cameroon, was very present in classical Athens as well. If a citizen was
slandered by someone who put into doubt his citizenship, he could sum-
mon the slanderer before a city tribunal. However, this involved a huge
risk: if the slanderer were judged to be in the right, his challenger would
lose not only his citizenship but also his liberty: he could be sold as a slave
(Loraux 1996:195).

The above may indicate why the present-day New Right in Europe
is tempted to quote the celebration of autochthony in classical Athens
as a precedent to be respected. However, Loraux and Detienne convinc-
ingly show that on closer reading these texts actually highlight the basic
impossibilities of autochthony thinking: its tortuous struggles to come to
terms with history, which always undermines the apparent self-evidence
of chtonic belonging, and, even more, the great uncertainty it creates
about "authentic" and "fake" autochthony and hence an obsession with
purification and the unmasking of traitors-in-our-midst.[17] These complications will prove to be all too relevant for autochthony's present-day
trajectories

French West Africa: A Colonial Version of Autochthony

For present-day developments the classical Athenian version of autochthony may serve to highlight certain inherent tensions. Yet the concept's
complicated trajectories on the African continent were much more directly shaped by the colonial intermezzo. As noted earlier, the term was
abruptly introduced on the continent by French colonials around 1900,
when they were struggling with the question of how to administer the vast
territories they had conquered in a few decades in West Africa. In the
French colonial conception developed during the French conquest of the
West African Sudan in the 1880s and 1890s, *autochtonie* was to become

the very first criterion for bringing some order into the confusing proliferation of diffuse groupings—some more or less integrated in larger state
formations, others constantly splitting up in segments—that confronted
the new conquerors.[18] *Autochtonie* was the basic principle of *la politique
des races*, elaborated by Governor-General William Ponty around 1900,
which for the French was, at least in the first decades of colonization,
their alternative to British Indirect Rule.[19] While to the British it seemed
increasingly vital to identify the "real" chiefs in order to base the native
administration on them, the French were initially rather bent on circum-
venting at least the higher chiefs, who in some parts of the Sudan had
offered determined resistance.[20] This policy called for homogeneous *cantons* to be formed, populated by people of the same *race* (here used in the
sense of what today is called an "ethnic group") and administered by local
power-holders who would constitute the building blocks for *le comman-
dement indigène*. It was urgent to discover within the confusing medley of
groups and subgroups, more or less related but constantly splitting up, the
real *autochtones* who were so central in this conception of the *politique des
races*.

A typical example of the French approach is provided by the huge,
three-volume book *Haut-Sénégal-Niger* (from 1912 but based on research
in the 1890s) by the French ethnographer-administrator Maurice Delafosse, who was to become very influential in the building of French
colonial empire. A recurrent principle in the book was that "some *indigènes* are autochthons, whereas others are definitely not" (see Delafosse
1912/1972:280; cf. also Arnaut 2004:207). Thus a vital question in his en-
cyclopedic description of the various groupings in this area was whether
a given group was or was not autochthonous. Yet despite his determined
search for autochthony, Delafosse was clearly much more interested in
migrating groups. Invariably, once he has finally found an autochthonous
group, it gets only a short description in somewhat condescending language (they are characterized as *malheureux*, poor and backward—see
Delafosse 1912/1972:238; see also Triaud 1998). In contrast, Delafosse de-
votes more than forty pages to, for instance, the Peul/Dyula ethnic conglomerate: he was clearly fascinated by their peregrinations throughout
West Africa and their reputation as empire builders.

This makes his book a striking example of a widespread colonial paradox, of crucial importance to the vagaries of autochthony and belonging
in postcolonial times. On the one hand, there was a heavy emphasis on the
urgent need to "fix" the local populations: only thus would it be possible

to administer them—more specifically, levy taxes and labor.[21] The *politique des races* and the principle that the new administration should be built upon autochthon groups, the true locals, fit in with this localizing approach. Yet on the other hand, most colonial governments showed in practice a clear preference for migrants, who were seen as more energetic and entrepreneurial—and therefore much more interesting for launching projects. In practice, the *politique des races* seems to have foundered rapidly on this penchant for migrants among the new colonial authorities, who tended, just like Delafosse, to oppose migrants' dynamics to locals' indolence and resistance to change. In many areas the French soon became inclined to appoint chiefs from such more "enterprising" groupings over "backward" locals.[22] Still, ephemeral as the *politique des races* may have turned out to be, it did introduce the term *autochtones* and its counterpoint *allogènes* as some sort of primal criterion in the French colonial context.

One of the reasons that the term did flourish in this new setting was that it easily articulated with distinctions existing already locally, though these often had a quite different tenor. Indeed, the varying trajectories of the autochthony notion even within Africa reveal the ways in which colonial terms were appropriated locally, acquiring a dynamic of their own. Especially in the interior of the West African Sudan, local patterns of organization turned on a sort of complementary opposition between "people of the land" and "rulers." The latter were (and are) often proud to have come in from elsewhere, and they referred to their external origin as their justification to rule; yet the "chief of the land" formed (and still forms) a ritual counterpoint to the chief of the ruling dynasty. To the French ethnologists, *autochthony* was an obvious term to describe this counterpoint position.

The vast literature on the Mossi (the largest group in present-day Burkina Faso) exemplifies this. For generations of researchers, the opposition in Mossi society between what they termed *autochtones* and "rulers" became the central issue inspiring highly sophisticated structuralist studies (Zahan 1961; Izard 1985; Luning 1997; see also Gruénais 1985). In this context, the notion of autochthony took on somewhat primivitist overtones, similar to the image of primal chtonic creatures in Athens's mythical history. Sabine Luning (1997:11), for instance, points out how in the prevailing discourse of the Mossi Maana, the *tengabiise* (a term now currently translated, also among the people themselves, as *les autochtones*), were characterized as some sort of "presocial," "terrestial" beings, who

were fully humanized—that is, included in a society—only by the coming
of the *naam*, their foreign rulers. In practice *naam* power was limited in
all sorts of ways by the *tengabiise*. Nonetheless, the *naam* as foreign rulers
were formally at the apex of the prestige scale, dominating *les autochtones*. Here, this latter term had a strong chtonic meaning, reminding one
of Erechtheus, the Athenian king who was so graphically "locked in the
earth" by Poseidon and whose temple thus became the very place to celebrate "autochthony."[23]

This was certainly not the meaning Delafosse had in mind in his search
for *autochtones* for *la politique des races*. It was also not the meaning that
came to the fore with so much force in the 1990s with democratization in
this part of Africa. Among the main targets of the upsurge of autochthony
in neighboring Ivory Coast, under Houphouët-Boigny's successors, first
Bedié and then Gbagbo, were precisely these Mossi immigrants who were
supposed to have taken the land of the "autochthons" of the rich cacao
belt in southern Ivory Coast (see chap. 4). In this version of the term—
as in the version propagated by Delafosse and *la politique des races*—an
autochthon is certainly not a subordinate; on the contrary, the notion implies a claim to priority and the right to exclude strangers. The reference
to the soil in this context expresses a right to possess. Clearly, despite its
self-evident or even "natural" appearance, a term like *autochthony* can
take on very different meanings in different contexts and times.

Nevertheless, for the African continent the colonial background provided a common framework. In all the African present-day confrontations
around autochthony discussed in later chapters, belonging and the exclusion of "strangers" turn out to be deeply marked by the paradox of most
colonial regimes: on the one hand, their insistence on fixing and territorializing people—which implied a determined search for autochthons who "really" belonged—and, on the other, a constant preference for migrants.[24]

Autochthony Now: Globalization and the Neoliberal Turn

Clearly, then, autochthony has a long history. The discourse of its present-
day protagonists is certainly not new. Yet it is clear as well that recently,
especially since the late 1980s, it has undergone a powerful renaissance. A
crucial question, if we want to develop a more historical view of this discourse, is why it became such a tempting discourse at the present moment
in many parts of the globe.

Tania Murray Li's notion of a "global conjuncture of belonging" seems to point toward various aspects of what has come to be called "globalization" that can serve as important leads. The rapidly increasing mobility of people, not only on a national but also on a transnational scale—which to many is a basic factor of globalization—has generated the wider context for people's preoccupation with belonging.[25] But Li's approach allows one to identify other more specific factors, which may vary among regions. While Li emphasizes global concern over the loss of biodiversity, "indigenous people," and "disappearing cultures" in the areas she studies in Southeast Asia, in the chapters below about Africa the focus will be on the twin processes of democratization and decentralization, both closely related to the new emphasis since the end of the 1980s on "bypassing" the state in the policies of the global development establishment.

Throughout the continent the wave of democratization of the early 1990s seemed initially to bring a promising turn toward political liberalization. Yet in many countries it inspired, quite unexpectedly, determined attempts toward closure in order to exclude certain groups from their full rights as national citizens—or at least to distinguish between citizens who "belong" and others who belong less. The tragic example of Ivory Coast was mentioned already, with Gbagbo's Opération Nationale d'Identification as an extreme manifestation. In Eastern Congo, the enigmatic Banyamulenge—opponents rather call them Banyarwanda (Rwanda people)—became similarly the object of fierce struggles over belonging and autochthony, fanned by Mobutu Sese Seko's Machiavellian manipulations in offering them full citizenship and withdrawing it at will. In Anglophone Africa as well, belonging became a crucial issue in the new style of politics. In Zambia, former national president Kenneth Kaunda could be excluded from the political competition by the simple claim that he "really" descended from strangers. In a completely different context, the new African National Congress democracy in South Africa became marked by furious popular reactions for excluding all *Makwere-kwere*—"those" Africans from across the Limpopo.

At least as important as democratization was the drastic shift, already mentioned, in the policies of global development agencies like the World Bank, the International Monetary Fund, and other major donors from an explicitly statist view to an equally blunt distrust of the state. While up to the early 1980s it seemed self-evident that development had to be realized through the state and therefore strengthening the state and nation-building by the new state elites were the first priorities, subsequently in the World Bank's official view the state was no longer a pillar but rather a major barrier to development.[26] Especially after the Bank's 1989 report on Africa, "bypassing the state," strengthening "civil society" and NGOs, and notably "decentralization" became the buzz words. But just as democratization turned out to open up unexpected scope for autochthony movements, the new decentralization policy and the support of NGOs, often quite localist in character, similarly turned questions of belonging and exclusion into burning issues. In chapter 3 we will see, for instance, how the new forest law in Cameroon, heavily supported by the World Bank and World Wildlife Fund, made autochthony – that is, the question of who could be excluded from the new-style development projects as "not really" belonging—a hot issue even in areas that were so thinly populated that there seemed to be no demographic pressure at all on the soil and other resources.

Such developments cannot be dismissed as just political games—maneuvers imposed from above by shrewd politicians or well-meaning "developers." Political manipulations and external interventions by development agencies certainly play a role in most of these cases, but they can work only because the very idea of local belonging strikes such a deep emotional chord with the population in general. Indeed, the force of the emotions unleashed by a political appeal to autochthony is often such that it threatens to sweep the very politicians who launched it right from their feet. This is vividly illustrated by the increasing importance, throughout the African continent, of the funeral "at home" (that is, in the village of origin), which is turned into a true festival of belonging—often to the discomfort of urban elites, who dread such occasions when the villagers can get even with their "brothers" in the cities. Marked by a proliferation of "neotraditional" rites that often involve great expenditure, these occasions show how deeply this obsession with belonging is rooted in society but also what a complex balancing act between returning and maintaining distance it requires from urban elites. In many regions there is a direct link between democratization and the increasing exuberance of the funeral "at home"—a clear sign how important local belonging has become. All this not despite but rather because of "liberalization." A major challenge for this book will be how to relate shrewd political manipulation and deep emotional involvement, since the combination of both seems to be at the heart of the autochthony conundrum.

Elsewhere, other factors have had similar effects, as my surprise at noticing the same language in Africa and on my radio "at home" clearly showed. One of the interesting aspects of the term *autochthony* is that it easily bridges the gap between "South" and "North."[27] Apparently it works as well in Flanders or Holland as in Cameroon or Ivory Coast. In the early 1990s, I became familiar with the Dutch version of it mainly from our southern neighbors in Flanders. But in subsequent years it conquered with surprising rapidity the Netherlands as well. The shocking murder in 2002 of Holland's most successful populist politician ever, Pim Fortuyn, made his heritage all the more powerful. Since his meteoric career, Dutch politicians have realized that electoral success depends on taking "autochthony" seriously. Since then the defense of the "autochthonous cultural heritage"—which for the Dutch, always proud of not being overly nationalistic, proved quite hard to define—has become a dominant theme, together with the idea that more pressure is needed to make immigrants "integrate" into this elusive culture. The term *autochthony* is now less current in France and almost absent from Germany or the United Kingdom, even though similar concerns about belonging are high on the political agenda there. Elsewhere it crops up in unexpected places. In Italy, Umberto Bosi has recently adopted it for his Lega Norte, and as noted earlier, it emerges strongly in the Pacific and in Quebec, albeit in a different sense.

. . . .

A brief illustration will show how great the confusion can become when autochthony, with its different meanings, crosses the dividing lines between continents. In 2006 I attended, together with several Africanists, a large-scale conference on the theme of autochthony at the École des Hautes Études en Sciences Sociales, Paris's leading institute for social sciences. The conference was organized through close collaboration among colleagues from Quebec and France. For the Québécois and their French counterparts, the meaning of the term *autochthony* was clear. In the 1980s they had decided that this was to be used as equivalent to the budding Anglophone notion of *indigenous*, clearly because since the colonial period the more direct French translation, *indigène*, has carried such a pejorative charge that it had to be avoided at all costs.[28] In the Quebec version of the term, *les autochtones* are "indigenous people"—that is, people in a minority position whose way of life is threatened by dominant groups. In this view, Quebec's Native Americans are the prototype of *peuples autochtones*. At the conference, however, our Quebec colleagues discovered to their dismay that in other continents the term had acquired quite different meanings. It was

difficult for them to accept that, for instance, in Cameroon and elsewhere
in Africa the term *autochthonous* does not primarily refer to groups like
the "Pygmies" or endangered pastoralists but is commonly claimed by well-
established groups who are in control of the state and wield the term against
immigrants who are still seen as foreigners. Even more surprising seemed to
be the fact that in Flanders and the Netherlands, the majority of the population is happy to be labeled "autochthons." As one participant from Quebec
put it most eloquently: "If the Dutch are so foolish as to label themselves
'autochthons,' it is their affair. But the United Nations Working Group on
Indigenous Populations have already decided that *autochtone* is the French
translation of *indigenous*.[29] And I think we should stick to this."

It was of little use to question the United Nations' mandate to decide
the meaning of a term that clearly had very different histories in different
parts of the globe. And to a large part of the audience, the suggestion that
the Québécois might be tempted to use the term for themselves in their
relation to Anglophone "latecomers" seemed to be even more hilarious.
Apparently, in Canada the *autochtone* has to be the Other, with his own,
endangered culture.

. . . .

It is tempting to see the recent upsurge of "autochthony" and related
notions of belonging in very different places of the globe as an unexpected
outcome of the neoliberal tide that swept our globalizing world with so
much force after the end of the cold war. It is true that democratization
and decentralization, the dominant trends in the African continent since
1990, fit in very well with the so-called Washington Consensus, tersely
summarized by Jim Ferguson (2006:39) as pretending to bring "less state
interference and inefficiency"—and, one might add, more leeway for the
market.[30] Still, the explanatory value of neoliberalism as a final cause may
lately have become somewhat overstretched.[31] In recent seminars and
conferences, many colleagues have warned that this notion, just like globalization, is rapidly becoming a blanket notion facilely cited as the cause
for a discouraging wide range of phenomena. So it might be necessary to
try and be a bit more specific.

A leitmotif in the chapters that follow will be the surprising penchant
of many advocates of neoliberal reform for "tradition" and belonging.
There is of course an interesting paradox here: how can one combine a fixed
belief in the market as the solution to all problems with far-reaching trust

in "the" community or "customary chiefs" as a stabilizing anchor?[32] In Africa, this penchant for "community," tradition, and "chiefs" seems to be a logical consequence of a drive toward decentralization. If one wants to bypass the state and reach out to "civil society," local forms of organization and "traditional" authorities seem to be obvious points of orientation. Unfortunately, as we shall see below, the new approach to development tends to ignore that most "traditional" communities are actually products of determined colonial and postcolonial interventions. Even more serious is neoliberals' supreme indifference to the fact that focusing on such partners inevitably raises ardent issues of belonging: chiefs relate only to their own subjects and tend to discriminate against immigrants (who, as said, were often encouraged to migrate by colonial development projects). Local communities are tending to close themselves and apply severe forms of exclusion of people who had earlier been considered as fellows.

For different reasons, the same paradox emerges with the protagonists of the New Right in Europe (and elsewhere). For instance, while liberalism on this continent used to be equated with various forms of anti-clericalism (or in any case with insistence on a strict separation of religion and state), neoliberal spokespersons now often plead for a resurrection of "Judeo-Christian values" as an anchor for society. More important, they manage to combine the good old liberal principle of reducing the interference of the state as much as possible with a vocal appeal to the same state to exercise almost total control over society (mostly against suspect immigrants)—thus strengthening the presence of the state in everyday life instead of promoting a withdrawal (see chap. 5). Neoliberalism as such may be a fuzzy phenomenon, but on the ground this surprising combination of market and tradition has very concrete effects.

Autochthony and the Tenacity of the Nation-State

The "global conjuncture of belonging" is certainly related to rapidly increasing transnational mobility of people, but it is so in a very special context: the tenacity of the nation-state that succeeds through a wide array of forms and processes in grafting itself onto increasing globalization. It may indeed be important to stress that all the mobility globalization seems to stand for cannot be interpreted as a "withering away" of the nation-state. On the contrary, as most eloquently stressed by Jean-François Bayart

(2004, chap. 2), globalization processes still take place within the frameworks created by the historical emergence of the nation-state. This holds certainly true for present-day migration currents, transnational as they may be. It is precisely this tension between global flows and the continuing importance of national controls that gives autochthony and other forms of belonging such a powerful impact on recent developments. Indeed, we will see that the varying articulations of autochthony movements with the nation-state are central for understanding their different trajectories.

The close link with the struggle over the nation-state, as still a crucial target, is most strikingly illustrated by President Gbagbo's 2002 plan for an Opération Nationale d'Identification in Ivory Coast, cited already as one of the most blatant examples of autochthony in recent years. The insistence by Gabgbo and his allies that every Ivorian had to go back to his or her village of origin to be registered and that people "without a village" could not pretend to national citizenship is strongly reminiscent of Achille Mbembe's fulminations against autochthony as a basic idiom of the *imaginaire identitaire* in present-day Africa: "The central preoccupation becomes the struggle over the appropriation of political power and the state apparatus by the autochthons. Everything boils down to the perverse structure of autochthony. The prose of autochthony seems to exhaust the possibilities for the constitution of the subject . . . a xenophobic way of thinking, negative and circular."[33]

In other respects as well, the vision of the nation-state as being overtaken by recent developments can be misleading. It might suggest that the present-day upsurge of autochthony expresses a return of "traditional" tensions, now that the pressure of the authoritarian state is defused—just as, for instance, in Yugoslavia the implosion of the authoritarian one-party state seems to have pulled the lid off the can of worms that was hidden underneath all the time. But this is too simplistic a view. In the same text just quoted, Mbembe emphasizes that the postcolonial preoccupation with autochthony has clear colonial antecedents rather than "traditional" ones. Indeed, as stressed above, it is all too often a direct product of (post)colonial state formation. In many respects the present-day manifestations of autochthony in various parts of the African continent refer to a colonial model rather than to a precolonial one.[34]

There are therefore good reasons to stress that the present-day preoccupation with autochthony and closure throughout the continent can hardly be considered as a traditional given that is typical for Africa. On the contrary, it is quite surprising that autochthony is becoming a seemingly self-evident frame for identity politics on that continent. After all, African traditions used to have a different orientation. Generations of anthropologists and historians characterized African societies as strongly inclusive, marked by an emphasis on "wealth-in-people" (in contrast to Europe's "wealth-in-things").[35] These societies employed a wide array of institutional mechanisms for including people from elsewhere (adoption, fosterage, the broad range of "classificatory" kinship terminology, and all sorts of clientelist relations). As noted above, ruling groups often confirmed their prestige by boasting that they came from elsewhere to rule the autochthonous group—supposedly it was only under their guidance that the latter had become "humanized" and part of a social order (see chap. 4 below). The growing closure of local groups in recent decades, culminating in the fierce defense of autochthony—especially after democratization—is thus a striking development. All the more reason to emphasize the crucial role of the colonial intermezzo and the vagaries of (post)colonial state formation in this respect—notably the paradox noted above that most colonial governments (and their postcolonial successors) tended to affirm the principle of building on *les autochtones*, while in practice they consequently favored migrants (see also Geschiere 2007).

The current prominence of themes of autochthony and belonging in Europe, promoted by a growing distrust of immigrants, has a similar, paradoxical background. Here also the state is struggling to contain tensions that follow from its earlier policies: the halfhearted support in earlier decades of immigration, for a long time (and against all evidence) still seen as only temporary; and the continuing reluctance of most governments to acknowledge that Western Europe is becoming an immigration region that needs foreign labor, just like former white settler colonies in other continents with their "melting pot" ideology. The consequence is quite paradoxical: as said, right-wing groups that are normally in favor of privatization and reducing the role of the state now try to force the very same state to intervene in drastic ways in order to contain the "migrant problem." Instead of trimming down the state, such "liberals" insist that it has to impose new forms of control and get involved into operations on a scale it can hardly handle.[36]

In both contexts, it would be clearly misleading, then, to see autochthony as trying to offer an alternative to the nation-state. It may be tempting, especially when one listens to its propagandists, to see it as affirming the local level as some sort of counterpoint to the global, with both levels appearing to drain the intermediate national level. In contrast to this neat but all too simplistic view, both the European and the African examples below fit rather with Bayart's emphasis, already cited, on the tenacity of the nation-state as the continuing framework in which an emerging *gouvernement du monde* is taking shape (Bayart 2004).

One of the nodal points in the ambiguities surrounding the upsurge of autochthony and other forms of belonging is, therefore, their relation to national citizenship. And this notion is undergoing important changes, both in its ideological status and in its practices. It may be overly simplistic to talk of a weakening of the nation-state, given its capacity to graft itself upon processes of intensifying globalization. However, these processes have affected the status of national citizenship as an ultimate identity. Being a national citizen used to be a very icon of modernity. As Gyanendra Pandey puts it so graphically: "To be civilised is to have a nation" (Pandey and Geschiere 2003:15). However, recently the very idea of national citizenship has become the subject of fierce debate. A clear sign of the growing uncertainty around this concept is that in America "citizenship studies" is now seen as *the* field for the future (cf. Isin and Turner 2002). The well-known Canadian political philosopher Will Kymlicka characterized the 1990s as "the decade of citizenship" (2002:284), thus highlighting both the continued importance of the notion and its loss of self-evidence. Clearly the vicissitudes of autochthony in the present-day world are deeply marked by such debates.

In North America, the new discussions on citizenship center on growing doubts about the old, liberal version of the notion, based on the formal equality of all citizens as autonomous individuals before the law. Many authors emphasize that in practice this formal equality entails advantaging well-entrenched groups that better know how to play the rules and, further, that it ignores differences between groups that are all too real. This inspired a plea for recognizing special rights for special groups by creating scope for "group-based" or "group-differentiated" forms of citizenship.[37] In the United States this translates, for instance, into recognition of special "women's rights" and "gay rights." However, pleas for group-based citizenship inevitably also create openings for protagonists in the struggles discussed above: champions of "indigenous peoples," whether abroad or at home, or defenders of autochthony in a situation of decentralization.

An opposite tendency, starkly emerging in Europe, and to a lesser degree in North America, is what has been called the "culturalization of citizenship"[38]—the search for a more pregnant formulation of the cultural consensus that forms the basis of citizenship and must be subscribed to by new citizens as proof of their "integration." Often an appeal to history as the mold of the nation is seen as essential for this. However, the difficult relation of autochthony to history, noted earlier, then generates problems. Advocates of such a cultural formulation of citizenship evoke a very special history: a condensed version, more or less fixed; recent demands for a historical "canon" in various European countries are good examples of this. Such a compression proves to be, time and again, highly precarious and even controversial. Indeed, the historical canons that have been produced in Denmark and the Netherlands offer striking examples of the confusion that results when academic historians try to honor the demand for such a canon. It might be interesting to relate this to well-known debates among historians over "memory" and "history." Pierre Nora (1989) contrasted the two, since in his view our time brings the dramatic collapse of a last effort to bring the two together—"memory-history"—around the nation ("memory-nation"). The consequence would be that "history"— especially academic history, always plural and distanced—therefore inevitably fragments *les lieux de mémoires*, so dear to the nation.[39] The protagonists of a culturalization of citizenship seem to ask for a return of memory-history, still around the nation. The question is whether this can work if "memory" refuses to allow for difference (see further chap. 5 below).

In the African context both tendencies emerge: efforts to purify the nation with an appeal to history (which often turns out to be a colonial history) and appeals to a special version of group-differentiated citizenship in which autochthons should have precedence over *allogènes,* even though the latter might still be recognized as citizens. In this continent, where national citizenship still has a very short history, any plea for differentiation will directly subvert the principle that all national citizens should be equal before the law. The new development policy of decentralization, referred to above—often applied in quite simplistic forms—undermines national citizenship, which had received such strong formal emphasis in the preceding decades of nation-building. With projects and development funds entering no longer through the state but rather through circuits of decentralization, regional or even local forms of belonging gain importance. This inevitably raises the by now familiar issues of belonging: who is to profit from the new-style development projects? and, even more urgently, who can be excluded from them?

In practice, decentralization has encouraged the reaffirmation of fuzzy identities and a constant search for the exclusion of "strangers" (often citizens of the same state). One question is whether the very idea of national citizenship, which at least provided some sort of fixed point, is not thus being dispensed with too easily. To put it in stronger terms: are currently fashionable ideas about surpassing the nation-state from America and Europe, where national citizenship is deeply rooted and provides strong guarantees, being too thoughtlessly transported to zones of the South where this notion is still quite ephemeral and backed by fewer guarantees? Another question is to what extent the very idea of group-based citizenship will prove to entail similar divisiveness in Northern countries as well. It is with such questions in mind that various articulations of autochthony (and similar notions of belonging) with the idea of national citizenship—whether autochthony claims to offer an alternative to citizenship or rather is aimed at its "purification"—will be traced in the chapters below.

Whatever the trend of such articulations, however, it is quite clear that at the present moment autochthony and the quest for alternative sorts of belonging remain deeply marked by the specific trajectories that nation-building took in different regions. In the present-day context, historicizing autochthony will always mean putting it into relation with the nation-state. In this sense, and only in this, autochthony can be termed to be inherently postnational.[40]

Historical Construction, Political Manipulation, and Emotional Power

The above discussion may suggest more specific dimensions for my explorations of the ambiguities and paradoxes of autochthony's trajectories in the modern world in subsequent chapters.

A first key aspect is autochthony's ambiguous relation to the local. As, for instance, Achille Mbembe (2001:7) and AbdelMaliq Simone (2001:25) have emphasized for Africa, it may seem logical to equate "autochthony," "indigeneity," and other notions of belonging with a celebration of the local and with efforts to close the community against global "flows," as a retrograde reaction. Yet in practice these movements are often directly linked to processes of globalization. Simone is right to insist that "the fight is not so much over the terms of territorial encompassment or closure, but rather over maintaining a sense of 'open-endedness' " (2000:25). What is at stake is often less a defense of the local than efforts to exclude others from access to the new circuits of riches and power. This is why it is

misleading to see the upsurge of autochthony movements in Africa as reflecting attempts to return to "traditional" realities: as if the cover of the
pot (state authoritarianism?) had been lifted and the old tensions began
to boil over again. Such a traditionalizing view severely underrates the degree to which the autochthonous subject is shaped by broader processes:
struggles over local belonging are closely intertwined with the desire to
be recognized as a citizen of the world. A key role in this is played by
les originaires—the "sons of the soil" who left the village and made their
careers elsewhere, in the city or even in diaspora. They are often central
in raising the autochthony issue, but mainly as part of their struggle for
special access to national or global circuits.

A second crucial point in the chapters that follow is the strong *segmentary* tendency of discourses on autochthony and belonging. In line with its
"naturalizing" capacity, autochthony discourse will always make the basic
distinction between autochthons and others appear to be obvious. But,
as stressed above, in practice any attempt to define the autochthonous
community in more concrete terms will give rise to fierce disagreements
and nagging suspicions of faking. The preoccupation with purifying the
community of alien elements leads people to redefine autochthony at
ever closer range, especially when certain "spoils"—resources, political
posts—have to be divided. In one of the examples examined in chapter 3,
a Cameroonian village was confronted with new opportunities to create
a "community forest." This immediately triggered fierce debates on who
"really" belonged and, more particularly, who did not. Initially, recent
immigrants were pushed out of the project, but subsequently all sorts of
latent divisions within the local population itself became exacerbated, and
finally people started to classify even their own relatives as *allogènes* when
their lines of descent did not perfectly correspond to patrilineal principles.

There is a direct link here to the paradox, already noted, between apparent certainty and a practice of great uncertainty. Autochthony's appeal to the soil seems to promise some sort of primal belonging: what can
be more secure than the knowledge that one is born from the soil? Yet the
notion's self-evident, natural appearance is time and again undercut by
this elusive segmentary quality. An obsession with purifying the community generates constant redefinition of the "true" autochthon, with ever
smaller circles being drawn. This goes together with an obsession with unmasking fake autochthons inside—people who pose as autochthons but
are really traitors. The violent implications of such an obsession were most
horrifyingly illustrated by Radio Mille Collines in Rwanda in 1993–94

with its terrible warnings against the *cancrelats* (cockroaches) hiding inside that had to be identified and exterminated.

Third, and most important, there is autochthony's uneasy relation with history. In her masterful study of classical Athens cited above, Loraux puts it most pregnantly: autochthony's claims of having stayed always on the same spot are historically impossible—after all, history is movement (Loraux 1996:36, 95). The Athenian aristocratic families' embarrassment over their histories of origins elsewhere has striking parallels in present-day Africa and Europe. Such carefully guarded secrets can explain why the language of autochthony is a "nervous" one, as Stephen Jackson puts it so strikingly in his studies of East Congo, where rumors of alien origins haunt fierce debates of autochthony (Jackson 2003; chap. 4 below). Any claim to be "born from the soil" seems to sit uneasily with history, either denying it or trying to strictly control it.

Despite its heavy appeal to the soil, autochthony turns out to be quite an empty notion in practice: it only expresses the claim to have come first.[41] It is precisely this emptiness that makes the notion so pliable: autochthony's Other can be constantly redefined, entailing new boundary marking for the group concerned, which may be one reason it fits so well in a globalizing world. As several recent authors have emphasized, globalization entails not only "flow" but also "closure";[42] yet the boundary making that accompanies global flows is constantly shifting, just like the definitions of the Self and the Other in autochthony discourse. This pliability is part of autochthony's considerable uncertainty: an obsession with traitors inside and constant fears of being unmasked as a "fake" autochthon (recall what was said about the notion's segmentary quality). Autochthony discourse may seem straightforward, yet on closer inspection its apparent self-evidence hides great uncertainty and confusion. An important challenge is, therefore, to return it to history in all the different settings where this discourse emerges powerfully: this might be an obvious way to try to denaturalize it.

*   *   *

Yet historicizing may be only half of the job to be done. Following the varying trajectories of the autochthony notion in different contexts may relativize its pretense of constituting some primordial and self-evident truth, but will this indeed relativize its mobilizing force and the hold it has over people's minds? The question remains why this notion and the link to the soil it postulates have such powerful emotional appeal. It is not clear how historicizing can help us to understand this.

Recently, several authors have expressed a certain fatigue with the emphasis on the historically constructed character of phenomena and the concomitant obsession with deconstruction or even debunking that, after cultural studies, increasingly affected anthropology as well. As Mattijs van de Port (2004; 2005; 2006) puts it in a series of publications on such varying topics as Serbia, homicide in the Netherlands, and *candomblé* in Brazil: the recent anthropological predilection for debunking authenticity does not preclude people's powerful cravings for the authentic—maybe especially in "modern" circumstances.[43] The same applies to autochthony. History may highlight its volatility underneath a natural appearance, but this only makes the question of the reasons for its high "performative quality" (to quote Ruth Marshall again) in widely different situations all the more urgent. How can it evoke such deep emotions and a sensation of deep truth despite all the variations involved? Are there any limits to its apparent self-evidence?

An obvious starting point for explorations in this direction is to take the reference to the soil, basic to the notion, seriously and to try to follow it in its different implications and elaborations. Even in such places as present-day Flanders and the Netherlands, where people hardly seem to be conscious any more that the notion is centered in the soil, the reference still has power. A striking example of this is provided in the Comaroff and Comaroff article cited above (2001). A widespread panic in South Africa about a huge fire on the Cape Peninsula, which risked destroying the country's cherished heritage of *fynbos* (unique in the world), fed into national concerns about the postapartheid swell of immigrants from other parts of Africa. In popular perceptions, the menace to the autochthonous *fynbos* came to stand for the South African population's risk of being overrun by hordes of strangers from across the Limpopo (the *Makwere-kwere*). For the Comaroffs, this initially surprising transfer of anxiety from botanical to sociopolitical "aliens" is symptomatic of the powerful naturalizing capacity of autochthony discourse. The discourse's capacity to appeal to what seem to be primordial truths is indeed quite striking. The link with the land, central to the notion of autochthony, gives it a strong territorializing capacity, outlining—in a more or less symbolical way—a clearly defined "home."

Of course, it is important in all this not to lose sight of the direct, economic importance that the soil has in many of the examples considered here, both for the locals and for "sons of the soil" living elsewhere: land to make farms on, plots to build houses upon, forests in which to hunt and gather. Thus protecting the land against foreign invaders is of very direct economic importance. In autochthony notions, however, such economic interests seem intricately intertwined with a more general emotional involvement. In many settings (though in this too there are great differences), the soil as such seems to raise deep feelings that easily surpass economic calculations. As noted, in many parts of present-day Africa the funeral "at home"—that is, in the village, even for urbanites—has become one of autochthony's major rituals, a veritable test of where one "really" belongs. There is a noteworthy parallel here with the central role, already mentioned, of the *epitaphios* (funerary address) in Athenian autochthony or with the role of the cemetery in European nationalism.[44] The funeral offers an occasion to link "soil" and "body" in all sorts of naturalizing ways. Funerals among the Maka (Cameroon), for instance, require a division of roles between patrilineal descendants and the various groups of in-laws that is graphically inscribed on the body. Patri-kin are painted white, a sign of mourning; meanwhile the "daughters-in-law" (that is, all the women married into the village of the deceased) have to dance with great frenzy all night long (see chap. 6). And of course, the climax of a funeral anywhere is when the body of the deceased is committed to the soil. Below (chaps. 5 and 7) it will become clear that, in comparison, in Europe the autochthony notion seems to be much more uncertain precisely because of its problems with pegging itself onto similar "chthonic truths."

It is tempting to ascribe the emotional power of an appeal to autochthony in many situations to such powerful naturalizing icons as the soil and the ways it is linked to the body. However, this may still be too simplistic. Below, a brief comparison among the rituals of nation-building that marked the first decades of independence in Cameroon and those in other African countries—roughly from 1960 till the end of the 1980s—will indicate that these rituals too invoked the soil (in this case the national territory) and strove to impose special disciplines of the body (military-style parades, special clothing, sometimes also special dances). However, generally these rituals seemed to lack the visceral quality of the funeral at home, and in most cases the nation-building rituals disappeared leaving scarcely any trace. New-fangled autochthony rituals in the Netherlands, as elsewhere in Europe, play with similar icons but retain an artificial or even insipid quality (see Verkaaik forthcoming). Clearly, not every appeal to the soil or the body "works."[45] Is it possible to outline more finely tuned approaches that can help us take both the constructed character of these notions and their emotional appeal seriously?

Approach: From Identity to Subjectivation and Aesthetics

Autochthony's puzzling ambiguity between, on the one hand, emotional power and "natural" self-evidence and, on the other, haunting uncertainty raises questions of a more general nature. If historicizing its claims—which often boils down to debunking them (see van de Port 2004 and 2005; Latour 2005)—is only one step and the main challenge is how to understand its emotional appeal despite blatant historical inaccuracies and unsettling elusiveness in daily life, then what concepts can help us to analyze and compare the different manifestations of this notion? An obvious starting point might be the concept of identity, all the more so since autochthony with its earthy references—the soil, funerals, belonging—presents itself as a sort of primal identity. Yet in recent years the problems with that notion have become clear.[46] It has an unfortunate tendency to fix what is in constant flux (which is often exactly what its protagonists are striving for), and it often acquires teleological implications, suggesting that there is a basic need for a group or a person to produce a clearly outlined and unequivocal identity. Indeed, the way in which, in the last decades of the twentieth century, the notion of identity rapidly spread from psychology to the social sciences in general, more or less replacing "class" as a key notion, could well be further explored and problematized (see Shami 1999).

In practice, the concept of identity seems to be employed in widely different senses. Sometimes it is used in a more or less essentializing way, in the sense that a given identity seems to determine a person's behavior. In other contexts it acquires overtones that correspond to an actors approach: actors are depicted as shaping identities and using them to further their interests. Neither use, however, is very helpful for explaining the variable and shifting ways in which autochthony and people's preoccupation with belonging manifest themselves in the present-day world. An essentializing view of identity risks taking autochthony's deceiving self-evidence for granted, thus neglecting its constant shifts and reorientations. But an actors approach has even more serious limitations: it risks resulting in a kind of instrumentalist view, reducing the impact of these notions to conscious choices and strategies of key figures. Thus it becomes

almost impossible to address what was identified above as the main challenge: understanding the impressive emotional power these notions can
have, at least in some contexts. The chapters that follow will offer many
examples of how politicians are almost literally swept of their feet once
they let loose the emotional tide of this notion—this despite the fact that
it is clearly historically constructed and is undergoing drastic shifts and
reorientations. But how to take this emotional force into account without
succumbing to the notion's apparent self-evidence?

Recently some promising propositions have been forwarded to dy-
namize the notion of identity and overcome the stalemate between sub-
stantialist and actionist approaches. Most interesting for our topic is a
focus on how identities can shift from inclusive to exclusive tendencies.[47]
Arjun Appadurai (2006) has raised the question of why and when identities become "predatory"—that is, under what circumstances they begin
to refuse pluralist coexistence with other identities, claiming for themselves all available space (see chap. 5 below). Gerd Baumann (2004) has
followed a similar track with his different "grammars of identity and alterity." The merit of his approach is that he is determined to move beyond the rather basic truth that a "Self" (an "identity") logically needs
an "Other" ("alterity") in order to profile itself. Instead, Baumann tries
to distinguish different ways ("grammars") of relating to the Other, each
with its own implications: orientalizing; segmentation; encompassment.[48]
His distinctions suggest also the possibility of historical shifts from one
"grammar" to another. This might be helpful for understanding the
present-day turn to special forms of belonging, both in Africa and in Europe. A basic but sound idea might be also his plea to take the word *belonging* itself more seriously and to follow its different languages that so
strongly assert themselves in quite different recent configurations. One of
its advantages over identity is that it is at least in the *-ing* form.[49]

A determined processual approach may be crucial for interpreting autochthony's riddles, precisely because of the notion's inherent tendency to
deny change and history. This makes it all the more tempting a topic for
trying to explore the practical relevance of notions like subjectivation—
following Foucault's vision of the *sujet* in the double meaning of the word
as both agent and being subjected—and its more concrete associate, "techniques of the self,"[50] as crucial to *dispositifs* of (auto-)disciplining. These
notions are certainly in fashion now—which makes it all the more challenging to try to test their practical relevance. For instance, can they be of any
help to break out of the stalemate in which "identity" seems to lead us?

My main inspiration in working with these notions is not so much the-oretical but rather a hunch that they might highlight aspects of the dra-matic Maka funerals, already mentioned as festivals of belonging, that have puzzled me ever since I began doing fieldwork in this part of south-eastern Cameroon in 1971. My puzzlement has deepened into amazement that at these occasions people's behavior—fairly wild, elated forms of behavior—seems to follow fixed (traditional?) patterns in a ritual that at the same time is constantly changing. Yet there seems to be no director who is in charge of all these dramatic performances, directing the innova-tions and people's improvisations. The subjects in their different roles—remember what was said above about the strict division of roles between patrilineal and matrilateral kin at these funerals—seem to emerge from the ritual. But there are all sorts of switches—some people manage to play two different roles interchangeably—and constant innovations, often with a pseudo-traditional appeal and related to money: women impose new pay-ments on the men, "daughters-in-law" ask to be "paid" for the deceased's body, and so on. All these innovations are presented as completely self-evident (even as "traditional") and are most graphically inscribed in the body: in the ways in which people are decked out or marked, in specific forms of dancing and rhythms. No external disciplining seems to be nec-essary; people seem to "automatically" discipline themselves—in all their outrageous behavior—within the role they enact for a given moment.

The result is an occasion of impressive power. Most urbanites express great reluctance to make the trip to attend a funeral in the village—for good reasons: many innovations of the ritual focus on reminding wealthier visitors of the urgent need to redistribute some of their wealth—but very few of them fail to attend. As soon as they arrive in the village, they seem to be sucked into the ritual, and they perform in high-spirited style. With the upsurge of autochthony as a major political issue in many countries of Africa (see chaps. 2 and 4), it is no wonder these funerals have grown in size and intensity: in them the emotional appeal of autochthony seems to be publicly condensed in a visceral involvement of body and soil. For me, the literature on subjectivation and techniques of the body irresistibly evoke these events, all the more powerful since they seem to unfold by themselves.

However, as noted already, such inscribing in the body and the soil does not always "work." To put it more bluntly, the notion of *techniques du corps* cannot be invoked as a *passe-partout* explanation. The earlier rituals of nation-building in Cameroon and elsewhere in Africa and the new autochthony rituals in many European countries do address notions of soil and involve special bodily disciplines, but they conspicuously lack this visceral quality (see chaps. 5 and 6). Is it because they are so blatantly "made up"?[51]

In addressing such questions I am especially inspired by the way Jean-François Bayart works with the Foucauldian notions in a compelling mix of theory and historical examples from all over the world.[52] His original approach has the great advantage of outlining the concrete relevance of these notions. Especially inspiring is the way he shows that people feel dominated by identity's illusions or by processes of globalization but at the same time are deeply involved in shaping them. Changing techniques of the self, mostly centered on the body, are obvious entrance points for trying to understand how the subject is both shaped by and participates in evolving processes of subjectivation. Also important is Bayart's emphasis, following Deleuze, that subjectivation is a never-ending process. This corresponds particularly well to the always unfinished nature of the autochthony discourse (like other discourses of belonging). Its protagonists may see themselves as fully shaped subjects, but the figure of the autochthon is constantly reshaped and further specified. This unfinished quality is precisely what makes the discourse such an uncertain one.

In a related perspective, equally focusing on experiences of the self and bodily techniques, Birgit Meyer has recently developed a seminal approach for understanding how some religious images can convince while others do not (Meyer 2006 and 2008). Especially the latter might be relevant for understanding autochthony's highly variable performance at different times and in different parts of the world. Key notions in Meyer's approach are "style" and "aesthetics" as bringing a "concentration" that can create "a shared sensorial perception of the world" (Meyer 2006:7).[53] Her focus is on the "comeback of religion" that announced itself so emphatically in recent decades, upsetting current assumptions of ongoing secularization as a self-evident process. In her view the strength of religious images rests on their capacity to evoke a holistic sensorial experience, shared among a broader community and thus overcoming the *Zerstreuung* that marks the modern world (interestingly, this German term means both "distraction" and "fragmentation"). With this capacity, religious experiences can evoke a feeling of "authentic belonging" in the midst of a world that seems to be fragmenting. However, the degree of success in evoking such authentic feelings depends on the aesthetics of the images— that is, on the degree to which their aesthetics is indeed able to bring about a shared sensorial perception. Style, as a concentrating force, is a crucial variable: "Thriving on repetition and serialization, style induces a mode of participation via techniques of mimesis and emulation that yields a particular habitus" (Meyer 2006:25; see also Meyer 2008). Religion depends on aesthetics and style, then, for being convincing.

The question is whether such an approach can be transferred from the field of religious studies to help us understand the appeal of alternative forms of belonging, like autochthony. Particularly a focus on style "as a concentrating force" bringing a "shared sensorial perception of the world" in the face of threatening disorientation might help to understand autochthony's emotional appeal in highly different situations, despite—or maybe because of—its unsettling elusiveness. Another question, especially in chapters 6 and 7, will be whether this approach can explain why in some situations autochthony's impact remains limited.

Yet in all this it may be wise to stick to the concrete maxim chosen earlier as our anchor and take the reference to the soil, central in any appeal to autochthony, most seriously (whether it is historically correct or not). The special and highly variable meaning imputed to the soil—and notably the different articulations of conscious socioeconomic interests and broader emotional appeal—can offer a vantage point to explore the relevance of these sophisticated approaches, in terms of subjectivation, disciplining techniques of the self, aesthetics and style, for explaining autochthony's varying trajectories in a changing world.

Chapter Overview

The order of this book's chapters follows from my central concern to place the upsurge of autochthony and belonging in Africa and Europe—and its varying articulations with the nation-state—in a global perspective. The focus is on the question of how similar languages of autochthony can acquire great persuasive self-evidence and hence great mobilizing force in widely different circumstances.

Chapters 2 through 4 take up spectacular but quite differently oriented outbursts of autochthony on the African continent. Chapters 2 and 3 are based on research I undertook with a number of Cameroonian colleagues—notably Francis Nyamnjoh, Antoine Socpa, and Basile Ndjio—in different parts of Cameroon. Chapter 2 discusses violent manifestations by autochthons in close relation with the politics of belonging of President

Paul Biya's former one-party regime. Indeed, it was its support for autochthony movements that explains how his regime managed to hold on
to power despite democratization (in 1990) and an initially very successful opposition. This betting on autochthony marked a dramatic shift. Up
to 1990, the Biya government, like other one-party dictatorships in the
continent, had always emphasized nation-building and the unity of all
Cameroonian citizens. Its sudden choice to play the autochthony card—
actively supporting all sorts of regionalist movements—proved to be an
ideal strategy for neutralizing the effects of multipartyism. However, the
autochthony movements were particularly unstable. Despite strong government support, segmentary tendencies asserted themselves as soon
certain political gains had to be divided.

The third chapter discusses autochthony in a very different part of
Cameroon—the very thinly populated forest area, only of marginal interest in national politics—and against a very different background. Here the
drastic application of a new policy of decentralization triggered fierce confrontations over belonging and exclusion at the local level. Cameroon's
new forest law (1994), dictated by the World Bank in close collaboration
with the World Wildlife Fund, gave local communities strong rights as major stakeholders in the exploitation of the forest. In itself, this initiative
was certainly justified (this region had always been severely neglected).
However, a major problem was that here the local units were (and are)
particularly unstable—segmentary—in character. The law avoided defining the crucial notion of "community" in any detail. The consequence was
that belonging became a major issue and that people tended to redefine
autochthony at ever closer range, even excluding their own relatives as
allogènes.

Chapter 4 follows parallel developments elsewhere on the African continent. Its main focus is Ivory Coast, where local violence against *allogènes*
has recently taken on particularly shocking forms. The obsessive insistence of the regime of Laurent Gbagbo on trying to reconstitute a puri-
fied nation, cleansed from all foreign elements, led to a fierce struggle over
the definition of who is and who is not an autochthon. It is not only a matter of southerners' claiming to be autochthons and thus excluding northerners. Within the South, notions of autochthony have tended to shrink
progressively, leaving the Baoule—who until Gbagbo's election as president (2001) had been in control of the state—in a highly uncertain situation. Similar uncertainties mark the struggles over *autochtonie* in Eastern
Congo/Zaire, notably because of the difficulties in situating the Banya-

mulenge (or Banyarwanda). Here again, the present-day violence has a
long history: Mobutu's manipulations, affirming and then again denying
Congolese citizenship for the Banyamulenge, make possible very different interpretations of their history and their belonging. In South Africa,
rising xenophobia, notably in Johannesburg, against the *Makwere-kwere*,
African immigrants from across the Limpopo, is expressed in a different
language. But the implications are similar: the perceived pressure of these
foreign immigrants offers South Africans, many of whom managed only
quite recently to settle in the city, the possibility of affirming their belonging there. These three cases of violent localist reactions represent strikingly different patterns in the ways the government relates to them. But
in all three cases local struggles are clearly centered on the nation-state.
The present-day predicament of many "Pygmy" groups shows another
catch in autochthony discourse. Even though everybody agrees that they
are the "real" autochthons, they cannot deduce any claims from this since
the are not "really" citizens.

Chapter 5 discusses autochthony movements in Europe, where the language of belonging and autochthony spread especially in relation to popular concerns about immigrant labor. This chapter focuses on the Netherlands and what seemed to be an abrupt switch in this country after 2000—
marked by two shocking political assassinations—from a multiculturalist
approach to a forceful policy of cultural integration. The new and much
stricter approach toward immigrants was based on the idea that, rather
than socioeconomic marginalization, a lack of cultural integration was
the main problem. More coercion would be needed in order to force *allochtonen* to integrate into Dutch culture. However, this begged the question how to define Dutch culture. In this context the autochthony notion
again showed its receding quality. The efforts to define a clear cultural
and historical core as an anchor for integration policies ran into all sorts
of difficulties. Frequent references to the idea of autochthony, as a self-
evident opposite to the influx of *allochtonen*, went together with an appeal
to highly simplistic notions of culture and history as obvious tools for enforcing integration. The main lesson of the Dutch example seems to be
that only concepts of culture and history that address differences—rather
than trying to ignore them—are relevant to the present-day context.

Chapter 6 focuses on the striking emotional appeal of rituals of autochthony in present-day Africa. It offers a comparison, based on my fieldwork in East Cameroon, between the rituals of forceful nation-building
of the 1960s and 1970s and the funeral "at home" that has become a high

moment for celebrating belonging in the present-day context. Since the 1990s, "nation-building" seems to have become a slogan of the past. Yet if we want to understand subjectivation as an ongoing process, the period of forceful nation-building and its quite artificial efforts to shape subjects into citizens may be of particular importance. Mbembe (1992) is certainly right in emphasizing that we must take the clumsy rituals imposed by the first national leaders much more seriously. After all, they did outline new forms of discipline in which the dominated were often eager to participate, and thus set the stage for the upsurge of autochthony with its special implications for processes of subjectivation. Yet one must also ask why these rituals always seemed so shallow in comparison with present-day rituals of autochthony and how they could disappear with hardly a trace left behind.

Chapter 7 offers, finally, a comparison with similar shifts elsewhere in Africa and in Europe, focusing again on the very different forms rituals of belonging take in these contexts. The question is whether different aesthetics and styles, in Birgit Meyer's sense—that is, different ways of invoking key referents like "soil" and "body"—can help to explain the variable impact of appeals to autochthony as an ultimate form of belonging.

*   *   *

Clearly autochthony's techniques of the self are quite different in Europe and the African continent. But they have one thing in common, and that might be the leitmotif of this book: the paradoxical combination of autochthony's promise of creating a safe kind of belonging and its practice of nagging uncertainty, since the "real" autochthon always seems to be receding. This relates to what might be the basic tension in this discourse: it celebrates the primacy of being rooted as something self-evident, but it does so to enable participation in a world shaped by migration.

CHAPTER TWO

Cameroon:
Autochthony, Democratization, and
New Struggles over Citizenship

On February 14, 1998, a train car full of petrol capsized near the station of Yaoundé, the capital of Cameroon.[1] As was only to be expected, people rushed to the place in order to profit from the accident and fill their jerry cans with the precious liquid. Unfortunately, someone lit a cigarette, and the terrible explosion that followed produced dozens of victims. Strikingly, the terrible event was immediately interpreted in terms of the split between *autochtones* and *allogènes*. Comments by Radio Trottoir and on the Internet (the most modern variant of the former) were that "of course" all the victims were autochthons, since they had already chased away the *allogènes*. The accident had taken place in "their" territory, so the petrol was only for those who really "belonged."[2]

Noteworthy in this incident—and in many others since the 1990s—is that it apparently was self-evident to people to refer to notions like *autochtone* and *allogène* in their comments This was "not done" in earlier decades when "nation-building" was the all-overriding theme in national politics. Under President Ahmadou Ahidjo, the nation's founding president, who ruled from independence (1960) until 1982, it was bad taste to mention someone's ethnic affiliation, let alone to qualify someone openly as an *allogène*. This was seen as a shocking transgression of the cornerstone of the ideology of Ahidjo's one-party state: the unity of the Cameroonian people, which was repeated *encore et toujours* at any official meeting.[3] In those days the standard answer to prudent enquiries about someone's ethnic or regional background was "Il est Camerounais comme moi," and the word *allogène* was used only in nasty backbiting.[4]

All this changed rapidly in the 1990s. Already in the 1980s, after Paul Biya succeeded Ahidjo (1982), ethnic differences became more pronounced, even in official discourse. But especially since 1990, with the onset of democratization and the return of multipartyism—which President Biya had to accept with great reluctance and under direct pressure of his close ally French president François Mitterand—autochthony became the all-overriding issue in Cameroonian politics, and with it claims to special rights for those who "really" belonged in the area where they lived. Struggles over the exclusion of *allogènes* from access to political influence, land, and jobs—even when they were Cameroonian citizens—became part and parcel of everyday life. Even the churches could not escape deep divisions over the issue. In 1999, the Vatican's nomination of Msgr. Wouking (a Bamileke) as archbishop in Yaoundé raised fierce protests from self-styled autochthonous priests. The Vatican's reply was to appoint the same year a Beti bishop (that is, an autochthon of Yaoundé) as bishop in Bamileke-land.[5]

The upsurge of autochthony in all walks of life became a subject of fierce debates in newspapers and other periodicals among Cameroonian intellectuals of varying backgrounds, and also among foreign and Cameroonian academics.[6] Nearly all these writers have related the upsurge to the renewed importance of elections under multipartyism and to the Biya regime's encouragement of autochthony movements in order to divide the opposition. Yet the "global conjuncture of belonging," noted in the previous chapter, had broader implications for Cameroon as well. The next chapter will highlight other factors behind people's increasing obsession with autochthony: the new emphasis on "decentralization" and "bypassing the state" in the policies of the development establishment and global concern for the environment or the survival of "indigenous peoples."

However, it is clear that in Cameroon, as in other African countries (see chap. 4), political liberalization—centered on democratization and a return of effective multipartyism—played a prominent role in the upsurge of issues of autochthony and belonging as dominant themes in the new style of politics. In Cameroon this implied a particularly dramatic *volte-face* of the national regime. Up to the end of the 1980s, the Biya regime retained an extremely authoritarian control over politics, forbidding any form of association outside the one party, since this would endanger the unity of all Cameroonian citizens. But in 1990 the same regime abruptly began to encourage autochthony movements, proclaiming its duty to protect "minorities" against immigrants (even if the latter were equally Cameroonian citizens). In this chapter I will highlight the dramatic consequences this switch had for the very notion of national citizenship. Noteworthy are the "natural" appeal of autochthony discourse (reinforced now that it was formally supported by the government); its ways of condensing highly complicated histories; and its segmentary character as soon as new prizes—such as political posts—had to be divided.

Belonging to a Nonexistent Province

The enigmatic Association of the Elites of the Eleventh Province that in the 1990s emerged in coastal areas of South-West Province (in the country's Anglophone part)[7] is a striking example of how pervasive the autochthony issue had become and how severely it could put into doubt people's citizenship and thus their very right to participate in the new politics. The association's name itself is both a riddle and a challenge. Everyone knows that Cameroon has only ten provinces, so what is this Eleventh Province?

I stumbled upon the association when I read an interview in the *Herald*, an opposition newspaper from Buea (capital of South-West Province), with the association's chair, Professor Beltus I Bejanga from Kumba.[8] The journalist's first question to Bejanga was a request to explain this strange name. The latter's answer was that the association's members "are the children or the grandchildren of our forefathers who came over from the former French Cameroon to the then Southern Cameroon [British]. . . . These children or the grandchildren of these migrants had their education, training and everything in the British Cameroons and therefore they are members of what we call the Eleventh Province Association."

This brief answer serves to highlight the considerable historical complexities of the region concerned. There are special reasons that immigration and consequently the autochthony conundrum became particularly virulent here. The South-West is one of the more economically developed parts of the country. In the 1890s the Germans (the first colonizers of Cameroon) developed a large-scale plantation complex on the fertile volcanic slopes of Mount Cameroon, generating an ever-growing demand for labor which the local population could not satisfy. In 1914, at the outbreak of World War I, Cameroon was divided between the British and the French. The latter's military effort was considerably larger, but the former quickly conquered this most valuable part of the colony and appropriated the large-scale plantations. Under British rule, the inflow of labor migrants from other parts of Cameroon and, later on, also from Nigeria continued. The "real" locals, notably the relatively small Bakweri group, soon felt threatened by all these immigrants.

Since the 1920s, the Bakweri have complained insistently that they are becoming a minority in their own territory due to the increasing influx of these *came-no-goes* (as the immigrants are called in local pidgin English). It is to these issues that Chairman Bejanga was referring in his answer to the journalist's first question. Apparently the members of his Eleventh Province association are children and grandchildren of the labor migrants who had fled from the former French part of Cameroon—often under pressure of the *corvées* (the feared coercive labors imposed by the French)—and settled in the South-West to work on plantations.

The *Herald* journalist then asked the next obvious question: why does Bejanga proclaim himself and his friends as belonging to an Eleventh Province "instead of identifying with where he was born?" Clearly, Professor Bejanga expected this question. He replied with some heat:

> Exactly, we thought we belonged to where we were born, until recently SWELA [the new South West Elites Association] was formed. In one of their meetings some of us attended but were driven out and called strangers who have no right to take part in the meeting. So we concluded that we didn't belong to English-speaking Cameroon, nor are we accepted in French-speaking Cameroon.... We want to draw the attention of the government to tell them that we are here, we are Cameroonians but have no statehood. The government should decide what to do with us.

This raised the central issue in the whole affair: where does one "really" belong? The Herald journalist tried to kindle the fire by quoting another elite from Kumba—probably a member of SWELA—who proposed to "refer to somebody's home as the place where he is buried when he dies." At this Professor Bejanga became really excited—evidently because he foresaw that this criterion would make him a stranger in the area he considers to be his own: "Will I claim my home when I am dead and buried? I think my home should not be where I will be buried, because I could die in the sea and my corpse never seen.... The government should step in and stop people from calling others 'settlers' or 'strangers.' It is sometimes provocative. The government should say no to this."

Thus, the interview, and especially this dispute over the criteria for someone's belonging, provides a graphic illustration of how thorny an issue autochthony had become in the area. Of special interest are Bejanga's last remarks, since they highlight two crucial aspects of the issue to which I will return in this and subsequent chapters: (1) the role of the government and (2) the meaning of the funeral as the ultimate test of where one belongs. Bejanga's appeal to the government "to step in" and do something about his loss of "statehood" must be ironic. He must have understood by then that, on the contrary, the Biya regime was betting on the "autochthons" as its obvious allies. Indeed, SWELA—the South-West Elites Association, accused by Bejanga of brutally excluding him and treating him as a stranger in his own home region—was a stark example of how deeply the Biya regime was already involved in what rightly could be called the politics of autochthony.

Elite Associations and Autochthony: Different Degrees of Citizenship?

A crucial factor in the upsurge of autochthony, in Cameroon as elsewhere on the continent, was the quick realization by leaders of the former one-party regime that supporting regional elite associations was an ideal strategy to try and circumvent the effects of multiparty democratization and divide the opposition (see Nyamnjoh and Rowlands 1998). For Cameroon this switch was, as noted, particularly dramatic.

In general the ongoing relation of urban elites to their village of birth is of great salience in Africa. It is also of crucial importance to our theme. In Africa, urbanization is not a once-and-for-all choice. Anthropologists refer to "a rural-urban continuum" that is particular to the continent, since people keep moving between the city and the village.[9] Urban elites, even though their career prospects lie in the city, still emphasize their attachment to the village of birth. Some see the village as a more reliable source of social security than the provisions in the modern sectors of society, and nearly all elites feel that the link with the village remains crucial as a source of belonging and identification.

Under Ahidjo in Cameroon's first decades as a nation-state, official policies were emphatically aimed at limiting this ongoing involvement with the village of birth—or at least to keep it outside the formal political framework. Any form of regional association was severely discouraged.

Many analysts have written already about Ahidjo's authoritarianism.[10]
Under his one-party rule, any form of association outside the *parti unifié* was
strictly forbidden. In order to efface the traces of the violent Union des
Populations du Cameroun (UPC) guerrilla,[11] the new president reminded
Cameroonians time and again that they had to unite under his strict rule.
Any sign of autonomy would be interpreted as a form of potential subversion—in those days a particularly threatening notion. This meant, for
instance, that politicians who took their relations with grassroots supporters too seriously and tried to form regional associations could be accused
of being subversive, and this was often enough to justify banishment to
Tcholliré, Ahidjo's feared concentration camp in the north. Politicians
at every level were constantly admonished to remember that they owed
their political success to the favor of the party apparatus and to no one
else. Efforts to build up one's own power base were seen as an attempt to
create division, and this was a cardinal sin against Ahidjo's ideal of national unity, constantly repeated at all levels of the party organization.

· · · · · · · · · · · · · · · ·

To give just one example of the paranoid climate of those days: in 1971 I
witnessed a very rough police raid in an East Province village where I was
doing fieldwork. A group of young men were arrested because they had
founded a checkers club without asking the approval of the party. The gendarmes accused them of subversion and of going "behind the president's
back"; they took them to their station in town and gave each of them a severe beating. They boys were lucky to be released after this.

· · · · · · · · · · · · · · · ·

Even after Biya took over as president (1982), there was initially no
change in this respect: the party's central role as a monolith encapsulating
all forms of organization remained a fiercely defended principle.

This made the change around 1990 all the more dramatic. When Biya
had to give in to international and national pressure to allow multiparty
elections, the regime suddenly became highly conscious of the political possibilities of elite associations, based as these were on the ongoing involvement of urban elites with "their" region or village. Already for the crucial
1992 presidential elections, the regime made it clear in no uncertain terms
that things had changed and that from now on elites—mostly employed
in public service—had better take their relations to their region seriously.

Clearly the Biya team had realized that regional elite associations offered special possibilities in the new political configuration. A year later, I did a series of interviews with civil servants from the East Province (my main fieldwork area), and they all explained to me that they had been ordered to create their elite association and go "home" in order to campaign for Biya. Whatever their political persuasion—and even among elites of the East Province there were some who were flirting with the opposition—they simply could not refuse the order if they wanted to keep their job. What only a few years earlier had been strictly forbidden now became an obligation.

Clearly, the sudden blooming of regional elite associations all over the country had one reason. Leaders of the regime had realized that its hold over the elites, in great majority *fonctionnaires* of the government and therefore under its direct control, offered an alternative channel for marshaling votes now that coercive mobilization via the one party's channels was no longer possible. This was also the origin of the South-West Elites Association that had excluded Bejanga in such unpleasant ways. But in South-West Province there were even stronger reasons for the Biya regime to try to relate to the regional elites, since they would play a key role in the newly emerging political constellation. A brief overview of the turmoil of Cameroonian party politics is necessary here to set the stage (see Takougang and Krieger 1998).

After Biya had finally been forced to lift the ban on freedom of association in 1990, there was a proliferation of all sorts of political parties. However, soon three stood out as the major ones, each with its own regional base. Thus it has been common to analyze the new political constellation as a tug-of-war between those three:

- the CPDM (Cameroon People Democratic Movement), Biya's party, which was supposed to have its main support in the Greater Beti region (Centre, South, and East provinces) and which remains in power today
- the very first opposition party, John Fru Ndi's SDF (Social Democratic Front), which from the start was generally associated with the Anglo-Bami (the Anglophone area, including North-West and South-West provinces, and Bamileke-land, that is, the Francophone West Province)
- the UNDP (United Democratic Party), whose base was mainly in the northern provinces

Thus the three parties appeared to represent the main ethnic blocs, each with its own region: the Beti in the south, the Anglo-Bami in the west, and the Fulbe in the north.

It is important to underline, however, that in practice all these areas were deeply divided. The "Greater Beti" have manifested themselves as one bloc only since the rise to power of Biya, himself a Bulu. Before this, the term was little used; rather, one would speak of the Eton, the Ewondo, the Bulu—groups that now see themselves as subgroups of the Beti. In the north, the Fulbe had established a violent dominance in the course of the nineteenth century, but many local groups—the so-called Kirdi—kept a certain autonomy. In the western parts of the country, there was the divide between the Anglophones and the Francophones, while among Anglophones were clear tensions between inhabitants of the highlands and the southwestern forest area.[12]

Biya and his team were quick to profit from such divisions. The UNDP, supposedly the party of the north, was soon confronted by independent "Kirdi" parties that sought to emancipate themselves from the Fulbe hegemony with the help of the government. But the regime's policies of belonging proved to be even more effective in the case of the Anglophones, who in the early 1990s became the main source of opposition. In those years, the SDF seemed to be able to mobilize an important bloc of support in the two Anglophone provinces (North-West and South-West), West Province (Bamilekeland), and also Littoral Province (with Douala, the country's economic capital). Biya's stubborn refusal to convene a national conference—in contrast to, for instance, Mathieu Kerekou and even Mobutu Sese Seko—triggered the impressive "Ghost Town" operation (Opération Ville Morte), which paralyzed all major cities month after month and brought a definitive victory of the informal over the formal sector (since shopping went on, but now only at the back door).

Yet already in those years, when the Anglophones seemed to become the vanguard of a new national élan, it became quickly clear that there were deep internal divisions among them. As noted earlier, the people nearer to the coast—in the Anglophone South-West Province mainly the Bakweri, but the same applies to the Douala or the Mbo in the Francophone Littoral Province—felt swamped by immigrants from the densely populated Grassfields: "Bamenda" from the Anglophone North-West and "Bamileke" from the Francophone West. These two provinces formed a sociocultural continuum; both were populated by a conglomerate of larger and smaller chiefdoms. In subsequent years the label *anglo-bami* was increasingly used for this conglomerate of migrants, in implicit opposition to the "autochthons" in South-West, Littoral, and Centre provinces.

It was in this context that, in 1991, SWELA was founded, as an association to defend southwestern elites against the encroachment of northwestern elites with their "treacherous" appeal to a common Anglophone identity (Nyamnjoh and Rowlands 1998; see also Konings and Nyamnjoh 2003). Initially launched as a "nonparty association," SWELA sent a delegation to meet with Biya in Buea already in September 1991.[13] Piet Konings and Francis Nyamnjoh (2003:114) rightly emphasize that the ensuing alliance was highly advantageous to both the regime and the southwestern elites. For the first it meant driving a very effective wedge into a threatening Anglophone unified bloc. For the latter, who represented fairly small ethnic groups, it meant that they suddenly got much more than what would have been their fair share of political posts under Ahidjo's old *politique d'équilibre régional*. In 1992 Biya appointed a northwesterner, Simon Achidi Achu, as his prime minister, clearly in the hope of penetrating the region of his main opponent, Fru Ndi. However, when Achu failed to deliver his province in subsequent elections, he was succeeded by a southwesterner, Peter Mafany Musonge, a Bakweri.

Thus the latter group, until then seen as being marginalized, made a spectacular comeback.[14] Musonge was determined right from the start to deliver "his" province. At the reception in Buea after his appointment was announced (September 1996), he made a speech about the "politics of back scratching" that was to become quite famous in Cameroon. Interestingly—and characteristic for autochthony discourse—the theme of the speech was gratitude, a theme Musonge developed in two ways. On the one hand, the South-West's gratitude to President Biya for appointing its son to this high position; Musonge put it quite graphically, "President Biya has scratched our back, and we shall certainly scratch the head of state's back thoroughly when the time comes."[15] On the other hand, the gratitude immigrants owed to the southwestern autochthons for allowing them to come and live with them; in a subsequent speech, they were reminded by Musonge that "even if you have a long hand you cannot scratch your own back. You need someone to do it for you." The latter phrase was apparently supposed to mean that these immigrants should go along with the political choices of their "hosts" if they did not want to be treated as ungrateful *came-no-goes*.[16] The message was clear: if the South-West wanted to retain the unexpected blessing of special access to the summit of the state—a southwesterner as prime minister—not only the locals had to vote for Biya's CPDM but their "guests" also must be forced, one way or another, to do the same.

In the course of the 1990s, CPDM politicians' hammering on belonging and the special rights of autochthons paid off in the national power struggle. Indeed, one of the most remarkable aspects of Cameroonian politics over the last decades has been how the Biya regime survived a particularly tight situation in the early 1990s and subsequently succeeded in completely dividing the opposition. In the first years of the 1990s the opposition seemed to have the winning hand. "Operation Ghost Town" showed its strength throughout the country. The crucial 1992 presidential election generated a scandal, since it was quite clear that Biya obtained his narrow victory over his main rival, Fru Ndi of the SDF (officially 38% against 35%) only through massive vote-rigging.[17] The fraud was so blatant that all European governments withdrew their development assistance—except for France, whose support saved the regime from immediate financial collapse (the close links of Biya with the Mitterand family have been a true leitmotif in Cameroonian politics). In subsequent years Biya held out against all pressure. His party won all the following elections, and the 2004 presidential election even brought him a landslide victory—more than 70 percent—over his main rival, Fru Ndi, who this time obtained only 17 percent of the votes.

President Biya's capacity for survival has been impressive—all the more so since the regime's gradual recovery took place in the context of a severe economic crisis. One telling indicator of this was that the government was forced by International Monetary Fund dictates to impose dramatic salary cuts. Coupled with a devaluation of the CFA franc (no longer supported by the French franc), this meant that around 1994 salaries of the *fonctionnaires*—always the government's main supporters—dwindled to less than 40 percent of their former value. Actually in those years most salaries were not paid at all, except those of the police and the army. The regime is generally counted among the most worrying examples of the "criminalization" of the state (cf. Bayart et al. 1997); indeed, under Biya Cameroon rose rapidly to the first position on the list of the world's most corrupt states. Yet Biya's personal charisma is almost nil: he has become increasingly invisible to the population, spending much of his time abroad and keeping his public appearances to a minimum, for he fears a repetition of the failed attack on his life in 1984.

Biya's capacity for survival is thus quite enigmatic. It can certainly not be explained by economic success or personal charisma—on the contrary. A more mundane reason is the successful autochthony politics of his regime. Just as in the South-West, where the government's support of

SWELA and the regional elites was very effective in shattering the apparent unity of the Anglophone opposition, the regime succeeded in the Littoral and the northern provinces in mobilizing so-called autochthons against its opponents.[18] Already in 1998, observers were concluding that the CPDM was the only party that could claim to be national; all the opposition parties had been contained in specific areas and could therefore hardly form a real rival in national elections.[19]

In retrospect, this autochthony strategy may seem to have been the obvious one for the Biya regime to follow. Yet it must be emphasized again that this constituted a drastic turnabout from Biya's policies before the onset of democratization. In his first years in the presidency, as noted, Biya—adhered—at least formally—to his predecessor's celebration of national unity as the overarching goal. In Biya's 1986 book, formulating his government's political ideology, "national integration" was still a central goal; and even now it remains present in the government's official statements. However, in practice, the ideal of nation-building that in the 1960s and 1970s was hailed throughout the continent as the remedy for Africa's problems seems to have been forgotten and replaced by divide-and-rule policies in Cameroon—as elsewhere in the continent.

To return to Professor Bejanga, the unhappy founding president of the Elites of the Eleventh Province: the above suggests that his appeal to the government to intervene and protect the "statehood" of his people who did not seem to "belong" anymore must have been merely rhetoric. In the neighboring city of Douala, the government manifested itself even more ruthlessly as the new champion of autochthony, even though this undermined the very idea of Cameroonian citizenship.

The "Sea People" Protected by the New Constitution

The violent 1996 demonstrations in Douala by the Sawa (sea people), mentioned in chapter 1, highlighted crucial reasons that belonging had become such a central obsession among both politicians and the people. As noted, the first multiparty elections at the municipal level were held in 1996 and raised in a particularly pregnant form questions that have haunted the democratization process in Cameroon since its beginnings: Who can vote where? And even more important, who can run for office where? Or to put it more concretely: can an immigrant be a candidate in an area where he or she does not "really" belong?

In a city like Douala, such questions arise inevitably. The Douala ethnic group, which claims to be autochthonous to the area, has become a small minority in the huge city that grew up on its territory. Hard figures are difficult to come by because both urbanization processes and ethnic identity are in constant flux. The city's population is now believed to surpass two million, while the number of ethnic Douala would not be more than twenty thousand (Austin and Derrick 1999:1). The Douala consider the great majority of the city's population to be immigrants, even those who have lived there for generations. Bamileke alone, generally seen as faithful supporters of the SDF, the major opposition party, are believed to make up 70 percent of the city's population (Konings and Nyamnjoh 2003:118).

Not surprisingly, in the elections of January 11, 1996, the SDF won in five of the six municipalities that constitute Douala. In four of these municipalities its candidate for the mayor position was a Bamileke. This led to the Sawa demonstrations of February 10. Douala people, mainly young men, marched the streets in a rowdy parade displaying placards with telling texts: "Let All Tribes Vote in Their Place of Origin," "Mayors Should Be Natives," "Yes to Democracy, No to Ethnic Expansionism," and "No Democracy without Protection for Minorities and Indigenes." They sang songs in Douala with titles like "This Shall Not Happen in Our Homeland," "These People Lied to Us," and "Where Are They Going to Dump Us?"[20] The same day the *ngondo*, the neotraditional council of Douala chiefs,[21] convened and addressed a letter to President Biya to complain of "Bamileke domination" and "gross violation of the Constitution in relation to human rights." They asked him to deal with the threat posed to national unity by the attitude "of certain ethnic groups who are bent on flouting the spirit of peaceful coexistence among all Cameroonians." They requested him also to enact "ordinances and laws aimed at defending and protecting the interests of minority groups." Only this, the chiefs maintained, would "safeguard our sociocultural and historical heritage for posterity...and maintain our identity as a minority group in Cameroon."[22]

The government clearly lent a willing ear to these protests from a city that in preceding years had been a bulwark of the opposition SDF. The Sawa chiefs' complaint that the elections had been "a gross violation in relation to the protection of human rights" referred directly to a recent government measure of great formal significance: the proclamation of a new constitution, not by coincidence, just before these elections were to take place. The new constitution was to play a crucial role in justifying the regime's interventions in situations like the one in Douala. It is of some interest to compare the earlier constitution, of 1972, with the new one. The 1972 one starts with a preamble that states:

> The people of Cameroon, proud of its cultural and linguistic diversity,... profoundly aware of the imperative need to achieve complete unity, solemnly declares that it constitutes one and the same Nation, committed to the same destiny, and affirms its unshakable determination to construct the Cameroonian Fatherland on the basis of fraternity, justice and progress.... Everyone has the right to settle in any place and to move about freely.... No one shall be harassed because of his origin.

This is very much the language of nation-building and national citizenship, in those days strongly emphasized as the precondition for development. The 1996 constitution maintains most of these formulations, but it adds small but highly significant elements that seem to go in a very different direction. Special attention is given to "minorities" and "indigenes." The 1996 preamble lists as one of the first duties of the state that it should "ensure the protection of minorities" and "preserve the rights of the indigenous populations in accordance with the law." In part 10, "Regional and Local Authorities," the notion of "indigene" is further emphasized: "The Regional Council shall be headed by an indigene of the Region." Such notions come from a discourse that is, indeed, very different from the earlier language of nation-building and national citizenship. Notions like "indigene" and "minority" seem to be borrowed—or rather hijacked—from the discourse on development now promoted by the World Bank and other global institutions. Clearly, the 1996 constitution is permeated by the spirit of decentralization, albeit a special Cameroonian version.

It is striking that the Cameroonian lawmaking bodies have made no further effort to define notions like *indigene* and *minority*. In development parlance these terms refer to local groups whose culture and survival seem to be endangered, like "Pygmies" and certain nomadic pastoralist groups. But in the Cameroonian version the terms remain completely open and fluid. The consequence is that the government can recognize at will a specific group as "indigenous" or as a threatened "minority," depending on the political situation. As Henri David Kala-Lobé puts it in his comment on the new Constitution, "People only have to constitute themselves as a minority."[23]

Clearly this implication had been quickly understood by the Sawa. Their demonstration of February 10 and their chiefs' letter to the president

the same day appealed directly to these passages in the new constitution. And the government was quick to follow up on its new obligation
to "protect minorities." A few weeks later, by special decree, the function
of a "government delegate" was created as a kind of counterweight to
the elected mayor; of course this new official would be appointed by the
government. This decree was a good example of how the regime sought to
neutralize the impact of elections. It also proved to be a very useful tool in
the politics of autochthony. The first delegates were appointed in Douala,
and of course all were "indigenes" and faithful supporters of the CPDM.
This was the occasion for Sawa meetings to send their "congratulations to
the Head of State for heeding their call to put a check on the hegemony
of 'non-natives' in their cities" (Yenshu 1999:69).

However, the government also quickly learned to use the idea of belonging in more proactive ways. A series of electoral laws of the 1990s
seem to be mainly intended to protect "locals" from being outvoted by
"strangers." An elaborate set of rules and stipulations determines who is
to vote where. For instance, one has to prove a continuous stay of at least
six months in a given locality to qualify to vote there. To stand candidate in
elections in a locality one must be an "indigene" or a "long-term resident."
Other requirements, not explicitly formulated in the law, are invoked to
disqualify opposition candidates by the Ministry of Territorial Administration (MINAT), which is charged with overseeing electoral procedures
but is of course closely linked to the CPDM regime.[24] During the presidential, parliamentary, and municipal elections of the 1990s, MINAT de-
vised and applied additional conditions and diversionary tactics before
approving candidacies. In practice, the complicated electoral laws provide the government with precious opportunities to manipulate the electoral roll in its favor while making matters extremely difficult for the opposition. For instance, it is not uncommon for urban migrants (many of
whom supported the opposition) to be told that they cannot vote in the
city where they live but must go "home" to their village of origin to vote.
But once there, they are informed by the authorities that they have to vote
where they live—that is, in the city. In this way many voters never make it
to the polling station on election day. Moreover, at every election, newspapers are full of stories about opposition lists that have been disqualified
by the Ministry (generally at the very last moment), either for failure to
"reflect the sociological components" of the locality concerned or for including candidates who did not "belong" to the locality. Belonging has
become a choice weapon for manipulating elections.

Debates in the Cameroonian Press

The new emphasis in the government's policies did not escape the attention of the Cameroonian public. Especially after the Sawa demonstrations and similar events in Yaoundé (see below), a fierce debate developed in various newspapers and periodicals on the autochthony issue and how the government was using the new constitution and other legislation to develop an active politics of belonging. In progovernment papers like *Cameroun Tribune*, *Le Patriote*, and *L'Anecdote*, writers—mostly Sawa or Beti—hailed the constitution as a necessary step to protect minority groups from the "asphyxiating grip" of "expansionist" and demographically stronger groups such as the Bamileke.[25] Articles in the antigovernment press with mainly a Bamileke or Anglophone background rather attacked the new constitution as a recipe for national disintegration. Dieudonné Zognong (1997), for instance, emphasized that instead of promoting "national consciousness," it encouraged ethnic discrimination and therefore a "false consciousness," substituting an "ethnic citizenship" for the "civic citizenship" defended by the 1972 constitution. According to Zognong, the term *minority* was deliberately kept ambiguous and therefore open to manipulation. Others like B. Nantang Jua (1997) and E. Tatah Mentan (1996) blamed the CPDM government for championing a divide-and-rule politics to the detriment of nationhood.

At the end of 1996, Ethnonet/CIREPE, a Cameroonian research center that includes academics from various universities, organized a large-scale survey in various regions of the country on issues of autochthony and belonging in politics. The researchers were happy—but apparently quite surprised—to report that the majority of Cameroonians did not support the growing emphasis on the *autochtones-allogènes* tandem; at least this followed from the replies to their questionnaire. More than half of the respondents said they opposed the use of such notions, and less than a fourth stated that such issues influenced their voting behavior (Zognong and Mouiche 1997:15). However, the authors themselves were clearly somewhat worried that the survey might have elicited normative replies rather than reflecting actual political practices. Other contributions in the Zognong-Mouiche volume point, indeed, to how difficult it is to escape the apparent self-evidence of autochthony.

Earlier, in May 1996, the Cameroonian journal *La Nouvelle Expression* dedicated an entire issue (no. 1, May 23) to "minorités, autochtones, allogènes et démocratie." Most of the contributors made a serious and consistent attempt to deconstruct these notions and highlight their dangerous political implications. Professor Ngijol Ngijol (Yaoundé University I) provided a historical analysis of consecutive versions of "autochthony" and emphasized the dangers of including such an ambiguous notion in the constitution of the country. Bertrand Toko showed how difficult it is to apply the notion, notably in cities like Douala and Yaoundé that from the very start were populated by immigrants. It was all the more worrying, said Toko, that in these cities people invoke *autochtonie* as a self-evident base for political and economic claims. Philippe Bissek raised the question of why so many African regimes had recently begun to appeal to such primordial slogans.

However, other voices in this special issue seemed to have more impact. The same volume of *La Nouvelle Expression* (p. 18) featured a long interview with Roger Gabriel Nlep, then professor of political science at the University of Yaoundé II. Nlep's "theory" of *le village électoral* was to become a key reference point in subsequent discussions. To him, "integration" remained the central issue in Cameroonian politics: people should be fully integrated in the place where they live, "but this supposes that there is not *un autre chez soi* [another home area]." Therefore, if somebody who is elected in Douala defends the interests of "his" village in another region, this should be deemed "political malversation."

Nlep formulated this as a matter of course. Implicitly, however, he gave the notion of *intégration* a completely novel tenor. Ever since independence, this term had played a central role in Cameroonian political discourse, as in many other postcolonies. However, under Ahidjo, with his untiring emphasis (at least at the ideological level) on national unity, *intégration* meant "national integration." Initially Biya seemed to follow in his traces: his 1986 book still extolled "the realization of national integration, the *étape suprême* of national unity" (Biya 1986:30). Nlep rather related the notion of integration to the local level—which, of course, corresponded very well to the new divide-and-rule course the Biya regime chose after democratization. Thus integration suddenly acquired implications that make it the very opposite of national unity: it now referred to integration in the local setting and to some sort of local, instead of national, citizenship. The implication of Nlep's "theory" was clear: migrants should go "home"—to the village of origin—to vote, since they clearly feel that they belong there. In these discussions, as in the interview with Prof. Bejanga, president of the Eleventh Province, the place of burial was cited as the final proof of where one belongs.

Autochthony's "Naturalness": The Funeral
as a Final Test for Belonging

Nlep's theory of *le village électoral* has a self-evidence that seems difficult to escape. "Of course" one belongs in the village of one's ancestors—certainly if one wants to be buried there. Nlep's approach is therefore a good example of what was called above the "naturalizing character" of autochthony discourse (cf. Comaroff and Comaroff 2001). In the popular understanding, this idea of *un autre chez soi* is especially marked by the continuing habit of migrants to be buried "at home"—that is, in the village. In many parts of Africa it is still considered a social disgrace to be buried in the city. The general idea is that this is the fate of people who do not have any relatives; a person who still has family will at death be brought back to the village to be buried there (see Geschiere and Gugler 1998). Big cities like Yaoundé and Douala—and many other African cities—hardly have cemeteries.

In the new political configuration, the Sawa people and other self-styled autochthons tend to emphasize the political implications of this. If migrants want to be taken to their family's village at the *moment suprême* of the funeral, this is clearly what they consider home. So while they're still living they should get involved in politics in that village, instead of trying to dominate their "hosts" in the latter's own territory. This brings us to the second issue that worried Professor Bejanga, the unhappy chairperson of the Association of the Elites of the Eleventh Province quoted before: the funeral as the ultimate test of where one belongs.

The fact that the issue of the funeral came up at the end of the interview with Professor Bejanga was certainly not accidental. It is precisely this link with the funeral "at home" that gives the autochthony discourse its broader implications in many parts of Africa. The inherent link with the place of burial indicates that the upsurge of issues of autochthony and belonging in general is not just created by shrewd politicians and their manipulations to gain support. Clearly their appeals to autochthony strike a deep emotional chord among the population. The "naturalizing" tenor of the autochthony discourse—its appeal to heavy chtonic rituals like the funeral—gives it such strong resonance.

In many parts of Africa the funeral "at home"—in the place where the deceased was born and not where (s)he lived—is acquiring an ever more explicitly political significance. Simultaneously there has been a spectacular proliferation of funeral rituals—often emphatically "traditional" performances that in fact contain many *neo*traditional additions. These occasions become true festivals of belonging (see chap. 6). The Cameroonian economist Célestin Monga (1995), concerned about the rapidly growing expenditures for these lavish ceremonies, even speaks of *une mauvaise gestion de la mort* (a bad management of death). This is, of course, strong language, probably inspired by his concern that these apparently private occasions are becoming highly politicized, precisely because belonging has become an all-overriding criterion in democratic politics.

As Samuel Eboua, a true *eminence grise* of Cameroonian politics,[26] put it most clearly: "Every Cameroonian is an *allogène* anywhere else in the country...than where his ancestors lived and...where his mortal remains will be buried. Everybody knows that only under exceptional circumstances will a Cameroonian be buried elsewhere" (*Impact Tribu Une* 5 [1995]: 14, my translation). Again, very powerful language. Any concept of the equality of all Cameroonian citizens before the law—for instance, the principle that every citizen had the right to settle anywhere in the country (emphasized in the 1972 constitution)—is lost here. The whole notion of national citizenship seems to be overshadowed by the natural truth of the autochthony appeal: a person belongs where he or she will be buried.

All the more important to highlight that even this natural truth has its history. In many contexts, the very idea of the funeral at home seems to have a neotraditional character. Moreover, its importance seems to increase, rather than decrease, in many areas, despite continued urbanization and migration. For some groups, notably in the western highlands, the tradition of bringing the body back to the village is older; here the old rituals are elaborated constantly with new—and often quite costly—elements stressing the ongoing commitment of the urbanites to "their" villages. But in other areas, for instance in the southern forest regions, this is a clear neotradition. There groups remained quite mobile up to the colonial conquest (around 1900), and people buried their dead in newly settled lands.[27] Yet now these southerners also heavily emphasize the need to bring back the deceased to the village and bury them there.

In the new political order, proving one's autochthony has come to have supreme importance, and there is no better way to do this than through elaborate funeral rituals "back home." The consequence is a rather macabre traffic in bodies: people digging up their father's body and burying it in a different site in order to fortify their claims to belong there; gendarmes interrupting funeral rites to "arrest the body" and bury it elsewhere so as to safeguard a claim to belonging by an elite member of the family. Yet we will see below (chap. 6) that these earthy rituals—despite all their dynamics and innovations—give the appeal to autochthony a deep emotional charge.

A Tortuous History

Thus far I have focused on a special part of Cameroon, South-West Province and the adjacent metropolis of Douala, which for obvious reasons became a hotbed of autochthony. These areas were particularly affected by an influx of migrants from the interior. For the self-styled autochthons in this area, theories like Nlep's *village electoral* therefore became particularly self-evident. So it might be all the more worthwhile to go further back into the history of this area. Already in chapter 1 I emphasized autochthony's difficult relation with history. Indeed, in a longer time perspective all the inconsistencies mentioned there—the contradictions inherent in colonial labor policies, changing self-identifications among local groups, and especially the uncertain, "segmentary" implications of autochthony discourse—come to the fore again.

Nowadays, to many Bakweri "autochthons"—and notably to their elites—it seems self-evident that fellow Anglophones from Grassfields in North-West Province are their main rivals. People often say that this threat is as old as the plantations created by the Germans after 1890: after all, they triggered the labor demand that led the northwesterners to arrive in ever greater numbers. However, in his fine-grained studies of the plantation laborers, Piet Konings (1993 and 2003) shows that it was only after 1960 that northwesterners really began to dominate within the plantations' labor force. Before this, it were first Francophones from eastern Cameroon, and later Igbo from neighboring Nigeria, who constituted major contingents among plantation laborers. In those days, they—notably the Igbo—were the main "Others" by whom the autochthons felt threatened.

Striking in Koning's historical study of the building up of the plantations' labor force is—again—the clear preference of colonial authorities for immigrant laborers. As said, the colonials' distrust and their condescending views about the local populations constitute a true leitmotif in the history of autochthony discourses in many present-day African settings. Quite soon after their first penetration into this area (early 1890s), the Germans despaired of the Bakweri's "apathy," their reluctance to work on the plantations, and their utter unreliability as laborers.[28] A strong argument for *Strafexpeditionen* (punitive expeditions) into the interior was that new labor reserves could be opened up of people more fit for productive labor. This stereotype of a somewhat tragic apathy or "indolence" was to stick to the Bakweri throughout colonial times. British authorities worried about the rapidity with which the Bakweri "sold"— mostly in a very informal way—land to immigrants who chose to stay in the area after expiration of their contract on the plantation.[29] The authorities worried even more about the apparent collapse of Bakweri marriage, since many women seemed to prefer to live as concubines with immigrants rather than stay with their husbands. In the 1950s the colonial authorities asked the anthropologist Edwin Ardener to conduct an in-depth study of "divorce and fertility" among the local population (Ardener 1962), since they feared—apparently like the Bakweri themselves—that the whole group would soon be extinguished (cf. also Ardener 1956:16 and 1958/1996:228–29). As late as 1982, George Courade published an article on the Bakweri with the title, quite striking in retrospect, *Une marginalité volontaire* (a voluntary marginality); he refers also to *une conduite volontaire d'échec* (a voluntary tendency toward failure). In 1987, when I first did some research in the area, the condescending stereotype of Bakweri men as "not being able to retain either their land or their women" was still quite current. However, the fierceness with which many Bakweri now defend their autochthony claims against *allogènes* and the prominent role of southwestern elites in national politics show not only how quickly stereotypes can change but also how conducive the present-day political setting is to autochthony endeavors.

The colonial intermezzo had similar effects in the case of the Douala grievances against immigrants. German colonial administrators were very skeptical of the Douala, even though the Douala chiefs' acceptance of a German "protectorate" had permitted the very beginning of the German colony. The first decade of German rule was dominated by the colonizers' determined efforts to break through the control Douala "middlemen" retained over the trade with the interior (Austen and Derrick 1999). Subsequently the Douala were pushed off their land in order to make it available for expanding European settlement (see Eckert 1999). Eventually the Germans broke Douala control over a budding, indigenous cocoa plantation sector in the Douala hinterland. As a consequence the area, especially the fertile land along the Mungo River, was opened up for increasingly rapid immigration by Bamileke from the overpopulated Grassfields plateau (Eckert 1995). In this area as well, the recent reversal in relation between autochthons and *allogènes* is quite striking. In the second half of the twentieth century, Douala seemed to have become an immigrants' city, until the vociferous protests of the Greater Sawa Movement in the 1990s. Apparently autochthons fare considerably better in the postcolony than in the colony.

The present-day tensions have interesting precedents in the later years of colonial rule, when democratic experiments were very gradually introduced. During a brief interlude when colonial authoritarianism was decreasing and before postcolonial one-party authoritarianism had asserted itself, elections had real meaning (cf. Lentz 2003 and 2006). In the South-West this led to fierce confrontations because of the immigrant problem. Especially after World War II, the British had started to experiment with local government as a more democratic form of indirect rule. However, in this area the British adage of "no taxation without representation"— meaning that anybody who paid taxes had a right to vote—created serious problems. Indirect rule had meant a constant search from the side of the British for the "truly" traditional authority holders, leading to repeated reshufflings, since each new divisional officer set out to correct the work of his predecessors. Among the locals, it engendered an equally determined search for ways to make the colonial authorities recognize each group's claims to traditional pedigree over those of rival factions (see Geschiere 1993; Nicolson 1969). But in those struggles it was clear in any case that the only ones involved were the natives—in this area, the Bakweri.

Reforms from the 1940s on, leading up to "local government," threatened to change all this and to open up the new political arenas to the numerous immigrants—in those days still notably Francophones and Igbo from eastern Nigeria, who paid their taxes in the area and therefore, in the British view, should be represented.

• • • • • • • • • • • • • •

How threatening all this was to the Bakweri leaders is clear from the minutes of a 1944 meeting of the "Bakweri Clan Council" in Buea. The DO opened the meeting by sternly admonishing the council to make at last a definitive decision on the reform of the "Native Administration." The councillors were clearly impressed by this opening shot and approved all his proposals without any discussion—until the issue of the "strangers' representation" was raised. Then, a true firework of protest exploded. One after another, the councillors passionately argued why "strangers" could never sit on any council of the Bakweri Native Administration:

> In our tradition, a stranger cannot become a chief—how can we call a stranger *sango boa* [lit.: "father of the village"]? We very much oppose it.

However, the DO stood firm:

> Here you are, the Bakweri Native Administration receiving approximately L 1500 a year in tax money of which the strangers in your midst pay almost exactly half. You benefit by their money and you decide how their money shall be used. This is absolutely contradictory to the things we British believe in, and it is against the very things for which we are now fighting a war.

In spite of this passionate speech, the meeting broke up in complete chaos:

> Whereupon all shout: "We will not admit strangers."[30]

· · · · · · · · · · · · · · ·

The same question was to come up time and again in the last years before independence, forcing the British to experiment with highly complicated compromises: a fixed percentage of seats (but always a minority) for stranger representatives and so on. However, after independence, the whole issue was settled in a quite unexpected way. The reunification in 1961 with former French Cameroon, where the new president, Ahmadou Ahidjo, had already succeeded in consolidating his regime, meant that within a few years in Anglophone Cameroon as well a one-party regime was established under which elections had only symbolic importance, as a tightly controlled manifestation of support to the government.[31] Under Ahidjo's rule, it was the party elite that made decisions on all candidacies, down to the lowest level. Only one list was submitted to the electorate, and voters were allowed only to pronounce their support of this list. A refusal to vote, let alone any attempt to vote for other candidates, was severely sanctioned (see chapter 6 below on the "techniques" of nation-building).

"Regional equilibrium," the cornerstone of Ahidjo's policies, meant certainly that each group had to have its own representatives within the political-administrative hierarchy of the one-party state. However, it was the party–elites—Ahidjo and his close collaborators—who decided on who was to represent which group or region, and there was no space for any debate about whether the candidate was "really" from the region concerned. On the contrary, any discussion in that direction was forcefully repressed as a sign of incipient "subversion" and an effort to create dissension among the Cameroonian people, who had to stand united behind their president. As noted, in those days terms like *autochthons* and *immigrants* may have been used frequently in everyday life, but they were hushed in public political speech.

All this changed dramatically with the return of multipartyism, which brought a reemergence of the kinds of debates that plagued the Bakweri council in 1958 in its indignation over the British insistence that strangers should be represented. The difference is, of course, that now the split between autochthons and immigrants has become a major issue at the national political level as well, and that state authorities no longer see fit—as the British did—to try to mitigate the local contradictions. On the contrary, the regime seems intent on fanning them. Yet in this respect as well, things can apparently change rapidly. For instance, since the end of the 1990s the Greater Sawa Movement, which for a few years had great salience, seems to have lost its momentum. One reason might be that the Biya regime has less need of it, now that it has been so successful in dividing and cantoning the opposition. Autochthony discourse may seem to be self-evident and even "natural," but it becomes virulent under specific political conditions. One of these is hotly contested elections.

Autochthony's claims seem to have a quite surprising historical changeability in another respect as well. At present, nobody seems to doubt the Bakweri self-definition as the autochthons of the Mount Cameroon area along the southwest coast. Yet since the time of Edwin Ardener—the British anthropologist who with his wife Shirley undertook path-breaking research in the area from the 1950s on—Bakweri elders invariably start their histories with an account of a migration (see Ardener 1956). This is to be expected: remember Nicole Loraux's insistence in her study of classical Athens, the cradle of autochthony, that history is always about an initial migration and that therefore autochthony can be only a negative notion, a denial of an original movement (Loraux 1996). What is more surprising in the Bakweri case is that their histories seem to hesitate between two opposite origins. Especially around Buea, on the slopes of the huge Mt. Cameroon, elders point to "the other side" of the mountain, the inland-looking northern side, as their land of origin. This is the version that is confirmed in most of the literature.[32] However, in 1987 I found that at least in those days among the so-called Lower Bakweri, closer to the coast, many elders categorically refused this tradition (especially in the area around Bonjongo, where the colonial authorities had instituted a regional subchief who soon developed a rivalry with the paramount chief in Buea).[33] Here, informants insisted that, on the contrary, they had come from the southwest, together with their "brothers" the Douala. The contrast between these traditions brings out Bakweri uncertainties between being a people from the mountains or from the sea (Sawa).

· · · · · · · · · · · · · ·

A graphic example of such hesitations can be seen in the metamorphosis of the present chief of Buea, Samuel Endeley. In 1987 I did an interview with this prominent Bakweri elite (brother of Emmanuel Endeley, who in the last years of British rule had been prime minister of "Southern Cameroons"). At the time, the Buea chieftaincy had been vacant since the death of chief Gervase Mbele Endeley III (Samuel's father's brother). It was clear that Samuel considered himself to be the obvious candidate to succeed his uncle. However, the government seemed reluctant to fill the vacant seat.[34] In those days, Samuel, who had just retired from a splendid career in the judicial hierarchy—first as chief justice of Western Cameroon and then as judge at the High Court in Yaoundé—presented himself very much as a British gentleman, receiving me wearing a three-piece suit and opening a bottle of claret. I met him again in 1993 at a conference in Yaoundé. In the meantime he had been finally appointed chief of Buea,[35] and this had led to a spectacular transformation. He was now clad in all sorts of "traditional" gear: a little raffia crown, a wide white jacket, a wrapper around his waist, and strings of beads and cowries around his torso. This time he refused to shake my hand, as a chief would do; he motioned for me to kneel beside his chair and talk to him from this position.

Apparently his appointment had led also to a drastic change in his viewpoints. In 1987, he asserted that the Bakweri, as people of the mountain, had nothing in common with the Douala, "those people of the sea" of whom he was very critical ("liars", "traitors"). However, at the very end of 1991, when he finally had become chief, Endeley joined the Douala chiefs in a spectacular revival of their annual *ngondo* ritual, in which they enter the sea in order to ask the water spirits for their blessing for the coming year.[36] The "man of the mountain" had abruptly turned into a "man of the sea."[37]

. . . .

Of course this metamorphosis fit in with the general rapprochement under the new political constellation of the 1990s between the southwestern elites and the Sawa. In 1996, SWELA (the South-West elite association, already mentioned) formally joined the Greater Sawa Movement.

An Empty Discourse with Segmentary Implications

This fusion of elites of various "autochthonous" groups is a striking example of how useful the very emptiness of the autochthony notion can be (cf. chap. 1). Mountain people can turn into sea people (Sawa) at will, since both claim to be autochthonous. However, a fixed corollary of this emptiness is the highly segmenting implications of this discourse, equally emphasized in chapter 1. This was soon to manifest itself among the new-fangled Sawa as well. In 1996, a split arose in the Greater Sawa Movement when the government appointed a Bakweri, Peter Musonge, prime minister. In a subsequent Sawa meeting, Jean-Jacques Ekindi, a Douala and the initiator of the Sawa movement, accused the South-West delegation of trying to sideline him and dominate the movement: "Sawa cannot complain of Bamileke domination and later accept South West domination" (quoted in Nyamnjoh and Rowlands 1998:333).

SWELA itself was plagued by similar segmentation. As noted earlier, Oben Peter Ashu, the feared governor of South-West Province, commanded the "strangers" in his area to vote for the CPDM, now that the president had been kind enough to name a son of the area as prime minister. However, Ashu is himself a Banyangi from Mamfe, so at other times he can be heard complaining bitterly of how the government is always favoring the Bakweri (the present prime minister's group).[38] Autochthony ideas may allow "fusion" with a kind of massing effect and thus offer solace to smaller groups like the Douala or the Bakweri. However, "fission"—the segmentary tenor of this discourse emphasized above—is always quick to follow.

Conclusion

Here I have focused on a specific part of the country, South-West Province and the adjacent Douala area. But there are striking parallels in the upsurge of autochthony in other parts of the country, for instance in the capital Yaoundé. In a study of developments in this city, Antoine Socpa (2002) highlights the crucial role played by the new style of elections and the ways the regime tried to manipulate these. In Yaoundé, Beti autochthons also fear being overrun by Bamileke immigrants.[39] The basic issue here is plots for building houses. The concomitant stereotype is that shrewd Bamileke are profiting from the Beti's proverbial taste for red wine; deals are supposedly made strategically in bars—"a few bottles of wine and the land is handed over."[40]

In his second chapter Socpa points out, however, that negotiations over land have a much longer history and indeed still go on, despite all the consternation about them among the "autochthons." It was only with democratization in the beginning of the 1990s, when immigrants founded SDF cells and started to vote for the opposition, that small-scale violence against Bamileke newcomers became rampant. As in the South-West, the former owners of the land complained about the immigrants' "ingratitude." They should consider themselves guests, since their true belonging was in the village where their family had originated. Was it fitting for a guest to go into politics and dominate his "landlord" in the latter's own home?

As in Douala and the South-West, the government firmly backed the autochthons' cause. The violence in Yaoundé was partly caused by the regime's strong encouragement to make these immigrants go "home" and vote there instead of forming a fifth column in CPDM heartland. However, here as well the Beti's rapport with the regime was quite ambivalent. Socpa (chap. 3) notes that in many quarters of Yaoundé it was the government that had expropriated land to divide it into plots and sell those to richer Bamileke. Segmenting tendencies manifested themselves here as well. After the autochthons of the CPDM had won the elections, fierce debates followed about who "really" belonged. Apparently some Beti candidates were more autochthonous than others, so some were scrapped from the list and others were downgraded to a lower place (Socpa 2003: chap. 5). The precise spoils of autochthony may differ, like its icons.[41] Yet the basic–characteristic—the notion's emptiness, allowing for great elasticity and constant fusion but also making it vulnerable to equally constant fission—is the same.

Thus the various examples above point to one common trait that might be the main strength of autochthony discourse. In all these cases a great complexity of layers and ambiguities is swept together with surprising ease into one apparently self-evident opposition: between people who belong and those who came from elsewhere. It is its natural appearance that gives the autochthony category unifying force, bringing together highly local preoccupations with national rifts and even beyond this. My examples may show also where its main weakness lies: the whole category seems to evaporate through an inherent but highly unstable segmentary logic as soon as a battle is won and assets have to be divided.[42]

Cameroon: Decentralization and Belonging

In the Cameroonian context it was to be expected that autochthony and belonging would become hot issues in the South-West and the Mungo, densely populated and economically developed regions where a constant influx of immigrants caused a growing pressure on land.[1] The same applies to the country's two big cities, Douala and Yaoundé. This chapter focus on a completely different part of Cameroun: the dense forest area of East Province, which was always seen as the most backward part of the country—of very difficult access and so thinly populated that large parts of this province still seem to be completely empty. This was one of the regions on which the Ahidjo regime focused in its 1970s campaign to raise the birth rate, with the motto that the *sous-population* was one of the main reasons for *sous-développement* (a definition of underdevelopment that is quite striking in retrospect). Several *arrondissements* in this area still have figures of 3 or 4 inhabitants per square mile. All the more surprising that in the 1990s even in these almost empty areas autochthony and the exclusion of "strangers" became hot issues.

The background to this turmoil was quite different from that for the regions discussed in the previous chapter. In the East it was not so much the new style of elections and the locals' fear of being "outvoted" by more numerous immigrants that ignited the autochthony issue, but rather the development establishment's new advocacy of decentralization, "bypassing the state," and reaching out to "civil society." As noted in chapter 1, these new accents in development interventions were as dramatic a reversal for the African continent as the sudden wave of democratization and political liberalization around 1990. In many ways they were closely related, both arising out of the new context created by the end of the cold war. In the second half of the 1980s, the World Bank rapidly switched from a highly statist and centralist conception of development—stressing "modernizing state elites" and "nation-building" as prerequisites to development—to a deep distrust of the state as a barrier instead of a support to development. The new view on development, announced as "neoliberal," emphasized the need to bypass the state as much as possible through decentralization and support for civil society—which in practice meant support for the nongovernmental organizations that have been the objects of fierce debate ever since.[2]

Like political liberalization, this approach to development had quite unexpected effects on the ground. The older statist conception of development had certainly raised many problems: in retrospect it is clear that it often served as an excuse for Western donors to support highly dictatorial regimes as indispensable allies in the cold war context. But simplistic applications of the new development creed soon turned out to be haunted by their own problems. For instance, many proponents of the neoliberal style of development in the 1990s hardly seem to worry that decentralization and greater autonomy for local communities might turn issues of belonging—who "really" belongs to a certain region or village, and who is therefore entitled to profit from a new development project?—into explosive issues. As for the NGOs, it is now increasingly recognized that in practice it is often problematic to characterize them as "nongovernmental." Many of these organizations are initiated by former civil servants who maintain close contacts with their former colleagues in the state's bureaucracy. A related and often overlooked implication of this is that such NGOs are often highly localist in orientation. Urban elites who launch an NGO are intent to use their contacts in order to further the development of their region or village of origin—often with a keen eye to their own interest. Villagers may look with mixed feelings at this sudden return of their "brothers" from the city now that they can take advantage of new opportunities in the village. Such new opportunities to gain access to the development manna therefore raise issues of belonging similar to those raised by the political changes discussed in chapter 1: who is "really" local and thus entitled to profit from the new project?

For Cameroon's East Province, the ideals of the new development policies were condensed in the 1994 Forest Law—no wonder, since timber, the province's main resource, had become highly important to the national economy. The new political tensions had mostly bypassed this part of Cameroon, since even though the population here never tires of complaining about the utter neglect of the province by the political establishment in Yaoundé, people remained staunchly united behind the Biya regime and the CPDM.[3] The opposition hardly gained a foothold, since support of the SDF has been time and again interpreted by the population as support for the Bamileke. Even though the latter are not particularly numerous in the area, they have acquired a central position in regional trading networks, and for many this seems reason enough to fear a regime change. Voting for the opposition is thus seen as selling out to "the Bami." However, the impact of the new approach to development was very direct in this province, especially because the country's main forest resources are concentrated here. Indeed, the new forest law, marked as it was by the novel buzzwords of decentralization and reaching out to civil society, was the main catalyst in turning autochthony into a crucial issue in this almost empty area.

The forest law is, moreover, of special interest here because of the central role it assigned to "the" local community in its blueprint for the exploitation of the forest. In chapter 1 I discussed a somewhat unexpected aspect of development initiatives that subscribe to a neoliberal agenda: the trust they put in "traditional" entities. The central role the Cameroonian forest law attributes to "the community" is a striking example of this. In many respects the Cameroonian forest law—as said, heavily promoted by the World Bank—followed the so-called Washington Consensus, which might be called the neoliberal Vulgate. The basic principles of the law were to limit the role of the state and allow locals to profit more directly from the market. However, this was supposed to require a strengthening of the local community, which, characteristically, seemed to be taken for granted by the legislators. The text of the law includes no further effort to define this community, even though in the eastern forest region the composition of local formations is quite volatile. In practice, the consequence of this peculiar combination of economic rationality and trust in tradition was that belonging became all the more pressing an issue.

Below I will first sketch the general contours of the forest issue and the growing importance of Cameroon's East Province in this context. Then I will briefly discuss the new forest law as a typical example of the new approach to development. The last sections will consider its effects on the ground, notably the struggles over belonging it triggered with similar implications as in the political context discussed in the previous chapter. The tension between autochthony's apparent self-evidence and its receding qualities in practice comes again sharply to the fore.

The East and the New Importance of the Forest

In the spring of 1971, when I had just begun my fieldwork in the East Province, I witnessed a memorable scene in Abong-Mbang, one of the main towns of the province.

. . . .

The new minister of territorial administration, Victor Ayissi-Mvodo—at the time a rapidly rising star in Cameroonian politics (even tipped by many as President Ahidjo's crown prince)—was to come and visit the province; Abong-Mbang was to be his first stop. For days the regional authorities— both the civil servants and the politicians of the UNC, the one party—had been busy preparing for the event. The square in front of the Préfecture had been swept, a canopy had been erected for the guests of honor (including of course all the town's whites: the priests, the nuns, the traders, the development workers, and even the town's new anthropologist). On the day itself, the schools were closed and all the schoolchildren marched in uniform to the square. The women of the OFUNC (the party's women's league) were lined up in their colorful wrappers with the president's image; occasional passersby were forcefully stopped by the omnipresent gendarmes and forced to join the crowd as well. However, at the appointed hour (10 o'clock in the morning) nothing happened. It got hotter and hotter, but the crowd remained standing in the full sun, supervised by the gendarmes. Only toward noon a dust cloud appeared, and then we saw a cortege of about ten cars approaching at full speed. Orderlies ran up to the first cars to open doors, and out of the biggest black Mercedes stepped the minister. The applause master behind the pulpit motioned the crowd to clap their hands, which they dutifully did.

There followed a long series of highly laudatory speeches by the various dignitaries of the province, praising first of all the president and his love of the people, and secondly the minister who had come all the way down to visit the town. But the most memorable speech came from the minister himself. After having listened somewhat condescendingly to all the speeches by others, he rose to make his own speech, starting with the memorable words: "Before I came here I always thought the East was a backward area, inhabited by people who only drink *arki* [home-distilled spirits] and practice witchcraft." He clearly intended to go on and say that his visit (which had only just started) had taught him differently. But unfortunately, the applause master signaled the crowd to clap already after the minister's first sentence—which, again, they dutifully did. Most remarkable in all this was that nobody seemed to see any irony in the crowd's applauding the current stereotype of themselves as *arki* drinkers and witches.

. . . .

The whole scene offered a striking example of what kind of subject the new regime tried to create as *le citoyen camerounais* and what kind of disciplinary techniques it used for this. But this is the topic of a later chapter (chap. 6). Here it may suffice to signal that the minister had succeeded in summing up in one striking phrase—underlined by the crowd's applause—the current stereotype of East Province as backward, inaccessible, and even dangerous. Among civil servants transfer to East is seen as a serious punishment. One of the reasons that in the 1980s state courts in this province started to convict "witches" seems to have been the magistrates' own fear of having to serve in what was reputed to be a witchcraft-ridden area (see Fisiy and Geschiere 1991).

However, all of this changed dramatically toward the end of the 1980s. With the collapse of the world market prices for Cameroon's main cash crops (cacao, coffee, and cotton) and in view of the apparent limits on the country's oil resources, logging suddenly became the main export product and the regime's major hope for redressing its economic ills. The main untapped forest resources were to be found in East Province. The effects were quite spectacular. Whereas in the 1980s irrigation had been a central focus in development, with projects mainly focused on the semiarid zones of the country's northern parts, around 1990 a sort of turnaround took place and development efforts were largely reoriented to the southeastern forest zones. Many Cameroonian colleagues who in the 1980s had launched themselves as irrigation experts now presented themselves as having equal expertise on the rainforest and the social issues raised by its exploitation.

This reversal acquired all the more momentum because donors proved to be willing to invest significant sums of development money into projects that might help to steer the ongoing exploitation of forests in the right direction. In the present context it is impossible to do justice to all the complexities of the rainforest issue that became the topic of so much debate in the 1990s. The central question will be obvious: how can an ongoing exploitation of this highly valuable resource—so profitable not only to larger logging companies but also to national governments of countries in dire financial need—be reconciled with the increasingly powerful global concern over the depletion of rainforests, seen as the "world's lungs"? In the course of the 1990s, this dilemma was further complicated by the main development agencies' new policies of seeking to "bypass the state" and get into direct contact with the population—in this context, the people who actually live in these forests and whose interests do not necessarily correspond to those of their government. In this complex configuration all sorts of unexpected alliances emerged. Striking is, for instance, how strongly ecologically oriented the World Bank, a major player, has become in this context. This was certainly not always the case. In Cameroon circa 1980 the World Bank had provided important subventions for parastatals to create huge agroindustrial complexes in the forest zone, which had the inevitable consequence of large-scale deforestation. Nowadays, however, the main priority of the Bank's representatives in the zone—often biologists or other ecologically minded experts—is to stop such deforestation.[4]

At least initially, the interests of the (usually expatriate) logging companies seemed to converge with the ecologists' viewpoints: both saw the local population as the main culprits of ongoing deforestation because of their slash-and-burn agricultural techniques. In the early 1990s, for example, one of the major ecological projects in this zone, financed by both the World Bank and the SFID (Société forestière et industrielle de la Doumé, the area's major logging company, an offshoot of Rougier, an important French business empire), proposed to literally fence off a significant part of the forest so as to keep out the locals. Later on, however, ecologists of the World Bank came to see the locals instead as major stakeholders whose role would be crucial for maintaining the forest.

The key question is how a "sustainable" exploitation of the forest can be realized—that is, how can logging contribute to the national economy and local development without endangering the regeneration of the forest? Despite a host of studies, basic questions remain unanswered. For instance, how long does the forest take to regenerate? To what extent does logging indeed damage the forest? Are the locals' slash-and-burn agriculture and hunting more damaging to the forest than logging? An even thornier

question: Who is to undertake such sustainable exploitation? Privatization, which now seems the obvious answer in many contexts, would mean
opening up this sector to mostly foreign capital. The national government
instead advocates privatization with national capital, which in practice
means allowing members of Parliament and other politicians to obtain
major logging permits. This leads, moreover, to fierce struggles between,
on the one hand, "strangers" from other areas (especially Bamileke entrepreneurs from the west, who are supposed to have more capital at their
disposal) and, on the other, the elites of the zone itself, who insist that as
"autochthons" they should be privileged in the attribution of the highly
coveted logging concessions. An even more sensitive question: To what
extent can these elites be assumed to represent the locals' interests? Or do
the villagers have to be protected not only from foreign firms eager to log
in their territories but also from their own elites? The staff of some development projects in the area, run by expatriate developers, seem inclined to
confirm the latter. But village committees for their part are inclined to complain of the meddling and the paternalist attitude of these developers.[5]

It is in the context of this Gordian knot of conflicting interests, unclear
alliances, and oppositions that Cameroon's forest law was launched, turning belonging and autochthony into hot issues in this region as well.

The New Forest Law

The 1994 forest law carries, as noted, the signature of the World Bank,
which in this context worked closely together with the World Wildlife
Fund.[6] No wonder it is heavily ecological in tenor. Its major concern is to
ensure "sustainable" exploitation of forest resources. Of special importance is, moreover, that it applies new insights in forest ecology, in that it
treats the participation of the local population as vital to the forest's conservation. One of the most revolutionary aspects of the law is that it institutes a whole series of new arrangements to safeguard the role of "the"
local community as a main stakeholder in any form of forest exploitation.

There are good reasons to sympathize, therefore, with the overall tenor
of the law. Until now, the local population hardly profited from the logging in "their" forests. Logging companies were (and are) mostly run by
expatriates (French, Dutch, Lebanese, and also Malaysians for a time, but
they left after a few years when their main concession was exhausted).
Under the earlier rules, a company was required to come to some sort
of agreement with the population, and this frequently took the form of *a*

cahier de charges (a written list of obligations). In practice these amounted to a series of ad hoc *cadeaux* (grants of food, palm wine, shirts for the local soccer team, etc.) and sometimes assistance for constructing a school or a bridge. However, there was little that villagers could do to exert pressure on the company when they felt that it had not kept its promises. In case of conflict, the administration invariably sided with the company, and in those days the gendarmes knew how to quench any resistance. After all, as in other former French colonies, the postcolonial state maintained the legal principle that all forest that is not cleared and cultivated belongs to the state's domain.[7] Therefore the idea was that the companies should compensate the state, rather than the locals, for exploiting forest resources.

The new law, in contrast, intends to empower the local population. The latter is recognized as an important—maybe even the most important—stakeholder, next to the state and the *concessionaires* (the logging companies that acquired a concession from the government). Thus, the law offers local institutions, both the municipality and the "local community" (an entity that, as noted, is not further defined in the law's text), the possibility of creating their own forests and managing them collectively.[8] Moreover, the law assigns—in line with the now fashionable emphasis on financial decentralization—half of the taxes on all logging activities to the local communities on whose territory the logging takes place. In principle such decentralization would have quite dramatic consequences: municipalities of a few thousand inhabitants would suddenly be entitled to massive sums of money. Of course, the reality is different. The extremely centralist tradition of the Cameroonian administration guarantees that most of this tax money will never arrive at the local level. Still, this new formal arrangement in itself has created great excitement and expectations among local populations.

Positive as this emphasis on local participation might be at first sight, it is at the same time somewhat naive. First of all, it remains to be seen to what extent the aim of increasing local participation can be reconciled with the law's main aim—that is, to guarantee the sustainable exploitation of the forest. Expatriates who run development projects helping local communities to create community forests[9] are highly concerned that once the community finally gets its forest legally recognized, the local committees will succumb to the seductive offers of logging companies. Thus the creation of a new community forest might even speed up the depletion of remaining forest resources. Most foreign experts believe that their presence is indispensable as some sort of counterweight against the pressure of these logging companies. However, in view of the broad resonance of the law and the new possibilities it opens up throughout the East Province, it is to be expected that all over the province people will take initiatives to constitute their forest, including outside the areas covered by development projects. And what external institution will offer some counterbalance there against the temptation for the villagers to strike a quick deal with a logging company, so that the new community forest would be quickly depleted?

An even bigger problem is that the legislative bodies seem to have had good reasons to avoid specifying what is meant by "local community."[10] Precisely in the forest area, local communities are notoriously diffuse and floating in their composition. This has been the despair of a long series of development projects in the area. Local forms of organization are still marked by strong segmentary tendencies and a constant seesaw between fission and fusion. Groups that make common cause against an outsider quickly split up when resources have to be divided internally. Moreover, the "village" as such has a checkered history: it is mostly a creation of successive colonial governments (German and French), which forced small family hamlets to join in larger settlements along new roads (see below). Hence villages remain riven with internal tensions. In such a context the forest law's heavy emphasis on "the" community as a major stakeholder without further defining it must lead to practical problems in defining who is "in" and who is "out."

Participation in Practice

Another problem is the great complexity of the law, which makes participation for the locals not an easy thing. A complete overview of all its intricacies would require too much space here (but see Karsenty 1999 and Oyono 2002). Yet the unexpected effects of the law's application are of broader interest, since they might be typical of what decentralization and bypassing the state—aspects of the new approach to development—mean in everyday practice, almost inevitably giving rise to fierce struggles over who "really" belongs.

The forest law provided three main openings for increasing local involvement in the management of the forest:

- the fiscal decentralization, already mentioned, of tax revenues on forest exploitation: no less than 40 percent of this tax is to go to the municipality concerned and another 10 percent to the villages adjacent to where the logging has taken place

- the new opportunities for creating forests to be owned and managed by local organizations, notably municipal forests (to be run by a municipality) and
community forests (to be run by a village or an even smaller community)
- a new measure fixing a remuneration for the villages on whose territory logging
is taking place, to be paid directly to the villagers by the logging company (on
top of the tax owed to the government); in 1996 a separate circular from the
Ministry of Environment and Forests fixed this rate at 1,000 FCFA (USD 1.30)
per cubic meter of logged wood

The second innovation, the institution of municipal and community
forests, seemed to hold the most promise for encouraging local participation in forest management. However, starting such a forest involves such
a complicated procedure that the local communities are hardly capable
of undertaking this without strong outside support—in practice, from either an expatriate development project or the "external elites" of a village
("sons" of the village who have made their career in the city but still feel
involved with their village of birth). First, a special association with a corporate status that will be entitled to manage the forest must be founded.
Next a *réunion de concertation* (consultation meeting) with all parties involved has to be held in order to ensure the representativity of the new
association. Then a detailed map specifying the limits of the new community forest has to be drawn according to precise guidelines. Finally a
plan de gestion (management plan) has to be presented, and this, again,
requires expertise that is hardly present in the villages. All this demands
considerable expenditure and, even more important, considerable political clout in order to "follow the file" at the various administrative levels.[11]

These complexities make it all the more seductive for villagers to try
to profit in a more immediate way by encouraging logging companies to
come and exploit the forest resources in their vicinity. Hence the new obligation for the logging companies to pay fixed amounts to the villagers for
each piece of logged wood becomes especially attractive. Relatively low
as this rate is in relation to world market prices for tropical wood, it can
still add up to significant sums. Philip Burnham and Monica Graziani, for
instance, report on a village in the Messok area that in 1997 received the
sum of USD 14,000 (Burnham and Graziani 2004). Of course, the fiscal
decentralization under which 50 percent of the taxes on logging is supposed to go to local institutions would, in principle, involve much bigger
sums. In a 2000 paper, Christian Adonis Milol and Jean-Michel Pierre
arrived at quite spectacular calculations of the sums involved, taking into
account the low population figures for the forest area. According to them,

an amount in the order of 1 billion FCA (USD 1,350,000) would yearly be destined for a region with about 320,000 inhabitants. A municipality like Messok (near Lomie) with 8,340 inhabitants would be entitled to a yearly income of more than 35,000,000 FCFA (USD 50,000). However, these authors emphasize also that most of this money does not arrive on the ground—which, as said, is hardly surprising in view of the extreme centralist administrative traditions (especially when finances are involved) that the Cameroonian state inherited from its French colonial predecessor. Still, such potential revenues do raise high expectations and contribute to the wide resonance of the new law throughout the forest area.

In 2001, a British project from DFID (Department for International Development) was involved in developing quite complex models for a *peréquation* (equation) of local communities' revenues from logging so as to even out regional disparities and spread the revenues over a broader zone. The great complexities of this scheme may make it hard to apply, particularly given the vague and overlapping claims that have been actually put forth by the diffuse local communities. The width of the unit over which such a *peréquation* can be realized remains moot: *commune*, *arrondissement*, or even wider areas? More generally, it remains to be seen how fiscal decentralization can be achieved without creating glaring regional inequalities that will undermine the very idea of national Cameroonian citizenship. A practical problem is that the different possibilities the new law offers to the local population—for instance, to create a community forest or profit from their share of the taxes on logging companies—may not always be compatible. People's enthusiasm for reaping large revenues in the short term may make the long-term option of instituting a community forest less attractive. Yet the latter option does have the advantage of safeguarding the local community's entitlement to at least some part of its forests. In any case, the varying options have one thing in common: they all raise the issue of belonging. Who are the "real" autochthons who are entitled to profit from local forest resources?

The Elusive Community

There is some irony in the legislature's optimism in giving the notion of "local community" such a central place in the 1994 forest law while, as noted, precisely in the forest area the application of this notion is highly problematic.

On a broad level it may be important, even urgent, to study more closely the genealogy of the notion of "community," which is so closely related to the idea of belonging and plays such a central role in development discourse on Africa. Why do many developers see it as self-evident that in Africa development has to be realized through "communities"? The notion seems to have acquired a new lease of life with the neoliberal agenda for development—remember what was said above about the unexpected trust that proponents of a neoliberal style of development seem to put in traditional entities like "the" community or "customary chiefs." In the case of the forest law this was reinforced by the input of ecologists, who are equally fond of this notion. The 1994 forest law of Cameroon is certainly not the only example of an important document in which a glib use of this notion leads to all sorts of confusion. Of interest is especially the tendency to take the community as a self-evident, "traditional" given.[12] However, the forest area offers telling examples of how the notion of "community" always has a specific situationally determined history and is subject to constant (re)construction. In this area its history has been particularly rocky.

In the literature on the area, local societies are generally described as strongly segmentary in their organization and subject to constant rearranging.[13] For instance among the Maka in the East Province prior to colonial conquest, small patrilineal family groups lived in autonomous hamlets dispersed in the forest. Family elders and local big men exercised considerable authority over their descendants, but there was no central authority above these units; at the most, related settlements might collaborate against a more distant group. Inside the local units, the elders' authority was circumscribed by various leveling mechanisms—notably the constant threat that a discontented section of the group would split off and create its own settlement further away in the forest. Fission and fusion, combined with considerable mobility of the settlements, made for a highly fluid organizational framework. After 1900, however, the new colonial authorities—first the Germans and after 1918 the French—went to great lengths to try to stabilize the population. In order to obtain administrative control over this fluid population—for taxation, but even more for allowing regular levies of forced labor to meet the new administration's desperate need for carriers and other laborers—the small family groups were resettled along the new roads and in larger villages under the authority of one village chief. As a consequence, most present-day villages are constituted by two to four *grandes familles*. Sometimes these families emphasize their common ancestral descent, but in other cases people do not recognize any common origins, maintaining rather that prior to the Germans each family lived in its own part of the forest.

Village unity remains therefore quite precarious. During the last century the village acquired a certain coherence as an administrative unit under the village chief, who had to execute administrative orders from above. The villagers will also stress their unity against outsiders—for instance in football matches between villages, which to a certain extent have replaced the old *dombe* (wars) between family settlements. But as soon as something is to be distributed inside the village, whether it be possible revenues, benefits from development projects, or onerous government charges, the old segmentary idiom reasserts itself and members of a dissatisfied family will grumble that in the olden days this would have been reason enough to split off and create a new village elsewhere.

Ever since the imposition of the state in the region, colonial officials complained about the lack of authority in these fluid societies. The Germans even spoke of *einen Mangel am staatenbildendem Sinn* (a lack of state-forming capacity) which would explain while people in the East Province belonged to *die Primitivsten aller Primitiven*. Their successors— first the French *Commandants* and, after Cameroon's independence, the development experts—have similarly complained about a lack of leadership. Indeed, it still remains difficult to find leaders inside a given village with sufficient authority to speak on behalf of the whole village. The village chief is first of all an auxiliary of the government. His role in imposing official measures, which are often quite unpopular, hardly helps to raise his prestige. Even when some chiefs succeed nonetheless in acquiring some ascendancy, time and again they run the risk of being reproached for defending especially the interests of their own *grande famille*. Other potential leaders—teachers, successful farmers, officials of the local party organization—are equally vulnerable to the strong leveling mechanisms at work in everyday life in the villages. Under such circumstances, mobilizing villages for joint initiatives—for instance, for creating a community forest—is not an easy task.

A clear precedent—one that at least in some areas has affected people's reactions to the new forest law—is found in the problems of the ZAPI de l'Est, a government cooperative that tried to develop cash-crop production through popular participation in the 1970s and 1980s. There are striking parallels with the ways in which development projects now try to channel local participation in the application of the forest law.

· · · · · · · · · · · · · ·

The model of the ZAPI (Zone d'Actions Prioritaires Intégrées) was developed by French experts who were heavily inspired by the *animation* ideology (a French variant of community development). The government granted it a monopoly over the commercialization of cash crops in the Abong-Mbang–Nguelemendouka–Doume region that has been since the 1940s the richest cacao- and coffee-producing area of the east. The ZAPI instituted a complex hierarchy of local committees—*comités de village, de secteur, de zone*—that were supposed to enable farmers to manage the commercialization of their products themselves. This triggered a fierce competition among villagers and factions, both within the village and between villages, for the presidency of these various committees. But the strong segmentary tendencies in village life often paralyzed the functioning of the committees. Another problem was that government representatives, accustomed to a highly authoritarian style of intervention, had little patience with these experiments in local democracy.

After the withdrawal of the French experts in the 1980s, the ZAPI suffered severe financial difficulties (there were constant rumors about large-scale embezzlement of funds by both ZAPI and state officials). It went definitively bankrupt at the end of the 1980s with the collapse of cacao and coffee prices. It is quite shocking to find nowadays that the whole impressive organizational structure of committees and official positions disappeared without leaving a trace. The only thing that seems to remain from the ZAPI is the local name for *Chronolaena odorata,* an obnoxious weed that rapidly spread in the area in the 1970s—that is, the same time that the ZAPI was imposed on the region. The villagers still call this weed *zapi.* At the time they explained to me that it was similar to the ZAPI, which "also comes and does not go away"—a prophecy that proved to be singularly inapt.[14] There is some sad irony in that even the development experts who are now helping to set up organizational frameworks for their forest projects seem to be oblivious to the history of similar experiments by the ZAPI only a few decades ago. In 2001, when I tried to warn a highly committed and intelligent representative of the World Bank, who had been working in the area for more than a year, that certain interventions might repeat the misguided efforts of the ZAPI, he answered me with some amazement: "What do you mean by ZAPI? It is just the name of a weed." The villagers involved will certainly have a longer institutional memory.

The ZAPI was part of a longer historical series of SIPs, SAPs,[15] and other externally imposed forms of peasant cooperatives under French rule. For the local people, the recent proliferation of new forms of organization (committees, associations, etc.) in relation to the 1994 forest law has, therefore, its prehistory.

. . . .

The 1994 law posed, therefore, a very real challenge: how to channel popular interest in the new opportunities for community forest management into organizational forms that would prove to be less ephemeral than the ZAPI committees.

Such problems are further complicated by the fact that the village as such has no corporate status, while the 1994 law stipulates that only a corporate body can submit a demand for the creation of a community forest. This requires therefore the institution of a separate association, which, again, can raise the issue whether all parties concerned are actually represented. The practice that has emerged over the last few years is that the village figures as the community behind the constitution of a community forest. However, the village as such is not recognized by the law as a corporate entity. This means that a special body has to be created, usually an *association* as defined by the 1989 law guaranteeing freedom of association (the same law that triggered the democratization process and the proliferation of political parties, referred to in the preceding chapter). Founding a new association means the formation of a committee that has to function alongside the existing village council presided over by the village chief and his notables. Moreover, it becomes a moot point how the representativity of this committee can be guaranteed.

In several villages, associations seem to have been created by ambitious individuals, often in direct connivance with representatives of a logging company, to submit a demand for a community forest although the association in question could hardly be seen as representing the village as a whole. In some of these cases, the village chief even intervened asking the *autorités administratives* to halt the process since it had been initiated by only a few individuals who were trying to promote their own interests. To avoid such problems the ministry's manual requires a *réunion de concertation*, as mentioned above, where the village as a whole can express its support for an application for a community forest. However, the highly democratic tenor of deliberations in the village council—where each man and even each woman can intervene, and where the chief and his notables often succeed in reaching some sort of compromise only after considerable rhetoric exertion—makes it a forum that is more equipped for conflict resolution than for reaching a common decision (see Geschiere 1982).

It is therefore not easy to unite all villagers behind a new association and its proposal for a community forest. Moreover—and this is in practice often an even more serious obstacle—all the problems with ascertaining a committee's representativity seem to provide the administration with handy excuses for returning an application or for long delays in its treatment (cf. Nguiffo and Djeukam 2000). Indeed, the combination of the local, often quite rowdy, style of "tribal democracy" with the administration's deep mistrust of any initiative from below—and since Independence the Cameroonian government bureaucracy has become notorious for its high-handedness—risks making the submission of a community forest project a very precarious and lengthy undertaking.

The Community as Stakeholder: Belonging and Exclusion

In recent years, the crucial role attributed to the "local community" in the new forest law has proved indeed to lead to explosive tensions endangering the very unity of the village. First of all, the stubborn competition between *grandes familles*, which had often been brought together forcefully in one larger village by the colonial authorities, has been intensified since the law has forced people to discuss how the cherished rights of different groups in certain parts of the forest could be amalgamated into a proposal for one community forest. Another sensitive point has been the involvement of the external elites and how this was viewed by the villagers. On the one hand, these elites seemed to be the obvious intermediaries for helping to move a community forest proposal through all the complicated procedures. On the other, their claims to still "belong" to the village have been critically weighed by their former "brothers," now that local forest resources had become so valuable. But the most incisive issues of belonging have come up at the very local level, between near neighbors and even between those who seemed to belong to one family. The very idea of "the community" as a major stakeholder in the surrounding forest has triggered fierce debates about who "really" belongs to the village or even to the family.

In itself, this obsession with exclusion and closing the local group is quite new. Until recently, Cameroonian forest societies have been quite inclusivist and open in their forms of organization. As emphasized in chapter 1, historians and anthropologists tend to characterize African forms of organization in general as dominated by the notion of "wealth in people" (in contrast to, for instance, Eurasian societies where wealth was—and is—rather expressed in things). Forest societies must have offered optimum examples of this. The Maka elders told me stories about the olden days, about feuds between the villages and how they were reconciled by an exchange of women, that resonated with the adage that wealth lies in attracting people. The more persons a leader could attract to his village, the more powerful he became: more women meant more food farms and therefore more food; more men meant more warriors to defend the village and to loot other groups. Polygyny, adoption, fosterage, and, more generally, the attraction of clients were crucial to establish oneself as a "big man."

Local kinship terminology—in these societies particularly open and elastic—is in many respects reflective of this inclusivist tenor. One of the most unexpected "discoveries" in my fieldwork among the Maka in the 1970s was how utterly misleading it is to equate of kinship with "ascription," as many observers and even anthropologists still tend to do.[16] My new fellow villagers turned out to be true masters in working with their kinship terms. I was constantly nonplussed by the highly ingenious ways in which they succeed in capturing yet another relation in kinship terms. Even increasingly complex genealogical drawings were of little help for tracing all the complex equations and shifts that enabled them to claim again another kinship relation. My assistant, who had come along from another village and received a very chilly reception in the village where I lived, soon "discovered" a very narrow kinship link with our landlady, to the satisfaction of both. And I was constantly bombarded with exogamy warnings—"no, no, you can not marry this girl"—which completely baffled me, since I had not paid any special attention to the girl. Later I understood that among the Maka any kinship link excludes the possibility of marriage. So by emphatically excluding marriage, my host automatically adopted me as his kin.

This view of kinship as a highly dynamic principle rather than an order that "ascribes" fixed positions is not without importance for our discussion of belonging. The central role that kinship continues to play among the Maka, as in many other African societies, may appear to offer fixed frameworks for belonging—certainly if one continues to think in the stereotypical opposition of fixed "traditional" societies versus increasingly mobile modern forms of organization. In practice, however, in many of these "kinship societies" the kinship terminology rather seems to offer a highly flexible framework in which all sorts of relations and links can be captured and reinterpreted. This elasticity may explain the resilience of kinship as an organization principle, despite all the modern changes.

With the Maka—and in other forest societies—kinship does not necessarily mean closure. On the contrary, the very open kinship terminology confirms the inclusivist tenor of local forms of organization. Clients (or even "slaves"—see below) are easily turned into kin, and stretching one's kinship network in order to include ever more persons, even in faraway places, is a true art—all the more useful now that rapid urbanization often makes finding a point of support in a new environment particularly urgent. However, in the second half of the twentieth century, changes became apparent in this respect. The increased significance of cacao and coffee farms brought a tendency toward closing the family units. In the past, a heritage of a man had consisted only of some personal possessions and his dependents. Land as such had no value, since food farms were abandoned after a few years. With the new, more permanent cash-crop farms, the distribution of a father's heritage amongst his sons became a hot issue. Sons would also object to the adoption of cousins (let alone of more distant kin) who might claim their part of the inheritance (see Geschiere 1982). The very idea of a community forest and, more generally, of "the community" as stakeholder seems to raise similar issues—but now for the village as a whole, inciting further closure and efforts to try to separate those who "really" belong from other villagers with only second-class status.

Village or *Grande Famille*?

Within the forest area, local reactions to the new law have been quite different in those areas where externally financed developments projects are active—mainly around Lomie, Dimako, and Messamena—compared to other areas. The already quite voluminous literature (mostly papers and research reports—see Geschiere 2004a) on the effects of the law and the problems in its application tends to focus especially on those areas where expatriate projects have been active. However, the resonance of the law has been much broader. It is quite striking that even in parts of the East Province where logging used to be of little importance, villagers are now quite excited about the new possibilities for creating a community forest.

And in those areas where outside projects—with their heavy presence of expatriate experts—do not function as an uniting factor, divisive tendencies can come to the fore all the more readily.

• • • • • • • • • • • • • •

For instance, on my return in 2001 to the area where I have regularly done fieldwork since 1971, I was quite surprised to find that the village of Bagbeze II—which I had chosen at the time for a pilot study since it was reputed to be one of the most dynamic villages along the *piste*—had not yet developed any plans for submitting a proposal for a community forest. In contrast, the neighboring village of Andjouk, much smaller and in general seen as a somewhat backward place, was already quite far advanced in constituting a dossier for such a forest.

My informants explained that this was for quite obvious reasons. For Bagbeze, constituting a community forest was a highly explosive issue, putting the unity of the village to a severe test. In fact, people clearly did not like to discuss the new possibilities at all. This village consists of four *grandes familles*, which are not tied together by a clear notion of common descent. On the contrary, each *famille* points to a different part of the forest as the place where the ancestors used to live—often at considerable distance (more than half an hour on foot) from the present-day village. It was also in these ancestral domains that, in the 1940s, men from each family began to lay out their cacao plantations. However, in those days these rights were hardly seen as really exclusive. People from other *grandes familles*—certainly when there were marriage relations—could always get permission to cultivate food crops and even create more permanent cacao and coffee farms in the ancestral domain of another *famille*. This seems to change with the new possibility of formalizing rights to parts of the forest by the institution of a community forest.

For Bagbeze, the irony is that the smallest *grande famille* of the village, Bandjag, can lay claim to a relatively vast forest territory, stretching all the way down to the river Nyong to the south of the village. The Bandjag people used to resent the dominance of the village's largest *grande famille*, Balamkoas. Bandjag people tended to complain that Balamkoas, through sheer numbers, had succeeded in monopolizing the position of village chief ever since the French colonizers instituted an electoral procedure for this office. The ancestral domain of the Balamkoas group is, however, limited by parts of the forest claimed by other *familles* (including Bandjag). No wonder the village had been unable to come up with any initiative for constituting a community forest. People from other *grandes familles* fear that the small Bandjag group, supported by a relatively large number of external elites, will opt for a community forest of its own. Clearly the very possibilities opened up by the law with its emphasis on an undefined "local community" reinforce the segmentary tendencies ingrained in the local forms of organization and jeopardize the unity of the village as such.

The situation in Andjouk, Bagbeze's smaller neighboring village, was quite different. Here, people had already taken initiative toward assembling a dossier for the recognition of a community forest for the village as a whole. Andjouk consists of only two *grandes familles*, whose members claim that they already lived together in the same part of the forest before the Germans forced them to resettle along the road. Consequently, there are no sharp divisions between their ancestral forest domains. The Andjouk village chief explained to me how everybody had worked together for demarcating a community forest that would guarantee the village control over its very rich forest domain—still largely untouched because their ancestors lived quite far from the site of the present-day village. A year earlier, two external elites of the village—brothers who both worked elsewhere in the east but were regularly in Yaoundé (the oldest was a pastor, the other a high-up police officer)—had launched the idea of a community forest. Prospects looked very bright, all the more so since an Italian agent from a company in Mbalmayo had confirmed that there was a great deal of valuable wood (Moabi and Sapelli) in the Andjouk forest.

However, even for this village, the complicated procedure risked to encourage divisive tendencies. The chief had approached the Ministry's service in Abong-Mbang and had indeed been shown the manual prescribing all the steps necessary for composing an application. He foresaw that all this would involve an important amount of money. But the phase he feared most was the organization of a *réunion de concertation,* in which the villagers' support for the whole plan had to be ensured. Already, people in the village had the most exaggerated expectations of the revenues of this community forest. Moreover, some had questioned the elites' leading role in the whole undertaking: "Why were they so interested? Wouldn't they use their personal contacts with officials and logging companies to profit from the project in their own ways?" The chief sighed that it might be very difficult to make the villagers agree with any plan. Even in a more coherent village like Andjouk, the new possibilities created by the forest law risked to undermine the very unity of the village community.

. . . .

The Halfhearted Belonging of the External Elites

As the examples above show, the law may encourage the segmentary tendencies that are already strong in everyday village life, aggravating the hidden tensions between the constitutive *grandes familles*. But the second example, the village of Andjouk, shows that a different conflict can also arise: there the villagers questioned whether the external elites who had played a key role in launching the forest project really belonged.

The relation between urban elites and their village of birth is particularly complicated in the East Province. In the previous chapter the special importance of this link was emphasized as characteristic of many parts of Africa: urbanites continue to go to and fro between city and village, while villagers try to involve their "brothers in the city" in all sorts of ways in village affairs. However, there are considerable regional variations in elites' involvement with the village (see Geschiere and Gugler 1998). In the Cameroonian forest area these relations are quite precarious from both the perspective of the villagers and that of the elites. The former often confess to being very proud of the "sons of the village who now live in the city." They see them as obvious points of support in the confusing outside world; they can help in obtaining lodging and jobs in the city or scholarships for the children, and more generally they can intervene when somebody is in difficulty with the gendarmes or the government. But these high hopes are often disappointed. A general adage in the East (see also Burnham and Graziani 2004) is that the villagers see their external elites as prone to neglect their village of birth. As one of my neighbors in the village used to say in the 1970s: "They do not even build a house here, they only think of themselves. So how can we have development here?" Such complaints are invariably followed by comparisons with elites from the west (the famous Bamileke) who do invest in the development of their village.

The eastern elites, for their part, emphasize their emotional involvement with their "brothers" in the village but dwell also on the impossible mentality of these people who only ask, ask, ask. Many feel that they have to keep at least some distance, else—as several of my informants expressed it—there is the danger of "being eaten," an expression that most graphically summed up their deep fear of the powerful leveling mechanisms that mark everyday life in forest villages.[17]

Until quite recently there were also good political reasons for them to maintain a certain distance. As said before (chap. 2), under one-party rule (that is, until 1989) it was even dangerous for an ambitious politician to maintain close relations with his supporters in the village. This could easily be interpreted as an attempt to build up personal support outside the one-party system, and jealous rivals were quick to denounce such incipient "subversion" to the hierarchy. However, all this changed with democratization, which brought a true proliferation of elite associations. As highlighted also in chapter 2, the regime of President Biya, which used to strictly forbid any form of association outside the one party, suddenly began to actively encourage the founding of regional elite associations, since they seemed to offer a welcome alternative for marshaling votes and thus neutralizing the effect of multipartyism. The elites from the East Province are almost all in public service, and so they could hardly refuse orders from above to go back at election times to campaign for the president (see Geschiere 1997:128). In the new political configuration, the eastern elites need to take their belonging seriously. The best proof that they did was that many of them started building a house in the village. In the course of the 1990s there was a mushrooming of villas in a dazzling variety of styles in many villages in the east. Now the villagers could no longer complain that "their" elites were too stingy to build a house there.

In economic respects as well there are now good reasons for the elites to pay more attention to the village.[18] The pushy ways in which representatives of all sorts of logging companies—large expatriate and smaller Cameroonian ones—seek access to new areas make the increased value of the forest resources ever more obvious. Elites, who often have prior contact with these companies, can play an important role in introducing them to the villagers. Often they also use their knowledge of administrative procedures to launch a proposal for constituting a community forest under the new law (as in the example of the small village of Andjouk, above). Indeed, most of these elite associations emphasize contributing to the further development of their backward region of origin as their very first aim. No wonder that new elite organizations like REFID (which was presided over by none other than the former secretary-general of the Forest Ministry, Lazare Balla), Kul Bebend, and the Association des Elites des Maka Mboans—also led by powerful politicians—are deeply involved with the forest issue.[19]

However, this increased interest from the side of elites seems to elicit an equally increasing distrust on the part of villagers. The same people who used to reproach the elites for not taking any interest in the village were the first to denounce their secret dealings with logging companies or the ways in which elites from the area use the new law to try to claim promising parts of "their" ancestral forest. Expatriate development experts, too, have manifested deep distrust vis-à-vis the external elites. Representatives of the Dutch project in the Lomie-Messok area saw it as their task to protect the villagers against elites who had always neglected the area but now had begun trying in all sorts of ways to profit from the novel creation of community forests.[20] Philippe Auzel and Paul Nkwi (2000:30) even speak of "the mafia-like alliance between elites and logging firms." Thus, the new law served to further complicate the status of the external elites: can they claim to be part of the local community that is supposed to be a major stakeholder in the management of the forest, or do they rather belong to the city and thus should keep their distance from the local forest resources?

Indeed, interference of the elites with projects for a community forest or negotiations about the compensation to be paid by a logging company can evoke fierce reactions.

· · · · · · · · · · · · · ·

In 1999 friends, who are *originaires* from Mpoundou (one of the biggest villages in the Abong-Mbang area) and now live in Yaoundé, told me that they were quite upset about "their" villagers' having been cheated by an entrepreneur who opened up a *vente de coupe* (a very short-term concession) behind the village.[21] The villagers had received three oxen and a set of shirts for the local football team, while at the time there were already rumors that the ministry would fix a minimum remuneration in cash (the much-discussed 1,000 FCFA per cubic meter). However, my elite friends were even more upset by the fact that, when they wanted to intervene—after all, they were much better informed about developments at the ministry—they had been rudely rebuked by "our own brothers" in the village: "You people, you have already your salaries. So there is no need to come down here now and try to share in what we get for our wood."

· · · · · · · · · · · · · ·

The villagers complain that their elite "brothers" think they can get away with anything because they are from the region. People will say, for instance, that if a foreign entrepreneur, exploiting a small *vente de coupe,* has his workers log trees far outside the borders of his concession (this is indeed a normal practice), it is possible to put an end to this—for instance, by threatening to lodge a complaint with the ministry—and thus extort extra compensation from the entrepreneur. However, when an external elite—a "son of the soil"—is doing the same, it is much more difficult to obtain redress: how can one lodge a complaint against one's own kin? Local representatives often feel sandwiched between the powerful elites of the region in Yaoundé and international committees of control.

....

The mayor of Messok, for instance, complained that a recent mission of the World Bank had put him in an impossible position. The World Bank people had insisted that he should point out to them which *exploitants* were regularly surpassing their boundaries. But how could he do so? Among those *exploitants* were several powerful external elites from the region itself who could—and certainly would—make his life very miserable if he complained about them.

....

Thus the new possibilities opened up by the forest law tend to make even the local belonging of the elites uncertain, despite all their professed attachment to the "home" village. There is, again, a sort of irony here. Precisely at the time that the changing politico-economic context pushes the elites to finally take their local belonging really seriously—remember the renewed importance "the" village assumed under democratization with the politics of autochthony (see chap. 2)—the villagers seem to become ever more suspicious (at least in this region) that their "brothers" in the city might come back to try to get a share of the new revenues from the forest. Yet when all is said and done, they will need the support of their better-connected "brothers" to get a community forest going—certainly if the projects begun by expatriates, who cannot be present forever, are withdrawn. The ambivalence of the elites' "belonging" to the local community will be a crucial factor in the "development" of the region for the time to come.

Discovering *Allogènes* at Ever Closer Range

The fiercest struggles over belonging and exclusion develop, however, at the local level itself, inside the village. In many villages people's enthusiasm about the new opportunities opened up by the forest law and related de-crees goes together with determined efforts to unmask "fake autoch-thons" inside—persons who may have always been treated as fellow vil-lagers but are now marked as not really belonging in the community and not fully entitled to share in the new projects. In this context the segmen-tary implications of autochthony discourse, emphasized in chapter 1—its inbuilt tendency to draw its circles of exclusion at ever closer range—come to the fore particularly strongly, even within the family. An early example comes from Monica Graziani's seminal fieldwork in a few Nzime villages beyond Messok—a fairly inaccessible area that only by the end of 1996 was abruptly opened up by the intensification of logging in the region and concomitant measures under the new forest law.[22]

••••••••••••••

Graziani worked in the area at the end of the 1990s, prior to the constitu-tion of a ful-fledged community forest. However, the villages were already entitled to royalties on logging taking place in "their" part of the forest—as noted, 1,000 FCFA per cubic meter of wood—and additional tax remit-tances were to come. In each village the *autorités administratives* told the people to form a CDV (*comité du développement villagois*) in order to be able to benefit from the new remittances. From the start, considerable sums were involved. Graziani focuses on one (unnamed) village where in just the first year the committee had to handle about 14,000 USD plus gifts in kind from a logging company that had started to exploit its concession close by. She describes in detail how the committee's leadership—the village chief and his elderly notables, supported by the village's external elites—developed plans for using the money for projects that would benefit the community as a whole (the purchase of an electrical generator, the build-ing of wells, etc.). However, soon it turned out that the committee's legiti-macy within the village was severely limited, while people became increas-ingly excited over the tantalizing possibilities of wealth: to the villagers, the amounts of money involved are quite fantastic. A factional struggle followed, pitting the women and the young men against the chief and his el-derly followers. The youth and the women exercised increasing pressure for a distribution of the overall revenue on an individual basis, and after some confrontations, they prevailed.

However, as soon as it was decided to divide the total sum among the village's inhabitants, issues of belonging acquired increasing urgency. The overall principle of patrilineal descent, which appeared to provide a self-evident basis for the demarcation of communities, turned out to lend itself in practice to widely different interpretations (cf. what was said above about the practical flexibility of apparently rigid kinship classifications). To quote Graziani:

> The first instalment of "gifts" (money and goods like machetes, hoes, cacao pesticides, and sheets of aluminium roofing) was shared [by all], apart from the Baka,[23] in a rather equal way. But during the subsequent distributions, criteria of social differentiation (young unmarried women and "strangers"), social stigmatisation (illegitimate birth, descent from a slave and other secrets that had been previously jealously kept by the elders) became more overt and were used to legitimise biases in sharing and in deciding priorities for employment in the timber company. Even people who had long lived or were born in the village, were suddenly faced with this new social status of stranger.

In the end, Graziani says, "collective control over timber royalties was rejected in favour of an individualistic solution and unequal share-out." One could add that new differentiations—different degrees of belonging—had thus crystallized between those who "really" belonged and other who apparently could not be considered to be "true" autochthons.

• • • • • • • • • • • • • •

As was only to be expected, such struggles over belonging assume much more virulent forms in the rare villages where a community forest is already constituted and plans for its exploitation are to be executed. In 2001 there were already several cases where efforts toward exclusion became so intense that one might speak of an emerging xenophobia.

• • • • • • • • • • • • • •

Indeed, in Koungoulou, one of the very first villages in the Lomie-Messok area to constitute a community forest, a strong current to exclude "strangers" developed as soon as the exploitation of the new forest had to be taken in hand. This village—mainly inhabited by Nzime—had acquired a sort of pilot status for the Dutch project that was active in this zone. It was mainly thanks to massive support by this project that Koungoulou

village had succeeded as one of the first to complete the long and complicated procedure for getting a community forest recognized.

However, as soon as the Dutch began to help the villagers initiate the
next phase—executing the carefully formulated plan of exploitation of their
newly constituted forest domain—they were suddenly confronted with
strong complaints from villagers who called themselves *autochtones* and
insisted that managing the community forest could not be left to *allogènes*;
it was therefore unacceptable that the latter were so well represented in the
responsible committee. Indeed, it turned out that immigrants from other
districts (Hausa from Bertoua and Kako from Batouri) formed a majority
within this committee.[24] Apparently the locals had originally decided to
wait and see what would become of this whole new business of community
forests, but now that the stage of exploitation was drawing near, they did
not want to play second fiddle any more. In order to reconcile the so-called
autochtones—Nzime, who did form a large majority in the village—the
Dutch helped to constitute a new committee for which people from the
main kinship groups in the village were chosen.

But this certainly did not put an end to efforts to exclude "strangers."
Just as in Graziani's case above, there followed all sorts of additional skir-
mishes about different degrees of belonging among Nzime who always had
claimed as a group to be autochthons. The exploitation of the community
forest continued to be haunted by struggles to limit the group that could
rightfully share in the profits of the forest.

. . . .

Thus the segmentary discourse that dominates local forms of organization in the area leads to ever finer distinctions between "us" and "others."
Allogènes do not necessarily come from elsewhere. Even people who orig-
inate from the same village can be redefined as "immigrants."

Of special interest is, for instance, that Graziani in the example above
refers to "slave descent" as one of the more or less secret criteria on the
basis of which people can be relegated to a secondary status. Indeed, most
language groups in the East have a term that they now translate as "slave."
Among the Maka, this term is *lwa*. However, as I have sought to show elsewhere, there is good reason to suppose that this translation has misleading
associations.[25] The main implication of the term seems to be rather that
someone is not living in the village of his father (where he should live
according to the—at least formally—strictly patrilineal order). Thus even

the richest Bamileke merchant in Abong-Mbang, the main town in the Maka area, can be termed a *lwa*. One of my eldest informants told me the following story about these "slaves" in olden days.

••••••••••••••

One day Mpede of Bagonkou [patrilineage/village] was out fishing in his small boat on the River Nyong. Suddenly his sister came running toward the bank to warn him: his father and his brothers had been butchered by the other men of Bagonkou. They had fought because Mpede's brother had slept with the wife of one of his "fathers."[26] Mpede fled in his small boat down the river. When it became dark he hid himself under an overhanging tree. The next day he was discovered by fishermen of Wabelek. Mpede saw no escape: "Take me and kill me if you want."

But one of the Wabelek came forward and claimed him. This man had no children himself. Instead he took Mpede into his home; he even paid for a wife for him. Ever since, Mpede's children have been living in Wabelek.

••••••••••••••

The term *lwa* can, therefore, refer to anyone who is living "elsewhere": it can be a man who was born from a premarital love affair of his mother and whom she left with her own family when she got married in another village, or a man who had been brought by his mother to the village of her new husband, or even a man who for one reason or another chooses to live with his mother's brothers. The term is a real insult—this might be the reason it is now easily equated with "slave." In the 1970s I attended several palavers convened by a man whose fellow villagers had dared to call him a *lwa*—often at the climax of a fierce row. In all these cases the notables severely reproached the culprit, ordering him never to use such a term again and to duly compensate the other with a present (a chicken or a goat). Moreover, they solemnly confirmed the plaintiff in his full status of belonging to one of the village's families.

Yet recently in Maka villages I know—just as in the examples above of Koungoulou and the village where Graziani worked—gossip or even straightforward accusations that so-and-so is "really" a *lwa* crop up fairly frequently. The term no longer seems to denote a deep secret that should best remain hidden; it has rather become a not uncommon way of trying to marginalize a neighbor by "unmasking" him as not really an autochthon.

Often such accusations are clearly linked with people's excited expectations of the new bonanza that the forest law will bring. The implication is clear: such "strangers" should not fully share in the benefits of a community forest or in the taxes paid by logging companies.

Clearly, promoting a poorly defined local community as a major stakeholder in forest resources can have its dangers: instead of strengthening the community's unity it may reactivate older forms of social exclusion.

Conclusion

These examples from the forest area in Cameroon's East Province show again how elastic the language of autochthony is. It is clear that quite different issues play a role here compared to the South-West and big cities like Douala and Yaoundé. Yet people adopt the same discourse of autochthony, with considerable success: claims to a primordial belonging have great mobilizing force here as well.[27] Apparently economic liberalization—the new development policies with their emphasis on "bypassing the state" and decentralization—can have similar effects as political liberalization (democratization). In the examples from the forest area, neoliberal interventions triggered again an urgent preoccupation to purify the group of strange elements and thus draw the circles of "true" belonging ever closer.

In this region the decentralization impetus may be the main factor promoting the upsurge of issues of belonging and exclusion. Yet it is clear that it is closely intertwined with other trends mentioned before as part and parcel of the "global conjuncture of belonging." The forest law—the pivot of the decentralization approach in this area—was deeply influenced by global concerns over ecological damage and disappearing local knowledge among "indigenous" groups. The particular effects democratization had in Cameroon as a whole—notably the government's encouragement of autochthony—had some impact in this area as well. Even if opposition parties have hardly managed to gain a foothold here, the villagers are conscious of the new slogans at the national level, they are informed about changes in the constitution, and they know very well that autochthony is now "in" in Cameroon.

It is probably not very helpful to invoke a global neoliberal agenda as the ultimate cause of all these problems. As noted earlier, the notion of neoliberalism is rapidly becoming a blanket term. Still, on one point there is an interesting and intriguing link. As noted, in their efforts to reduce the role of the state, many development experts supporting a neoliberal agenda tend to put their trust in "traditional" institutes like "the local community," taken as some sort of given. But the examples above show that the fuzzy contours of such "traditional" entities make them little apt for playing a role in a modern development project, all the more so since attempts to define them inevitably turn belonging into a burning issue.

In the struggles in the villages of the East Province over the new opportunities to create a community forest, this problem came strongly to the fore, since here the autochthony idea is shrinking to a very limited scope: even relatives could be unmasked as *allogènes*. Apparently, there is no end to autochthony's segmentary implications. This is why the new forest law—despite its laudable aim of finally ensuring that at least part of the revenues from the forest return to the local population—offers a telling example of how new development policies can have quite worrying implications in practice. Indeed, one might wonder whether the principle of decentralization is not too rigidly applied in the new forest law. The older statist version of development may have had an uncritical emphasis on nation-building and strengthening the state as essential preconditions for economic growth. Yet the new style of development seems to exaggerate in the opposite direction. A financial decentralizaton in which suddenly 50 percent of the taxes on a crucial national resource are supposed to go to local authorities might be seen as all too drastic. Most developers would hesitate to apply such an innovation in their home country. Just as with the old version of development—or maybe even more so now—Africa still seems to serve as a laboratory for development experiments.

This is all the more worrying because the local tensions generated by the application of the forest law show that the decentralization approach not only encourages conflicts over belonging and exclusion but inevitably favors the upsurge of all sorts of fuzzy identities that dissolve as soon as too much emphasis is put on them. By their very vagueness they seem to encourage ever more violent struggles over redefinition and exclusion. The earlier emphasis on national citizenship may have had its disadvantages as well, but at least that identification had a clear formal basis— which is utterly lacking for the kinds of regional or even local identities favored by decentralization. Again, the microexamples from the forest societies are quite relevant here, since they show that issues of belonging can rapidly divide even such apparently close-knit societies. Even here the question of who is "really" autochthonous cannot receive a final answer.

Of course, the dangers implied by diffuse discourses on belonging and autochthony, directly encouraged by simplistic approaches towards decentralization, should not suggest that the solution is to return to a disciplinary kind of national citizenship, as was propagated at the time of nation-building. Still, given the strong tendency in many present-day writings on development to hold up decentralization as a sort of panacea, greater caution may be called for. An urgent question is whether the new approach toward development, with its distrust of the state, does not let the notion of national citizenship go down the drain too easily. But if we wish to rescue the citizenship concept, the question is then, of course, what kind of citizenship? I shall return to this.

What comes quite dramatically to the fore from the examples from the East Province is the basic insecurity of autochthony reasoning, already emphasized in the introduction. Apparently this basic insecurity can manifest itself at very close range. Even where the notion is combined with kinship—promising a most "natural" form of security—it cannot offer definitive certainty, since even among relatives belonging seems to manifest greater and lesser degrees. How then can one ever be sure of an unquestioned belonging as "really" autochthonous? As a friend complained: "This autochthony thing is terrible: you can go to bed as an autochthon and wake up to find that you have become an *allogène.*"

CHAPTER FOUR

African Trajectories

S elf-evident as autochthony discourse appears to be, its recent upsurge on the African continent follows remarkably varying trajectories. The aim of this chapter is to explore how core aspects of this discourse as outlined already—its segmentary nature, the paradox between apparent safety and deep insecurity, and above all, the naturalizing purport that gives it such high mobilizing propensity—take shape in different settings. Are these aspects of any help to explain the different implications autochthony can have?

The quest for belonging as a sort of counterpoint in a context of globalization takes so many shapes in present-day Africa that a full survey is out of the question. However, several cases stand out as possible comparisons to the Cameroonian examples in earlier chapters. An obvious one—because of the parallels but even more because of the differences—is Ivory Coast.[1] First of all, in this country the obsession with autochthony has reached an as yet unparalleled climax in the context of President Laurent Gbagbo's 2002 Opération Nationale d'Identification, already noted in chapter 1. Second, it has become a commonplace to compare Cameroon and Ivory Coast since the independence of both countries (1960), precisely because their apparently similar situations seem to generate striking differences. The recent upsurge of autochthony as a central political issue in both countries continues this intriguing mix of similarity and difference. Divergent expressions of the obsession with autochthony and belonging also emerge from Eastern Congo around the enigmatic Banyamulenge (according to some, "just" Rwandans) and, in a completely different setting, South Africa in its struggles with the *Makwere-kwere*, threatening strangers from across the Limpopo.

However, over and against all these examples where autochthony acquires a sweeping "performative quality" (Marshall 2006:12), it might be instructive to look also into a context where the discourse does not seem to work. A good example is the present-day predicament of "Pygmies" in the forest area of Cameroon and adjacent countries. This is not a minor example, since these "hunter-gatherers" are generally seen as first-comers in the forest area and therefore they seem to qualify as one of the continent's most autochthonous groups. Yet their autochthony seems to be of little avail in the new political context. Cameroonian villagers rather tend to see *themselves* as the autochthons; their reasoning seems to be that even if the Pygmies were first-comers they cannot qualify as autochthons since they have no citizenship. This last example highlights, therefore, in a negative sense what seems to be a crucial dimension in all autochthony's variations: its crucial but volatile relation with the nation-state and the idea of national citizenship.

Ivory Coast: Identification and Exclusion

Chapter 1 already made reference to the "National Operation of Identification" launched by Ivory Coast's president Laurent Gbagbo (in power since the beginning of 2001), which reduced the idea of autochthony to its very quintessence. So that autochthons could be separated from strangers, every Ivorian had to go back to his or her "village of origin" in order to be "identified" there. Only after such an identification could a person be registered as a full citizen of the country and claim full citizen's right—notably rights to own land and to vote. Cities like Abidjan (more than three million inhabitants), the country's capital, could not count as a place of origin. Urbanites could prove their citizenship only by returning to a village from which their family originated. As the "director of identification" of this operation, Séri Wayoro, explained it, "Someone unable to show his belonging to a specific village must be . . . a person without bearings and . . . so dangerous that we must ask him where he comes from."[2]

When this ambitious program proved to be too cumbersome to be carried out, it was adapted, though the central idea of a "village or origin" was retained. People were allowed to file for an identity card in the place where they lived, but they had to cite witnesses who knew their village of origin and could testify that the family really originated from there. If their statements seemed plausible, the applicant would receive a receipt. In each village, notables—chiefs, party officials, members of important families—had to form a committee that could verify such claims of autochthony. Only after such verification could people finally exchange their receipt for an identity card.

It is worthwhile to reflect upon the notion of *village d'origine* that is central to this national identification project. Notably, it does not necessarily coincide with *lieu de naissance* (place of birth). Already in 2000, when the military regime instituted the Consultative Constitutional and Electoral Committee to prepare the return to a democratic regime, the Front Populaire Ivoirien (FPI)—the party of future president Gbagbo— had insisted that the new identity card should mention not only the *lieu de naissance* but also the *village d'origine*. The importance of the latter is graphically explained by Wayoro, the director of identification mentioned before: "The village of an Ivorian, it's firstly from the ancient Côte d'Ivoire.... Authentically, people were sedentary, they stayed on their homelands, where their parents, their elders and ancestors were born. That's what we consider as a village, the place where a person finds members of his family at their origin, before the urban phenomenon."[3] The notion of *village d'origine* is obviously meant to separate the autochthons, who retain a link with "their" village even if they move, from more nomadic people who seem to forget where they come from. The parallel with current views of the immigrants (*came-no-goes*) among the coastal people in Cameroon is striking.

In Ivory Coast, the message was clearly understood by people from the northern parts of the country. Gbagbo's Opération Nationale d'Identification seems to have been the direct reason for the "rebellion" that broke out in the north in September 2002 and eventually split the country in two (a situation that still exists at the moment of writing, January 2008). One of the main fears of the northerners, who are easily associated with immigrants from adjacent countries like Mali and Burkina Faso, was that in the process of identification they would be allotted a "foreign resident card" and thus effectively lose their nationality. Ruth Marshall vividly describes the rage of rebel soldiers when at their new roadblocks travelers present the receipts they received in the context of the identification operation: as said, rebels often tear up them up and attack their bearers. One of the first things the rebel forces did in the towns they conquered was to destroy national identity records. Marshall (2006:26) quotes a northern *donzo,* one of the hunters feared for both their warrior's courage and their magical powers: "I joined the rebellion because the Malinké have been here since the 12th century, and soon they will be giving us a foreign resident's card to be able to live here."[4] For people from the northern parts of the country it was apparently crystal-clear that the new government's identification operation was meant to "purify" the nation of all elements that were seen as foreign by the southern "autochthons"—not only immigrants from Burkina Faso and Mali but also Ivorians who had joined the strong southward migration current. Even the latter were seen as belonging to one large category of "Dioula," associated with *le Grand Nord* (see Dozon 2000; Arnaut 2004: chap. 3) and therefore in serious danger of losing their citizenship in this process of reconstituting the Ivorian nation. In Cameroon, autochthony means distinguishing between citizens who belong and others who belong less. In Ivory Coast it rather implies a shrinking of the nation, and an effort to exclude not only foreigners but also former nationals from citizenship as such.

Ousmane Demblé (2003:43) sketches the constricting logic of autochthony thinking that led Gbagbo's FPI to adopt the *village d'origine* as the final test for who is in and who is out. Gbagbo's regime was certainly not the first that had tried to solve the question of Ivorian citizenship, for since colonial times the matter has been confused by large-scale migration to the more prosperous southern parts of the country. During the second half of the 1990s, President Konan Bédié's regime had tried to clarify this issue through an ideological effort to define the essence and the limits of *ivoirité.* But Gbagbo and his collaborators became impatient with the fuzziness of this solution and chose a more legalistic option that seemed to offer firmer criteria for in- and exclusion. Dembélé summarizes their logic as follows: "The only precise reference for people's status is their parents, since one acquires the Ivorian identity through descent. And the only reference of the parent's identity is the village—not the one of birth but the one of origin" (2003:43).

Yet the same author shows that such an apparently clear-cut, legalistic approach can have dramatic and chaotic consequences. In a context of rapid urbanization, ever more mixed marriages, and general mobility of people, the apparently simple idea of a return to the village of origin created great confusion that quickly led to violence. Gbagbo's identification operation is a telling example of how the basic language of autochthony promises a self-evident clarity that creates havoc in everyday life, precisely because it seems to be so "natural."

The unfolding of Gbagbo's FPI also highlights the pervasive nature of the autochthony issue. In the 1980s the party developed into the major (or even the only) opposition movement against the regime of Ivory Coast's founding father, Houphouët-Boigny, *le Grand Vieux*, who ruled the country for more than thirty years. In those days, the FPI presented itself as a socialist party with a strong anti-imperialist current.[5] It mainly attacked Houphouët-Boigny's neocolonialism, which had made Ivory Coast a showcase of capitalist development on the African continent but—according to his critics—at the price of complete dependence on the French. In those days the party included leading persons from the north, who defined themselves as leftist against the right-wing regime of Houphouët. The FPI is still a member of the Socialist International, but toward the end of the 1990s the autochthony issue came to dominate its profile ever more. Again, it was the identification operation that caused a final split within the party itself. Northern members withdrew and joined the RDR party (Rassemblement des Républicains, associated with the north) and even the subsequent northern "rebellion." This split was especially striking within the FESCI (Fédération Estudiantine et Scolaire de Côte d'Ivoire), the student movement associated with the FPI that had played an important role in paving the road to power for Gbagbo. The FESCI can also be seen as the matrix from which the "Young Patriots" movement emerged, which over the last few years acquired a high profile as Gbagbo's *troupes de choc* and the main perpetrators of the day-to-day violence that has been wrecking the country. Former FESCI officials, like the self-appointed *général* Charles Blé Goudé, now act as leaders of the Young Patriots. In their often vitriolic propaganda they especially target their former comrades-in-arms, FESCI fellows from the north from the days when the FPI still advertised itself as a socialist party but who opted out when autochthony became the central issue (Konate 2003; Arnaut 2004: chap. 5). Several authors (Marshall 2006; Dembélé 2002) emphasize in retrospect that the theme of autochthony was always present in the FPI's propaganda. However, it is striking how quickly the basic "realities" of autochthony could take precedence over themes like socialism and anti-imperalism.

The Chimera of Ivoirité

President's Gbagbo's Opération Nationale d'Identification may illustrate the problems of a legalistic attempt to resolve autochthony's ambiguities. His predecessor, Henry Konan Bédié (president from 1993 to 1999), experimented with a different, more culturalist approach by launching the notion of *ivoirité*. However, in practice this attempt got stranded in similar absurdities. The rapid rise and demise of the *ivoirité* notion might be revealing for the awkward and confusing implications of autochthony thinking, apparently so straightforward in its appeal to basic truths. Striking is, indeed, the heavily ideological purport of Bédié's project. Jean-Pierre Dozon (2000:51) notes that Bédié assembled "a whole areopagus" of intellectuals and writers in order to give substance to this idea. United in a working group with the proud name CURDIPHE (Cellule Universitaire de Recherche et de Diffusion des Idées et Actions du Président Konan Bédié; University Cell for the Study and Diffusion of the Ideas and Actions of President Konan Bédié), they published a series of texts intended to bring clarity to the Gordian knot of belonging. In practice, the whole operation became a vivid illustration of how tricky this was.[6]

The starting point of most of these texts was Bédié's cherished and rather bombastic notion of *le blanc manteau de l'ivoirité*. Bénoît Sacanoud, CURDIPHE's president, cites this image as a sign of the reassuring clarity of autochthony and belonging: "This mantle is visible, the ivory white is visible; so there is no problem with recognizing the Ivorian if he accepts to adorn himself with some white cloak of *ivoirité*." However, already in the next few lines the uncertainty that is so typical for autochthony discourse creeps in, and with it the need to unmask traitors:

> Like any new philosophical concept, the term *ivoirité* has is ambiguity....Its duplication leaves room falsification....Thus one cannot escape the crucial question, how can one distinguish the false certificate of Ivorian nationality from the real one? The false identity card from the real one?...From this viewpoint, *ivoirité* proves to be a system that for coherence's sake inevitably supposes closure. Yes, closure....Closure and control over our borders: to stand guard over the integrity of one's territory is not a proof of xenophobia. It is only possible to identify oneself if one differentiates the self from the other, and this demarcation implies, whether one wants it or not, discrimination. It is not possible to be oneself and the other at the same time.[7]

This rapid switch from self-assurance—*ivoirité* with its "white cloak" as self-evident belonging—to the great uncertainty that returns in so many versions of the autochthony discourse led CURDIPHE's chairman to appeal to an anthropologist to clarify the issue. In a subsequent article, Georges Niangoran-Bouah—at the time director of the *patrimoine culturel* at the Ministry of Culture and according to Karel Arnaut (2004:239) the country's leading anthropologist—tried to resolve the ambiguities of this seemingly natural form of belonging by putting together an impressive tableau based on historical, geographical, and linguistic data. A typical notion in his argumentation is *Ivoirien de souche* (lit. "Ivorian of the trunk"); the basic purport of his learned treatise is to prove that the people of this *souche*, as real autochthons, have always been on the spot and never migrated. He undertakes an impressive overview of different groups that do belong. Among the *Ivoiriens de souche*, he makes a first distinction between *autochtones à origine mythique* and *autochtones sans origine mythique*. Moreover, within the first group there is a subdivision between "the subterraneans" and the "extraterrestrials." Especially this last subdivision may surprise. However, its deeper reasons become clear in the anthropologist's triumphant conclusion: "This tableau shows that on 10 March 1893, at the moment that Ivory Coast was born, the ancestors of all the important ethnic groups were already there; they come from nowhere else than the soil, the water, and the air space of their present country."[8]

The reference to "subterraneans" and "extraterrestrials" may seem to touch on the burlesque. Yet the anthropologist's learned discourse expresses a struggle with history that is typical for the tension within autochthony reasoning. In certain respects autochthony needs history: its very essence is to make historical claims. The recurrent problem for its advocates is, however, how to fix the flow that emerges from any historical narrative. Remember Nicole Loraux's seminal analysis of similar inconsistencies in the archetype of autochthony thinking, the ancient Athenians with their claim to be the only autochthons in classical Greece. As Loraux puts it most trenchantly, history is basically about movement, and so autochthony's claim of a group's always having stayed on one spot is at loggerheads with history itself. Thus in Athens, as in Ivory Coast, the memory of earlier migrations becomes some sort of guilty secret.[9]

Niangoran-Bouah's celebration of subterranean or extraterrestrial origins therefore has a deeper meaning: if one's origins are in the sky or under the ground, one can still claim to be an autochthon; there is no risk of being unmasked as really an *allogène*, someone who was born elsewhere. The very rigidity of Niangoran-Bouah's ethnic classifications suggests what they have to hide: the evident fact that most of the groups mentioned have a long history of having come from elsewhere. Equally significant is his insistence on March 10, 1893, as a crucial moment for measuring who belongs and who can be excluded from *ivoirité*. This is the date of the colonial decree by which the French for the first time fixed the borders of their new colony (which was followed by a long stream of other decrees constantly changing those borders). This invocation of a colonial intervention as crucial to the substance of *ivoirité* may smack of a certain ideological poverty. But, again, it has wider implications. It shows very clearly how deeply autochthony thinking, despite its traditionalizing aura, is linked with the modern state, whether in its colonial or its postcolonial version. Autochthony's obsession with fixing people—whether by tying them to a village of origin or by classifying them in accordance with colonial boundaries—is strongly reminiscent of the colonial governments' obsession with *la population flottante* that one way or another had to be contained in order to make control and colonial rule possible (see Roitman 2005). In many respects, autochthony's protagonists seem to be heirs of this colonial tradition; but the forms of mobility they are trying to contain have increasingly global aspects.

Violence and Changing Images of the Stranger

Gbagbo's Opération Nationale d'Identification and the idea that it is possible to make all citizens return to their village of origin in order to be counted in a census, just like Bédié's belief that it is possible to return to the purity of *Ivoiriens de souche*, seems almost tragicomical. So it is good to emphasize that these ideological and juridical experiments took place in a context of rapidly growing violence as an everyday reality. Until the end of the 1980s, Ivory Coast still seemed to be a haven of peace on the continent and one of its few success stories. After 1995, all this collapsed. Claudine Vidal (2002) has collected eyewitness stories about *l'année terrible* (1999/2000), marked by General Gueï's military coup against Bédié in December 1999, unclear confrontations among various political parties in view of the coming elections, and finally a street battle between Gueï's soldiers and Gbagbo's Young Patriots over who had won the elections. These stories describe a frenzy of violence that was all the more disastrous because it often arose among people who had lived together for many years. Thus Ivory Coast quickly became an extreme example of the violent propensities of tensions over autochthony, belonging, and exclusion. Ruth Marshall, who was evacuated from Abidjan in 2002, sketches a picture of how all-encompassing such a violence without clear boundaries becomes:

> The southern populations had returned from the north. When it came to political enemies, the rebellion appeared to follow the policy of "taking no prison-

ers." In the *cours communes* of Abidjan, veritable ethnic melting pots, neighbours eyed one another with suspicion, speaking in whispers. A reign of terror had taken hold of the city, with the infamous "death squads" roaming the streets after curfew, army officials encouraging citizens to phone into hotlines to denounce "suspicious activity," the destruction of poor neighbourhoods and slums, regular round-ups...where northerners were carted off like cattle in trucks, after having been stripped to the waist and relieved of their documents. It was not uncommon to drive by naked corpses on the side of the road in the early morning, hands tied behind the back and a bullet in the...head. In what seemed like a from of collective madness, the only voices that made themselves heard were the "young patriots" filling the streets...with patriotic rallies, an the nationalist media, all screaming hate-filled insanities daily....On the one hand, it seemed that each new act or statement of violence constituted in itself an isolated event, one option among several, whose occurrence had nothing self-evident about it. On the other hand, the unfolding of events gave the impression of following an inexorable and terrifying logic, against which nothing could be done. (Marshall 2006:28)

Mike McGovern (2005) relates the "grammar of violence" in Ivory Coast to a "politics of resentment" that would notably characterize Gbagbo's propaganda but that seems to be a powerful undercurrent in autochthony discourse elsewhere also. There is a celebration of feeling oneself victimized, betrayed by guests once hospitably received, and misunderstood by an uncomprehending world. The resentment of being victimized seems to justify extreme verbal violence that complements and further inspires the violence in everyday life (cf. Marshall 2006; Mbembe 2000:35): "The Gabonese have chased the strangers and they are still alive. The Nigerians have chased the strangers and they are still alive. The Libyans chased the strangers out of their country, and they are still alive. So, if Ivory Coast chases the strangers, what is the problem?...Yes, I am xenophobe, so what?"[10] This pride in being politically incorrect, another recurrent element in autochthony discourse, translates itself also into furious attacks at outsiders who try to mediate the conflict—in Ivory Coast notably France, the former colonial oppressor. As Mamadou Koulibaly, the number two in Gbagbo's regime, put it, "To say that they're here to keep the peace is to ridicule the international community's intelligence. They're here to organise coups d'états, mass killings and pillage" (*L'Inter*, March 16, 2005, quoted in Marshall 2006:35). And in reaction to the UN report on the mass killing of 25 March 25, 2004, and the role of Gbagbo's Young Patriots in these events, "General" Blé Goudé had this to say:

"I've got to the point where I don't believe that Hitler was bad, or that Milosevic was bad. Because it's the same media networks that presented Hitler and Milosevic as criminals who today present me and the Ivorian patriots who suffer at the hands of the rebellion as the executioners, and the rebels as victims" (*Fraternité Matin*, May 11, 2004; see Marshall 2006: 36). The autochthons alone against the world?

In a seminal and detailed article on the (re)construction of the category "stranger" in Ivory Coast, Dembélé (2002) shows how this growing resentment was complemented by the rapid emergence of a new image of migrants. The abruptness of this transition might be typical of the volatility of autochthony reasoning. During his long rule of more than three decades, the country's "founder-president" Houphouët-Boigny had imposed an *esthétique de l'étranger*: the influx of migrants from the north—both the northern parts of Ivory Coast and neighboring countries (Burkina Faso and Mali)—was promoted as crucial to the spectacular development of the plantation economy (notably cacao) in the southern parts of the country and therefore as the key to *le miracle ivoirien*. The old institution of the *tutorat* was used in order to channel immigrants' labor into further expansion of the cacao farms, local ethnic groups proclaimed themselves proud of receiving strangers, and offering these strangers a piece of land was seen as bringing the sky's benediction (Dembélé 2002:145).[11] In this context the prevailing image—or at least the official one—of the stranger was that of a *travailleur* (a hard worker) whose labor was necessary to maintain the growth of the cacao sector.

In retrospect, already then there were signs that local communities were becoming worried about this influx (it was in those years that, especially in the southeast, locals became a minority—sometimes even less than 20 percent—in their own area). But it was only in the course of the 1980s that the *esthétique de l'étranger* was definitively broken with. Quite suddenly the media were spreading new images of the stranger: *l'étranger criminel* exemplified in the bodies of slain Burkina bandits shown on TV and in the newspapers; and also—another common type in autochthony propaganda—the stranger as an ecological malefactor, destroying the precious patrimony of the ancestral *terroir* by his indifference.[12] Interestingly, Dembélé mentions NGOs—in the 1980s still a new institution—as an important voice in the vilification of the strangers (2002:151, 160). Subsequent decades were to see many more examples of this.

As long as Houphouët remained alive (until the end of 1993), the regime tried to ignore these signs of a rapidly changing attitude vis-à-vis immigrants. However, under his successors—first Bédié, then Gueï and Gbagbo—there was a complete *volte-face* of the state's policies, from an inclusivist version of nation-building infused with Houphouët's ideas about a *fraternité africaine* to a vision of citizenship that was highly exclusivist and intent on protecting autochthons from foreigners, who were now officially seen as a grave threat. The central questions for the government now seem to be how exactly to protect autochthons' primordial rights and how the foreigners among them can be set apart. Just as in the Cameroonian case, the rapidity of the switch in state policies gave the ensuing developments a dramatic turn. Below we will see more examples, including some from Europe, of how concerns over belonging and autochthony can quite suddenly have a surging impact leading to abrupt reversals in the state's policies.

Moreover, it is again striking how quickly the changing perceptions of the stranger acquired the self-evidence that seems to be one of the secrets of the success of discourses on autochthony and belonging. In the Ivorian case, it became simply "logical" that northern immigrants and southern autochthons would eventually become locked in violent struggles because of their basic differences. The verbal violence of the propaganda of Blé Goudé and other Gbagbo disciples seems to vent a basic and inescapable truth. In Ivory Coast this apparent self-evidence was reinforced by the inevitability with which the vicissitudes of national policies became intertwined with local concerns.

The figure of Alassane Ouattara played a dramatic role in this intertwinement. Appointed prime minister in 1991 by Houphouët-Boigny, he was the first politician from the north to acquire such a prominent position. Because of his previous career at the World Bank and the IMF, he seemed the obvious person to carry out the humiliating structural adjustment dictates that the country, despite its former status as a model for Africa, had to swallow, after so many of its neighbors. But after Houphouët-Boigny finally died, Ouattara became almost by accident a key figure in the unleashing of the autochthony wave. As chairman of Parliament, Bédié took over as head of state. Fearing Ouattara's competition in upcoming elections, Bédié became preoccupied with how to exclude him. Rumors about his non-Ivorian background (Ouattara's father would have come from Burkina) seemed to offer a convenient rationale for this. Thus the struggle over the new constitution became focused on the notorious issue of "or" versus "and." Everybody seemed to agree that candidates for the presidential elections had to prove that they were Ivorian by birth.

But did this mean that their father *or* their mother had to be born Ivorian, or rather their father *and* their mother? Ouattara's candidacy became the occasion for numerous protest demonstrations, many of which turned bloody, and his person acquired emblematic dimensions in the struggle to exclude "foreigners" from citizenship.

An additional factor was that Houphouët-Boigny's victory in the tense presidential elections of 1990—the first democratic ones after many years, with a rival candidate (Laurent Gbagbo)—was, according to his opponents, mainly due to the fact that immigrants were allowed to vote. This had important implications for the political competition in subsequent years. One the one hand, it inspired Bédié (Houphouët-Boigny's successor as leader of the PDCI, Parti Démocratique de la Côte d'Ivoire, the former single party) to launch his ideological *ivoirité* offensive in the hope this appeal to all "true" Ivorians would compensate for the loss of the foreign vote (for immigrants, Ouattara as a northerner was the obvious candidate). On the other, it encouraged Gbagbo, who still blamed his 1990 defeat by Houphouët on the stranger vote, all the more to profile himself as a champion of autochthony, increasingly giving xenophobia precedence in his propaganda over his former socialist leanings.

The competition at the national level may have been full of surprising turns—at one moment Gbagbo's FPI was even in alliance with the northern RDR—but the controversy around the Ouattara figure and the stranger vote converged with the deepening split between the north and the south, between the *Ivoiriens de souche* and the immigrants, and made it appear ever more inevitable. However, a closer view into the backgrounds of these developments show that, in practice, other contradictions cross this apparently inevitable split and show that different scenarios might well have been possible.

Backgrounds: Different Implications

Two aspects are of interest to qualify the apparent self-evidence of a north-south divide as some sort of natural axis in the recent developments in Ivory Coast. First of all, the north-south axis of migration is crossed by a west-east movement of the cacao frontier in the southern forest; this means that the powerful Baoule group in the center of the country, which under Houphouët Boigny and Bédié dominated national politics, has a highly ambivalent position as both *autochtone* and stranger. Second, several authors emphasize that the autochthony wave that overran Ivorian politics and is interpreted so easily as an inevitable consequence of south-north tensions reflects a true social revolution by youth, who are placing themselves in the lead over their elders; somewhat paradoxically, this makes very young men the guardians of autochthonous "traditions" and seems to complicate tensions *inside* local communities (see Chauveau 2005; Chauveau and Richards 2007).

Many authors—especially from the *Politique Africaine* group[13]—have already written about the complex character of the cacao boom on which *le miracle ivoirien* rested. So just a few remarks on its relevance to the upsurge of autochthony in this country may suffice here.

Cacao cultivation started in the 1920s in the forested southeast part of the country among the Agni and other prestigious Akan groups. Since then the "cacao frontier" moved gradually in a western direction, through the forest area of southern Ivory Coast, first passing its center and toward the 1940s reaching the thinly populated southwestern parts of the country, the land of the Bété and other Kru groups. From the very beginning it attracted laborers from the northern savannah zone, especially the central Baoule, who still boast of their historical links to the Ashanti and other Akan groups in present-day Ghana and for centuries had been moving from there in a southeastern direction toward the savannah-forest divide in central Ivory Coast.

Chauveau (2000:100) shows how this cacao frontier was marked by specific and highly flexible institutions, the most important being the *tutorat*. The old possibility for a newcomer to be incorporated into a local community by attaching himself to a tutor acquired a new scope with the expansion of cacao farming: especially given the tendency of local youth to opt for a career in civil service rather than work on the farms, local farmers needed to attract workers from outside.[14] These immigrants would first work on the farm of their tutor but soon gain access to a piece of land to create their own farm. The rights and duties in such a relationship were far from clear: Chauveau characterizes the *tutorat* as an institution under permanent negotiation. Often immigrants had greater access to labor—they could invite young relatives from home in the drier parts of the north—and could thus rapidly expand their farms.

From the beginning of the cacao boom, this extension of the local *tutorat* system to accommodate immigrants from the north was encouraged by the state. In 1932, the colonial government even incorporated the much more populated colony of Haute Volta (the later Burkina Faso, which was already then seen as a labor reservoir) into the Ivory Coast colony in order to facilitate the recruitment of laborers for French planters in the south.[15] But especially after the abolition of *le travail forcé* in 1946, labor migration, still encouraged by the colonial state, took off. In the 1950s, the colonial government was actively supported in this by Houphouët-Boigny's local branch of the RDA (Rassemblement Démocratique Africain), the major nationalist movement in French West Africa. Houphouët's faction consisted mostly of richer Baoule farmers who had every reason to encourage further labor migration. After independence (1960), he further reinforced his support of the migrants. As said before, the new government actively promoted an open and inclusivist version of national citizenship, justified by the economic contribution of (im)migrants to the *miracle ivoirien* but also inspired by an appeal to *la fraternité africaine* related to Houphouët's old Pan-African ideals (cf. Yéré 2006). Thus immigrants received the right to vote, and local groups were reminded in strong terms of their duty under the *tutorat* to welcome strangers who could contribute to national progress.

The main bone of contestation in all this remained, however, the rights to the land. In many parts of the south, land tenure was organized in a bundle of rights, which meant that in practice it was far from clear who owned a particular piece of land. For the Bété, for instance, Dozon (1985:279) states that it was through offering a piece of land to a stranger that a local could manifest himself as its owner. The immigrants for their part sought to confirm and expand their rights by accumulating all sorts of informal contracts (*les petits papiers*—Chauveau 2000:108), without, however, being able to attain full juridical ownership. Houphouët-Boigny tried to sidestep this tricky issue by his daring statement of 1963—at a meeting of autochthons complaining of losing their lands to strangers!—that *la terre appartient à celui qui la met en valeur* (the land belongs to the one who works it; quoted in Chauveau 2000:105). Nevertheless, this issue led to local confrontations already in the 1960s. These occurred especially in the southwest, where locals—Bété and others—attacked Baoule immigrants (that is, people from President Houphouët's own group). However, in view of the continuing state support for immigrant farmers, most locals pursued another strategy, constantly augmenting the obligations called for under the tutorship of their "clients"—often much richer than they themselves. It was this increasing pressure that turned the *tutorat* into a "constant negotiation," becoming ever more explosive (Chauveau 2000).

Chauveau analyzes Houphouët's policies as a double compromise aiming to satisfy not only migrants but also local youth (Chauveau 2000:104). The constant support for immigrants, facilitating their access to land in exchange for electoral support, was balanced by the state's support of local youth—apparently especially sensitive to the adage *Ivoirien aime bureau*—giving them access to education and to employment in the city. However, especially after 1980 this double compromise ran up against its limitations. On the one hand, the cacao frontier had reached the country's western border, so that there was no more new land to be cleared. Typically it was in the southwest—notably among the Bété, where the average scale of farms was much smaller than in the areas of earlier colonization—that rural tensions first exploded. On the other hand, there were fewer and fewer jobs for educated youths; many were forced into a dreaded *retour à la terre*, and these young *rurbains* ("rural urbanites") took the lead in ever more violent attacks on strangers who were occupying "their" lands. The concomitant decline of the cacao economy forced the government to accept a structural adjustment dictate, and Houphouët-Boigny lived just long enough to experience the humiliation of seeing his country, once the "miracle" of Africa, cited by the World Bank—in the then still overly self-assured language of the first cohort of "adjusters"—as an example of "fettered adjustment" showing that "poverty can accrue when the politics of adjustment are applied incorrectly."[16] The final collapse of Houphouët's model of development through an open-door policy came in 1998, five years after his death, with the new land law reserving land ownership for Ivorians only, thereby abolishing any right to land that foreign immigrants might have appropriated under the earlier *tutorat* regime. Foreign donors may have approved of the law as a step forward in establishing individual land ownership. But within the country it was mainly seen as a smashing victory for the ideas of autochthony and *ivoirité* concerning the land issue (Fisiy 1999).

A prominent role in all these developments—and one that makes it impossible to see them as a self-evident north-south confrontation—was played by the Baoule. Culturally, this group, proud of its Akan ancestry, sees itself as part of the south (and is seen also as such by others) in clear contrast to the north, strongly influenced by Islamic culture. In political terms, the general notion that the Ivorian state belongs to the south (Dembélé 2002:167) is based on the long years that it was completely dominated by the Baoule. As said, the first two presidents, Houphouët and Bédié, belonged to this group, and especially during Houphouët's long tenure, key positions were occupied by his Baoule *barons*, mainly coming from an emerging Baoule cacao farmer bourgeoisie. This was further underlined by an often hardly hidden assumption among the leaders that the Baoule, as part of the Akan group with its proud tradition of state-building—they still see the Ashanti as their "brothers"—were the anointed rulers of Ivory Coast.[17]

However, in the context of growing tensions within the cacao economy, the position of the Baoule was less commanding. In many areas of this zone they were counted among the immigrants. In the southeast they had been among the first migrants who moved to profit from the incipient cacao boom. In this area many of them succeeded in creating large-scale plantations. But especially in the southwest, where the cacao frontier finally got clogged, Baoule farmers were still emphatically seen as "strangers" by the local population. Several authors (McGovern 2005:7; Marshall 2006) even report that the autochthons resent the Baoule in particular because of their arrogant behavior and their habit of creating their own *campement* near the plantations, while the Diola from the north and the Burkinabe live in the village with their tutor and try to adapt themselves at least in some respects to local ways.

This ambiguous position of the Baoule is again a good example of how deceiving autochthony's apparent clarity can be. The opposition between southern autochthons and northern immigrants seems to be self-evident, but on closer inspection the unity of the southerners as autochthons seems to dissipate. As in so many cases, autochthony's clarity turns out to recede: any effort to define its unity becomes mired in ambiguities. The ambivalence of the Baoule position is, moreover, not a minor one. Marshall (2006), for instance, warns that Gbagbo's rigidity in trying to fix who belongs and who does not can very well lead the local Bété and others to project their hatred of greedy strangers onto the Baoule rather than the northerners. The segmentary effect of autochthony discourse makes it very probable that in the future the unity of the south against the north will be further undermined.

*   *   *

Another and even more crucial point that risks disappearing from sight in simplistic presentations of the present-day crisis as a logical outcome of the tension between northern immigrants and southern autochthons is the leading role of the youth, especially in Gbagbo's autochthony movement. Marshall (2006:29) speaks of a "small social revolution."

Indeed, Gbagbo's road to power seems to have been paved mainly by his young *combattants*. And it becomes ever less clear to what extent he and the other FPI leaders are still able to control these unruly youths and their propensity to violence. Konate (2003:56) relates how the FESCI, a student movement that became ever more closely associated with Gbagbo, could terrorize a university campus already in the 1990s. As said, FESCI leaders came subsequently to dominate the Young Patriots, Gbagbo's private commandos who were to play a central role in the street guerrilla in Abidjan during the crucial changes in 1999–2000.[18] In 2002, just after the "rebellion" in the north, their self-styled General Blé Goudé[19] tried to reunite them in the Alliance des Jeunes Patriots pour le Sursaut National. Profiting from substantial financial support from the president himself, the movement succeeded for a time in mobilizing huge crowds at its rallies. However, popular enthusiasm rapidly cooled, and other groups emerged to fill the gap. Marshall (2006:30) notes that the "patriotic galaxy," as this diffuse set of groups came to be known, was basically schismatic, constantly producing new split-offs. Yet it was coherent enough to engage in a process of "gridding" the southern cities, "enabling the least compound and its occupants to be identified and watched, even going so far as to having painted marks on some compounds." A shocking climax of this diffuse but deadly violence was the killing of some three hundred supposed supporters of the rebellion, many of them in their homes, within a few days in March 2004.

However, this violent and high-handed behavior of gangs of youngsters is not limited to the cities. Jean-Pierre Chauveau and Koffi Samuel Bobo (2003) sketch a vivid picture of the role of the *barragistes* (roadblock people) in a rural area of the Centre-West region. Every village has its *barrage*, manned by young men. The *sous-préfet* and other local representatives of the government argue the necessity of arming the young and giving them a key role in controlling the area, notably in policing the numerous immigrants and hostile infiltration by "rebels" from the north and more recently the west. Within a few years the *barrage* has become a way of life for these armed youngsters. Constant "fines," imposed particularly on strangers, assure them of a regular and nonnegligible income (Chauveau and Bobo estimate that the daily income of a *barrage* could be around 20,000–30,000 CFA = around $40). Immigrants have no alternative but to pay, in view of their threatened position. Local *barragistes* are regularly involved in violent confrontations with strangers who are accused of supporting the "rebellion." Especially the Burkinabe in the area are terrorized by the tightening grid of *barrages*.

Most *barragistes* are so-called *rurbains*—sons of the village who tried to make a career in the city but had to come back because of high urban unemployment rates. Many of them feel they are entitled to the payments they impose on strangers through their *barrages*. Their elders receive rent for the land they have leased to these strangers, and as a consequence there is no more land for these *rurbains* on their return. So they make the strangers pay. The practice seems to lead to increasing tensions between the *rurbains* and their own elders. The latter often prefer to lease out the land to foreigners, who at least pay rent, rather than to their youngsters who return impoverished from the city. Moreover, some *rurbains,* if they finally get access to a piece of land, are so disappointed with rural life that they lease or even sell it in order to accumulate money for trying to get into Europe (Chauveau and Bobo 2003:16).

As in the cities, the lines of distinction between autochthons and those who do not "really" belong are getting ever more confused. In the southwest, for instance, the Baoule may now be seen as immigrants, yet on some barrages young Baoule men are prominently present. Even more confusing is the infiltration of militants from neighboring Liberia in the same area. Some local groups—like the Yacouba (or Dan), the group of General Gueï, supposedly murdered by Gbagbo's people—supported the two new "rebel" movements in the area, which worked together with militants of Charles Taylor (former president of Liberia and an archenemy of Gbagbo), while other groups, like the Guéré, side with the Gbagbo regime and collaborate with Liberian soldiers from other factions. Comfort Ero and Anne Marshall (2003:100) conclude that in this area the Ivorians had invited Liberians to join in their struggles over belonging but can no longer control them.

A closer look at what is going on at the ground shatters again the simplistic image of a self-evident confrontation between south and north. The Young Patriots and the *rurbains* on their *barrages* in the countryside have good reason to continue the violence—it has become their way of life. Yet they form an informal and sprawling network, and their autonomous activities constantly complicate the lines of opposition on the ground. The confused but all the more murderous violence, notably in the southwest, is a shocking illustration of how the segmentary tendency of autochthony thinking leads to constant redefinitions and shifts that inspire further violence in efforts to achieve an impossible purification.

Interpretations

Recent developments in Ivory Coast provide an extreme example of how quickly autochthony could transform an apparently peaceful country into a hotbed of ever more startling forms of violence. This makes the question of how to understand the striking mobilizing capacity—or what Marshall (2006:12) calls the "performative power"—of such a discourse of belonging all the more pressing. A related and equally urgent question is why it manifested itself especially in the last decade of the last century with such devastating force.

In a seminal article of 1997, Dozon showed, with considerable foresight, that 1990 and subsequent years can indeed be seen as a turning point in a much longer development. He emphasized that Ivorian subjectivity had always manifested itself as poignantly relational. Autochthony as such is nothing new to the country. Already in 1934, elites from the south (mainly Agni) founded the Association de Défense des Intérêts des Autochtones de Côte d'Ivoire (ADIACI), but in those days autochthony's "Other" was a very different one: this movement targeted especially Dahomean and Senegalese clerks, who were overrepresented in the colony's administration to the detriment of local elites. There was certainly some continuity with precolonial days in this. Unwittingly the colonials, with their preference for foreigners over supposedly backward locals (see above), continued a long tradition in which migration was celebrated. As noted already in chapter 1, precolonial rulers themselves often claimed to come from elsewhere, and, in general, local groups were proud of their migratory histories. Throughout the colonial period, the government continued to see migrants, in contrast to the southern forest peoples, as the most dynamic element of the colony.[20] Houphouët-Boigny's encouragement of further immigration, as a stimulus for economic development, and his ideal of an open, inclusivist citizenship equally fit in with this *longue durée*.

Dozon concludes, therefore, that the presidential elections of 1990—the first truly democratic ones in many years—constituted a true watershed. In these elections *Le Vieux* (Houphouët-Boigny) was for the first time opposed by a serious rival candidate, Laurent Gbagbo, and the latter did surprisingly well. His relative success (supposedly Houphouët won due only to large-scale rigging and the numerous strangers' votes) was clearly based on massive support among southerners due to Gbagbo's heavy propaganda against foreign immigrants and in favor of the rights of autochthons. Just as in Cameroon, democratization went together with an upsurge of autochthony—not to say xenophobia. The autochthons seemed finally determined to get rid of their more or less subservient position: at long last the state would have to recognize their position as first-class citizens with special rights.

Several factors specific to Ivory Coast can explain why in this country this upsurge of autochthony had particularly violent effects. On the ground this seemed more or less inevitable. As Marshall remembers: "As an observer... I was absolutely struck by the daily escalation of events. On the one hand, it seemed that each new act or statement of violence constituted in itself an isolated event. On the other, the unfolding of events gave the impression of following an inexorable and terrifying logic, against which nothing could be done" (Marshall 2006:28). This sense of inevitability was strengthened by a more or less fortuitous intertwinement of the vicissitudes of national politics with local concerns about belonging and exclusion. The controversial Alassane Outtara with his supposed Burkina origins happened to become an emblematic figure of the *autochtones-allogènes* opposition. Another specific factor was the crucial role, already mentioned, that the vote of the immigrants came to play in Houphouët-Boigny's last election (1990). Then there was the quite accidental political situation of the end of 2000, from which Laurent Gbagbo emerged as the only possible candidate for the presidency, which sealed the victory of autochthony.[21] Another factor special to Ivory Coast was Houphouët-Boigny's extremely open version of nation-building, welcoming immigrants as a sign of African fraternity but also to assist in further economic development. This large influx of immigrants triggered an all the more violent backlash against them in this country.

However, in a broader perspective the Ivorian developments were not exceptional. With the present-day "global conjuncture of belonging,"[22] all over the world more cosmopolitan forms of citizenship are being discarded in a return to highly exclusive definitions of the nation. Ivory Coast is a somewhat frightening example of a general trend toward a renaissance of the nation-state, which far from being surpassed by globalizing processes, becomes much more constricting than in previous decades.[23] The paradoxical example of Ivory Coast's young *rurbains*, who against their will are forced to return to the countryside and there become the main defenders of tradition, autochthony, and a purification of the nation, clearly has more general implications. It shows how closely this obsession with belonging and autochthony is intertwined with the formation of the nation-state. Rather than arising from a wish to withdraw into the local, it expresses a determined effort to get access to the national arena and through this to the processes of globalization. Or to put it more forcefully: autochthony presupposes national citizenship; it is not a contradiction of the latter but rather grafts itself onto that institution in highly variable and precarious patterns.[24]

Another more general aspect of the autochthony movement and its spectacular successes in Ivory Coast—and a possible explanation of its "performative power"—is its special capacity as a "politics of resentment" (McGovern 2004:11) to accommodate a wide array of shifting grievances. The young *rurbains* can oppose their own elders under the cover of acting as defenders of autochthony. Gbagbo's Bété, who lately have become the main champions of autochthony, can lead the southerners against the threatening wave of northern immigrants, but they can at the same time warn the Baoule, who formerly seemed to own the state, that they too could be redefined as immigrants who do not really belong. However, this elastic quality of autochthony logics also constitutes a weakness. Indeed, Ivory Coast exemplifies how quickly autochthony's apparent clarity dissolves when the common cause of those who really belong has to be defined more substantially. Both Gbagbo's Opération Nationale d'Identification, with the "village of origin" as a final criterion, and Bédié's effort to give substance to notions like *ivoirité* and *Ivoiriens de souche* highlight the impossibility of a final clarification of the question of belonging, whether by more ideological or by more legalistic criteria. The subsequent developments in the country graphically showed that the segmentary tendencies of autochthony thinking—the possibility of constant redefinitions—engender a special kind of violence, one that works especially at close range, because of the need to be constantly vigilant against fake autochthons, traitors who are all the more dangerous since they are so hard to recognize.

Marshall's powerful title "The War of Who Is Who"[25] effectively sums up the general problem. Autochthony promises to fix the subject—and, as said, in this obsession with fixation it echoes old colonial preoccupations with *la population flottante*—but like so many similar efforts, Ivory Coast's struggles over identification only added to the general confusion, with highly violent consequences.[26]

Elsewhere in Africa

Kivu in eastern Congo (Democratic Republic of Congo, or DRC) became another hotbed of internecine strife over autochthony and exclusion, at least as violent as Ivory Coast. Stephen Jackson (2006:99), who worked in this area around 2000, first for NGOs and then for his PhD research, notes that "the term *autochtone* enjoys striking currency in eastern DRC. It crops up continuously in everyday conversation as a way of delimiting

and distinguishing peoples and their associated rights...or political allegiance. Even when the language in use is not French—in Kiswahili, say,
which is the other lingua franca, or in one of the many languages local to
the Kivu—the French *autochtone* will be code-switched into an otherwise
'local' sentence." Jackson (2003:2) also quotes shocking figures of the violence all this created: between 1998 and 2001 nearly two million people
died out of a total population for the Kivu of nearly eight million.

At first glance, this seems to be quite a special case. The direct cause of
the local violence appears to lie in neighboring Rwanda and the particular (castelike?) hierarchy between Tutsi and Hutu that marks relations in
that country.[27] Since independence (1961), ever more spasmodic forms of
violence between these groups—culminating in the horrible genocide of
1994 of Tutsi and intellectuals among the Hutu—pushed growing waves
of emigrants toward the Kivu. The local violence in Kivu seems therefore an outcome of the Rwandan Hutu-Tutsi conflict, and the fault lines
within the Kivu region appear to be simple: local people defending their
rights as autochthons against recent Banyarwanda immigrants. Yet on the
ground, the—by now familiar—sprawling implications of discourse on autochthony and belonging manifest themselves in the Kivu as well. Jackson
speaks of "a vortex" of diffuse and constantly changing identities and of
a "nervous language of belonging":

> Particularly alarming has been the increased use of a vernacular concerning
> "autochthony."...Dangerously flexible in its politics, nervous and paranoid in
> its language, unmoored from geographic or ethno-cultural specificity, borrowing
> energy from present conflicts (genocidal cycles in Rwanda and Burundi, seven
> years of war in the DRC, and long-running arguments about entitlement to
> Congolese citizenship) and deep-seated mythologies of the past (the so-called
> Hamitic Hypothesis...and conspiracy theories about "Nilotic" machinations
> against "Bantu" autochthons), the idea of autochthony has permitted compar-
> atively localized instances of violence to inscribe themselves upwards into re-
> gional, and even continental mega-ethnic logics. (Jackson 2006:96)

In the Kivu as well, the certainty promised by notions of autochthony and
belonging seems to evaporate in practice, giving way to nagging uncertainty, precisely because the fault lines are far from unequivocal so that
"fake autochthons" and "traitors" seem to be all around. As in Cameroon
and Ivory Coast, autochthony discourse in the Kivu is beset by a "pro-
found nervousness": "[it] is obsessed with a purity that can never be

achieved, and as a result it is deeply unsettled by the thought of creeping impurity"(Jackson 2006:114). Here as well, it is this desperate search for purity that makes autochthony so prone to violence.

Indeed, in practice the simplistic contrast of Kivu autochthons (Hunde, Nyanga, Tembo, and other groups) versus Banyarwanda immigrants gives way to a kaleidoscopic confusion of identities. Jackson notes that on the local level, claims to *autochtonie* can also lead to conflicts between groups like the Hunde and Nyanga, which both pretend to be autochthonous. Further, the Banyarwanda cannot be seen as a uniform group. Some Rwandan groups claim to have settled in the Kivu centuries ago and try to distinguish themselves from more recent migrants.[28] But the main split, also among the migrants, is of course the Hutu-Tutsi division, which complicates claims of autochthony for this entire region. When after the 1994 genocide, Kagame and his Tutsi army succeeded in reconquering Rwanda and many Hutu—included the feared Interahamwe soldiers—fled into the Kivu, there were signs of a common "Bantu" solidarity of "autochthons" against "Nilotic" (Tutsi) invaders, especially when Kagame subsequently invaded the Kivu pursuing the Hutu Interahamwe. Thus autochthony can be expressed also on a transnational scale, covering the whole Interlacustrine region and evoking a general nightmare of "all Tutsi rulers of the region [working together to create a] . . . Hima/Nilotic Empire in Central and East Africa" for the ultimate subjection of all Bantu (Hutu) autochthons.[29] However, at other times it is Hutu immigrants in the Kivu who are branded as "Banyarwanda" and therefore as *allochtones* by the "real" autochthons—even if they are Bantu also.

What Jackson means by the "nervousness" of this language, its obsession with "purity" and its confusing capacity to switch from one level to another, is vividly illustrated in his analysis of the popular tracts—"dog-eared, continuously and poorly reproduced on cheap street-corner photocopiers and then re-corrected with ballpoint pen" (Jackson 2006:99)—that are locally produced in Goma and Bukavu (Kivu's main towns), circulate everywhere, and excel in verbal violence. For instance, the "Congo Dépec" (Congo Dismembered) tract by "L'Oeil du Peuple" warns that "the purity of the Bantu Congolese population is threatened by massive implantation and demographic inundation by Tutsi sponsored by a colonial administration and a Bank for Tutsi Implantation" (Jackson 2003:199). Another tract, with the challenging title "Race Pure" and attributed to "Le Représentant de la Race Pure à Kigali," that is, to a Tutsi (but clearly written by a self-styled autochthon), imputes to the Tutsi a similar obsession with purity. It opens with a warning: "The present circular is only for effective members of the Pure Race" (Jackson 2003: 274). Most spectacular—especially in the way in which it relates local autochthony to global constellations—is the "Mawe Mawe Antifada" (sic), which states, "Another reason that pushed the Mawe Mawe [a militia of 'autochthons'] to attack the enemy is the political repression and social cannibalism from which the autochthon population suffers under this Israeli-Anglo-American occupation via its mercenary Tutsi intermediaries" (Jackson 2003:204).

Kivu autochthony may, therefore, seem to be a kind of side eddy of the of the major Tutsi-Hutu current. Yet in a longer time perspective more general factors emerge that are evident as well in Ivory Coast, Cameroon, and many other settings. For instance, even though the Kivu case confirms again the emphasis of Mbembe (2002) that autochthony's present-day virulence appears to be a typically postcolonial phenomenon, colonial interventions played a crucial role here as well—notably the colonial government's preference for migrants as more "dynamic." From the 1930s on—when the Tutsi-Hutu opposition still seemed to be safely contained within the colonial framework—the Belgians forcefully encouraged the migration of large numbers of Hutu peasants from densely populated cantons in Rwanda into almost empty parts of the Kivu (Mathieu and Tsongo 1998). In 1937 a special agreement was signed between the administrative authorities in Rwanda and those in the Kivu (all Belgians, of course) to create a special project, Mission d'Immigration des Banyarwanda (MIB), to administer the immigrants in their new homes. One of the first things the new office did was to publish a manual of more than two hundred pages with detailed guidelines on how to install these *transplantés*: what kind of formalities had to be fulfilled upon their arrival, what salaries would be paid to the workers on European plantations, what kind of infrastructure the new immigrants had to create, and so on.[30] Especially in the fertile Massisi zone, local Hunde chiefs were heavily pressured by the colonial government to make land available for all this. To their outrage, the government even appointed a Rwandan chief to control the Hutu immigrants (and, in line with then current colonial policy, this Rwandan was a Tutsi). Apart from the idea that this would ease pressure on the land in the Rwandan highlands, colonial administrators believed that more dynamic migrants were needed for the *mise en valeur* of the fertile parts of the Kivu, either as independent farmers or as workers on European plantations.

However, since these immigration projects were accompanied by large-scale land expropriation for European planters and for nature reserves, land pressure started to mount rapidly in the Kivu as well. Just as in south Ivory Coast or South-West Province in Cameroon, the autochthony explosion of the 1990s in the Kivu can be understood only in relation to the mounting anger among the locals about gradually losing access to their "own" land because of government projects bringing in ever more strangers—who, moreover, seem to appropriate land on an ever larger scale. Mathieu and Tsongo (1998) document the rage among people who consider themselves to be autochthons but complain that large Banyarwanda landowners have emptied good agricultural land and turned it into huge cattle farms, especially since the 1970s, after a new airport in Goma made meat transports to Kinshasa and other cities possible and highly profitable.

The Kivu is also a striking example of how directly the vicissitudes of the idea of national citizenship during the proud period of nation-building affected the subsequent autochthony backlash. Here as well autochthony is very much a product of state formation in postcolonial times. Jackson (2006) shows how strongly present-day debates on the precarious status of the Banyarwanda are still affected by Mobutu's manipulations of the definitions of citizenship. With his usual expertise for divide-and-rule, the Leopard President knew how to make his presence felt in this faraway province. The 1964 constitution limited Congolese citizenship to those who had descended from an ancestor living in the colony before October 18, 1908 (the date that the Belgian Congo was officially constituted). However, in 1971 Mobutu allowed Barthélemy Bisengima, a Congolese Tutsi who in those years was his confidence man, to change the law to such an extent that persons from Rwanda-Burundi origin who had settled in the Kivu before January 1, 1950, were also entitled to Zairean (Congolese) nationality. But in 1978, Bisengima fell from grace, and in 1981 Mobotu's parliament reaffirmed the 1964 rulings on nationality, moving the crucial date, before which one's ancestor(s) should have settled already in the Congo, back to August 1, 1885 (an even more colonial date—the moment of the Berlin conference and the foundation of Leopold II's Congo "Free State"). Thus, with one legal change, hundred thousands of Rwandan immigrants lost the citizenship that had been offered to them just a few years before. The consequence of all this uncertainty was a hectic trade in identity cards—which again strengthened "real" locals' suspicions that they were surrounded by "fake" autochthons (Mathieu and Tsongo 1998:397–78; Jackson 2006).

But Mobutu's master-stroke was to insist, when he was finally forced to convene a *conférence nationale souveraine* in 1991, that only "autochthonous" representatives could participate on behalf of "their" province. In the Kivu, this had dramatic consequences. Already in 1991, an *opération d'identification des nationaux* was started—that is, more than ten years earlier than in Ivory Coast—in order to separate immigrants from those who had a right to vote, the "real" citizens (Mathieu and Tsongo 1998:394). It is tragic that even in this area, where there have scarcely been any elections because of subsequent waves of violence, democratization had the by now familiar effect of triggering fierce conflicts over who belongs and who can be excluded from the right to vote.

In the Kivu, as elsewhere in Africa, autochthony and history seem to fit together only with difficulty. Hunde, Nyanga, and other "autochthonous" groups invoke history in order to confirm their ancestral claims over against latecomers. However, Jackson (2006) notes that nearly all these groups have oral traditions about coming from elsewhere; in the present-day context such history is hushed since it might relativize their autochthony. The strongest example of such an attempt to fix history and deny any movement can be found in Liisa Malkki's magisterial study (1995) of the production of an extremely rigid historical orthodoxy by Hutu refugees in Tanzanian camps. Malkki (1955:63) speaks of an "autochtonization of history": the whole aim of Hutu history production seems to be to prove that they are true autochthons who never moved—in contrast to the Tutsi, who are only latecomers and therefore have no right at all. Yet Malkki notices a certain reluctance among the Hutu to use the term *autochthonous*. Her informants were clearly suffering under the Tutsi's contemptuous stereotype of them as being rude and uncivilized, so for them the term could easily become a double-edged sword. After all, the real autochthons in this area are the Twa "Pygmies," and who would ever want to be associated with those primitives? In chapter 1 this double edge was already noted: *autochthonous* can imply a claim to privilege, but it can also connote being primitive or even prehuman (cf. the Athenian and Mossi examples above). I will return later to this hidden ambivalence of autochthony discourse, as it comes to the fore in striking inconsistencies when it concerns groups like these "Pygmies," whose autochthony cannot be doubted but who are still considered to be more or less "subhuman" by many self-styled autochthons.

* * *

Southwest Cameroon, southern Ivory Coast, and eastern Congo are regions where popular preoccupation with autochthony and belonging has taken on particularly virulent expressions over the last decades. But under present-day conditions, there are parallels throughout the continent. Carola Lentz (2003; 2006) writes about similar developments on both sides of the Burkina Faso–Ghana border, where autochthony has a long history but became a violent political issue only in the 1990s. The term itself seems to spread from Francophone areas into Anglophone Africa: for instance in the Anglophone part of Cameroon (see chapter 2) or in the part of north Ghana that borders on Togo (Wienia 2003). But even where the notion as such is not current, similar discourses prove to be highly mobilizing. Achim von Oppen's 2003 *Habilitationsschrift* on "bounding villages" in Zambia highlights a similar, exclusionist discourse on locality and belonging that manages at the same time to remain open-ended and tuned in to globalization.[31]

Even more striking are the parallels with developments in a very different context, South Africa's highly industrialized society—notably with the rising popular concerns in this country about the *Makwere-kwere*, mentioned above, the ever more numerous immigrants from other parts of Africa.[32] In South Africa's major cities people tend to blame most daily problems—not only crime but also shortage of jobs and housing—on the influx of these "strangers" from across the Limpopo. Loren Landau (2006), who directs a research team investigating the often desperate conditions of these immigrants in Johannesburg, shows that in this context as well the preoccupation with separating those who do belong from those who don't leads to all sorts of apparently self-evident stereotypes that block insight into the situation.

Clearly, the *Makwere-kwere* serve as the Other for different categories of South Africans in the city, to reaffirm their own claims to belong, which in practice are quite new and not yet that stable. For the various "local" groups who came to live in certain parts of Jo-burg, scapegoating the feared *Makwere-kwere* automatically reinforces their self-image as autochthons who "belong." But this leads also to a projection of belonging: South African protagonists in the debate on the *Makwere-kwere* threat seem to assume that the latter are eager to put down roots in their new country and want to push a claim to belong there as well. Landau shows that actually many of these immigrants see Johannesburg only as a gateway to other locations. Autochthony is a catching discourse: sometimes it seems to reflect only itself.

"Pygmy" Predicaments: Can Only Citizens Qualify as Autochthons?

Recently, the obsession with autochthony and belonging has taken on the proportions of a huge wave sweeping over the African continent.[33] Despite the many variations and ambiguities underneath this deceiving appearance of uniformity, all of the preceding examples highlight the all-pervasive force these notions have acquired over the last decades. It might be helpful, therefore, to close with a counterexample so as to show that even this naturalizing discourse does not work under certain circumstances. The peoples of equatorial Africa commonly referred to as "Pygmies" provide a striking case, since they seem to play a particular role in the autochthony drama. Their inconsistent position in debates on autochthony—as eternal marginals, despite their unquestioned belonging—shows cogently how much this apparently primordial notion is related to historically constructed concepts of national citizenship.

In a very interesting publication on the relation between Baka Pygmies and the state in Cameroon—where state pressures toward the integration and sedentarization of Pygmies have probably been the most continuous and consistent in equatorial Africa—Alec Leonhardt (2006) points out certain noteworthy contradictions. Throughout this region, everybody agrees that the Baka were the first inhabitants of the forest. The "Bantu"—a scientific term that with the recent upsurge of autochthony talk has become very current in debates on the spot—may act as their "patrons," but nobody doubts that when they entered the forest they found the Baka "Pygmies" already there. Yet this unquestioned belonging hardly benefits the Baka in present-day struggles over issues of autochthony and exclusion; the contrary seems to be the case. Leonhardt explains this by making a contrast between "symbolical" and "substantive" autochthony. The Baka can certainly claim the first, but this is of little avail to them since they cannot make use of the latter. The reason is clear: they are still outside the field of the state, and "substantive" autochthony—the kind that counts in the struggle over political rights—is reserved for those who are considered to be citizen of this state.

In many respects the Baka, like most Pygmies, are clearly not citizens: they have great difficulty in obtaining a national identity card, since most of them have no birth certificate and Cameroonian citizenship can be claimed only if at least one parent can prove to be born in Cameroon. So for the Cameroonian state, they do not officially exist. In practice this has certain advantages: most Baka do not pay taxes; only successful hunters or healers are sometimes, and more or less unofficially, taxed by the administration.[34] But it is a severe handicap when they want to register for official projects or participate in regional or national politics.[35] All this may change in the future, since increasing numbers of Baka children go to school and there is growing international interest in both the conservation and the exploitation of the forest (remember the tug-of-war between logging companies, national politicians, and international conservationists discussed in chapter 3). The whole area has been invaded by all sorts of development projects, NGOs, and entrepreneurs who hope to profit, despite the ecologists' countervailing efforts, from further possibilities for logging. All this serves to make the Baka marginalization from the state even more problematic. Still, both national politicians and villagers have great difficulty in recognizing these "Pygmies" as full citizens of the Cameroonian state, even if they can claim to be some sort of arch-autochthons.

Clearly, autochthony discourse—the basic idea that a firstcomer can claim special rights—does not "work" in the case of the Pygmies.[36] There are several reasons for this. An obvious one is the special character of the Baka—or in general "Pygmy"—relation to the soil. Many Baka now practice some agriculture (even of cash crops), which means a certain sedentarization, but most groups still see themselves as primarily hunters and food gatherers, and this requires an at least seminomadic existence. As Leonhardt puts it: for them, the basic contradiction is not between village and city but rather between village and forest; being a Baka still means being a person of the forest. This does not imply that Baka, again like most Pygmy groups, see themselves as nomads without any link to the land. They do claim specific parts of the forest as their domain, but they tend to move through the forest in circles that overlap with the movements of other groups. The idea of being the "child" of a specific piece of "soil"—encased in the very notion of autochthony—is less self-evident in their case. Some authors on these groups emphasize that they tend to avoid the places where their ancestors are buried; these are dangerous rather than sacred places to them.[37] There is a sharp contrast here with self-styled autochthonous groups in Africa that nowadays boast of their autochthony, since for them the place of burial is rather becoming a final test of belonging (see chap. 6).

However, the most important reason that the autochthony upsurge seems to bypass the Baka is their highly ambivalent relationship with Bantu villagers, who claim the autochthon label for themselves. Most Baka groups—again like other "Pygmy" groups—have a special relation with a Bantu village or family, whose members will act as their *patrons*. The Baka groups may often wander in wide circles through almost empty forest, but their more permanent living places are mostly quite close to Bantu villages. The relation has sometimes been characterized as a sort of symbiosis. The *patron* has to provide "his" Pygmies with agricultural produce and market products (such as iron tools, notably arrowheads, and iron wire for traps, or even guns for hunting). In exchange, the Pygmies with their superior knowledge of the forest act as guides—and in former days also as spies during war expeditions—and offer forest products, notably the various kinds of bushmeat, still considered superior meat by both villagers and urbanites.

Lately several authors have criticized this notion of a symbiosis as far too ahistorical (cf. Biesbrouck 1999). It is indeed important to emphasize that these patronage relations have never been stable: Pygmy groups could and did switch to other patrons. Especially lately they are subject to rapid change, which leads to discontent from both sides. The establishment of larger concentrations of wage laborers in the forest—for logging companies and for large agricultural enterprises, often parastatals—offer the Pygmies new possibilities for selling their bushmeat instead of handing it over to "their" villagers. The ever more active *buyem-sellem* (informal traders, often women) along the roads into the forest further promote this commercialization process. The obsession of many Pygmy men with cigarettes and alcohol makes these new possibilities particularly alluring to them. However, the villagers often feel that "their" Pygmies are no longer sticking to their side of the deal. Thus, minor offences—like a Pygmy young man "stealing" a gourd of palm-wine which a villager has hung in the top of a palm-tree in order to fill up, or a Pygmy woman taking a bunch of plantains from a villager's farm—are now quickly seen as major "crimes."

In general, the villagers' attitude toward Pygmies—even of their "own" Baka group—is marked by deep ambivalence. They have deep respect for their knowledge of the forest. Pygmies are often said to have all sorts of secret and therefore dangerous knowledge. They are supposed to have special abilities as healers. In Abong-Mbang in eastern Cameroon, it was common knowledge that when the *sous-préfet* broke his arm in an unfortunate accident, he ordered his people not to take him to the hospital but right away to the Baka, since they knew how to set a bone far better than the doctors did.[38]

Yet cunning and dangerous as the Baka are supposed to be, they are also seen by the villagers as somehow prehuman. There are long series of standard jokes about Pygmies and apes. The same *sous-préfet* of Abong-Mbang who went to the Baka to have his arm set, used to organize—in the context of the government's project for the *intégration des Pygmées*—soccer matches for Pygmy teams. For this young Baka men were collected in the camps, put in lorries, and driven to Abong-Mbang's makeshift stadium. They were divided into two teams and told to play a match in front of a highly amused crowd of urbanites. After the match, a big heap of iron tools (cleavers, axes, cooking pots) was thrown on the field, and the players could grab what they wanted. People's reactions were again mixed: admiration for the players (some of the youth were very quick and clever with the ball), contempt for their lack of decorum in fighting over their heap of prizes, but also jealousy that the government gave them these tools.[39]

These soccer matches can be seen as a baroque illustration of a basic ambivalence in the state's policies vis-à-vis the Baka and the Pygmies in general. Ever since the colonial conquest, state authorities have intervened in all sorts of ways to try to integrate the Pygmies—or the *négrilles*, as many French civil servants used to call them—into the new politico-economic framework of the state; in practice this meant especially more or less coercive attempts to sedentarize them and turn them from hunter-gatherers into agriculturalists. Yet these halfhearted attempts toward integration were always pervaded—in postcolonial times as much as in colonial days—by an acute feeling of a basic incompatibility. For instance, in his long *monographie* on the area, a certain M. Siret, French colonial servant from 1946 till 1949 in Doume and Abong-Mbang (east Cameroon), has a fairly long chapter on *les Pygmées* or *négrilles*. Throughout the chapter, the focus is on difference: racial difference with the villagers, the Pygmies' complete integration with the forest environment, their shy disdain of the villagers and even of the Europeans. Yet in the last paragraph of this chapter, Siret suddenly emphasizes that sedentarization is an ongoing process—apparently already at that time many Baka practiced some agriculture—and that this, moreover, will lead to the inevitably disappearance of their special way of life (Siret 1946–49:42). However, this seemed to be more his conviction than an expectation borne out by his own data.

Indeed, more recent research suggests that the idea of an inevitable development toward sedentarization and integration of these Pygmy has to be qualified. For instance, among the Bagyeli, another Pygmy group in Cameroon living much closer to the coast, where the state's sedentarization offensive was much more intensive—and where it seemed to have had greater success (most Bagyeli are now officially considered to be sedentarized)—a kind of return movement seems to be taking place. Several Bagyeli groups that had settled close to the village of their Bantu patrons have opted to move again away, deeper into the forest—apparently because living so close to their patrons had created all sorts of difficulties (see Biesbrouck 1999).[40] Clearly, it is not self-evident that the "Pygmies" will indeed try to become ever more accepted as "citizens." Moreover, the villagers for their part will have great difficulties with accepting the Baka as fellow citizens, despite their uncontested autochthony.

• • • • • • • • • • • • • •

In 1994, people in Kribi, the capital of the Cameroonian department where the Bagyeli live, became quite excited when a Bantu villager was brought to trial for killing a Bagyeli boy. The young men had kept "stealing" gourds containing palm wine. One of the villagers had become so furious that he gave the Bagyeli a severe beating—with fatal consequences. Thereupon, a group of Italian nuns who had worked for decades among the Bagyeli helped the latter to press charges in the Kribi tribunal. The fact that this was at all possible and that the court was even willing to judge the affair came as a great surprise to many. The villagers were furious: the Bagyeli concerned were "theirs," and this young men did deserve a beating for all the stealing he had done.[41] People agreed that the law is there for all citizens but apparently hardly realized that this applied to "their" Bagyeli as well. Indeed, many villagers still hesitate to view them as fully human. The villager concerned was condemned for manslaughter and put in jail— clear proof that the law recognizes "Pygmies" at least formally as citizens. But the villagers had great difficulty in accepting this. After this and similar incidents, they put so much pressure on the nuns that a few years later the latter decided to evacuate the area and give up their projects among the Bagyeli.[42]

• • • • • • • • • • • • • •

Apparently firstcomers cannot always claim special rights as "autochthons"—for this they need to qualify as citizens. In practice, autochthony is less "natural" than it seems to be.

* * *

The examples of exclusion of the "Pygmies" show that even autochthony has its limits. They show also how intrinsically autochthony, despite its apparently traditional claims, is linked to processes of state formation. Autochthony can sometimes present itself as an alternative to national citizenship, as in southwest Cameroon, or as a principle that excludes people who unjustly claim to be citizens, as in south Ivory Coast or eastern Congo. However, it is always grafted upon the state. The Pygmies have only "symbolic" autochthony, as Leonhardt puts it, but they are outside the field of the state and therefore cannot deduce any rights from it.[43] Autochthony without citizenship is of little avail.

However, the main implication of the African examples above might be that autochthony's paradoxical combination of self-evidence and great uncertainty can be especially dangerous. The quest for an impossible "purity"—an obsession with purification of foreign elements in a world that has long been marked by constant migration—easily leads to violence. In the "global conjuncture of belonging," such scenarios are emerging in other parts of the world as well.

CHAPTER FIVE

Autochthony in Europe: The Dutch Turn

E urope is undergoing its own version of the present-day "global con-juncture of belonging." No wonder that here as well, the term *autochthony* has acquired new momentum.[1] Here too, however, its presence is a highly fragmented one, and the reference in the term to "the soil" is quite different from those of ancient Greece and present-day Africa. A rapid overview of western Europe shows that since the 1970s the term *allochtoon* and thus its inevitable counterpart *autochtoon* became ever more current in the Netherlands and Flanders (the Dutch-speaking part of Belgium) and dominated the debate about the "immigration problem." It is striking how quickly both terms, clearly *Fremdkörper* in the Dutch language, acquired a heavy emotional appeal. Meanwhile Umberto Bossi, a prominent leader of the New Right in Italy, seems recently inclined to adopt this terminology. Apparently he is trying to trigger a switch from the notion of "Padania" as a nation of true northerners, defined against the lazy and corrupt southern Italians, to a somewhat broader vision of true Italian "autochthons" against (Arab) immigrants. However, as yet his use of this term seems have little resonance in Italy.

Elsewhere in western Europe the terms themselves are less current, but the discourse of belonging is very much present, particularly for expressing both the feeling that new immigrants should adapt themselves to the culture of the national groups that do belong and the rising fear that especially the "second generation" of immigrants will refuse to do so.

Language variations in addressing this issue relate to broader differences among the various countries, while at the same time the terms used affect the ways in which people look for solutions.

In France, Le Pen and his National Front seem to avoid the term *allogène*—so current in Francophone Africa—mainly because its counterpart, *autochtone*, has highly ironic overtones in French: using this label for the group the Front wants to see as the bearer of the nation would open one to the risk of *ridicule*.[2] Therefore Le Pen and his followers rather speak of an opposition between *immigrés* and *Français*, which implies a denial of the universalistic notion of *citoyenneté* as the very basis on which the French nation-state is built. Le Pen's view is that some *citoyens*—for instance, the second generation of Arab and African immigrants—are not "really" citizens since they cannot be considered to be true *Français*. However, here again apparently self-evident concepts like *immigré* or *Français* exhibit tricky fuzziness when they have to be delineated. While *citoyen* had at least some juridical basis, these other concepts turn out to be very hard to define. It seems that in the 1980s Le Pen floated the idea of defining "real" Frenchmen—Francais de souche—as those citoyens who could claim four grandparents born in France. Yet, this idea was rapidly abandoned, since in practice it would have meant excluding a majority of the *hexagone*'s inhabitants. Indeed, a surprisingly large number of people who considered themselves true Frenchmen turned out to have at least one grandparent of immigrant stock. Since then, Le Pen and his followers have simply wielded these vague concepts without attempting to further define them.[3]

As far as terminology is concerned, Germany is a particularly interesting case, since its struggle with its recent past plays a complicating role in this respect as well. Several German colleagues have assured me that the term *autochthony* has no clear equivalent in German. They suggested that the language of belonging is condensed in the notion of *Heimat*. This is striking since this term, often formally translated as "fatherland" or *patrie,* has much more diffuse contours: it commonly refers not to the nation-state but rather to region or even village, denoting the place where one belongs in a vague but highly localized way. Clearly, the specific histories of nationalism within Europe—in this case the relatively recent unification of Germany as a nation-state—still affect the ways in which present-day immigration problems are being discussed.

Despite the insistence of my German colleagues on the absence of the notion from German, the term *autochthony* has turned up in German debates, but at a quite unexpected spot: with the towering figure of Martin Heidegger. In his writings from the 1920s and 1930s, Heidegger cited with emphatic approval the old Athenian ideas on *autochthonia* and proposed as a translation the term *Bodenständigkeit*, already current in agrarian studies (lit. "stemming from or even rooted in the ground").[4] *Bodenständigkeit*/autochthony is seen by Heidegger as the solution to give German nationalism a particular, more communitarian coherence. He proposed it as an antidote to "the Anglo-French model of nationalism and the whole Western Enlightenment definition of freedom, equality, individuality."[5] This idea led him for some time to sympathize with National Socialist ideas, as expressed in the slogan "Blut and Boden" (blood and soil). This is certainly not the place to discuss the highly complex aspects of Heidegger's philosophy on this point. Yet noting his 1930s views may show how powerful the notion of being rooted in the soil is and how prone to create confusion at the same time.

Yet Heidegger's defense of autochtony/*Bodenständigkeit* is complicated by the German emphasis on *ius sanguinis* (right of blood/descent) rather than *ius soli* (right of soil) as the basis for citizenship—this in contrast to most western European nation-states. The reference to soil (*Boden*) in the term *autochthony* is for Heidegger (as for the Nazis) very closely intertwined with *Blut*; one could even say that in this context "soil" has more or less disappeared behind "blood." For instance, the continuing emphasis on *ius sanguinis* meant that, still in the 1990s, people of German descent, no matter how far back in history their descent claims were—for instance, Baptists who had lived for centuries in Siberia and who, after the collapse of the Iron Curtain, had the possibility to return—could acquire German citizenship without any problem, while for Turkish persons who had lived in Germany for generations this remained almost impossible. This corresponded with the idea, maintained much longer in Germany (at least formally) than elsewhere in Europe, that *Gastarbeiter* (guest workers) would return to their country of origin. Only in the course of the 1990s did all this begin to change. *Ius sanguinis* is no longer all-determining for citizenship, which now can be given to inhabitants of non-German descent as well. Yet the intertwinement of "soil" and "blood" in this context still has special effects.

In the European context it was especially the Flemish and the Dutch who—apparently for quite accidental reasons—adopted the classical notion of autochthony and gave it new momentum in their struggle with the immigration issue. Here the notion was put in a precarious relation with "integration," an equally confusing notion. An additional reason to focus on the Dutch case is the abrupt reversal that took place in this country in the first years of the twenty-first century with the notion of autochthony—and especially the question as to how give it more substance—as a central issue. A rapid series of events, some of them quite dramatic, showed that abrupt explosions of popular preoccupations with belonging and exclusion are not limited to the poorer countries of the world. Until well into the 1990s the Netherlands saw itself—and was seen by others—as a *gidsland* (guide country) in the world for realizing a tolerant "multicultural" solution to the migration problem: in those days the dominant opinion was that the inclusion of immigrants in Dutch society had to be implemented with due respect for their own culture (*met behoud van eigen cultuur*). In only two years all this changed completely. Now, many Dutch see their country as a *gidsland* for attaining a forceful integration of immigrants with proper respect for the principles of Dutch culture (even though there is considerable uncertainty about what this is exactly). Indeed, several outside observers have noted a rising tide of xenophobia and a sudden switch in official immigration policies to a new approach that seemed to be increasingly attuned to an assimilationist model—all the more striking in view of the country's reputation for tolerance and openness.[6] Equally noteworthy were the ambiguities of the autochthony notion in this context. It was introduced in the Netherlands quite abruptly and in a somewhat artificial way. Yet it soon acquired a self-evident appearance, as in the African examples above. Again, this was accompanied with considerable vagueness: a central issue became how to give more substance to this notion, self-evident as it might seem. If the *allochtoon* had to integrate, an obvious question was how to define into what she or he had to integrate. However, defining this turned out to be not an easy job.

Central questions for this chapter are, therefore, how the autochthony terminology became implanted in the Dutch context and why it gained such resonance. Further, I will trace the special implications the terms acquired in this context—what did the reference to the soil implied in the term come to mean in this context? Clearly the link with the soil is quite different for many Dutch people compared to what it is for most Ivorians or Cameroonians. How could the autochthony notion nevertheless acquire such a mobilizing impact in the Netherlands as well? A rapid overview of recent developments in the Netherlands will help to set the stage for yet another performance of the autochthony notion—this time a European one.

The Dutch Switch: From Multiculturalism to Cultural Integration

It was especially two shocking events in recent Dutch history that drew a lot of attention abroad: the murder of populist politician Pim Fortuyn, who had made a rocket start in national politics, by a radical ecologist in 2002, and the even bloodier murder of filmmaker Theo van Gogh, after he made the film *Submission* with Ayaan Hirsi Ali, by an Islamic fundamentalist in 2004. Surprisingly, however, an event that was at least as shocking got much less international attention: the death of eleven "illegal" immigrants who, in 2005, burned alive when their provisionally erected prison near Schiphol Airport caught fire. The new policy of Minister Rita Verdonk, who in 2003 promised to arrange for the forceful extradition of no fewer than twenty-six thousand "illegals" within two years, required drastic interventions. Before the disaster in the Schiphol prison, some of the victims had been locked up already for six months or more, waiting for their extradition, under what an official investigation would later call completely "unsatisfactory" circumstances. The government treated the calamity as an unfortunate accident. To others it was the inevitable consequence of the new policy, which in haste to reach a final solution to the immigration problem overstretched the capacity of official institutions, leading to this unacceptable treatment of persons. Indeed, on several occasions, the European court in Strasbourg had criticized the new Dutch policy. What was new as well was that this hardly seemed to disturb the Dutch government.

To many people in the Netherlands, these three events marked an abrupt switch. Political murders were seen as highly "un-Dutch." That eleven people perished in a Dutch jail was equally unheard of. Yet within the country there was only a relatively limited political reaction to this last disaster. In Parliament only Groen Links (the Green-Left party) really attacked the minister for her handling of the disastrous affair. Other opposition parties clearly realized that Minister Verdonk's extradition policies had the full support not only of the cabinet but also of a large part of the population.[7]

The suddenness of the Dutch switch was directly related to the unexpected success of Pim Fortuyn, who had showed how much voting support could be gained by raising the immigration issue as a major shortcoming of government policies. Fortuyn had been a complete newcomer to the Dutch political stage. In 2002 he founded his own party, which he named after himself—again something unheard of in the Netherlands. Nonetheless, within only a few months, polls predicted that in the coming elections more than 40 percent of the national vote would go to him. In those days Fortuyn never tired of saying that of course he would be the next prime minister. Fortuyn had special talents: he was a gifted debater, very direct and with his own brand of humor. This was one explanation of the fact that he got away with behavior that Dutch voters would certainly not accept from other politicians: ostentatious snobbism, pseudo-aristocratic airs (he had, for instance, his own butler), and a flaunting of his homosexual practices that was clearly meant to shock.[8] However, the main reason his supporters forgave him for all this was his unrelenting pouncing on issues that until then had always been discussed with much more sensitivity—at least in public: the popular fear of criminality and rising Islamic fundamentalism, notably among second-generation *allochtonen*.

In order to understand the novelty of Fortuyn's approach—several of my friends who see themselves as progressive deemed him "refreshing," especially in the beginning of his political ascension—it is important to grasp how heavily national satisfaction with the Netherlands as a paragon of antiracism and tolerance had weighed in preceding years. The Anne Frank house was supposed to stand model for the nation,[9] and any remark with discriminatory implications was quickly condemned as racist. Fortuyn's secret was that he knew how to tap the pent-up popular resentment about ever more numerous immigrants that had been stifled by this national self-image.[10]

Other politicians learned his lesson very quickly. Already in 2002, the new cabinet, elected only a few weeks after the murder of Fortuyn (and in which his party played a tumultuous but secondary role), immediately announced a complete change, especially regarding treatment of immigrants: drastic curtailing of immigration, speedy extradition of "illegal" immigrants, and a new policy toward remaining *allochtonen* aiming at their forceful *integratie*, especially in a cultural sense. It was not their socioeconomic marginalization but rather their "refusal" to be culturally integrated that was now seen to be at the heart of immigrants' problems. Characteristic of the new configuration was that the main opposition parties—the Labor Party (PvdA) and the Socialist Party (SP)—were extremely weary of attacking the cabinet precisely on this point. Fortuyn had made it amply clear that opposing the new approach to the immigration issue might easily bring a loss of voter support. As said, popular discontent over this issue—and others—had been building up for a long period. Fortuyn's explosive presence made this issue break through quite suddenly in the formal political arena. After the 2002 elections, politicians of all feathers were quick to denounce their own "arrogance" for not listening to the people.

Fortuyn's impact in politics may have caused a landslide. For an insight into the substance of what was at stake, a series of articles by Paul Scheffer, published in 2000 in the leading Dutch newspaper, *NRC/Handelsblad*, may be more revealing than the more than thirty books Fortuyn prided himself on having written. In these articles, Scheffer—describing himself as a "publicist" and as "still" a member of the Labor Party—proclaimed the complete failure of preceding governments' policies on immigration. In his view, the capital mistake had been focusing only on the immigrants' socioeconomic integration while allowing—or even encouraging—them to retain their own cultural identity. This soft "multiculturalism" was the cause of increasing segregation, as many migrants had withdrawn into their own culture. The only solution would be a self-assured policy of cultural integration—that is, an integration of the immigrants into Dutch culture. In retrospect Scheffer's positions were not at all that new; it is even highly debatable whether the government's policies of the 1990s could be characterized as inspired by "multiculturalism."[11] Yet Scheffer's articles—which preceded Fortuyn's emergence on the political stage—caused quite a stir. There were critical reactions. But in general, his attack on what he saw as the political correctness of multiculturalism is still seen by many as a milestone; so is his plea for switching the attention from socioeconomic marginalization to lack of cultural integration as the major problem, and even more, his insistence that if necessary, such cultural integration had to be enforced.

In October 2007, Scheffer published his long-awaited book on the same issues—a very voluminous study (almost five hundred pages) bringing together a wide array of themes and authors. Clearly, his confrontation with all this literature and also his intensive meetings with people from different layers of society—notably with immigrants and their representatives—has helped to deepen and nuance his viewpoints. However, it remains to be seen whether the more nuanced viewpoints in this big book will acquire equal impact in society and politics as his more blunt 2000 articles, which went off like a bombshell, especially the first years after they were published. So it is still useful to follow the texts of these earlier articles. The development of his views evidenced in his book will be discussed later.

In his first 2000 article, with the telling title "The Multicultural Drama," Scheffer started with detailed demographic figures showing a threatening increase of "allochthonous" groups.[12] Next he enumerated equally worrying indications of increasing segregation and avoidance behavior among these groups[13]—notably a growing gap between "white" and "black" schools, and second-generation immigrants' conscious turn away from Dutch society. For him these were signs that "the multicultural society's house of cards is collapsing" (2000a:5). The current policy of integration *met behoud van eigen cultuur* (lit. "retaining the own culture") was typically based on the "cosmopolitan illusion" among many Dutch and their tendency that "national confidence" was "disposable." For Scheffer it was high time for a drastic change: the Dutch "should take their own language, culture, and history much more seriously" (2000a:6). Scheffer looked back with some nostalgia on the period when the political elite still felt it had a "civilizing mission" (2000a:9). The current Dutch bashfulness about their cultural heritage would be an obstacle to real integration. "If the Netherlands finally recognizes that it is an 'immigration country' it should at last do what any immigration country did—that is, emphasize the transfer of language, historical consciousness, and law-culture" (2000b:3).

Scheffer called urgently for increased reflection on how to give shape to a "modern citizenship" that could be shared by immigrants. A better knowledge of the landmarks of Dutch history, would be a first prerequisite to provide a common basis for this shared citizenship. One solution would be the formulation of a "canon"—that is "a core of historical and literary basic texts" (and apparently Scheffer had then only Dutch texts in mind)—that would provide "general points of reference" (Scheffer 2006:31). This canon would need to be central in schools so that immigrants' children could internalize it in their youth. But it should also provide a basis for the *inburgeringscursussen* (lit., courses to "citizenize") that immigrants-to-be, and also immigrants who were already in the country, must attend. In 2000, these courses already existed, but Scheffer urged that they be given much more weight; people should be forced to attend, if necessary.

A striking aspect of Scheffer's earlier interpretations is his tendency—like Fortuyn or, for instance, van den Brink (2006)—to explain the problems with immigrants in the Netherlands as a logical outcome of unfortunate policy choices of Dutch governments and, thus, as a typical Dutch way of mismanaging the issue. One almost gets the impression that this is a special problem for the Netherlands. It might be useful, therefore, to briefly situate here the Dutch experience with increasing immigration in its broader European context.

Overview: How the Netherlands Became an "Immigration Country"

Immigration into the Netherlands after World War II followed roughly the same trajectory as in other countries of northwestern Europe. The

1950s were dominated by the return of *repatrianten* (repatriates) from former colonies—in the Dutch case, Indonesia. In the 1960s, with the unforeseen expansion of the economy, recruitment of *gastarbeiders* (guest workers), or in more correct terms, *buitenlandse werknemers* (foreign employees), increased rapidly, first from countries like Spain, Italy, and Yugoslavia, later notably from Turkey and Morocco. In the 1970s it became gradually clear that large groups of the "guest laborers" were not at all inclined to return to their country of origin, despite economic stagnation and increasing unemployment. Moreover, with the approaching independence of Suriname (1975), a growing number of Surinamese used the last chance to immigrate to the former mother country without needing any special permission. The government reacted by trying to block further immigration. However, in these years "family reunion" was still an important factor in the further influx of people from Morocco and Turkey. In the 1980s, despite further government restrictions, "family formation" (younger and second-generation immigrants marrying a wife from the region of origin) led to a further increase. In those years the number of asylum seekers increased rapidly as well.[14]

The very fact that the growing concern about immigrants in the Netherlands corresponds to the general pattern in northwest Europe suggests that this should be seen first of all as a global problem that can hardly be explained by the mismanagement of earlier Dutch governments or a typically Dutch neglect of national culture and history. There certainly are unique Dutch variations, but in a truly historical perspective they may be somewhat different from the specificities emphasized by Scheffer and Fortuyn. One distinctive aspect is the striking official insistence, until well into the 1970s, that the Netherlands was an emigration country and *not* an

TABLE I. **"Non-Western allochthons" in the Netherlands, 1972–2007**

	1972	1976	1980	1984	1988	1992	1996	2000	2004	2007
Total (x1000)	162	320	475	631	774	986	1,171	1,408	1,668	1,738
Turkey	30	67	112	150	178	234	271	308	351	368
Morocco	21	38	68	105	139	189	225	262	306	329
D. Antilles	22	29	40	51	66	84	86	107	130	129
Suriname	53	124	157	191	219	251	280	302	325	368
Total pop. (x1000)	13,270	13,733	14,091	14,394	14,714	15,129	15,272	15,864	16,258	16,385

Source: Figures from CBS (Centraal Bureau voor Statistiek), Voorburg/Heerlen, www.CBS.nl (statline).

immigration country. Indeed, until about 1960 there was a constant flow of Dutch people emigrating, mainly to Canada, South Africa, Australia, and New Zealand, in numbers that still exceeded numbers of immigrants (even with the substantial influx of "repatriates" from the Dutch Indies). The general assumptions in those days were that Holland (the western part of the country) was far too densely populated; that the economy, destroyed by the war, could not sustain further population growth; and that, therefore, emigration was necessary in order to ward off the danger of continuing unemployment—else the country would risk sliding into a dip similar to the 1930s crisis, when unemployment had been particularly serious and prolonged in this country. A dogged fear of immigration played a decisive role in the strangely evasive and shifting terminology used to refer to incoming groups. Another special trait of Dutch policy was that during the 1970s—a crucial phase, when notably Surinamese, Moroccan, and Turkish groups were consolidating themselves in the country through family reunion—the government made access to the budding welfare state relatively easy. During the 1990s this was followed by increasingly determined measures to restrict such access.

Until 2001, major confrontations with youngsters from "allochthonous" groups—of the kind that took place in Britain (Brixton, Leicester), France (the *banlieues*), Germany (especially after the reunification), and even Belgium—failed to occur in the Netherlands. Yet since then, shocking events like 9/11 and the murder of van Gogh in 2004 led in the Netherlands to a particularly violent backlash against mosques and other Islamic meeting places. Moreover, ever since the 1970s, people have increasingly associated young men of the immigrant groups with crime and aggression. It is noteworthy, however, that stereotypes of the various groups shifted over time, even quite rapidly. Until the early 1990s it was mostly Surinamese boys who were feared as potentially criminal and aggressive. Only in the 1990s did Moroccan and Antillean youngsters come to be seen as the main problem groups. The Surinamese are now often cited as an example of relatively successful integration.

National Consensus and Its History—the Dutch Way

Another historical trait that is even more distinctive to Dutch society— and in a different way also Flanders—is a heritage of "pillarization" that still marks present-day debates about "integration" and the supposedly ambivalent attitude of the Dutch toward their own identity. Until well into the 1960s, Dutch society was divided among four competing "pillars"— Protestant, Catholic, liberal, and socialist—which exercised true hegemony over people's life: family, school, work, social and cultural activities, old people's homes, everything was fitted in the grid of this pillarization.[15] Scheffer (2000a:3) does mention the pillarized past, but he quotes Dutch American political scientist Arend Lijphart (1968) to show that it was a time when ideological differences were contained by one common history and commonly accepted values. Scheffer insists that precisely on this point there is a glaring contrast with the society that multiculturalism has created.

However, there are good reasons to emphasize that the national consensus of the days of pillarization was a very special one.[16] Precisely because this appeal to an earlier consensus is so central to Scheffer's argument, it might be worthwhile to note that (also in his 2007 book) he offers a version of Lijphart's views that is quite skewed. Lijphart has become the authority on Dutch pillarization and the ways in which this determined the twentieth-century history of the country. He indeed used terms like *pacification* and *consensus*, but it is important to stress that he did so in a very special way. For him, "consensus" was a consensus among the elites of the various pillars and definitely not among the population at large. He stressed that in early twentieth-century Netherlands, four "pillars"—the Catholics, the Protestants, the Socialists, and the Liberals—were about equal in size, so that none of them could be ignored. Lijphardt gives even more emphasis to the ideological rifts between these pillars; basic to his interpretation is that these rifts were so deep that the only way to save the "existing political system" was through negotiations between the elites. Confronted with an imminent breakdown of the state because of these internal tensions, these elites were willing to settle on a compromise: this was the famous "Pacification" of 1917, which was to determine the framework for Dutch policy for the next fifty years (Lijphart 1968:108, 117; 1986:111). There is a kind of paradox here: precisely because the coherence within each pillar was so strong, people were prepared to give their leaders enough scope for reaching a compromise. Lijphart also emphasized the flip side of this: such trust depended on the rift that separated each pillar from the others. For Lijphart, a "consensual democracy," as in the Netherlands, works because of the sharp border lines between the pillars, which he characterized as "mutually isolated blocs" (1986:78). The only consensus reached was a compromise about practical "rules of the game"—of which an important one concerned the necessary degree of secrecy surrounding the negotiations among the elites (1986:122, 131). In his view, this consensual democracy broke down in the 1960s, when the boundaries between the pillars started to evaporate (1968:11–13). Moreover, he emphasized (chap. 5) that history was a very sensitive aspect in the relation between the pillars—because it clearly opposed, on the one hand, Protestants as those who waged the nation's sixteenth-century liberation war against the Catholic king of Spain, and, on the other, Catholics, whose allegiance to the new nation remained suspect for a long time. In this view, national solidarity depended much more on pragmatic negotiations among elites who had their hands free than on a national consensus about values and history.[17]

The curious lack of *zelfbesef* (pride in one's own) among the Dutch—the lack of identification with the Dutch past which Scheffer so deplores—might indeed be directly linked to the pillarized past, yet not as a loss of former coherence but rather as a consequence of older difference. In the heyday of pillarization, Dutch *zelfbesef* was linked first to the pillar and only secondly to the nation. The pillars were the true sites of emotional belonging; they may have been coupled with national symbols, but many people's identification was primarily—and often quite passionately—with their pillar. Scheffer's sketch of pillarized Dutch society as "pillars under one roof" (2000a:10) underrates a long history of fierce confrontations and deep distrust. Such tensions went from the top to the bottom of society.

. . . .

For instance, a recent collection of articles in *De Gids*, a leading Dutch journal, includes a witty remembrance by Elsbeth Etty of her youth in the 1950s in a village close to The Hague which vividly illustrates this extremely segregated vision of society.[18] As a child from a well-to-do liberal family, she learned to associate Catholics with "stupidity" and Protestants with "uncivilized dogmatism." Of course, this did not stop her from playing with Protestant and Catholic children; sometimes she "even" felt jealous of the many, many Catholic children living in cozy proximity in small houses in the poorer parts of the village. But the splits were deep, and it was clear that these children would lead other lives. Her recollections are still quite friendly. I can go further back, to my youth in the 1940s, and I rather remember being beaten up—and a feeling of having to run for my life—every time I had to pass the public school next to our house (public = liberal + socialist) on my way to the Protestant school.

• • • • • • • • • • • • • •

The feelings of belonging internalized by members of the pillarized society were deep and highly exclusionist. It is too easy to remember it now as a safe haven of mutual respect. This might caution those who, complaining of present-day indifference to Dutch history and culture, hope for a "return" to the national élan of former days. During the greater part of the twentieth century, people in leading roles in the pillarized society—and also many of their followers—certainly had no hesitant attitude toward their own identity, but this identity rested on a strong identification with their pillar much more than with the nation. In practice, it often entailed a deep disapproval of the way of life of people around the corner.

Precisely because the appeal to a more homogenous past is such a recurrent element in recent debates on "integration" in the Netherlands, it might be useful to get a sharper picture of the country's pillarized past. Below I will take up other aspects of history and culture that play a central role in this debate, as in Scheffer's approach. The above may already have shown that, in view of certain special traits of Dutch history, the plea for a return to some sort of national élan buoyed by a common framework of reference may not be realized so easily.[19] Another question is whether such recourse to a well-defined common cultural core is indeed a means to reach a better integration.

Alternative Solutions

A few years after Scheffer's 2000 articles, an interesting collection with the polemic title *Kiezen voor de Kudde* (lit., Choosing for the Flock)—clearly written in reaction to Scheffer's challenging argumentation—proposed a radically different view. The editors (and main authors), Jan Willem Duyvendak and Menno Hurenkamp (2004:218), signaled rather a growing consensus among various groups in Dutch society concerning many apparently superficial aspects of everyday behavior. Instead of an increasing individualization since the liberation from a pillarized society, they observe increasing conformity in everyday life. For them it is precisely this kind of "community lite"—conformity in styles of dress, consumer preferences, career planning, and so on—that might serve as a framework for the further integration of immigrants. Such integration could become a problem, not because of over-the-top multiculturalism or the Dutch lack of national pride that Scheffer bemoaned so much, but rather because of the rise of a new and quite pompously "decked-out" Dutch identity. In important respects, the "increasing monoculturalist character of dominant Dutch cultural values" of the postpillarization period, propagating principles like the freedom and basic equality of the individual, is less tolerant of cultural differences. In practice this must sharpen the gap that seems to separate the Dutch from many immigrants (Duyvendak and Hurenkamp 2004:218). Instead of the more usual version of a community united around certain principles (as Scheffer seems to have in mind), Duyvendak and Hurenkamp therefore stress the idea of a "community lite": a light association around common consumer preferences, emotions, and fashions but allowing for difference—they refer also to Maffesoli's notion of "neo-tribes" of "skilled consumers"—as a more promising context for integration. Indeed, the studies bundled in their collection suggest that such an integration is already taking place.[20]

In an earlier reaction to Scheffer's first article, Anil Ramdas (2000)—an eloquent journalist of Surinamese-Indian background, well known for his challenging interventions in debates on immigration—voices a question that is similar but, as is usual with him, hidden in an argument that at first seems to lead in the other direction. Ramdas starts by emphasizing how strongly he agrees with Scheffer. He has always been amazed at Dutch squeamishness about their own identity. How then can they expect others to be interested in participating in this identity? However, the main part of his article recounts how Ramdas visits a sophisticated party of young *allochtonen* who clearly know how to use the opportunities to get ahead in their new surroundings. For Ramdas, this example points apparently in a very different direction. Clearly these youngsters are hardly interested in basic values of Dutch life, whatever they may be. They feel integrated—that is, they "behave"—because they participate to the full in modern cosmopolitan life. The question for Ramdas is whether common national values are indeed so important for realizing "integration."

The same question is raised by an intriguing confusion in the references by Scheffer and other advocates of enforced cultural integration (cf., for instance, van den Brink 2006:21, 301) to models from elsewhere. As said, there was initially a strong tendency—also, for instance, in Fortuyn's highly influential speeches[21]—to depict the immigration problem as just an unfortunate result of bad management by earlier governments in the Netherlands and not as a general European problem. Interestingly, when parallels abroad were mentioned, they nearly always concerned the United States, as an example of a better handling of immigration (Scheffer 2000a:7; van den Brink 2006: 21, 301). The old idea of the United States as a "melting pot" still seemed to play a role. However, more recent developments in that country hardly conform to Scheffer's (and van den Brink's) plea for more forceful cultural integration. In the U.S. context, economic pressure seems to be much more important for integration than a purposeful cultural policy.[22] Linguistic pluriformity becomes increasingly marked, in the country's centers (even in the Upper West Side and other posh parts of Manhattan it has become easier to shop in Spanish than in English) and elsewhere.[23] The strong emphasis of Scheffer and others on cultural integration seems to conform much more to the French model, which, indeed, left little scope—at least officially—for the "preservation" of the immigrants' own identity; all immigrants were made to rapidly learn the language.[24] This implicit leaning toward the French model is striking because this model is generally seen as radically alien to Dutch society, where pillarization taught people to live with differences rather than conforming themselves to one national culture.[25] Indeed, neither in Scheffer's texts nor in Fortuyn's reflections is France ever mentioned explicitly as an example to follow. This confusion of models from abroad can indicate that, in his earlier publications at least, Scheffer seems to be asking for a very complicated turnaround. Behind his version of the American model there looms instead a French assimilation model; but if the old assimilationist ideal has become increasingly precarious even in France, how could one ever hope to realize it in the Netherlands?[26]

A More Forceful Integration

However, despite such criticisms and considerable unclarity as to how "cultural integration" was to be effected, Scheffer's plea in his 2000 articles for a complete turnabout—supported as they seemed to be by Fortuyn's philippics—had concrete effect. After the 2002 elections, which brought a dramatic shift in the Dutch political landscape (it might have been even more dramatic if Fortuyn had not been murdered two weeks before), a new center-right cabinet made forceful integration and restriction of immigration into one of the cornerstones of its policy. The new minister of immigration and integration, former prison director Rita Verdonk, launched her drastic program, already mentioned, for the extradition of illegal immigrants (among whom were many asylum seekers whose asylum request had been denied). As noted earlier, the sheer size of the operation—twenty-six thousand persons to be extradited within two years—put the capacity of Dutch services concerned to a severe test. And, indeed, at the end of the cabinet's term, the target was still far from being reached. However, it did result—as had been predicted—in the internment of an increasing number of people for long periods in provisional prisons of the kind that led to the tragic deaths of eleven persons near Schiphol Airport. An unknown number of persons—up to eight hundred at one point—remain locked up on so-called *bajesboten* (prison boats) in the harbor of Rotterdam and Dordrecht; these have been depicted by journalists of highly different backgrounds as nightmarish and should have been closed down as ordered by the mayors of these cities. However, at the moment of writing they are still in use due to the central services' delaying tactics.

Another set of measures that directly coincided with Scheffer's exhortations were the *inburgerinscursussen* mentioned above (courses to "citizenize"), which were accompanied by ever heavier sanctions. Minister Verdonk waged trench warfare against judicial authorities concerning the question whether immigrants who had already acquired citizenship could still be forced to take such a course and incur the same heavy fine if they fail the *inburgerings* final exam. Would-be immigrants had to prepare for the exam in the country of origin; a special procedure was created to administer their exam by telephone and computer. Despite strongly expressed doubts about the technical validity of this procedure—the computer has to test, for instance, the candidate's ability to speak Dutch—Parliament approved the proposal. Politicians had learned their lesson from Fortuyn's spectacular success at winning votes.[27]

More recently, the pendulum seems to be swinging back again. Especially since the summer of 2007, other voices are in ascendance, pleading for an opener approach to immigrants and more room for differences in integration policies. The 2007 elections were clearly crucial to these switches. At the 2006, the Balkenende III cabinet (a center-right coalition of Christian Democrats and Liberals) fell in the wake of the very complicated affair of Minister Verdonk's withdrawal of the passport of "her friend" Hirsi Ali.[28] The new elections brought another cabinet under Prime Minister Jan-Peter Balkenende, but now his Christian Democrats had to govern with the socialists. In the meantime, Parliament had (with only minimal majority) passed a general amnesty for "illegal" immigrants who could prove that they had spent more than seven years in the Netherlands. The new "secretary of state" for immigration, Nebahat Albeyrak (socialist and born in Turkey), seems to opt also for an opener policy. The new minister for integration, Ella Vogelaar, even openly criticized the policies of her predecessor, Verdonk. The latter, now back in Parliament, staged several couplike efforts to become the leader of the Liberal Party, but without success; in the end she had to leave the party. At the time of this writing, she was trying to launch her own "movement," called Trots Op Nederland (TON, Proud of the Netherlands).

Moreover, there have been various significant initiatives in the broader society. The WRR (scientific advisory board for the government) produced a report, *Identificatie met Nederland* (Identification with the Netherlands), which typically replaced "identity" by "identification," pleading for an opener approach in trying to outline a Dutch identity, with room for input from groups with a different cultural background. Princess Maxima, the very popular wife of the crown prince, was courageous enough to express doubts about the existence of "the" Dutch identity—which brought upon her quite vicious attacks from a number of opinion leaders. Former prime minister Ruud Lubbers published a book, *De Vrees Voorbij: Een Hartekreet'* (Beyond Fear: A Heartfelt Cry), expressing his worries about growing xenophobia. The queen, in her annual Christmas address, emphasized that there were "no simple formulas for integration" and pleaded for tolerance instead of a worrying tendency to "sharpen contradictions" (this earned her a direct attack from Geert Wilders, the leader of the main New Right party in Parliament, who protested against such "multicultural claptrap"). And while in the first post-Fortuyn years "the voter is always right" had become the mantra of Dutch politics, at least some politicians now dare to say that their task is not only to follow the voter but maybe also to try to lead him or her.

Yet this thaw is only very partial. Toward the end of 2007, both Verdonk and Wilders emerged from the polls as the most popular politicians of the year. Verdonk's TON "movement" would, according to recent polls, obtain more than twenty Parliament seats.[29] If she would accept a fusion with Wilders's party, together they might make up the biggest party in Parliament. The main hope is, therefore, that the schismatic tendencies that haunt the New Right all over Europe—whether in France, Germany, Italy, or the Netherlands, New Right leaders seem to be true champions of fission—will prevent such a fusion.

Scheffer's 2007 book seems to fit with this partial thaw (the new minister of integration, Vogelaar, is clearly inspired by it). Many of the principles from his earlier publications are still present: the emphasis on cultural integration as a more pressing issue than socioeconomic marginalization, the need for a more forceful approach in order to realize such integration, and the appeal to a common history and cultural consensus as beacons for all this. But the title, *Land van Aankomst* (Land of Arrival), itself indicates that Scheffer has become more sensitive to the need to offer immigrants at least some opportunities to feel at home in the Netherlands. Possibly because of his many meetings and conversations with migrants, which are recounted throughout the book – and maybe also in response to the wide reading he has done—he now places more emphasis on the need to accommodate different elements. The "common stories" that he emphasized so strongly in 2000 are now seen as stories that can accommodate difference; they are not just Dutch stories but open up to new elements. He relates history now to "a society that emerges from the interaction between different groups" (2007:438). Especially toward the end of the book there is a strong emphasis on migration as a positive force that can "innovate society" (433). Even Islam is now given its place in the Netherlands. "In certain respects we are all newcomers to a past that we must assume" (437; all translations are mine). Below I will further explore how these new accents compare to Scheffer's earlier, fairly monolithic conceptions of culture and history, viewed as essential to integration.

Allochtonen: A New Term on the Dutch Scene

How do these fairly dramatic and confusing developments affect autochthony terminology, the central theme of this book? A first question is, of course, how this terminology actually emerged on the Dutch scene. Its entrée there was quite unexpected; terms like *autochtoon* and *allochtoon* were not at all current in the Dutch language. How then, did they come to play such a central role in the debates in the Dutch context and also in Flanders? It is striking how quickly these *Fremdwörter*—introduced precisely because they were not current but had a cool, more or less scientific aura—acquired a highly emotional charge in everyday language.

In the Dutch case, the term *allochtoon* seems to have preceded the spread of *autochtoon*. Elsewhere—for instance in the African cases examined earlier and in classical Athens—the claim to autochthony as a primal form of belonging seemed to have come first, while the various terms for denoting the others, the *allogènes* or allochthons, followed from it. In the Netherlands the order was the reverse: the need to find a neutral common term for various groups of immigrants led to the adoption of the term *allochtonen*. However, in reaction to this, the Dutch had to define themselves as *autochtonen*—which, as said, proved to be anything but easy.

The first documented use I have found of the term *allochtonen* was in a collection of articles edited by Hilda Verwey-Jonkers in 1971.[30] This collection, published by the Ministry of Culture, Recreation, and Social Work, was the result of a first official effort to gain an overview of the various groups that had recently immigrated to the Netherlands. The various contributions concerned *Repatrianten* (repatriates) from the former Dutch Indies, Surinamese, Dutch Antilleans, Chinese, "foreign laborers," and refugees. The term *allochtoon* figured in the very title of the book and in several of the texts (but interestingly not in the text by van der Staay on the "foreign laborers"—that is, the group that later would become the quintessential *allochtonen*). Yet there was no discussion in any of the texts of why this term was adopted. The choice of the term had apparently been quite an abrupt one, which makes it strange that there was no explanation of the reasons behind it.

In early 2007 I had a brief but most interesting interview with Hans van Amersfoort, a colleague in geography at the University of Amsterdam, who had written three chapters in that volume. He remembered quite vividly how the choice of this new term was made. One of the problems in editing the volume had been that there was no ready-made term to cover all the groups concerned. The obvious terms were, of course, *migrants* and *immigrants*. However, in those days the official line was still that the Netherlands was definitely not to be considered an immigration country. As noted earlier, for several decades after World War II immigration was seen as a threat: the Netherlands was viewed as severely overpopulated (indeed, official reports emphasized that it was the most densely populated country in the world); after the destruction of the war, the economy would not be able to sustain an influx of new laborers; and therefore, until far into the 1960s, emigration rather than immigration was propagated, since this seemed to be the obvious remedy for population pressure. The inflow of a considerable number of loyal subjects from the former Dutch Indies after the end of colonial rule was seen as a particularly serious threat. Of course, it was difficult to refuse them access, but there were several semiofficial initiatives to encourage them to try to settle elsewhere (notably in a "true" immigration country like Australia,

South Africa, or the United States; van Praag 1971:21; see also Ellemers and Vaillant 1985). Under these conditions the term *immigrant*, and even the more neutral *migrant*, remained anathema in official parlance.[31] For the refugees from Indonesia, the term *repatrianten* was specially coined (even though this was somewhat misleading: many of them had never been in the Netherlands, so there was no question of a *re*turn). But of course this term could not be used for the other groups that were discussed in the Verwey-Jonkers collection.

Searching for an alternative term that could not offend anybody, Hans van Amersfoort, as a geographer, proposed a term from physical geography: *allochtoon*, used, for instance, in expressions like *allochthonous sediments*.[32] Precisely because of its neutral, scientific flavor, the term was adopted by Verwey-Jonkers as the editor of the volume and by several other members. However, at first the term did not strike root.[33] During the 1970s, it was rather *ethnic minorities* that came into use in official discourse.[34] Yet this term turned out to have its own disadvantages, while the need for a general term became all the more pressing.[35]

In the meantime the rapid growth of the group of "foreign laborers" (*buitenlandse werknemers*) made the official fiction of the Netherlands as an emigration rather than an immigration country less and less tenable. Already in 1955 an official Dutch delegation had been involved in the recruitment of laborers in Italy (even though the responsible minister, Ko Suurhoff, emphasized that this was only a "temporary emergency measure"; Schuster 1999:165). Clearly the economic recovery after the war went much more quickly than had been foreseen, and unorthodox interventions became necessary in order to cope with a rapidly growing labor shortage. Especially in the 1960s, workers were recruited on an ever larger scale—first in Spain, Italy, Portugal, and Yugoslavia, and later more and more in Turkey and Morocco. In popular parlance this rapidly growing group became labeled "guest workers" (*gastarbeiders*). But apart from considerations of political correctness, this term became practically untenable, because it implied that these people's stay in the Netherlands would be only temporary. Already in 1970, official figures indicated that at least 25 percent of this group planned to stay permanently.[36] And this number would rise rapidly in subsequent decades.

Against this background, the notion of *allochtonen* finally took root, since it seemed to be a neutral term that could cover all the various groups of immigrants. In 1989, theWRR chose the title *Allochtonenbeleid* (lit., Policy on Allochthons) for its report on the immigration issue. The board made a conscious choice of this term: it argued that this term was more satisfactory than alternatives like *migrant* (which still was seen as having the unfortunate implication that a permanent migration was at stake) or *stranger* (WRR 1989:61). Moreover, *allochtonen* had the great advantage of being a "neutral" notion (25). The board actually specified its own definition of the term—and a very challenging one at that. It decided that the term should apply even in the third generation, as long as people "identify to a certain degree with the provenance of their (grand-)parents." The board emphasized that the term would apply also to children from marriages of an allochthon with an autochthon. In practice, this would mean that even a person with one "allochthonous" grandparent (out of four) was to count as an allochthon.[37] Of crucial importance was that the CBS (the national Central Office for Statistics) decided to adopt the new term and its quite audacious definition by the WWR. On only one point was the CBS somewhat more nuanced: in practice it counts only through the second generation as allochthon.[38] But the "one-parent" criterion was strictly maintained in official statistics. Thus, the WWR Board's launching of the term was to have far-reaching consequences: it became central to official statistics and demographic prognoses, with severely contested implications.[39]

These terminological vicissitudes reflect the country's uneasiness with the whole immigration issue. Clearly the Dutch government was particularly reluctant to recognize that the Netherlands, like other West European countries, had to redefine itself as an "immigration" rather than as an "emigration" country.[40] This might explain why official language was to be determinant for the popular language on this issue. The consecutive and more or less artificial choices of names and terms in official reports, committees, and decrees were quickly adopted in everyday language. However, in this process the terminology acquired a life of its own, and problematic implications of the terms were to emerge at unexpected moments.

One unexpected consequence was that the term *allochtoon*, meant as an umbrella word for all groups that had recently immigrated into the country, was increasingly restricted to the main groups that had earlier been called "foreign laborers" (or "guest workers"): the Moroccans and the Turkish, which were also the two main Muslim groups.[41] The term is now used less and less for persons from Suriname, who, after having been strongly stereotyped in the 1980s and early 1990s as being potentially "dangerous," are now increasingly seen as examples of quite successful integration. And even for people from the Dutch Antilles—though the young men from this group are still seen as a problem group—the term is now less current. Moreover, while the term was originally chosen for its "neutral" and "coolly scientific" implications, it rapidly acquired highly emotional and stigmatizing implications, because of its increasing limitation to the two main Muslim groups.

A concomitant problem was the quite confusing division in official statistics of the *allochtonen* notion into "Western" and "non-Western." This meant that, for instance, people born in Japan and Indonesia are seen as "Western" (apparently people from Indonesia are still equated with the *repatrianten* of the days of decolonization), while Turks are as a matter of course classified as "non-Western" (see Bovenkerk 2002). Coupled with the broad interpretation of the *allochtonen* notion as such (the second-generation criterion and the one-parent rule), such muddying helped to give demographic figures alarmist implications. To give just an example: on January 8, 2007, the country's most respected newspaper, *NRC/Handelsblad*, announced in an article on the first page that recent CBS figures indicated that in 2050 the country's population would consist of 29 percent *allochtonen* (compared to 19 percent at that moment). Due to the unclearness of this term, many people associated the figures immediately with Muslim immigrants. It is true that the article concerned (like the CBS report on which it was based) does offer some clues as to how to further unpack the key notion of *allochtonen*: the accompanying graphs show that almost half of these *allochtonen* will consist of "Western allochthons." But such nuances are easily forgotten in subsequent debates. Clearly, the notion of *allochtoon,* originally intended to be neutral and cool, had become a very explosive and confusing one. Already in 1989, Bovenkerk had warned in a column in *De Volkskrant* (at the time still a newspaper with leftist leanings) that the notion as such seemed to work to create distance and to oppose "them" to "us."

The most contested aspect of the way the term would be used in statistics—at least for experts—is the calculation of the number of *allochthonen* on the basis of the "one-parent" criterion, so that mixed marriages, in themselves a possible sign of integration, increase rather than decrease the number of allochthons. In practice it is quite difficult to find out to which degree this affects the official figures. It is especially this last implication that made van Amersfoort, in my recent interview with him, complain that he wished he had never launched the term.[42] Yet one might wonder whether another term would have done better. The complexities of the immigration issue and the impossibility of controlling it in the present-day global context will make any terminology potentially explosive.[43] However, it is clear that especially the heavy implications of the second part of the term, *chtonos,* that links "belonging" to the soil, were to leave their mark on the development of the Dutch debate on the migration issue.

The current use of the term *allochtoon* in the Dutch setting inevitably implies a certain blurring of the notion of citizenship, which used to be considered the cornerstone of any state that claims to be modern. In this respect the Dutch use of the term clashes significantly with the classical Athenian use. In Athens a citizen had to be an autochthon; foreign descent (stemming from "another soil") excluded citizenship at least formally: *ius sanguinis* and *ius soli* had to coincide (again: at least in principle). In the Netherlands, however, many "allochthons" are citizens, either since they have been "naturalized" or by the simple fact of being born on Dutch soil; in Dutch law, *ius soli* in principle prevails over *ius sanguinis.* However, maintaining the *allochtoon-autochtoon* opposition for the second—and (who knows?) possibly for a third—generation seems to return *ius sanguinis* through the backdoor and thus introduces a split within the citizenry. I will come back to the precariousness of, on the one hand, using the opposition between autochthon and allochthon as given and, on the other, proclaiming the need for allochthons to "integrate." If even people who have been born on Dutch soil are still to be called allochthons, this throws some doubt upon their being "really" Dutch citizens: indeed, can an *allochtoon* ever become an *autochtoon?*

Recently, there has been a growing consciousness of the anomaly of applying a term like *allochtoon* to people who were born on Dutch soil. Several spokespersons of the "second generation" of Moroccans have protested against this denial of their birthright and proposed the term *Nieuwe Nederlanders* (New Dutchmen). In 2006, Paul Scheffer himself acknowledged the problematic implications of the term he had used so much; he even called for a certain reserve in using it in public debates (although he still defended its use in official statistics – apparently for pragmatic reasons, yet without signaling that the use of the term in official statistics has had complicated effects). However, in his 2007 book he takes the logical step of consistently avoiding these terms, using "migrants" or "children of migrants" instead (Scheffer 2007:427). Already in 2005, even Minister Verdonk, the powerful advocate for limiting the number of immigrants and of enforced integration, advised her civil servants to avoid the use of the term *allochtoon* as much as possible because of its stigmatizing implications. But until now her intervention has had little effect. Clearly, the term has become deeply rooted and will not disappear so easily, neither from popular nor from official parlance.

It is striking that the Dutch—whether the experts who use the term or people at large—do not seem to be conscious of its powerful "chtonic" root. As said earlier, autochthony with its direct reference to the soil was some sort of negative choice. In the Dutch case, the term *allochtoon* came first, and it was only in reaction to it that the Dutch had to define themselves as *autochtonen*. However, it is clear that the terminology, originally meant as "cool" and "neutral," introduced highly charged issues regarding who belongs and who does not. In this sense it is like an iceberg, having an invisible depth that proves to have consequences of its own. The Dutch, neglecting the original meaning of the notion, may have used it originally as an almost empty signifier. This did not stop it from rapidly acquiring highly emotional overtones, but these remained quite diffuse. In the Dutch case the term lacked the clear substance the appeal to the soil had in the African cases and in classical Athens. This may explain the current uncertainty as to how give it a firmer expression.

Elusive Autochthony

In the Dutch language *allochtoon* was much more of a *Fremdkörper* than *autochtoon*, which was already in use (albeit with an archaic slant) in the sense of "original" and "authentic" to a certain area. The way in which it was now coupled to the first notion was to give it a more specific meaning, which soon acquired the kind of natural self-evidence that seems to cling to this term in all the different settings where it emerged. The exact delimitation of the *allochtonen* category might have been open to debate in the Netherlands, but everybody seemed to know who was to be qualified as *autochtoon*. For instance, in 1993 Joop de Beer, former director of CBS (the Central Office for Statistics mentioned before as a key player in the application of these notions in the Netherlands) proposed defining *allochtoon* in relation to its opposite, *autochtoon*, since in his view it was much clearer who fell under the latter category.[44]

It is all the more striking, then, that in practice the term proved, quite paradoxically, to have the same elusive, receding quality as elsewhere. Despite its apparent self-evidence, it became increasingly difficult to make out what was "truly" autochthonous. Indeed, the more prominent the notion became in the immigration debate and the more ardent therefore the attempts to grasp it, the more evanescent it turned out to be. In France, Le Pen and his National Front may have had difficulties in defining his notion of *Français de souche* (Frenchmen "of the trunk"). In the Dutch case, the problem became rather how to define the Dutch culture that was supposed to carry the common identity of the *autochtonen*. Especially after 2000, when opinion leaders like Paul Scheffer and Pim Fortuyn started to propagate forcible cultural integration as the only solution to the immigrant problem, it became quite urgent to define more clearly into what immigrants needed to integrate. With this, the apparent unity of the *autochtonen* category proved again to be quite elusive.

In the late 1990s, some historians and authors started to explore what was "typically" Dutch, seeking some sort of counterweight against a multiculturalism that was already then seen as too relativizing. Journalists like Herman Vuijsje and Jos van der Lans (1999) tried to do this in a somewhat folkloristic way by composing a *vademecum*—a kind of dictionary—of all sorts of things that could be considered "typically Dutch." Historian Herman Pleij (2004) published on an emerging Dutch identity in the history of the Lowlands.

However, after the turn of the millennium, with the increased attention to forcible cultural integration, the tone hardened. In Scheffer's pioneering 2000 articles the term *cultural integration* is used time and again without being given much substance. Some politicians tried to be more concrete. Thus, Balkenende—who, in the gap left by Fortuyn's dramatic eclipse, emerged somewhat surprisingly as the prime minister for the next decade—launched his plea, repeated time and again, for a *Herstel van Normen en Waarden* (redressing of norms and values), but had little impact. Other politicians ended in a sort of split in their search for Dutch values. Wilders—for many voters on the right the successor to Fortuyn—surprised his constituents with a sudden celebration of Christian values. Wilders had belonged to the Liberal Party (which, in the Dutch context, means anticonfessional in politics), but in 2004, he made a dramatic exit from that party. As leader of his own new party, he began to call for a recognition of Christian values as basic to the Dutch culture, even advocating that the teaching of these values be made a central part of the curricula of all schools at all levels.[45] This about-face did bring him considerable electoral success (nine seats in Parliament in 2007). Yet it was also a clear demonstration of a quite desperate search for a fixed footing in the elusive Dutch culture.

History and Culture

Culture and history thus became central themes not only in Scheffer's articles but also in the Dutch debate on integration in general. However, both were invoked as more or less self-evident notions, without further specification or consciousness of their highly complex character. The danger is that thus they will be used as a kind of black box that is expected to provide a solution in an almost magical way. Precisely because these notions are so central in the debate, it might be helpful to try to unpack them a bit.

A certain naiveté can be detected in the call for the formulation of a "canon," which became a central issue in the Netherlands as in several other European countries after 2000. The idea was that a succinct catechesis of the national culture should be drawn up and would serve as a beacon for immigrants' cultural integration, so shockingly neglected by earlier governments. Scheffer, in his 2000 articles, called for such an initiative, saying that it would provide a better knowledge of central events in Dutch history. Being acquainted with this history would be an absolute condition for the successful integration of immigrants; on the other hand, the Dutch lack of pride in national history—which he saw as typical for the Netherlands—would be one of the main reasons for a lack of cultural integration, and therefore of commitment, among immigrants. Scheffer was also quite outspoken on what such a canon should contain: "access to common stories" that would provide common points of reference and thus promote cultural integration. To him, criticisms of such attempts to fix a national heritage were signs of the squeamishness characteristic of the Dutch when culture and history are at stake (2006:30–31).

In these early texts Scheffer seems to take the idea of "culture," as a well-outlined totality, for granted. He apparently saw no problem with basing his argumentation on a fairly simplistic opposition between "traditional" and "modern" culture—in which, as usual, the "traditional" pole turned out to be in all respect the negation of the qualities of the "modern" one (2006:23–24, 30).[46] He seemed completely oblivious of all the problems such binary oppositions have raised in, for instance, anthropological explorations of culture. In his 2007 book, Scheffer emphasizes, in contrast, that he will "draw freely on anthropological literature" (48). Unfortunately, he seems to have stopped at the anthropological debate on "cultural relativism" of the middle of the last century.[47] For his appeal to culture as a condition for integration, the lively 1980s and 1990s debate in anthropology on the very notion of culture would be much more relevant.[48] A brief digression on this debate might be useful here in order to highlight the dangers of the culture notion that so suddenly became central in the debate on integration in the Netherlands and elsewhere in the West.

Central in this debate was a protest against an "essentialist" notion of culture which older anthropologists had adopted quite uncritically and propagated outside the discipline. The success of this older notion of culture—Ruth Benedict's *Patterns of Culture* (1934) is often cited as a characteristic example—worried many younger anthropologists. To them, the notion was becoming increasingly untenable amid intensifying globalization and cultural mingling. In the older "essentialist" vision, each culture was seen as a closed totality, centered in its own essence. Thus culture became a static notion, and cultural dynamics and interaction with other cultures were seen as an anomaly. A logical implication of this view was that cultural mixing can only be superficial and that intensive culture contact inevitably leads to a painful "bend or break" situation. Some of Benedict's reflections were highly suggestive in this sense; consider her quote from an old chief of a group of Native Americans in California: "In the beginning God gave to every people a cup, a cup of clay, and from this cup they drank their life.... They all dipped it in the water... but their cups were different. Our cup is broken now. It has passed away" (Benedict 1934/1953:19).

In the 1980s James Clifford and anthropologists like Arjun Appadurai (cf. his 1996 book) began to warn that this culture concept risked making anthropologists blind to the powerful dynamics of local cultures in articulation with increasing processes of globalization. They emphasized that, culturally, globalization does not simply bring increasing homogenization, in the sense of a worldwide dominance of Coca-Cola or McDonald's culture. To the contrary, the globalizing world seems to be marked by increasing emphasis on *cultural difference*, with modern elements acquiring different shapes and expressions across the globe and older cultural elements exhibiting new dynamics in interaction with globalization. Clifford warned that the essentialist view of culture is a very dangerous concept in this context: it pictures "other" people as locked in their stubborn cultural convictions, and it denies all the creativity with which people take up cultural elements to deal with new challenges. In his 1988 book he even warned anthropologists that it might be better to stop using the notion of culture altogether (Clifford 1988:9). Yet apparently he realized that there was little chance that the notion would disappear—anthropology

has been too successful in propagating it in the broader society. Therefore, he pleaded for using it in a new sense: a "Caribbean concept of culture," in which culture is seen as a continuous process of emergent hy-
bridization. Culture contact should not be seen as exceptional but as vital
for cultural reproduction (Clifford 1988:64). In other words, people use
their cultural heritage creatively in finding "their own path" through the
modern world. Such creativity is certainly not always positive. But seeing
the other as captured in a rigid cultural heritage—or trying to condense
Dutch culture and history in a simple formula—blocks comprehension of
what is going on.[49]

Clifford's plea for a transition from an "essentialist" to a "Caribbean"
concept of culture might be highly relevant for the debates on integration in the Netherlands and in immigration countries in general. Already
Scheffer—to return to him as one of the most outspoken advocates of
increased attention to culture in the Dutch debate—seems to have gone
through a transition of this kind between his 2000 articles and his 2007
book. In the earlier articles, the emphasis seems to be mainly on "fixing" Dutch culture: it has to be condensed in a canon and a certain set
of principles, and thus the choice left to immigrants seems to be indeed
something like "bend or break."[50] In the 2007 book, especially toward the
end, a more open view of culture seems to prevail: integration still must be
achieved through common stories, but now there is at least the suggestion
that these stories must address difference; symbols have to be shared between immigrants and Dutch people, and this is possible only when they
are *verbindend* (linking; Scheffer 2007:438). The anthropological debate
on how to achieve a more open view of culture and exchange might be
highly relevant to such a process.

*   *   *

A similar constriction seems to take place in the appeal to history—at
least as complex a notion as culture—and, again, a certain shift between
Scheffer's earlier viewpoints and his more nuanced position of his last
book may be symptomatic here. There is some tension in Scheffer's 2000
articles between, on the one hand, his heavy emphasis that there used to
be a national consensus even in the heyday of pillarization and, on the other,
his recurrent reproach that the Dutch do not have enough respect for their
own history and national heritage (2000a:6). On both points some nuancing might be necessary in a more long-term view. People of my generation

vividly remember how, in the late 1940s and early 1950s, we were taught a whole series of highly nationalistic songs in primary school: "Wien Neerlands Bloed door de Ad'ren Vloeit" (For Whom Dutch Blood Flows through the Veins), "Hollands Vlag Je Bent Mijn Glorie" (Dutch Flag, You Are My Glory), "Op de Blanke Top der Duinen" (On the White Top of the Dunes), and so on. Especially in the first decade after the German occupation during World War II, nationalist feelings were intense among many Dutch people. Yet it is not clear whether these strong appeals to history created a broader consensus. As said, history is as layered as culture: it can unite, but it can certainly also divide.

Indeed the nationalist fervor of my youth was strongly linked to the "pillar" that even in the last days of pillarization deeply marked people's commitment to a national past. In the songs I learned at a Protestant school, it was the proud history of a Protestant nation that was idealized. "Wien Neerlands Bloed" (from 1815 till 1932 the official national hymn) and "Wilhelmus van Nassauwe" (the hymn of the royal house, which subsequently replaced "Neerlands Bloed" as the national hymn) both celebrate in fact the victory of the Protestant Dutch over Spain. For Dutch Catholics, that victory meant that for a long time they had to hold their religious services in hiding—not only because they adhered to the wrong religion but also because they were seen as potential collaborators with the enemy and therefore not entitled to full citizenship. Even in the early 1960s, the *vaderlandse geschiedenis* (history of the Fatherland) taught in the Protestant Free University in Amsterdam differed markedly from the version taught at the Catholic University of Nijmegen—or from the socialist version taught at the University of Amsterdam, in those days the bulwark of secularization and socialism.

It is true that already in the 1960s these nationalistic songs of my primary-school days were remembered only with great irony or even ridicule. Yet it is debatable whether this was a sign of a declining nationalism. In the 1970s, the unexpected successes of Dutch soccer teams at the European and world championships—something completely unprecedented for the Dutch public—led to new climaxes of nationalist fervor. The growing irony surrounding nationalist symbols of the past was in the Dutch case closely intertwined with the implosion of the pillars. Characteristically for Dutch society, true emotional involvement used to be with the pillar and only through it with the nation. As noted, history is not necessarily a unifying force. Yet the call, by Scheffer and many others, for a historical canon as crucial for enforcing the cultural integration of newcomers seemed to assume that history has this magical power.

In this context, it might have been wise to listen to historians who can be credited with some experience of what history can or cannot do (just as anthropologists have some familiarity with the ambiguities of culture). Of special interest in relation to the idea of a canon is the debate, mentioned earlier, on memory and history that preoccupied historians in the 1980s and 1990s. As said in chapter 1, in this debate "memory" stands for emotional and even spontaneous identification with the past; "history" rather refers to academic history as practiced by professional historians. The first can be defined as "simplifying...impatient with ambiguities...expressing some eternal or essential truth about the group whose memory it is"; in contrast, the latter focuses on "complexity,...multiple perspectives,...ambiguities" (Novick 1999:3–4; Pandey 2001:8; see also Halbwachs 1950). Pierre Nora gave new vigor to the debate with his well-known collections *Les Lieux de mémoire* (1992). His quite special reason for emphasizing this distinction was that he felt that our times—at least in France—witnessed the implosion of the last effort to unite the two, *mémoire-histoire*, around the nation. This precarious unification gave way to a history that annihilates memory.[51] Concretely, the professional attitude of academic historians trained in dissecting the past, bringing in multiple views and radical uncertainties, would increasingly undermine the power of nationalist memory. However, the recent demand for national canons in various European countries seems to reflect a determined effort by dominant groups to reverse this trend. This may relate not only to rising worries about the nonintegration of immigrants but also to the fear of a loss of identity with ongoing European unification. Indeed, it was striking that it was two smaller countries that took the lead in this. Denmark was the first to publish its canon, in January 2006, and the Dutch followed in the spring of the same year. In both cases the government launched the project with expectations similar to those Scheffer had in mind in his articles. The Dutch minister of education, culture, and science, Maria van der Hoeven, explicitly asked the committee in her installation letter for a canon that would promote integration and *burgerschapsvorming* (citizen education) especially among the younger generations (Canon van Nederland 2006:96).

However, the committee, in which historians played an important role—the chairman, Frits van Oostrom, is a prominent expert of medieval literature—was much more cautious in its final report. It warned against unrealistic expectations: a canon could certainly not be imposed; if coupled with national pride it could easily constrain people's knowledge; therefore it should certainly not be equated with Dutch identity (*Canon van Nederland* 2006:19–23). The committee even expressed doubts concerning the notion of a "national identity" as such. A canon might be associated with *inburgering* (learning to be a citizen), but even here the committee was prudent: this should certainly not be seen as the main motive behind its canon (24). Its main aim had rather been to formulate a canon "of the country in which we live together... offering society a common framework of reference for mutual communication and for operating as a Dutch person in the world. Thus, the canon for Boulahrouz and Beatrix."[52] Clearly, the committee was very conscious of the risk that identifying a canon might imply the fixing of something (culture?) that is always in flux. It proposed a quite original solution for this by constructing its canon from a series of "windows" rather than from specific events or facts. Each of its fifty "windows" opens up to a branching set of stories and links with related topics and aspects. With this the committee hoped to provide a common but open framework for the teaching of history, one that could constantly be adapted to changing circumstances.

The reactions were, of course, highly diverse. Public figures who had advocated such a canon were disappointed. No wonder. To put it simply, they had called for "memory"—the minister's assignment to the committee to produce a canon that would "promote integration and citizenship education" clearly asked for this. But she had assigned the task to professional historians. Thus the result was "history"—pluralistic and with due attention to ambiguities. This was not what many people had hoped for. The most critical reactions came from the press that is usually equated with the right. For instance, in the weekly *Elsevier* (October 21, 2006, 14) Robert Stiphout reproached the committee for having missed its chance, for not daring to couple history to national identity in a time when there is a dire need for this in view of the general individualization and adaptation problems of immigrants. Laudatory comments, however, came from the leftist press: Hubert Smeets praised the committee in *De Groene Amsterdammer* (October 20, 2006, 12) for refusing to link history and national identity. But even *NRC/Handelsblad* (middle-of-the-road to rightist) complimented the committee for not having followed the minister's instructions to link the canon directly to the integration issue (October 16, 2006, 1).[53] The Dutch committee had succeeded in maintaining a prudent distance from the political aims behind its installation. The idea of taking "windows" as building blocks showed a keen sense of the fluidity of culture and history, which would make any use of them in the service of clear-cut political aims quite difficult—much more so than many protagonists in the Dutch immigration debate seemed to realize.[54]

With a prudence that was probably wise, the committee seemed intent on avoiding taking a clear stand on two major issues. First, not one of the fifty windows refers explicitly to the historical heritage that immigrants brought along when settling in the Netherlands.[55] This leaves open the question to what extent a canon should provide space for groups that insist on their rights to "differ" (not only immigrants but also groups that claim some other kind of minority status). A second and related point concerns the question, raised above, whether a common core of values and historical knowledge is indeed a precondition for living together in one country. The committee seems to have hesitated here. It clearly hoped that its fifty windows would provide a common framework of knowledge that could strengthen citizenship. But it was also clearly concerned that a canon might serve efforts to fix and impose a core identity—which in practice might rather reinforce divisions. The overall lesson of this nuanced effort to launch a common canon seems to be that the Dutch identity, so easily assumed by *autochtonen* when they oppose themselves to *allochtonen,* is much less self-evident when it has to be given more concrete form.

Similar defusing effects marked the other mainstay of the new policy for forceful cultural integration of immigrants, announced with considerable fanfare: Minister Verdonk's promise to further enforce the *inburgeringscursussen* (training for citizenship)—notably by complementing it with an exam with the necessary sanctions. Here again, the main issue soon became how to define into what the immigrants-to-be needed to be initiated. A good example is the confrontations and partial misunderstandings that arose around a film, *Naar Nederland* (To the Netherlands), which was to play a central role in the information campaign for persons who were considering emigration to the Netherlands. The official idea was that the film would give immigrants-to-be a realistic idea of what to expect in the country of their choice; however, critical voices soon commented that the aim seemed to be deterrence rather than providing information.

Early in 2005 the ministry launched a first version of the film, showing it only behind close doors. Yet soon rumors were circulating about it, especially two moments in it: a shot of two men passionately kissing each other after they had been officially married by the mayor of their municipality, and a longer shot of young women sunbathing topless on a beach. Fierce protests ensued. Some people commented that the aim of the film was clearly to deter Muslim immigrants, to whom such scenes were expected to be particularly shocking. However, a much stronger protest was voiced by those who thought it was a shame to characterize Dutch society by such scenes. And, indeed, to a considerable number of Dutch "autochthons" topless sunbathing and same-sex marriage, especially if the latter leads to two males passionately kissing each other in public, are almost as shocking as they would be to many Muslims. Apparently the minister reacted by ordering that these scenes be taken out of the film. But this led to further loud protests, this time from gay action groups: the Netherlands had been the first country in the world to officially recognize same-sex marriage; deleting this scene from the film would mean that the minister was covering over a Dutch reality and giving in to Muslim prejudices.

In the end the film became part of the package immigrants have to study for their *burgerschapsexamen* (the exam includes questions based on the film). However, Dutch embassies in several countries warned that they would be in difficulties if they circulated what would be seen locally as pornography. So now two versions of the film are offered: one that includes the controversial scenes and another one without them. The vicissitudes of the project show again the evanescent quality of Dutch culture. Like autochthony, it seems to be quite clear at first, yet the harder one tries to formalize it, the more elusive it becomes.

Comparisons

It is tempting to take a quick look across the Netherlands' southern border, since the *allochtoon/autochtoon* terminology fed into equally explosive confrontations among the Belgians. Apparently the terminology itself was borrowed from the Dutch, but in Belgium it acquired a high profile much more rapidly, especially in the Flemish part of the country, because of the electoral upsurge of the neo-right Vlaams Blok party.[56] In other respects as well, the trajectory of these terms—notably the way they introduced notions of culture into politics—was to be quite different here. An obvious reason was that the Belgian configuration is characterized by a deep split between two language groups: the Francophone Walloons and the Dutch-speaking Flemings. This split gained new momentum with a dramatic reversal in the relation between the two groups. After World War II, Flanders became the richer region—it is now one of the most prosperous areas of Europe—which further eroded the former cultural dominance of the Walloon group. It is, indeed, striking how deeply here the new discourse on autochthony, as menaced by an invasion of allochthons, became enmeshed in the older struggle between the two language groups over rights to language and belonging. In the propaganda of the Vlaams Blok, autochthony is marked by uncertainty about who the "Other" is. Bambi Ceuppens (2006) shows that in the party's statements there is a constant switching back and forth from one "Other" to another: from the Arab *allochtoon* to the Francophone (in a certain sense seen also as an allochthon who does not belong on Flemish soil) and back again.

In other respects as well, developments in Belgium take unexpected turns (see Ceuppens 2006). For instance, the language of autochthony is employed much more in the Flemish part—and notably in Antwerp— although the main concentrations of allochthons are in Wallonia and Brussels. The adoption of this language suited the Vlaams Blok party, since it offered a new terminology to relate to older Nazi currents among some parts of the Flemish population.[57] Strikingly, however, the currency of the *autochtoon/allochtoon* terminology did not lead, as in the Netherlands, to an uncomfortable search for a proper Flemish cultural identity. Apparently, the long-standing confrontation with a most present Other, the Francophone Walloons, had made people less uncertain about this identity.

A concomitant effect was that such cultural issues were far less allowed to penetrate into policy making. The *cordon sanitaire* that the older parties imposed around the Vlaams Blok—especially after it became the largest party in Antwerp in 1991 and the third largest in Flanders as a whole in 1999—limited the effect its ideology could have on government measures. More generally, the particularities of the Belgian setting may have made people more conscious of the dangers of trying to manipulate culture or language. Indeed, in 2005 when Minister Verdonk in the Netherlands, with her own kind of fervor, proposed that people should be obliged to speak Dutch in public spaces—all those foreign (read: Arabic) sounds in shops and streets might frighten people—many Belgians reacted with deep amazement: did this minister realize what she was saying?

Yet elsewhere in Europe there are clear parallels to the Dutch effort for defining a cultural core to serve as a beacon for more forceful integration policies—again, with similar confusing consequences. In 2005, for instance, Germany launched its own citizenship exams, with explicit reference to the Dutch precedent. Here, however, the exam was given form not at the national level but rather by the *Land* (the semiautonomous province in the German federation). The consequence was that criteria for accepting someone as a German citizen were strikingly different, even between neighboring *Länder*. A target of much ironic comments became, for instance, the glaring contrast between the exams in Hessen (more conservative) and in neighboring Baden-Württemberg (more progressive). In Hessen the candidate citizen had to show considerable knowledge of German history and national symbols (what is the first line of the national hymn? mention three German philosophers; etc.), while in Baden-Württemberg, citizens-to-be were tested, for instance, on how they would react if their son told them he was a homosexual and wanted to live with another man. Thus formulating a common cultural core proved to be highly complicated in Germany as well. Moreover, a standard reaction to the question about the homosexual son was that a large number of home-grown German citizens would surely lose their own citizenship if required to answer such a question.[58]

In France, Nicolas Sarkozy's initiative to create a ministry for *immigration et identité nationale* immediately after he was elected as president (2007), brought furious reactions from historians. Eleven prominent historians decided not only to step down from the national board for the history of immigration (Cité Nationale de l'Histoire de l'Immigration, CNHI) but also to found a Comité de Vigilance aux Usages Public de l'Histoire (CVUH)—that is, a "Committee for Vigilance against Official Abuse of History"! Further, they organized a petition that within a short time had been signed by more than ten thousand historians and others from all over the world. Clearly the mixing of memory and history makes an explosive cocktail.

One of the spokespersons of the group, prominent historian Gérard Noiriel, explains in a recent publication why these historians saw the bringing together of immigration and national identity as so dangerous (Noiriel 2007). In his view, Sarkozy's strategy of putting the issue of *identité nationale* at the center of campaign debates (thus marginalizing the social issues his opponent Segolène Royal tried to put forward) was crucial for his election victory. The notion of national identity as such was not new—in any case less new than Sarkozy made it out to be—but the way he linked it to the immigration issue turned out to be decisive: the message was that French national identity was under direct threat from new types of migrants who clearly refused to integrate. To drive home this message, Sarkozy made ample use of history, but—and this is why French historians felt attacked on their own turf—this amounted time and again to a distortion of history.

To highlight all the ambiguities behind Sarkozy's apparently self-evident position, Noiriel briefly traces the vicissitudes of the notion of national identity and its precursors in France.[59] Ever since the end of the nineteenth century, such notions have always related to issues of immigration, but mostly in a very different sense than in Sarkozy's use. Central to Noiriel's analysis is the fact that already in the nineteenth century—that is, the period in which the idea of a nation took concrete shape—France was an immigration country. This was further reinforced by the industrial revolution, which triggered a rapidly increasing demand for labor (Noiriel 2007:21). Only then did elites become preoccupied with turning immigrants into Frenchmen.[60] In Noiriel's view, this is one of the reasons that France adhered strictly to the *ius soli* for determining nationality while Germany and Italy, at the time both emigration countries, rather favored the *ius sanguinis*. At the time, then, French national identity was highly inclusive. However, there was an opposing conservative current of which, since the end of the nineteenth century, Maurice Barrès was an oft-quoted spokesman. In the latter's view the immigrants were becoming ever more an internal threat; therefore it was urgent to distinguish the *vrais Français* (the real Frenchmen) among the mass of citizens. For Barrès the *personnalité nationale* had to be constructed on the axis of *la terre et les morts* (the soil and the deceased).[61] In this view, there is apparently a crucial distinction within French citizenship: immigrants may become citizens, but they can never become *de vrais Français* (or, as Le Pen would put it, *des Français de souche*). In Noiriel's view, Sarkozy, himself the son of Polish immigrants, owes his success to giving this old conservative view a new twist: his discourse on immigration seems to be based on a distinction between older generations of immigrants that did integrate and newer groups that refuse to do so and therefore form a threat. This is why his linking of *identité nationale* to *immigration*, construed as a basic danger, is so vicious. Noiriel calls on historians to be *vigilants* against such "entrepreneurs of memory" (2007:8)—a powerful expression—who use history for creating a memory that suits them.

The current fierce debates on history in France—the debate started by the *comité de vigilance* is just one of them—show that even in that country, often seen as the classical locus of nationalism, it is not easy to frame history and culture in the service of a national consensus. Even here, the very notion of national identity seems to be relatively young and constantly contested. The fierce involvement of many historians in these debates shows that, indeed, history can divide as much as unify.

* * *

Despite these parallels in other European countries where immigration likewise became the dominant issue in the 1990s, the rapidity of the Dutch switch from being a *gidsland* (guide country) of tolerance to placing an impatient emphasis on forceful cultural integration is quite striking. This switch seems to be a strong example of Appadurai's reflections (2006), quoted before, on how identities can become "predatory"—that is, can start cannibalizing other identities instead of accepting a pluralist configuration. The Dutch government's new measures to force immigrants to integrate, the emphasis on cultural rather than on socioeconomic integration, and the insistence in Scheffer's earlier texts and by other opinion leaders that such cultural integration will necessarily be a wrenching process—a "painful" loss of earlier attachments (Scheffer 2000a:7; van den Brink 2006:21, 301)—smack, indeed, of a "predatory" approach. So does the clear impatience of many politicians with the "soft" pluralism defended by proponents of the earlier "multi-culti" approach. The idea seems to be, indeed, that Dutch identity must "cannibalize" other identities in order to turn immigrants into reliable citizens. All the more surprising that the overall profile of this identity—the vagueness of its contours and the great problems in giving it a more concrete shape—is hardly what one would expect from a "predatory identity." What will become of an identity that hardly knows itself yet refuses to leave space for other identities?

The Dutch case is equally difficult to place in Gerd Bauman's typology, also cited above, of different grammars of identity and belonging (Bauman 2004). As said, Bauman tries to move beyond the basic truth that a Self (or "identity") logically needs an Other (or "alterity") to define itself. Therefore he distinguishes different ways ("grammars") to relate to the Other, each with its own implications. The earlier "multi-culti" approach is easy to fit into this typology as a clear example of "encompassment": an effort to include different identities within a wider whole. But the subsequent switch to forcible cultural integration is more difficult to place. Bauman emphasizes that there always must be room for "alterity"—for some sort of a relation to the Other—in order to keep the specificity of a group's own identity alive. The problem is, again, that in the policies called for by Scheffer (at least in his earlier articles) and Verdonk—to cite just two advocates of this direction—Dutch identity, vague as it might be, is suddenly supposed to claim all the space. Or as Mbembe summarizes it so powerfully: autochthony is basically an impossible vision, since it conjures up an "Otherless universe."

The basic tension between the two terms, *autochthonous* and *integration*, that loom so large in the recent Dutch approach to the immigration issue may well be more than just a terminological quibble. As said before, in principle autochthony rules out integration of "strangers." In the African examples, even someone who has lived most of his or her life elsewhere remains an autochthon—as becomes clear, in most unfortunate forms, by the key role young urbanites have played in the upsurge of violence in Ivory Coast now that they feel forced to return to "their" village to claim their rights. In classical Athens, the mere suspicion that a citizen was hiding descent from elsewhere could make him lose his citizenship. The Dutch seem to deploy a watered-down version of this rigid definition of belonging: with them allochthons can become citizens but on the condition that they culturally integrate. Yet by relating integration to an "essentialist" culture concept—the Dutch culture, at least in the conception of Verdonk, Wilders, and others, is supposed to have its own essence, and the immigrants have to choose between this and their own culture— the heavier interpretation of the autochthon concept is smuggled back in. One might wonder, indeed, whether integration is at all possible with such an approach.

The central question raised by the Dutch experience, and by developments elsewhere in Europe, is whether giving greater substance to the national culture—especially if it is done in such contrived ways as in the Dutch examples above—makes integration of immigrants easier.[62] In practice, this seems rather to work toward a deepening of the divide and make integration all the more difficult. "Culture" in these contexts reminds one of "witchcraft" in Mary Douglas's famous characterization of it as a "clumsy and double-edged weapon" (Douglas 1963:126). It seems to be a useful tool, but it can easily turn against the one who tries to use it. The insistence on the need to outline a fixed cultural core as a precondition for the integration of newcomers comes from authors who seem to have surprisingly little experience in studying what culture can do and how it works.

All the more reason to take alternative approaches more seriously, like the one outlined for the Netherlands by Duyvendak and Hurenkamp (2004), who rather put their faith in an emerging "community lite" of similar lifestyles and everyday behavior (see above). The increasing conformity they note in everyday practices might seem quite superficial, but it could still be a more realistic means of achieving integration than a cultural offensive enforced from above—notably if this acquires such artificial overtones as it does in the Dutch case.[63] Of course, a certain consensus is necessary—Scheffer and others are certainly right to insist on this.

But it is questionable whether it necessarily must be a consensus on basic values. The great originality of Lijphart's analysis of Dutch pillarization is that he shows such consensus to have been highly limited in a key period in Dutch history. More important might be that any form of consensus—as in Lijphart's version of pillarization—must leave room for difference.

In his 2007 book Scheffer seems to be more conscious that "the Land of Arrival" has to offer openings for the migrant to feel at home.[64] In his explorations on how cosmopolitanism and identity can be combined, Kwame Anthony Appiah emphasizes, like Scheffer, the importance of "common stories," but he adds most importantly that stories of identity risk deepening gaps between different groups in society, unless they assume the character of "conversations" that respect difference: "What makes such conversations possible is not always shared 'culture,' not even, as the older humanists imagined, universal principles... it is the capacity to conjure a world" (Appiah 2005:245, 258).[65] Culture is a useful notion in debates on how to live with immigration only if it includes difference rather than excluding it.

CHAPTER SIX

Cameroon:
Nation-Building and Autochthony as
Processes of Subjectivation

The African cases and the Dutch trajectory of the autochthony notion, as discussed in the previous chapters, raise the challenge of how to understand its emotional force in such widely different settings. Clearly, the self-evidence that the notion acquires, despite all these differences, has to be placed in specific historical contexts. But as emphasized in chapter 1, such historicizing is only one step. Another challenge, and probably a more difficult one, is to understand that even if autochthony, again like other forms of belonging, is historically constructed—and can even be "debunked" as blatantly incorrect—it still takes on a "naturalness" that gives its considerable emotional power and concomitant mobilizing force. For instance, we saw that it seemed to apply as easily in present-day Europe as in Africa. To protagonists of autochthony claims, it seems of little concern whether these claims rest on a highly special interpretation of history or even a downright distortion: its emotional persuasiveness seems to be no less—at least in some situations. However, it is important to emphasize that this does not always "work" to the same degree—in this respect as well there are considerable differences. In the Dutch case, it proved to be much more difficult to give substance to the autochthony idea. The appeal to the soil remains quite empty here, and autochthony rituals remain hesitant and open (consider the citizenship exams and the canon). Still, even in this context, the notion seems to acquire an emotional charge, though with the sense of a much more diffuse belonging to the soil.

This chapter is an attempt to respond to this challenge to go beyond a historicizing of autochthony claims as determined by specific histories and rapidly changing politico-economic circumstances. The main question will be how to analyze the emotional power autochthony can assume. Is it possible to analyze more closely how it can take on a natural appearance in highly different situations? When does an appeal to the soil acquire a momentum of its own—as in the funeral rituals in both Cameroon and classical Athens, mentioned above; or think of the visceral quality of the Sawa demonstrations in Douala and the passionate references to the village in the Opération d'Identification Nationale in Ivory Coast. What does it take to acquire such a concentrated effect? Why do references to autochthony remain looser in other settings?

Chapter 1 has already indicated the lines along which I propose to address such questions. Rather than taking the problematic notion of "identity" as a starting point, I will focus—following Jean-François Bayart's elaborations upon Foucauldian notions—on processes of subjectivation that both shape and are shaped by the subject and on "techniques of the body" as central to the crystallization of changing patters of (auto)disciplining in such processes of subjectivation. A key role in such disciplining processes is played by certain ritualized or in any case recurrent moments.[1] To understand why such moments acquire extra power—or fail to do so—I will use Birgit Meyer's explorations of "style" and "aesthetic concentration" in order to understand how certain moments impress "a shared perception of the world" on people, "inducing an authentic feeling of belonging" which seems to surpass other identifications or preoccupations.[2]

In this chapter, I will try to go deeper into such questions by focusing on the recent transition in Cameroon, already touched upon, from nation-building as the overriding issue in both national politics and development to the more recent preoccupation with autochthony as a somewhat surprising outcome of processes of democratization and decentralization. In practice, this meant a switch between quite different forms of belonging: from a focus on national citizenship, as at least formally the most important form of belonging, to autochthony as a crucial criterion, aptly summarized by the elderly statesman Samuel Eboua in his statement that "every Cameroonian is an *allogène* anywhere else in the country than ... where he will be buried." Noteworthy in this comparison is that all the highly ritualized emphasis on nation-building of the 1960s and 1970s seems to have disappeared, almost without leaving a trace. It is tempting therefore to see the period of nation-building as an intermezzo of lesser importance—all the more since the rituals of nation-building seemed artificial and imposed from above, often quite clumsily.

Recently, several authors (Mbembe 2003; cf. also Bayart 1979) have emphasized that this is too simplistic a vision. Nation-building may have been deeply marked by the authoritarianism of one-party regimes, but people certainly did become involved in it. Both Bayart and Mbembe emphasize the "connivance" of the *dominés* in these authoritarian rituals: under the one-party states, politics were mostly marked by a dictatorial top-down approach, yet many people were eager to participate whenever they could. Precisely because of this, the different trajectories of nation-building are still very important for understanding present-day issues—for instance, the varying expressions of autochthony and belonging in different countries. It is high time, then, for a return to the topic of nation-building, especially since we know little of how it was carried out on the ground—how exactly the various regimes tried to shape their subjects into responsible citizens. To put it bluntly: political scientists have mainly studied the process with a top-down approach (which mostly remained concentrated on the top), while anthropologists, who at the time witnessed the realities of nation-building at the grassroots level, seem to have been more interested in other topics (for a more nuanced overview, see the next section below).

In the context of this book, nation-building is, moreover, of special interest for a comparison with present-day rituals of belonging. Of course, mundane interests played a crucial role in the transition from nation-building to autochthony, for both elites and villagers (see chapters 2 and 3). Access to the state was and is as important for the villagers as for the elites in their efforts to create or keep a stake in the budding urban sector; it as important for both to defend a special hold over local resources such as land and forests. Nevertheless, it may be clear from the above that reducing people's involvement in projects like nation-building or autochthony to such socioeconomic interests would provide an incomplete understanding. If we want to understand the worldwide appeal of autochthony and other forms of belonging in our globalizing world, its emotional appeal—and its capacity to appear "natural" in such highly different situations—remains a vital issue. Hence a focus in this chapter on special moments—mostly of a more or less ritualized character—at which a special form of subjectivity seems to take shape (or fails to do so). Precisely in this respect interesting contrasts will emerge between the rituals of nation-building and autochthony in, for instance, Cameroon. As noted earlier, there was a considerable effort in Cameroon, as in other African countries, to shape a national citizenry, but nowadays little remains of these elaborate national rituals of the 1960s and 1970s. Is it possible to pinpoint where exactly the difference lies with present-day rituals of autochthony, which seem to have a more direct emotional appeal?

In the next chapter I will complement this further with short comparisons to trajectories elsewhere in Africa and in Europe.

Nation-Building as an Everyday Reality

During the first decades after independence, in almost all African countries "nation-building" became a central issue, and its political importance was equaled by the attention it received in African studies. At the time it was generally seen as one of the most urgent conditions for a "take off" of development in what were then generally called "the young states of Africa." In line with this perspective, the topic was mainly studied by political scientists (Apter 1965; Deutsch and Foltz 1963), and this implied some limitations. As said, it was mainly looked at top-down—both by social scientists and by the politicians who carried out these projects—and as a functional necessity: it was the aims and the possibilities of nation-building that received the most attention, much more than what all this meant at the grassroots level. Anthropologists did witness how these lofty aims were carried out in everyday practice, but they often had other interests. Especially in the 1970s they were often searching for counter-movements or even resistance, rising from below, against the increasingly authoritarian regimes. In such a perspective, the local realities of nation-building seemed to be artificial, pompous, and hardly worth any attention.

I started my fieldwork in Cameroon in 1971 with the explicit aim of studying local effects of state formation, and I vividly remember my disappointment—and that of a few students I took along—when we realized what this topic would boil down to in practice. These were the post-1968 days, when younger generations in the West, disappointed with the political stalemate at home, looked to the Third World for new beginnings. Fidel Castro and even Mao Zedong were still seen as heroes. In such a perspective, nation-building in Cameroon could only seem amazingly uninspired. We were confronted with political rallies in which the public seemed to be mainly bored, giving clear signs of having been more or less forced to attend. The rhetorical prowess of most politicians was severely limited. President Ahidjo himself set the tone: dry, didactic addresses that seemed intended to keep the masses quiet and orderly rather than to stimulate enthusiasm. The one party produced a stream of publications, but these mainly offered monotonous reports on the main politicians' activities in pompous jargon that clearly was intended to impress rather than mobilize enthusiasm among the people. The burlesque and often quite vulgar show of wealth by the new elite of bureaucrats and politicians seemed intended to frighten the masses and keep them in their place. These were not the scenes I had hoped to study, and the consequence was that I mainly tried to avoid these quite boring events.

In retrospect my response is now quite regrettable—all the more so since apparently I was not the only observer who reacted in this way. One of the consequences is that we have surprisingly few studies of what nation-building meant on the ground: how exactly the new regimes tried to groom their subjects into the role of responsible yet acquiescent citizens, and the complicated and often contradictory implications of these disciplining apparatuses.[3] Among the great merits of the early work of both Jean-François Bayart and Achille Mbembe is that they took these experiments with nation-building seriously, burlesque and gross as they may have been. Bayart warned already in his 1979 study of the state in Cameroon that any opposition of the state and its coercion, on the one hand, and the oppressed masses, on the other, was far too simplistic; instead he called for closer attention to the constant interaction between *dominants* and *dominés*, those in power and the dependents (Bayart 1979: 277). Mbembe, in his much quoted 1992 article "Provisional Notes on the Postcolony," similarly attacked the obstinate quest for resistance that marked so much work in the field of African studies in those days. Researchers—mostly social scientists from the West—looked desperately for the beginnings of opposition against all this show of authority. In contrast, both Bayart and Mbembe emphasized the "connivance" of the dominated with the dominants and their rituals. Artificial as they may have seemed, these rituals were not ineffective, since people were often eager to join in them.

Another reason for the relative neglect of nation-building as an everyday practice was the emphasis—pervading African studies especially after the spread of *dependencia* ideas in the 1970s—on continuity from the colonial to the postcolonial period. In the *dependencia* vision, independence was only apparent; in practice, the colonial relation was continued, and the new African elites simply stepped in the traces of their colonial pre-decessors. In many respects there was indeed continuity. Yet the deter-mined efforts to "build a nation"—in those days heavily supported by the development establishment—did create a host of new institutions and in-terventions. Bureaucratic and imposed from above as these were, they did involve the people, and this involvement left its traces also after the stiff rituals of nation-building—the endless, disciplined political rallies and the regular party meetings at every level for the *formation* of the population—imploded in the 1990s.

It is in retrospect that one can see that nation-building, despite ap-pearances, had some effects. For instance, in order to understand the quite different courses that ideas of autochthony took in Ivory Coast and Cameroon, one has to return to the period of forcible nation-building and the quite different approaches of Houphouët-Boigny and Ahidjo—which were again circumscribed by distinctive historical circumstances. There seems therefore to be good reason to take the rituals of nation-building, tedious as they were, seriously; after all, they did have practical effects in the grooming of national citizens.

The brief sketch of the 1971 visit of the minister of national adminis-tration to the main town in Makaland in chapter 3 has already suggested how people on the ground in Cameroon were confronted with the lofty ideals of nation-building.[4]

• • • • • • • • • • • • • •

The rally was marked by strict discipline. People waited patiently in the sun for hours until the minister finally arrived. They had been more or less forced to attend: chiefs had been called upon to send an important dele-gation from their village, and all schools had been closed. Schoolchildren in their uniforms marched like troupes of Boy Scouts, strictly controlled by their teachers. The women of the OFUNC (the women's association of the one party) were a little bit more spontaneous, waving at the crowd and chanting, but their flowing robes, all of the same cloth with the portrait of the president printed all over, likewise gave the impression of a uniform. The role assigned to the crowd was entirely passive: they were to applaud when the applause master behind the podium gave a sign. This led to a particularly tragicomic moment when, after the minister's first sentence, which repeated the general stereotype of the East as a country of drunkards and witches, everybody duly applauded. But even this did not lead to any hilarity. The national hymn was played from a tape without any invitation to the people to join in. The omnipresent gendarmes, with their usual bullying behavior, made it very clear that any form of dissent or failure to conform would have serious consequences.

The speeches followed a fixed pattern. Regional party leaders profusely congratulated the minister and through him the president for all their wise decisions and especially for sending such excellent civil servants to the province; indeed, they never tired in emphasizing how wonderfully they worked together with the regional DOs in further affirming the glorious *unité nationale*—all people united behind the president. The only surprise came from Raymond Malouma, the regional MP, who compared the joy Christians feel about the coming of Christ each Christmas to the elation of the population now that the minister was here. But he was also the one who raised the somber theme of vigilance, which would be more necessary than ever in view of hidden traitors inside; in fact, this was his favorite theme and made him especially feared among the population. The minister, in his turn, spoke like a teacher, slowly and patiently. He emphasized the potential riches of the province; however, the population lacked two things: *orientation* and *encadrement*. Both were now provided by the president: the third Five-Year Plan offered *orientation*, just as the *grand parti national* assured the *encadrement* of the people. So all had to work united behind the president.

· · · · · · · · · · · · · · ·

The observance and the speeches effectively condensed not only the national ideology preached by the president and the party leaders but also the role it assigned to the subjects as good *citoyens camerounais*. The national ideology in those days was simple and straightforward. It was based on a Manichaean opposition between *unité* and *subversion*, which logically implied a third term, *vigilance*; since "national unity" was supposed to be under constant threat of "subversion," there was a heavy emphasis on vigilance as an urgent necessity.[5] The severity of this ideology—and notably the constant urging of *vigilance*—was historically circumscribed by traumatic developments around national independence (1960). However, any reference to that episode was completely anathema as long as Ahidjo was in power (until 1982). Of course, this strictly enforced silence on what everybody knew made the secret bear down all the more on everyday relations.

Indeed Ahidjo's pronounced authoritarianism had historical roots. As said, he had closely collaborated with the French in the bloody suppression of the country's first nationalist movement—the UPC, the first movement on the continent to claim complete national independence (already in 1948).[6] Ahidjo was later catapulted by the French colonials into the position of national leader, since as one of the representatives of the Islamic north he seemed more reliable than someone from the turbulent (and more developed) southern parts of the country.[7] Many (including the French *Haut-commissaire*) saw him as a temporary figure. But once in control of the state apparatus, he showed himself an astute politician, outmaneuvering all rivals. Already in 1962, he succeeded in eliminating all opposition parties, forcing rival politicians to either join his *parti unifié* or withdraw from politics.[8] Thereafter Cameroon became a particularly authoritarian one-party state, in which the president with his close followers tried to maintain an almost total grip on politics throughout the country.

Thus developments in Cameroon followed a pattern similar to that of other one-party states throughout the continent. The group that captured the state at the time of independence was able to quickly eliminate all formal opposition, on the one hand through its control over army and police and on the other through co-opting other politicians by offering them posts among the many vacancies that had to be filled because of the "Africanization" of public services. Moreover, in the context of cold war, Western powers were inclined to give the need for "stability" priority over the desirability of more effective forms of democracy. A consequence was that the postcolonial state in Cameroon—as elsewhere in Africa—seemed to defy any class analysis. Power became concentrated in the hands of the new president and his *barons*—in many respects a quite accidental faction shaped by the vicissitudes of independence, which was not so much wrestled from the former colonial power as negotiated with it. From the perspective of villagers in the early 1970s, the state looked like a sort of balloon—a concentration of power—drifting above society. A few people had managed—again for apparently quite accidental reasons—to become part of this concentration of power (we already met a good example of such a *baron* in the figure of Malouma, for a long time the MP and the main party boss in this part of Cameroon, who figured so prominently at the visit of the minister). But other people hardly had any access to the party leadership All decisions, even concerning political posts of very little importance, were made at the top. In the course of the 1970s this changed gradually as more people got access to important posts in civil service and clientelistic ramifications spread more widely, linking people in more informal ways to the state. Yet the composition of such networks and the reasons for the rise and fall of central persons in them remained highly unpredictable.

In Cameroon, Ahidjo's regime, like most of the "young states" on the continent, developed an extremely authoritarian version of this top-down approach. The persistence of UPC "rebellion," especially among the Bamileke in the western part of the country—but which in 1965 proved capable of suddenly opening a new front in the extreme south—inspired a true obsession with control: endless roadblocks and police checks throughout the country and, most important, a strictly maintained interdiction on any form of association outside the one party.[9] There was absolute censure on any reference to the UPC and its charismatic leader, Um Nyobe (killed in 1958), but precisely this made the shadow of both the movement and its leader omnipresent.

All this coercion was accompanied by a determined and rigid ideological offensive to mobilize the people behind the regime around the disciplinary triangle of the national ideology of *unité, subversion*, and *vigilance*. In 1963 the party headquarters started to print a weekly, *L'Unité*, which was distributed throughout the country; in 1971 it was available even in the little accessible East Province, because it was distributed through the omnipresent party organization. For some time it was complemented by a second publication, *Union et Vérité*, which contained longer articles. Moreover, the regular visits of both leading politicians and higher civil servants throughout the country had to be large rallies—as described above—in which the simple message of the national ideology, *unité* versus *subversion = vigilance*, had to be repeated time and again. The DOs were required to confront their subjects with these themes during their annual *tournées administratives*. Indeed, the principle of close collaboration between party and *administration* at all levels often made it hard to distinguish between the roles of the DOs and the regional party officials.

However, the main channel—at least on paper—for spreading the national message was the party organization, which was rapidly extended over the whole country. In the Francophone part, Ahidjo's Union Camerounaise (later Union Nationale Camerounaise) became the de facto one party in 1962. In the district where I was working, an elaborate party organization down to the very local level had been built up already by 1966—even though this was always seen as one of the most backward parts of the country. Each village had its *comité de base*, each *arrondissement* its *sous-*

section, and each *département* its *section*. On paper the party organization was even more impressive, since under each *comité de base* several *cellules* had to function. However, these *cellules* mostly had only a shadowy existence, even in the 1970s during the heyday of the one-party organization. In the villages where I worked, some people claimed to be the chairman of a *cellule*, but this was invariably contested by others. The *comités de base*, however, were fully installed, each with its own *bureau* (board) and its own chairman. Bayart speaks with good reason of the *quadrillage politique* of the country: the party was everywhere, even in the smallest village, and any form of association outside it was quickly repressed.[10]

The question remained, however, what this omnipresence of the party amounted to in everyday practice.

. . . .

When I could finally start my research in the village—after a long quest for the necessary research permits at all levels of the bureaucratic hierarchy— I was agreeably surprised to find that the chairman of the local *comité de base*, Pierre Nkal, had no objection at all to showing me his archive. This was unexpected, since in those days research into anything that smacked of politics was highly discouraged. However, when I went next day to his house—a relatively sumptuous construction with an iron roof—I was quite disappointed. The "archive" turned out to consist of two recent copies of *L'Unité* and three sets of minutes of meetings from some time ago (actually only the agenda for those meetings). According to the official guidelines, a *comité de base* had to assemble all *militants* at least once a month for a reunion; a *sous-section* had to meet each third month, and a *section* twice a year. The general aim of such meetings was described as *formation* and *encadrement*.

In 1971, Nkal was still quite young (late twenties), yet he claimed to have been chairman of the *comité de base* already for four years. He emphasized that in the beginning he had organized regular meetings. However, the problem was that there was hardly anything to discuss. The minutes he had kept mentioned indeed the two points of *formation* and *encadrement*. Nkal had a clear idea of what to do under these points. Under *formation* he had to go through the last issue of *L'Unité* with the *militants*. Under *encadrement* he had to inform the people about recent initiatives of the DO and other civil servants and exhort them to duly participate. Moreover, he had to admonish them to join every Thursday in the *investissement humain* that President Ahidjo demanded from all citizens as their personal contribution to national development.

This simple overview made it amply clear why Nkal had so few minutes in his archive: people simply did not turn up for meetings, since they were sure that nothing new would come up. He told me that after some time he had stopped convening meetings. What was the use of it when nobody would attend? His problem was not only that his *reunions* had such a repetitive agenda but also that the points he had to raise were quite unpopular. The *investissement humain* was massively sabotaged by all villagers, since it boiled down to working for the *ngomena* (government)—for instance, making the village youth plant poles all along the road, every fifteen meters, and paint these white with chalk before the DO's visit to the village. Neither did *formation* and *encadrement* offer Nkal—who certainly did not lack personal ambition—much scope to give his position more substance. The articles in *L'Unité* were strongly repetitive, and *encadrement* implied discussing all sorts of demands by the DO that resembled the loathed *investissement humain* and were as unpopular.

. . . .

Clearly, at the heart of this whole problem of blowing some life into the party organization, so impressive on paper, and of mobilizing the people for its meetings was the total lack of any possibility of interest articulation from below. The national ideology was most explicit on this point: the party was there to support the bureaucracy in executing orders from the top and not to articulate demands from below. Communication within the party organization was as top-down as in the bureaucracy.[11] The consequence was that, in practice, the party functioned as an extension of the DO and the *administration* in general (cf. Bayart 1979:247).

Another ritual of nation-building had similar implications: the regularly recurring elections, which acquired a distinctive format under one-party rule. A fixed principle was that for all elections at any level—the municipality, the parliament, the presidency, and within the party—there would be only one list or candidate. Moreover, even for the lowest levels like the municipal council or the *comité de base*, all candidates would be appointed (*investi*) by the party leaders—President Ahidjo himself and a small clique around him. The consequence was that the word *investi* acquired a magical ring. Once an ambitious politician was *investi* by the party top, he (or in rarer cases, she) was sure to be elected.

On the ground, elections thus became an extremely disciplined occasion. There were only ballots with "Yes," with which voters could support the only list; often the ballot was already in an envelope. All villagers had to queue and go one by one to a table. There they would get first a stamp on their party card proving that they had voted; then they were handed the envelope with the ballot, which they had to put in the ballot box next to the table. There was no screened-off booth, so there was not even the possibility of not putting the envelope in the box. No wonder that the party's scores were impressive. Once our village even obtained a score of 103 percent *Oui* (by including the votes of a few passersby), and this was celebrated as a winning rate that would certainly attract the DO's favors to the village.

Indeed, the regime did everything to divest elections of their political character. What political competition there had been had taken place before the elections, when ambitious politicians were trying to outmaneuver each other in efforts to ingratiate themselves with the party leaders in order to get the much desired *investiture*. But of course that took place behind tightly closed doors. The regime celebrated the elections as symbolic occasions, offering the population a chance to express massive support to Ahidjo and its regime.[12] This was the message repeated time and again in *L'Unité*, the party's journal—in such repetitive wording that the articles became quite redundant. For the voters themselves, the elections were also quite important, but for completely different reasons. As the village chief commented on one occasion—and apparently without a trace of irony: "Of course the people are *heureux*. There was palm wine to drink and some music. But most importantly, they got the stamp on their party card, so they will not be in trouble with the gendarmes at the next control." Formally the elections were organized by the party. But in practice it was again the DO who really handled matters. The chairman of the *sous-section* was certainly present, but it was the DO who told him what to do. Also during the elections, the party officials manifested themselves as being lackeys to the bureaucrats.

This blending of the party with the *administration* had special implications. The *administrateurs* operated decidedly according to the old colonial adage of the *civis miles*, "the citizen as soldier." For their French predecessors it had been a fixed principle, up to the end of their rule, that the colonial subjects needed to be commanded—and *encadrés*—like soldiers in order to make them work for the *mise en valeur* of the colony. Their Cameroonian successors made it amply clear—by an unremitting show of authority and the omnipresent gendarmes—that this was still the principle on which the *ngomena* (government) based its interventions. No wonder the villagers perceived a clear continuity with colonial times in this respect.

When people had to go to the government post in the capital of the *arrondissement*, they would say, "I am going to *le pays des Blancs* [the land of the Whites]." This was a kind of joke, since they knew very well that the DO was a Cameroonian now. But it was also stating the obvious. *Blanc* stood for commandment and the threat of violence, and this were still the main principles in any DO's approach to the villagers. The constant threat of violence was indeed another aspect that marked the continuity with colonial times for the villagers. Behind all the rigid rituals sketched above—the political rallies, the elections, the party meetings—there was the constant shadow of arbitrary violence by the state. In many respects the special rituals of violence bore a clear colonial mark.

· · · · · · · · · · · · · · ·

For instance, my cook—even though I lived in a simple *poto-poto* house, the village had insisted that I had to recruit a whole staff—would talk with some longing of his days as *para-militaire*, when he was sometimes summoned to assist the gendarmes in a round-up. He remembered, for instance, how only a year earlier the governor of the East Province had ordered them to go "and punish the town of Bertoua" (the province's capital). They entered all houses and told people to get out and stand in line in the street. If they did not obey quickly enough, they were beaten up. Once in the street, they ordered all people to sit down. It was the rainy season, so the streets (all unpaved) were very muddy. People protested that their clothes would get dirty, but the *para-militaires* had no mercy and pushed them down in the mud.[13]

· · · · · · · · · · · · · · ·

This was (and to a certain extent still is) a recurrent scene—for instance at the endless controls at the roadblocks, when people refuse to pay for supposed infractions or show signs of impatience, but also at sudden controls of whole town quarters. During my first survey in the village, I was quite impressed that nearly all adult villagers had their party card.[14] However, it soon became clear that this had a very pragmatic reason: they had to show the card at each roadblock, and it had to bear all the required stamps to show that they had voted at recent elections—else they would be in serious difficulties. The ritual of forcing *coupables* to sit in the mud was an initial humiliation. In more serious cases, people would be taken to the gendarmes' office, and everyone knew that there you would get an *avertissement* (a warning—that is, a lighter or heavier flogging, depending on the gendarmes' mood).

*   *   *

In many respects there was, therefore, a clear continuity with colonial times: the DOs—*les nouveaux Blancs* as the villagers called them—were hard to distinguish from their colonial predecessors in the way they approached their subjects; in everyday life the party seemed to hide behind the *administration*; and the violent performance of the gendarmes in support of this strongly reminded of the vivid scenes in novels like *Houseboy* by Ferdinand Oyono (which in fact was set in the same area, during the late colonial period). Yet, as emphasized earlier, it would be too rash to conclude from all this that independence did not bring anything new. Especially in two respects did the whole ideological offensive by the party and its impressive institutional presence create new openings—even if these did not exactly correspond to democratic ideals. One was the call to people to be constantly *vigilant*; the other was new career opportunities for ambitious politicians. Both added new touches to the way people felt they could manifest themselves as citizens—new turns in the process of *subjectivation*.[15]

The theme of *vigilance* was the only one in Ahidjo's ideology that directly called for initiative from below—in this sense it was the most mobilizing element. And indeed, the call did not go unheeded. The feared secret service may have regularly changed its name, but it had nonetheless a marked continuity as the regime's mainstay, certainly in the eyes of the population. Its importance was effectively symbolized by the towering presence of Jean Fochive, who remained in charge of the service until far into the regime of Biya (Ahidjo's successor)—always half hidden behind the president himself, yet generally seen as one of the secrets behind the regime's stability. Moreover, around this dark presence a culture of denouncing developed that might be seen as truly postcolonial in character: it certainly had colonial roots, but it acquired a life of its own in the postcolony. The awareness that any accusation of *subversion* might suffice to have someone spirited away to Tchollire or another one of Ahidjo's concentration camps, where people just disappeared,[16] had a double effect. On the one hand, it made people very careful not to meddle in politics. Any comment on the political situation could be passed on. So most of my spokespersons would clam up as soon as they thought the discussion was touching on such topics. A constantly returning adage in those days—in striking contrast to the present day—was *La politique, c'est l'affaire des grands.* However, the other side was that this did activate people to spy upon each other and pass on any dangerous bit to a party official or directly to the secret service. During those days, someone would just come up and sit at your table in a pub or restaurant, whereupon the other people at your table would suddenly fall silent and seek to get away as quickly as possible.

Especially inside the party hierarchy, it became standard practice to denounce one's superior by passing on information to the official at yet a higher level—apparently an obvious way to climb one step on the ladder (since then one could hope to get the other's position). However, this might easily backfire, since such an accusation could also be turned around, and the favors of the party leadership remained wrapped in mystery. The obsessive preoccupation with *subversion* and *vigilance*—clearly related to the trauma of independence and the arbitrary way in which Ahidjo succeeded in making his way to the top—thus had a double and paradoxical effect: on the one hand, it effectively paralyzed any open political discussion or political initiative, yet, on the other hand, it did activate people, and especially ambitious politicians, to all sorts of covert pursuits. In practice, politics were certainly not *une affaire des Grands* only: the regime's obsession with subversion gave others opportunities to try to join in, but always in a secret way since it was a dangerous and highly unpredictable field.

The second novelty relates to the new opportunities that the party hierarchy—despite all the controls—offered to those who dreamed of making a political career.[17] But again, the particularities of nation-building under a one-party regime gave this aspect unexpected forms. A major theme, to which Ahidjo and his barons returned time and again, was that each candidate owed the *investiture* for his post to the party leadership and not to his personal support among the voters (whose votes, after all, counted only symbolically, as a demonstration of support to the regime and not to the candidate in question).

> Indeed, the candidate nominated by our Party does not have to conduct his own election campaign and does not spend any money on it....Nevertheless some *militants*, once they have been elected, deem it necessary to make themselves

"popular" and to create an electoral clientele. Therefore they feel obliged to indulge in demagogy.... Thus, they create rival factions within the party. The inevitable result is friction with the *autorité administrative*, for the latter does not hesitate to draw the attention of the *autorité supérieure* to such a situation. (Kwayyeb 1967:126)

Given the discussion so far, it may be clear that the last phrase of this statement directly invited *les militants* to inform on the activities of any overly ambitious politician. Indeed, how paralyzing the emphasis on complete loyalty to the top could become is evident from an article from the same year in *L'Effort Camerounais* (a Catholic weekly, in those days the only paper that sometimes voiced somewhat different opinions): "An official, for instance, is working in Yaoundé and has a certain amount of support from the youth of his village, and would like to get work parties going there. But he cannot. He is afraid. He has been active at some time or other in such and such political party. It wouldn't be well regarded if he put himself at the head of some association, even just a work party."[18]

The result was remarkable: a political configuration in which local and regional politicians were involved in fierce rivalry, yet with their back to the people. All that counted was the favor of the top in Yaoundé. Popular support was no asset; on the contrary, any attempt to build up a local base would be counterproductive since rivals could denounce it to the party leadership as an attempt to disturb the unity of all *militants* behind President Ahidjo—that is, as *subversion*—and such an accusation could be literally lethal.

· · · · · · · · · · · · · · ·

For instance, a few months after I had settled in the village there were strong rumors that developments in a neighboring *arrondissement* were getting out of hand. In this area, the rivalry among politicians had always been particularly fierce. In colonial times two leading figures had come to blows in front of the DO; more recently there had been persistent rumors that they had been attacking each other through witchcraft. Apparently one of them had not accepted that his rival had recently been *investi* as MP and had written a letter of protest to the president himself. It was clear, then, that strong disciplinary measures would follow. Yet the villagers had no idea of what was actually going on. At night, and more or less in secret, people loved to gossip about it, launching all sorts of guesses, mocking *les*

Grands for their exaggerated ambitions but at the same time speaking with some awe about their intrepidity in confronting each other. However, in no way would the villagers themselves become involved in all this. The only clear sign that something was wrong was that Mr. Malouma's black Mercedes—as an MP he had a particularly big Mercedes, since this was *the* status symbol of the new elite at the time—kept passing on the road, on his way to and from the *arrondissement* concerned. People would say, "There he goes again. *Ils vont avoir chaud* [they are going to be roasted]." But that was all. None of the rivals tried in any way to involve local supporters. Indeed, that would have been really disastrous for them.[19]

• • • • • • • • • • • • • •

The pressure to contain political rivalry within a strictly closed circuit was reinforced by another particularity of politics under Ahidjo: his policy of *équilibre régional* (regional equilibrium), already mentioned (chap. 2), which was celebrated by the regime as one of the cornerstones of Cameroon's stability. The principle was simple: each region was entitled to a fixed quota of posts in the party hierarchy and the higher echelons of government. Many other African leaders followed such a policy to a certain extent.[20] But Ahidjo was special in the strictness with which the idea was applied. It was possible—as several authors have done (see for instance Ngayap 1983:68) to reduce this political principle to an almost mathematical formula for determining appointments throughout the Ahidjo period. In practice, "region" was equated with "ethnic group," so that this policy had another special effect: officially it was supposed to reduce ethnic tensions—since each group had its fixed quota—yet at another level it reinforced ethnicity as the grid on which politics was based.

Since the *équilibre régional* principle was common knowledge on the ground, it had a direct effect on the practice of political competition: it strongly reinforced the tendency, noted above, to denunciations and infighting within the party hierarchy. For an ambitious politician it was of little use to attack a rival from a neighboring region or ethnic group, since he could in any case not take the place of the latter. Within the *équilibre régional* grid, one's obvious rival was always close by: for my friends it had to be another Maka, since one could go up only if another Maka fell, since there was a fixed quota for the whole group. Thus, *équilibre regional* and the strictness with which Ahidjo's team maintained it again reinforced among politicians a feeling of absolute dependence on those at the top.[21]

All this was graphically expressed in another ritual that had very direct implications for the perception of the self in the period of nation-building: the one o'clock news as the hour of decision regarding personal careers. In the first months of my fieldwork I was struck by the obsession of my elite friends—in the regional towns or in the capital—with the one o'clock news. At that hour they were all glued to the radio. It seemed impossible to miss it. Yet the news in itself was not that interesting. Like the official newspaper, *Cameroon Tribune*, it mainly reiterated monotonous reports on the president's visits in and outside the country and so on. However, I soon understood that the general interest was in the appendix to the news, when *affectations* (appointments and transfers) were announced. It took me some time to realize that it was only on the radio that any *fonctionnaire* (and most elites depended completely on their position in public service) would hear that he (or less often she) would be appointed or transferred to a given place. My friends had a standard joke about a former colleague—a DO—who heard on the radio that he was to be transferred to Mouloundou (far out at the southeastern point of the country, deep in the forest and hardly accessible for a good portion of the year) and had burst into tears on the spot. Clearly, this way of announcing decisions that were crucial to people's lives was again an almost physical demonstration of power: it drove home once more how much everybody—including elites who felt that they had become *un Grand*—depended on the unpredictable goodwill of the party leadership.

The highly authoritarian tenor of these rituals—the key role of the one o'clock news, the autocratic style of elections, the rigor of the *équilibre regional*, the strictly orchestrated political rallies emphasizing the passivity of the masses, the party's celebration of *formation* and *encadrement*—evoke the contours of a highly rigid *dispositif disciplinaire* with new aspects. But did this inspire special "techniques of the self"? At the time, all this seemed to be rather imposed from above with a very coercive approach. Yet even then there were already clear signs of a *vulgarisation* of these new forms of power (see Bayart 2004) that might have escaped the attention of observers who were looking only for resistance. Moreover, the new power rituals did connect with preexisting forms of discipline, albeit in somewhat unexpected ways. As said above, the authoritarian approach to the villagers—the emphasis on *encadrement*, on a strict *quadrillage politique* by the party, and especially on the dominant role of the *administrateurs* as the backbone of the new regime—was nothing new to the villagers. It was the old colonial modus operandi of the *civis miles*. Even the political rallies and the elections—the very moments when the popular masses were mobilized to show their support to the regime—fit at least in some respects with this colonial pattern. After all, these occasions were dominated by the DOs and their ways of continuing the performance of the colonial administration.

· · · · · · · · · · · · · ·

Elsewhere (Geschiere 1982:210) I have sought to analyze the quite surprising combinations of very different styles of behavior by one and the same person during a public performance within the village, for instance in the lively village palavers or when in front of the DO and other officials. The villagers were conscious of such differences, but they seemed to see this as self-evident. As one of my friends always concluded: "Every time the *ngomena* [government] sends someone from town to command us, we are like women. We can only say 'Yes.' "[22]

This was indeed very different from the way people were supposed to behave in the village. The same man who, the Sunday before, had defended his cause in the village palaver with great rhetoric prowess, refusing to be shut up by the village elders and cleverly denouncing inconsistencies in the declarations of his opponents, spoke to the DO with his head down, strictly obeying the official's orders to be brief and stick to the matter at hand. But to the villagers, such differences were no cause for surprise—they had learned long ago that this was the way one had to live with *les Blancs*, whether the old or the new ones.[23] Indeed, for quite some time I never knew when someone might confront me in the boisterous, quite aggressive way for which the Maka are famous—asking for a cigarette or palm wine— or suddenly address me humbly as a *patron* (with the maddening stock reply "Oui, patron"). Often people could switch in a moment from one style to the other.[24] Clearly, the period of colonial rule—even if it was relatively short in this area (scarcely fifty years)—had internalized certain forms of behavior quite deeply. My friends' favorite joke, quoted above, whenever they went to the see someone of the *ngomena* (government)—"I am going to the land of the Whites"—had similar implications: it served to set apart a sphere where another code of behavior held sway. Apparently this separation had become ingrained in everyday life.

· · · · · · · · · · · · · ·

In other respects, the new accents introduced by nation-building echoed even older patterns of behavior stemming from precolonial times.

For instance, the unremitting emphasis on *vigilance* coupled with the strict principle that any political rivalry should be played out inside the party apparatus and therefore in absolute secrecy, made it very difficult to distinguish politics from the hidden world of witchcraft (*djambe*)—which to the Maka is in any case closely related to power and inequality (see Geschiere 1997). The need for absolute reliance on the party leadership if a politician wanted to ensure the strongly desired *investiture* for any position of power may have added a new, highly hierarchical element to the imaginary on the occult. But in other respects the fixed rules of the *politique d'équilibre regional* converged with the old discourse on the occult. The necessity to compete with colleagues from close by is reminiscent of a basic idea in witchcraft perceptions that the most dangerous attacks come from close by.[25] Or to put it differently: for the regime this was an ideal form of divide-and-rule, since it made people deeply distrustful, as in the witchcraft perspective, of their close colleagues in their myopic struggles to ensure the support of the top. This whole grid produced specific forms of self-styling, partly novel, partly continuing older patterns.

....

I was, for quite some time, extremely puzzled and fascinated by the figure of Monsieur Malouma, the MP who among the Maka was both celebrated and deeply envied as the quintessence of success in the new configuration.In everyday life Malouma exhibited a self-conscious style of behavior that was quite distinctive but for my new friends apparently completely normal.

Malouma always refused blandly to have an interview with me. Even my most unctuous approach—I sent him a note saying that since his life had been such a success, I was very interested in writing down his life story as an example for others—did not work with him. He clearly felt that a suspicious attitude toward me was more fitting to his important political role.[26] However, when I was in Yaoundé friends often invited me to Sunday gatherings of Maka elites that Malouma would attend as well. There also he kept his distance, but sometimes he did allow me to exchange a few words with him. His behavior at these parties—and also at other occasions where I saw him—was markedly different from the behavior of other Maka elites. It was obvious that he wanted to set a special example. Whereas most people would drink heavily and become very boisterous after some time, he would sit sternly and quite pompously in a corner of the room, with a few *gorilles* (private guards) around him and with a big glass of milk (regularly refreshed by the hostess) in front of him. All those present would be quite formally dressed (suits or jackets), but most men would include some colorful details (light brown or blue suits or gaudy shirts). However, Malouma—at the time a heavy man in his fifties—invariably wore a dark blue three-piece suit with a dark tie. I hardly ever saw him laugh at such events. And only once did I see him get angry. This was when all those present rushed to the balcony to see an impressive cortege of Bamileke women passing by on their way to their *tontine* (credit association). The cortege represented quite a contrast to the small and rowdy *tontine* that the Maka elite women had been staging. At all other times, Malouma would sit and watch people with a stern, suspicious look. I was not the only one to feel somewhat ill at ease at his heavy presence.

Malouma's everyday persona—at least at these semipublic gatherings—was very much in line with his performance at public rallies and smaller meetings. When reading the endless admonitions in party literature on how *les cadre*s should behave, I could not help thinking of him. In his official speeches Malouma could go on endlessly about the unfortunate behavior of some officials who seemed beset with jealousy and rivalry, instead of working together under the president's banner. In practice he was, of course, a champion in political intrigues and untiring in undoing any upcoming rival from within the new Maka elite. But apparently he saw this as part of the necessary *encadrement* of his followers, required by the party's ideology.

There was certainly not a complete breach with the past here. In some respects Malouma tried to relate to local ideas about prestige and power. He would, for instance, provide broad hints at the powerful protection he received from a *nganga* (healer) deep in the forest, which would render ineffective all hidden attacks against him.[27] In other respects, his persona contained colonial elements: the three-piece suit, the behavior of a DO. But Ahidjo's party ideology had clearly added certain touches: Malouma seemed to be the personification of the need for *vigilance*—in fact, this was his favorite theme, very effective for frightening off potential rivals—but he was also an expert in celebrating the president and his close collaborators,[28] thus creating a kind of symbolic mobilization of the masses that remained at the same time completely disciplined and controlled.

．．．．．．．．．．．．．

The MP apparently set an example of the kind of subject that befitted the *dispositif disciplinaire* of nation-building. His sudden fall in 1980—when he in his turn was accused of *subversion*—also fit in with this. People never knew the reason for his loss of favor, although they kept speculating. Malouma himself became more or less invisible, withdrawing to his village.

Ahidjo's nation-building project aimed to groom its subjects—*les Grands* as much as the masses—into particularly well-disciplined citizens, completely dependent on the president and his *camera*. However, soon people who wanted to succeed in politics would be forced to add new touches to their self-styling.

Rituals of Belonging: The Funeral at Home as a Celebration of Autochthony

The new rituals of citizenship and nation-building were—also in the 1960s and 1970s—of course complemented by other, more private rituals of belonging, in Cameroon as in all nation-states. The particularity of developments in Cameroon and many other African countries is, however, that in the 1990s these complementary, more private rituals increasingly invaded the public sphere, relegating the rituals of nation-building to a more or less secondary role. Recall what was said in chapter 2 about the quite unexpected role that the funeral came to play as a final test of belonging in the new political debates triggered by political liberalization and democratization. To quote the Sawa (sea people) demonstrators of Douala: "If Bamileke immigrants in the city insist on still burying their deceased in the village, then it is clear that they belong there. So they should go home and vote there, rather than in the land of their 'hosts.' "

The funeral is of special interest, then, for exploring autochthony and local forms of belonging as a new turn of subjectivation. An obvious way to do so is to take a closer look at the ways in which the funeral was and is ritualized. Why did funeral ritual come to play such a central role in the new politics of belonging? What kind of subject is outlined in these dramatic rituals? A brief ethnography of the funeral in Makaland, where I did fieldwork for more than thirty years, and its implications for issues of belonging might be helpful here.

Funerals are (and were) no doubt the most important ritual in Maka village life, as elsewhere in the forest zone of Cameroon and indeed in many other parts of the African continent. They are the occasion for enacting a dynamic series of ritualized actions and roles, involving the whole village and numerous delegations from related villages, which confirm the position of all people involved—not only of the deceased person but also of all those related to him or her—in the ramifications of the kinship organization. There is a marked contrast here to the stiff rituals of nation-building or of colonial subjection. Funerals are extremely animated occasions full of excitement, especially because they offer a channeled expression—a sort of social drama—for the feelings of aggression and reconciliation between the kin groups involved. This unsettling mix of aggression, rejoicing, and mourning can be read as a powerful moment of *subjectivation*—each individual both assuming and shaping his or her proper role. Moreover—and here Bayart's emphasis on subjectivation as a never-ending process is most welcome—it is a most dynamic occasion, constantly taking on new aspects and capable of addressing novel issues of belonging. A brief sketch of the main moments of the funerals I attended in the village in the early 1970s can serve as an illustration of the unsettling power of these rituals. Reading again in my notebooks from those days made me realize how confused I was by these wild occasions that nonetheless seemed to follow a clear script, each person playing his or her role with abandon, yet sticking to that role. Almost as confusing was the constant innovation: at nearly every funeral new touches were added, especially having to do with money, which nonetheless seemed to fit in seamlessly with older elements.

The central importance of the funeral in village life was brought home to me right from the start. Beginning on the third day of my fieldwork, the whole village went into uproar for two days and one long, long night (with a lot of deafening drumming) with the burial of an important elder. At such occasions there is always a massive attendance. Especially if the dead person was a senior man, people will come from all over the *canton* to attend his funeral.[29] These larger funerals offer a quite staggering mixture of mourning and merrymaking, solidarity and aggression, with a dramatic condensation of everyday tensions. The night after someone passes away there is a long wake, enlivened by constant drumming and dancing but also by fierce outbursts of grieving. A long series of ostentatious exchanges and gifts follows the next day, culminating in a mock fight over the body, which will be finally buried in the course of the afternoon. After this, people gradually make their way home. On rare occasions a family will stage a repetition of this ritual one year later to formally end the mourning. In most cases, the descendants talk about organizing such a second event but keep delaying it—supposedly because there would not be enough money for it.

Only gradually did I discover—mostly thanks to the patient explanations of my assistant, Meke Blaise—some pattern in all the tumult and outbursts of emotions. My assistant and my other friends emphasized especially the division of roles in all these dramatic performances between the patrilineal descendants of the dead (the people of his *njaw boud* = people of the house), on the one hand, and, on the other, those who were related by marriage (*ompombelou*)—the sister's sons and the mother's brothers.[30] Of course all these terms have to be taken in what anthropologists term a "classificatory" sense: they refer to whole categories of people. The "daughters-in-law" (*otsjol*) include all women who married into the deceased's group (or even the whole village); similarly, the "mother's brothers" (*ikougou*) constitute the whole group to which the deceased's mother belonged, and so on. One of the confusing things of a funeral was (and is) that a wide array of persons can be included in each category. The delegation of the mother's brothers at the funeral could include any person who can claim some sort of relation to the group concerned. The same applied to the sister's sons or the sons-in-law.

This play of substituting and equating often meant that one person attended the funeral in two different capacities. During the first funeral I witnessed, I was completely confused by the performance of Djenadek, the mother of my assistant. Sometimes she was weeping frenziedly next to the bier, as a descendant should do, but the next moment she would be happily dancing and mocking the mourners, as is expected of the daughters-in-law. My assistant explained that his mother could actually claim that she was both a descendant and a daughter-in-law—which is in principle impossible since to the Maka kinship excludes marriage. It required some complicated genealogical reconstruction to understand through what kind of substitutions and equations Djenadek managed to claim the double role she acted out with such abandon.

A big funeral thus becomes a dramatic acting out of the map of kinship and affinity that links persons and groups. It highlights also the staggering scope of this network: as in the case of Djedanek's double role, strenuous genealogical efforts may be necessary in order to reconstruct all the links that seem to be self-evident to the people concerned. Funerals graphically illustrate the seemingly boundless elasticity of Maka kinship.

· · · · · · · · · · · · · · ·

From the onset of the mourning ritual, the *otsjol* (daughters-in-law) play a key role. As soon as the drummers begin to beat the rhythm of mourning to announce that someone has died, the daughters-in-law put on their dancing gear (especially a tuft of raffia fiber attached to the backside so that it moves frantically with the shaking of the hips) and start to circulate with much *animation*, as people would say. With a big pot of chalk in their hand, they must "catch" all the descendants of the deceased in order to paint their faces white. This effectively sets apart the group that must mourn because their group "has suffered such a big loss." In stark contrast, the daughters-in-law themselves must enliven the long nightly wake with happy and often aggressive dancing. They often pull some of the descendants out of the mourning group around the bier and engage them in a sort of dancing duel. People explained to me that the elated dancing is an expression of their rejoicing, as members of a rival group, over the humiliation of their husband's family, which has lost such an important member. They sometimes literally dance one of the mourners into the mud as a dramatic expression of their "victory."

The Maka have a saying "Marriage is war" (*Ba djisse domb*), meaning that one can marry only outside one's kinship (*bjel*)—that is, into a potentially hostile group.[31] All relations with in-laws are, therefore, marked by a precarious mixture of aggression and solidarity. Anthropologists call such relations a "joking relationship," but this term can have the unfortunate implication that any show of aggression in such a context is only a joke. The Maka funerals are good evidence that there is, indeed, an attempt to channel the aggression involved, but these occasions also show that such "jokes" can easily get out of hand.

In the course of the night the daughters-in-law will be joined by other in-laws—the "sons-in-law" and the "sister's-sons"—who will engage in similar outrageous behavior. For instance, one of the sons-in-law will enter the circle of dancers, stop the drum with some exaggerated dancing steps, throw some money in a pot in front of the main drum, and give a speech that is clearly meant to shock. He may say that the deceased was already too old to satisfy all his wives; or that he was impotent from syphilis; or he may complain about the meager reception. At the same time the sister's-sons will prowl through the compound and grab any chicken or pork they can lay their hands on. All this behavior is all the more shocking since in everyday life daughters- and sons-in-law have to show so much respect to their father-in-law that it resembles a relation of avoidance. However, according to my friends, the deceased is meant to be pleased by all this aggressive behavior. His *djim* (ghost) is still hovering around and will be proud that now everybody can see what "dynamic" daughters- and sons-in-law he attached to his group. Indeed, people say it is an "obligation" of the in-laws to behave in such a way.

Toward noon, the funeral ritual reaches its climax with the *kombok*. The daughters- and sons-in-law gather in the bushes outside the village and form a sort of warriors' column. They are strangely attired. Some carry items associated with the warriors of former days (old spears, branches to camouflage themselves); women sport men's clothes—jackets, caps—preferably of the deceased. In front stands a man with a big spear. All of a sudden, yelling loudly, the whole group will rush into the village and charge the house of the deceased. The house is shaken to and fro; the bereaved relatives offer some symbolic resistance but are chased away from the bier; furniture is thrown outside and set on fire, animals are clubbed to death, sometimes even guns are fired, and the whole village is in uproar. The daughters-in-law grab clothes of the deceased and put them on, dancing frenziedly. At one funeral I attended, one of the women came rushing out of the deceased's room sporting a topee that clearly had belonged to him. The women may perform elaborate pantomimes for bystanders: one woman will "challenge" another, who will seek cover behind the back of a bystander. The first one will make furious "attacks" until both of them get some money from the harassed onlookers; then they dance on, contentedly. The *kombok* is generally associated with mocking and scorn; people do everything in a crazy and deliberately wrong way—you throw a fowl still with its plumage in the frying pan, you burn chairs, you "cook" palm nuts on an unlit fire, women dress as men, and so on.

After a while, the *kombok* will calm down somewhat. Food is distributed, and the descendants take up their positions around the bier. This is the time for negotiations and payments. The groups of the various "houses" (patrilineages) each take up their own position in front of the house. First it is the turn of the sons-in-law. They are called upon one by one by a blood relative of the deceased who, brandishing a long spear, runs around and points his spear in the direction of the village of a particular son-in-law. In a booming voice he will make a few nasty remarks (for instance, "Isn't this the village where no cacao can grow?" if the people of this village have a reputation for being lazy). The son-in-law concerned then must step forward, stop the drums, give a speech (once again full of insulting jests about the deceased or the meager reception), and throw some money in a bowl. The amount is carefully written down by one of the descendants of the deceased.

Next the daughters-in-law must be paid. They will assemble, dancing, in front of the house, still in their *kombok* attire. They sing all sorts of songs: French songs they learned at school, modern Cameroonian top hits, but also songs about the deceased—how stingy he was, how hard they worked for him, that he lived so long only because they took such good care of him. The favorite theme of these songs is *minkounde njame* (now the vengeance is mine). The elder of the deceased's group offers them some money on the order of a few thousands francs CFA (a few dollars), but the daughters-in-law indignantly refuse the amount with shrill cries and much laughter. Encouraged by the sons-in-law, they chase the mourning descendants away with hilarious mirth, grab the bier, and rush off with it on their shoulders—the corpse bouncing up and down—to "hide" in the bushes behind the house. The elder must then follow them in order to "buy back" the corpse by making a higher bid. As a rule the women will send him away scornfully a few times, but in the end they will accept the money.

Then follow the most difficult negotiations: with the deceased's mother's-brothers, who must dig the grave and be paid for their labor. But more important, the corpse must again be "bought" from them: the deceased was also their blood relative, and if they are offered too little money, they might take the corpse along and bury it in their own village. These negotiations often develop into a long palaver in which the elders of both groups confront each other with much rhetorical prowess. The elders of the deceased's group will stress that they have little money at their disposal since the coffee and cacao crops are not yet sold, or that the deceased never received much from his mother's brothers. The elder representing the mother's brothers will argue that he and his people came from afar, that the bride price of the deceased's mother was never paid in full, and so on.

When the elders finally reach an agreement (in the 1970s, up to thirty dollars might be paid), the time has come for the actual burial. The mother's brothers carry the corpse to the grave, and there is a highly emotional speech—in former days by the elder of the deceased's group, but now increasingly by one of the deceased's sons, who reads out a written statement in French accompanied by a translation in Maka. Often a Christian catechist (Catholic or Presbyterian) will say a prayer, and then the body is put into the grave. This is the moment when the mourning becomes general: the blood relatives writhe with grief, and even the sons- and daughters-in-law now show themselves deeply moved.

Once the grave is filled up, the funeral is over. Further exchanges are settled behind close doors, and most of the people begin the journey back home.

. . . .

The above is only a very condensed summary of all the complexities of the funeral ritual. But it may suffice to give an idea of the power of this ritual in affirming someone's belonging within the kinship order. Especially the vivid confrontations of aggression and humiliation between the different groups—maybe part of a "joking relationship" but nevertheless heavy with emotions—give a strong sense of rootedness. As the elder of my village explained to me: "The funeral is very important. If an old man dies, an important link disappears. We must remember that we are related. So all the people concerned have to be there and show how they are related."

However, it is also important to emphasize that the sketch above applies only to a given moment in time. Funeral ritual is extremely dynamic, and throughout the 1980s and 1990s I noticed constant innovations and additions. Characteristically, these had to do especially with the payment of money. Already in the account above from the 1970s, it is quite striking how central a role money payments had come to play throughout the duration of a funeral. As elsewhere in Africa, the Maka were constantly complaining about the rising costs of funerals.[32]

The newer additions often express other tensions than the one between grieving "descendants" and aggressive *affines* highlighted above. Especially at the moments when money is involved, the funeral becomes also a locus for acting out gender oppositions. In the late 1970s, I noticed that at the funeral of an elderly woman, the other women of the village were gathered around a cord they had stretched across the road. They stopped all the male passersby and demanded money from them. Apparently this surprised my assistant. He muttered angrily to me, "This is completely new. These women are turning the funeral into a market."

Such innovations can give the funeral ritual an ambivalent tenor. The emphatically "traditional" character of the ritual drives home how much each person is subjected to the kinship order: people "belong" because they have their place in this order. Yet at the same time people are actively involved in this subjectivation by constantly adding new elements and extending the scope of these rituals. This is what makes the funeral remain so relevant in new contexts.

*   *   *

In the 1990s these kinds of funeral rituals quite unexpectedly became a central element in the new-style political debate, as an ultimate test of belonging (and thus also of exclusion). Remember how Professor Bejanga, the unhappy chairman of the Association of the Elites of the Eleventh Province, became quite angry when the *Herald* journalist confronted him with the statement that "someone's home is where he is buried when he dies" (chap. 2). Apparently he felt that this seriously endangered his own belonging in the South-West. Similarly, in the debates about Professor Roger Gabriel Nlep's "theory" of *le village electoral*, so often cited by advocates of autochthony, it was precisely the ongoing practice of Bamileke immigrants in Douala and Yaoundé of burying their deceased "at home"—that is, taking their corpses back to the village—that led to the conclusion that they should also go home to vote, since that was apparently were they belonged. The most pregnant postulation of the funeral as the supreme test of belonging came, however, from Samuel Eboua, the éminence grise of Cameroonian politics, quoted earlier, who in 1995 categorically stated that a Cameroonian was a stranger anywhere in the country except "where his mortal remains will be buried." This is indeed a far cry from the principle emphasized in Ahidjo's constitution in 1973, during the heyday of nation-building, that every Cameroonian citizen "has the right to settle in any place...no one shall be harassed because of his origin"(see chap. 2).

This marked turnaround coincided with certain changes throughout the country in the celebration of funerals. The rituals came to emphasize increasingly the obligation of urbanites and especially the new elites, who had emerged so quickly in the decades after independence, to return "home" for a funeral—of course for their own funeral but also to attend those of their relatives. In 1991 I had the honor of presiding over a jury at the University of Yaoundé which had to judge a *thèse de troisième cycle* by Luc Mebenga on funeral rituals among the Ewondo.[33] This was a special time. The whole continent was being abruptly affected by a wave of democratization, and, as mentioned, this led to particularly fierce riots in Cameroon. Indeed, at the very moment of this defense, the university was occupied by gendarmes, who sought to quench ongoing student protests against President Biya's stubborn refusal to convene a national conference, as other authoritarian African leaders had agreed to do. The gendarmes' presence on campus was highly shocking to both students and staff; there was no precedent for it. The soldiers swaggered around the buildings making it clear that they considered the whole campus occupied territory.[34]

In this tense atmosphere, somewhat to my surprise, considerable attention was given to a topic that was not really central to the thesis.

Mebenga's descriptions of Ewondo funeral rituals were reminiscent in many respects of the patterns sketched above regarding the Maka: here also the different kin groups confront each other in fierce performances of aggression and humiliation. Mebenga analyzed the funeral as a highly collective moment, affirming the individual's belonging to the kinship group. The members of the jury focused, however, on another aspect: the precarious role of urbanites in these ceremonies. In fact, the central case of the thesis was the funeral of Mebenga's own father, for which he had returned to the village, accompanied by other "sons of the village" who had made their careers in the city. A few passages in the thesis highlighted the author's own commitment to the obligation "to come home":

> Every Ewondo knows very well that, though one is allowed to leave one's natal village, coming back to it—be it to live there or to be buried—is a moral obligation that no one can neglect. This idea finds its concrete expression in the burying of the placenta of a newly born child. This is to remind the child that even if he becomes a vagrant [*vagabond*], he should never forget to return to the place where his placenta is buried. This act ties any Ewondo to his village, as a child is tied to his mother by the umbilical cord. Indeed, this conception demands that every Ewondo be buried in his village of origin so as to reaffirm this union forged by his birth. Even the authorities nowadays respect this custom—which one finds nearly everywhere in Africa—by facilitating the transportation of the corpse of all its civil servants to their village in order to be buried there. This is one of the few customary norms that are still respected today. (Mebenga 1991:234, my translation)

Mebenga analyzed this aspect of present-day funerals especially by contrasting the emphasis on the collectivity and solidarity in the "traditional" funeral on the one hand (without, however, clearly specifying to which period he referred) and the rise of individualism marking present-day relations on the other. He saw urbanites' enduring commitment to being buried in the village as a highly positive sign, indicating that some of the old emphasis on the collectivity still remained. While their socioeconomic interests oblige them to orient themselves toward their new surroundings (the city), their "spiritual interests" make them retain their links to "the sacred place" of the village; and, still in Mebenga's words, this is why they keep wanting to be buried in their native soil, "which does not move despite all social change" (Mebenga 1991:235).

However, during the public defense, a quite different view on the funeral "at home" came to the fore, notably from the interventions of jury members from the same area. Professor Marcien Towa congratulated the candidate on his courage, since everybody knew how difficult it was to return to the village for a funeral. Professor Jean Mfoulou emphasized this even more strongly: "It is like this among us: anybody who emerges has to excuse himself constantly with those who do not emerge." And both professors stressed that the funeral in particular was an occasion when the villagers could make urban elites "excuse themselves" in the most distressing ways. Indeed, many of my colleagues from the forest area had told me stories about how they dreaded the moment of return, especially for a funeral. The wild behavior of the sister's sons of the deceased on these tumultuous occasions could easily be directed against urban visitors, who are always reproached for not sharing enough of their new riches. The funeral constitutes an ideal moment for villagers to get even with their "brothers" from the city.

The role of urban elites at the funeral expresses, therefore, a deep paradox. On the one hand, they feel ill at ease. It is a dangerous moment, as they are being forced to venture again into the intimacy of village brothers. They know that they will be assailed by all sorts of requests, and it is risky to refuse these outright. Everybody knows what disastrous consequences the jealousy of relatives can have if it is not appeased by sharing—after all, there is a direct link between jealousy, intimacy, and witchcraft.[35] Yet this does not erode their commitment to the village as a basic principle. As Mebenga emphasized, the obligation to be buried "at home" in the village remains unbroken. He seeks the explanation for this in the elites' moral commitment to this "sacred place," where they know that the placenta was buried at their birth.

The main cities in Cameroon, as in many other parts of Africa, lack major cemeteries. As noted above, it is seen as a social disgrace if someone has to be buried in the city, for it means that he has no family anymore; apparently there is no one waiting in the village to bury his body there.[36] There is a strong reminder here of the remarkable statement, quoted in chapter 1, by the director of the recent Opération Nationale d'Identification in Gbagbo's Ivory Coast that "whoever claims to be Ivorian must have a village.... Someone who is incapable of showing he belongs to a village is a person without bearings and is so dangerous that we must ask him where he comes from" (quoted in Marshall 2006:28).

Yet despite all this apparent authenticity, there is good reason for relativizing this principle of the need to be buried "at home" which now seems to be so sacred. The present-day preoccupation with this issue was encouraged by a special political setting: the new "autochthony" strategy of the Biya regime that allowed this regime to survive democratization. As indicated in chapter 2, when the institution of multipartyism could no longer be avoided, the regime reacted rapidly, ordering all civil servants to organize themselves in *associations des originaires*, go to their region, and bring back the votes of "their" people. The Maka elites whom I interviewed a few years later were still overwhelmed by it. They were being ordered to do exactly what had been anathema ever since Ahidjo's rule: marshal local support rather than depending on the favors of the party leadership. Elite associations, which had always been seen as signs of division since they were not sanctioned by the party, now became an important tool of the government to consolidate its position in the face of the return of multipartyism and democratic competition. The regime's shrewdness in suddenly opting for a completely different strategy is illustrated by the fact that none of the Maka *fonctionnaires* seemed to have considered not complying with it—after all, they depended on the regime for their salary (which in those days was highly precarious). This control over the bureaucrats turned out to be the regime's main asset in containing the opposition parties.

However, even if this switch took place without much noise—elsewhere also, the *fonctionnaires* accepted their new role in marshaling votes for the CPDM regime—it brought quite a different conception of how a politician should behave. The time when ambitious party cadres had to compete for the favor of the party leaders while keeping their back to the village—when fomenting local support was lethal since it laid one open to accusation of *subversion* by omnipresent rivals—was over. Anybody who wanted to climb in politics had to ensure support in his (or her) own area. Proving one's belonging to villagers who were often quite skeptical became an absolute must. It is in this context that the funeral at home became a central issue as a condensation of powerful preoccupations with belonging. Moreover, in this context the rituals of autochthony and belonging assumed the kind of self-evidence—typically appearing almost "natural"—that was repeatedly highlighted above.

· · · · · · · · · · · · · · · ·

In 1996 I visited Mamfe in the dense forest of southwest Cameroon on the Cross River, near the Nigerian border. Of course, people had warned me of how bad the road would be: the road to Mamfe enjoys general notoriety in Cameroon as one of the worst in the whole country. And indeed we spent a whole night on the *piste*, struggling and pushing the car to get it out of the mud. Upon our arrival in Mamfe, the many stories being told along the road suddenly took a new turn. The talk of the town was the burial of the wife of a general who originated from Mamfe—he was seen as one of the town's main elites. Of course, he had arranged for a spectacular funeral at home, but without taking into account that the rains had already begun. There was true *Schadenfreude* in people's stories about how all the region's elites, who evidently had to attend the funeral, had gotten stuck in the mud. Some had taken days getting their Pajeero (the new status symbol of the elites, replacing the Mercedes) through. Apparently, many people felt that this served them right—it was their own fault for not having done anything for so long to get this road tarred. For the burial of the general's wife the transport problems became so overwhelming that for a time it seemed it would have to be postponed to the dry season. But finally the general took a drastic decision: he "chartered" several helicopters from the army and had his wife's body, together with the main guests, flown in from Yaoundé.

It was noteworthy that people talked about this as if the whole exercise was more or less self-evident: "of course" urbanites had to be brought back to be buried in the village, so it was only "normal" that the general went to such great length to bring his wife's body back home. However, older informants had other stories to tell. To them this whole emphasis on burying "at home" seemed to be new.[37]

. . . .

There are many parallels elsewhere in Africa of similar debates on what appears to be an old tradition but, at least according to some, is a new issue in the context of the politics of belonging. The most well-known example is no doubt the case of SM in Kenya (see Cohen and Atieno Odhiambo 1992). The funeral of SM, a famous lawyer in Nairobi, led to a fierce fight—finally decided in the national Court of Appeal—between his Luo clan and his Kikuyu widow over where the corpse should be buried. The widow wanted to bury SM on their sumptuous farm in Nairobi and emphasized his identity as a modern Kenyan citizen. But the representatives of the clan insisted that modern or not, SM was a Luo and that a Luo should be buried "at home." Surprisingly enough in view of all this emphasis on "custom," Oginga Odinga, the grand old man of Luo politics, sided with the widow and declared that to him the stress on burying at home was new. According to him, the Luo, as an expansionist group, used to bury their dead in the areas where they migrated to, in order to confirm new claims.

In another example from the southwest, reported by Francis Nyamnjoh, similar concerns led to a violent struggle over the body and an armed intervention by the gendarmes. This funeral was a particularly tragic one: the deceased was a woman, a Banyangi from the Mamfe area, who unexpectedly died during a study period in the United States. Her husband, a Bamileke living in Buea (the province's capital), went to great lengths to have the body transported "home"—in his view, Buea—in order to have her buried near their house there. However, the woman's own family decided that her real home was in the family village near Mamfe. Therefore, they had the gendarmes interrupt the funeral (which had already started), "arrest" the body, and take it to Mamfe. Apparently, the husband's status as an immigrant weakened his claim to have his wife buried in Buea. So the forces of order were ready to intervene in support of Banyangi "custom" that the corpse should be brought "back home"—this is, to the village (see Geschiere, Nyamnjoh, and Socpa 2000).

Striking in this case is the tension between kinship—the claims of the wife's family—and autochthony. In most of the examples from Africa the strength of autochthony is that it seems to be closely intertwined with kinship: the soil of the village of birth is such a powerful referent since it is the place of the ancestors, so references to "soil" and "blood" seem to shade into each other. Yet even where the funeral becomes a celebration of belonging, as in the Maka example above, it highlights a potential tension between the two: kinship implies exogamy—recall the Maka proverb quoted above, "We marry our enemies"—and therefore the introduction of "strangers" into the local group. Maka funeral rituals center on this potential tension, with their heavy emphasis on the opposition between patrilineal descendants (the mourners) and "in-laws" with their festive ostentation. Thus it is only logical that among the Maka, as in other patrilineal social formations, the funeral of a woman can easily lead to a conflict over where she should be buried—in the village of her husband or in that of her brothers. Apparently she is not "really" an autochthon. Even in its articulation with kinship—soil and blood—autochthony is less "natural" than it pretends to be: the definition of which kin is to be considered autochthonous still depends on the context and can be open to contestation.

The idea of the funeral "at home," self-evident as it seems to be for the protagonists of autochthony, is clearly full of tensions, which come even more starkly to the fore now that the burials of important persons have become highly politicized. In a recent article, Nantang Jua (2005a) gives an overview of a series of recent cases that created quite a stir. The funeral "at home" of the famous novelist Mongo Beti, a staunch opponent of both Ahidjo and Biya, became a real scandal, since the widow refused any involvement by President Biya; but the village, eager to please the authorities, went directly against her wishes. Even more shocking—at least to many Cameroonians—was the case of a Bamileke living in France, who was cremated. When his French wife brought the ashes in an urn to the village, people were bewildered. Of course she should have brought back the body to be buried in the ground of their forefathers—this was where her husband belonged. Indeed, the Bamileke are often cited as a group for whom the tradition of bringing back the body to be buried goes back far into the past.[38] Yet precisely among some groups of Bamileke migrants, the custom of the burial at home seems to be diminished. For instance, in Yaoundé, rumors are circulating that the Bangangte (a Bamileke chiefdom) increasingly bury their deceased in the city, sending only a stone—symbolizing the skull—home to the village.[39] Clearly, even what seems to be a basic technique of the self—burial in the village as proof of one's belonging—allows for all sorts of variations and adaptations.

In general, the ambiguities and dynamics of the funeral at home highlight how much the *dispositif* of belonging that came so strongly to the fore in Cameroon and elsewhere in Africa in the 1990s draws other contours for the subject than did the official approach to nation-building during the preceding decades. While in the time of nation-building ambitious politicians had to learn the kind of tightrope act that was sketched above for Maka politicians—keeping careful distance from the village and launching uncertain forays into the higher levels of the politico-administrative hierarchies so as to attract the favors of a fickle and suspicious party leadership, they now have to do the opposite: they must ensure their belonging by showing themselves to be "men of the people" with carefully chosen ostentation. This balancing act can be equally tricky, as the uneasy position of urban elites, worried about being assaulted by their own "brothers" during funerals at home, shows. There is a hidden paradox: even if politicians can no longer allow themselves to turn their back to the village, their new interest in emphasizing how much they belong there does not concern the village as such; it rather has become an essential asset in their struggle to get access to the state.

* * *

The funeral has become one of the most important moments in this styling of the self. I have focused on it here since it is such a powerful element of subjectivation, producing its subjects but at the same time being (re)shaped by them. Yet there are other key moments in the crystallization of belonging. An increased emphasis on building a house in the village was noted in chapter 3. Among the Maka this was a significant change in the 1990s, for until then the elites had shown great reluctance to "construct" in the village, to the great annoyance of their "brothers." This has been rapidly changing.[40] The spectacular forms many elites choose for their new houses—one even built an imitation of an emir's palace from north Cameroon—highlight the deeper meaning they want to give to them.

Another aspect, already mentioned, is the formalization of *associations des originaires*, now also in the East Province. These associations were certainly not active only when the president ordered his bureaucrats to go home and campaign for him, in the early 1990s. Subsequently they acquired a life of their own. Many now seek to play a central role in development initiatives for "their" region. In 1996 I was invited to give a lecture for the new association of the Maka Mboans[41] in Yaoundé, and there was a marked contrast between this meeting and the informal elite parties I had attended in the 1970s. The 1970s gatherings emphatically shunned any formal profile—there was never anything like an agenda, and there was certainly never any discussion of politics: the dark presence of MP Malouma was a guarantee of that. In contrast, the new association in 1996 was fully formalized: a chairman, a whole board with all sorts of functions, and a clear agenda for the meeting. The agenda was also expressly political; the main question was what role the elites could play alongside the government in finally helping development take off in their area.

Elite associations are now often closely linked to NGO activities—they try to attract development funds in all sorts of ways—and this creates, at least in many parts of the East, new tensions between elites and villagers. While in the days of the one party villagers would reproach "their" elites for neglecting the village, the latter's new role as "men of the people" founding their own NGOs often raises suspicions among their "brothers" in the village. Local spokesmen are quick to denounce the elites for trying to exploit the village—all the more so since the new forest law opens up new opportunities for these urbanites to take the lead in the exploitation of local forest resources.[42] An even greater problem for the new elite associations is that the segmentary implications of local discourses of belonging—highlighted before in all sorts of contexts—manifest themselves here as well.

Compare, for instance, the fate of REFID, the large elite association for the whole *department* of the Haut-Nyong (mentioned in chap. 3), which manifested itself in the area in the 1990s when the exploitation of the rich forest resources of the East Province became a major issue. After an auspicious beginning as a major intermediary for defending regional interests at the national level, it soon got divided up, first among *arrondissements* and now even among *cantons*. This apparently inevitable process of fission into ever smaller elite associations provides again a vivid illustration of what was called above the "segmentary" quality of discourses of autochthony and belonging.

An equally telling illustration of how difficult it is to escape this divisive trend in discourses of belonging—which has come up already in various contexts—is the *feymen*, Cameroon's by-now famous equivalent to the Nigerian perpetrators of 419 fraud. The latter are better known in the West, with their intrepid e-mail messages and computer fraud. The Cameroonian *feymen* specialize in counterfeit money and casino fraud instead, but their overall profile is the same: lavish and ostentatious spending—always smartly dressed according to the latest fashion, flashy cars, showing off their *petites* (girls), living in huge mansions or renting entire floors in the Hilton and other first-class hotels. No wonder that both Dominique Malaquais (2001a and 2001b) and Basile Ndjio (2006) describe them as the new role model for the Cameroonian youth. The image of the old role model, the *fonctionnaire* who due to his education rose rapidly in public service, was severely damaged in the 1990s. As said (chap. 2), between 1994 and 1996, with the devaluation of the franc CFA coming on top of drastic cuts due to structural adjustment, the real value of government salaries decreased by 60 percent, and even these meager salaries were often not paid for months on end. This led to growing doubts about the value of education: why should parents sacrifice so much for the schooling of their children if even university graduates could not find a decent job? The real *nouveaux riches* were the young *feymen*, most of them with hardly any education at all. Ndjio describes with some relish how these new rich made it their specialty to humiliate ministers and other higher functionaries by ordering more champagne in a nightclub or by leaving with the *petite* who had seemed to be destined for the minister that evening.

Of special interest for our theme is that at first the *feymen* seemed to transgress current discourses of belonging and opposition. According to Ndjio, most of them were poor young men from among the Bamileke (supposed to be the country's most dynamic group, especially in economic respects). In the early 1990s, several of them participated in the *villes mortes* campaign to protest the devious ways in which the Biya regime tried to circumvent democratization. However, disappointed by the stalemate in which the promising political actions of those years ended, many of them later switched to informal or even illegal forms of enrichment, often with greater success. Ndjio emphasizes that they did so in ways that were highly shocking to older generation of Bamileke entrepreneurs, always seen as the most prominent group within the newly emerging bourgeoisie of Cameroon. Not only did these *feymen* seem intent on making a mockery of the creed of parsimony that was supposed to have been the secret behind the emergence of older Bamileke bourgeoisie, but also, even more shocking, they consistently refused to stick to Bamileke custom that any newly rich person will build a house in the village, marry a Bamileke woman, and provide jobs for young men from his village. Instead, the *feymen* behaved like real urbanites, constructing their luxurious villas in Douala or Yaoundé. Malaquais offers quite remarkable details of their peculiar but always flashy tastes, marrying girls from the city and refusing to act as brokers for "their" village.

However, Ndjio shows that toward the end of the 1990s all this changed, especially due to determined efforts of the Biya regime to co-opt these dangerous rivals. In the early 1990s the regime used to denounce the *feymen* as bandits and traitors—no wonder since, as said, the latter seemed to enjoy to personally humiliate the higher-level *fonctionnaires* who used to be seen by all (especially themselves) as the absolute pinnacle of Cameroonian society. But the regime changed its attitude toward the end of the decade and began to address the *feymen* no longer as bandits but rather as *jeunes entrepreneurs* and promising elements in Cameroonian society. Successful *feymen* were now invited to assume major political posts in the party hierarchy and in Parliament. Yet this clearly had a price: they had to conform to the existing order of belonging; only thus could they bring in the votes of "their" people. Ndjio offers fascinating cases of *feymen* who made an abrupt turnaround: divorcing their first wife and marrying a woman from the village, actively supporting the young men from the village, and above all finally constructing a proper house there. He shows also that all this had its flip side. One question is whether, thus captured in the discourse of autochthony and belonging that came to dominate Cameroonian politics in the 1990s, these "young entrepreneurs" can still function as proper *feymen*—after all, one of the secrets behind the latter's success had been their lack of commitment to any institutional setting. He shows also that not all *feymen* allowed themselves to be co-opted. Others rather preferred to steer clear of the regime's overtures and went even more determinedly "global," trying to succeed in ever more creative "coups" on new "fronts" (Europe, Southeast Asia). However, this meant that they increasingly turned their backs on their own country.

Striking in all this is the ease with which more cooperative *feymen*, who initially had seemed to break out of the political discourse of ethnicity and autochthony, were brought to heel—another graphic illustration of the growing emphasis on belonging and the rituals by which it is affirmed (building a house in the village, burying at home, and so on). The *feymen* example also highlights the limits of a notion like identity in such contexts. Clearly in this context "belonging" is not prescribing an identity with a fixed substance, determining people's behavior. But neither is it merely manipulated by the *feymen*, clever entrepreneurs though they may be. The approach outlined above in terms of subjectivation and *dispositifs disciplinaires* might have certain advantages for understanding this example as well. The rapid succession of turns and shifts in the *feymen*'s short careers seems to be related to different *dispositifs disciplinaires*. The state's efforts to bring these unruly young men to heel work only because they are intertwined with pressure from the village. Indeed, "the" village might constitute a *dispositif* that works to discipline at least as rigorously as the state's apparatus. Apparently different *dispositifs* can be articulated in quite unexpected ways. This suggests that subjectivation in such contexts might be marked by ruptures and tensions.

* * *

The above outlines a clear contrast between the rituals of nation-building on the one hand and those of autochthony on the other. The latter seem to offer good examples of what has been called "aesthetic concentration," resulting in a "shared experience" among the participants (see Meyer 2006 and chap. 1 above). The rituals of nation-building seemed to be much less engaging, and indeed they disappeared almost completely when the political context changed.

How are such differences to be analyzed? First of all, it is important to historicize this transition in order to bring out the complex layeredness of the processes concerned. The great danger is, of course, assuming the up-surge of apparently old rituals of belonging, like the funeral, to represent the return of some sort of "traditional" identity now that the state has been weakened—as if these traditions themselves had not been affected by processes of change. A more historical view of the 1990s switch can bring out more complex articulations. The autochthony discourse, cen-tered as it is on the village, in many respects follows a colonial model—much more than a precolonial one.[43] As emphasized above, in most of the forest zone the social formations were seminomadic and highly inclusive in character up to the colonial conquest (around 1900), and it was only the colonial state—with its obsession to fix people[44]—that forcefully created more or less stable villages. Nation-building, in contrast, sought to impose a wider territoriality—the national space—as the proper context for be-longing. In line with this, it strongly discouraged elites from building up their own clientele in the village; instead, these elites were made to under-stand most forcefully that they depended only on the national leadership. The national ideology also included recurrent references to the soil—*la patrie*. However, this soil reference was quite a novel one, constructed re-cently and lacking the "traditional" trappings that make the appeal to the village seem so "natural"—even if in most cases the village hardly goes back further than colonial times.

Yet as noted, historicizing autochthony's appeal—relating it to chang-ing politico-economic contexts—has its limits. What remains to be ex-plained is its great emotional appeal despite its tortuous history. Here, due attention to the layeredness of *dispositifs disciplinaires*—as central in ongoing processes of subjectivation—and the new articulations they al-low for in changing contexts may make possible a more nuanced insight into the changes in the 1990s: both in the apparent cogency of rituals of belonging and in the ways people are involved in their reshaping.

A term like *techniques of the body* applies very well to the autochthony rituals, which are most graphically inscribed in the body. During the fu-neral, the mourners (the patrilineal descendants) have their faces painted white, while the "daughters-in-law," as representatives of a potentially hostile group, dance in unremitting frenzy in order to express their theme of "vengeance is mine" and the sons-in-law disguise themselves in cam-ouflage outfits formerly worn by warriors. Such ritual indeed "produces a subject" in no uncertain ways. People clearly contributed to constant innovations in these rituals, and this did not require any explicit coordi-nation. The different roles were (and are) so much part of their behavior that changes can be included almost automatically. On all these points the rituals of nation-building were markedly different. The disciplining involved in those rituals had nothing inherent; on the contrary, the omnipresence of the threatening gendarmes underlined time and again how much the leadership insisted on retaining explicit control. Any spontaneous or excited behavior by the people was deeply distrusted and was generally quelled by violence.

The appeal to the soil and the techniques of the body that underline it "work" in the case of funerals. The power of the ritual in relating people to the village—including the urbanites who are often reluctant to attend but end up participating with ostentatious gusto—can hardly be exaggerated. Here one can certainly speak of an "aesthetic concentration" that brings a "shared experience of authentic belonging" (cf. Meyer 2006 and chap. I above). The particular mix of grief and frenzy that marks the funeral is a powerful reminder of the village as a crucial orientation point for those who belong there. However, such a concentration also has its weaknesses. Powerful as the rituals of autochthony may seem, they are at the same time highly confusing in their effects—precisely because they bring a narrowing of vision. In many respects the ritual seems intent on ignoring obvious facts. The consequence is that it produces subjects who have to deal with inconsistencies as a way of life. Remember what was said about the Cameroonian elites who participate in the funeral in the village as a sign of their belonging but do anything to maintain distance; clearly they would not dream of ever going to live there again. Similarly, the elite associations in southwest Cameroon, discussed above, stage cultural festivals in the village, but the clear aim of their leaders is to thus strengthen their position in national politics.[45]

Glossing over such apparent inconsistencies and making them livable is precisely what a ritual is supposed to do. Yet ignoring them has its costs in practice. As said, the appeal to the local in autochthony discourse is often about defending special access to the national or the global. Autochthony ritual seems to realize the concentrated sensorial experience, which gives it so much force in these contexts, by ignoring such articulations and focusing on the local to the exclusion of all other aspects. Hence its practical ineffectiveness in a world shaped by migration, and its succumbing to the local as a limitation—the endless tendency to split up into ever smaller segments, the destructive obsession with internal purification and the unmasking of fake autochthons.

The rituals of nation-building too made a formal appeal to the soil: *la patrie* that had to be defended against foreign incursions. There as well, the discipline that was imposed related directly to the body: the women of the party parading in their uniform outfits; the military order the gendarmes tried to maintain during rallies and parades; sometimes— in Mobutu's Congo much more than in Cameroon—special music and dances. Yet these rituals were much less effective in bringing about such a concentration and a sensation of a shared experience. People were certainly eager to join in them (the "connivance" emphasized by Bayart and Mbembe), but as soon as the politico-economic context changed, they lost their meaning. Of course, many of the "ideological apparatuses" of the state remained—the school system, the health service, the judicial apparatus. Yet as in the rituals of nation-building, a heavy authoritarian and top-down approach prevails in all these institutions. Discipline is constantly imposed in harsh ways. One can wonder whether this is a conducive context for the kind of autodisciplining that gives the funeral rituals such a "natural" profile. The strong emphasis on social engineering—in both the policies of the (post)colonial state and development discourse—gave the rituals of nation-building an artificial, "made-up" profile that hardly brought about a shared sensation of authenticity.

In the next chapter, the epilogue of this book, I will elaborate on this with the help of further comparisons. Here it may be useful to note the greater resilience of a less official element of nation-building that seemed to have emerged in its own right and that the regime was never able to control completely: soccer. In Cameroonian soccer games, bodily aspects—for the audiences as much as for the players—acquire the self-evidence and emotional power that characterize funeral rituals. It is therefore worth noting that soccer is one of the few elements of nation-building that remain important in the new political constellation, in Cameroon as in other African countries; it even seems capable of muting autochthony on certain occasions. Consider the upsurge of national pride in Cameroon any time that *les Lions indomptables*, the national team, seem ready to live up to their former glory. Compare the national excitement, despite major internal strife, in Ivory Coast in 2004 when the national team made it to the World Championships (cf. Yeré 2004). With soccer, and to a lesser degree other sports, the population feels free to participate in the vicissitudes of national teams in physical ways, which seem to generate their own forms of discipline. This was brought home to me during a soccer match in Senegal, when I forgot to rise when our cheerleader called on us to stand up and sit down (a version of "the wave"?). During the great soccer matches in Africa, the audience is expected to be as active as the players—supporting their team with magical rituals, led by a *marabout*,

and ensuring constant but disciplined movement on the tribunes. My failure to participate in due form broke the unity of the support of our team—
so people glared at me furiously when our team lost the match.[46] The contrast with the more official rituals of nation-building, with their coercive
orchestration, is telling.

Appeals to the body and the soil work only under certain circumstances. Only in certain settings can an appeal to autochthony evoke such
a powerful vision as in the African cases discussed above. It may be helpful, therefore, to conclude with a brief look at other transitions from
nation-building to autochthony in Europe as well as Africa.

CHAPTER SEVEN

Epilogue: Can the Land Lie?

Autochthony's Uncertainties in Africa and Europe

The foregoing has shown that the appeal to the soil, so central to the naturalizing tenor of the autochthony notion, can have quite different meanings. In the preface I quoted the eloquent slogan *La terre, elle ne ment pas* (the land does not lie) with which, in 1940, *Maréchal* Philippe Pétain tried to support his appeal to all French to "restore" France under the Vichy regime—that is, in close collaboration with the victorious Germans.[1] These poetic words sum up most cogently the appeal to the soil as an ultimate truth—an appeal that has emerged in many different guises in the preceding examples. Indeed, in comparative perspective the soil can say many things, depending on the context. The soil as such may be a powerful icon with a heavy emotional charge, but it does *not* speak for itself, even though autochthony's protagonists appear to think it does.

The comparison in chapter 6 of rituals of nation-building and autochthony in Cameroon already developed this point. Both kinds of rituals appeal to the soil, but only the rituals of autochthony—notably the funeral "at home"—feature the kind of condensation that gives the link with the soil so much emotional force. Or, in Birgit Meyer's terms (cited in chap. 1), only in this setting does the "style," or more broadly the "aesthetics," of the ritual acquire the kind of concentration that captures people in a "shared perception of the world." Chapter 6 showed that the rituals of the time of forcible nation-building (the 1960s and 1970s) serve as a marked contrast. At the time, people were eager to participate in these rituals as well. Yet the latter disappeared with the onset of democratization, almost without leaving any trace. The rituals of autochthony—particularly the funeral—seem to be made of hardier stuff.

It may be useful, though, to remember that the Cameroonian scenario of autochthony superseding nation-building as an alternative kind of belonging fits in a specific politico-economic context. As said, autochthony is certainly not replacing the nation-state—not even in Cameroon. It is rather grafting itself upon the framework of this state. One particular reason that nation-building and its rituals disappeared so quickly there may have been the extremely authoritarian approach of Ahidjo, Cameroon's first president. His style of nation-building betrayed a deep distrust of any form of popular excitement—possibly because of his bitter struggle with the country's first revolutionary movement (see chap. 6). Thus nation-building became an extremely pedagogic and even coercive affair. Another reason was the political choice of his successor Biya, once democratization was imposed on him, to play the autochthony card. This relates to the broader economic context, notably the fact that the opposition was mainly supported by the more entrepreneurial groups, whose members were migrating in large numbers to the country's main zones of economic activity. Hence access to land—to make farms or to build a house—became a crucial bone of contention with broad political implications. It was in this context that the appeal to the soil in the rituals of belonging described earlier acquired such a powerful emotional charge.

Yet as said, there is no automatism here. An appeal to the soil may relate to concrete political or economic interests, but this does not suffice to trigger the "aesthetic concentration" that calls forth a "shared perception of the world" with emotional cogency. A rapid comparison with parallel and different situations in Africa and Europe can help us to explore under what conditions autochthony can produce the "techniques of the body" and forms of "autodisciplining" through which an appeal to the soil produces an "authentic form of belonging" that can override other interests and preoccupations—and, even more important, when such an appeal lacks such cogency.

Varying Patterns of Nation-Building in Africa and Their Implications

Throughout the African continent, the 1990s brought a turn from explicit nation-building to other rituals of belonging. Yet the specific practices of nation-building continued to influence the crystallization of alternative forms of belonging in every part of the continent, albeit along quite different trajectories. This alone might justify a return to nation-building as a topic—which, as noted, was dealt with too one-sidedly in a modernization perspective. Especially the variable practices by which the new regimes tried to shape their national citizens merit closer attention. Even within the limited context of Francophone West Africa, there were great variations in this respect which still have direct impact on present-day preoccupations with autochthony and belonging.

Ahmed Sékou Touré's Guinea offers an interesting comparison with Cameroon. At a formal level there is a strong contrast between Sekou Touré's rigid (though quite personal) version of Marxism and Ahidjo's *liberalisme planifié*. But in practice there was a clear convergence in the strong emphasis of both regimes on *subversion* as an omnipresent danger. In Guinea, this was—again as in Cameroon—clearly related to the circumstances of decolonization. The growing paranoia of Sekou Touré was historically linked to the fact that he incurred the wrath of Charles de Gaulle by making his country opt for independence as early as 1958, thus staying out of the Union Française and obtaining immediate independence. With the ensuing fear among the new national elite, especially Touré himself, of a coup from outside, the regime's ever more paranoiac exhortations to *vigilance* against the threat of *subversion* became an important channel for mobilizing the citizens. Sékou Touré went much further in this than Ahidjo, turning the country into one great concentration camp.

Another special trait may have been of even more consequence for the shaping of national citizenship in Guinea: Sekou Touré's Programme de Démystification, launched immediately after independence.[2] Mike Mc-Govern's challenging PhD dissertation (2004), which will be published soon, depicts vividly how powerfully this operation came to affect everyday life, at least in certain parts of Guinea. The basic idea behind the operation was that all secret practices in local societies had to be exposed in public in order to break the mystifying spell of "tradition"—a blatant example of Marxism put into practice. The often violent ways in which this was imposed, especially on so-called animist tribes in the country's periphery (that is, the non-Islamized groups), made it a most dramatically enacted rupture. Local traditions might be conserved, for instance, as artifacts in national museums or as dances for public performances in the capital, but such public forms were designed to break their secrecy and hence their hold over people's minds. This demystification was deemed necessary in order to "liberate" people and open them up to reeducation as socialist citizens of a truly "modern" nation.

The success of this reeducation may have been limited, but it is clear that the Demystification Program had considerable effect at the local level. The main one was that the most affected "animist" groups became heavily marked as the nation's nonmodern Other. McGovern (2004, chap. 5) explains that under such conditions autochthony notions became quite powerful at the local level, especially among one of these marginalized groups, the Loma in the southeast of the country. There is now, again, a growing emphasis on the funeral as a test of belonging and also on other chtonic rituals (sacrifices that only autochthons can make). Apparently, even a draconian intervention like the Demystification Program could not thwart the resilience of such autochthony rituals. However, in Guinea the impact of autochthony discourse seems to remain limited at the national level. Sékou Touré's forceful efforts toward nation-building, shaped by a particularly rigid version of Marxism, were followed by a clear ethniciza-tion of national politics. But the ethnic mosaic of Guinea is such that it made little sense for Sékou Touré's successors—even though they as well were confronted with democratization—to play the autochthony card.

At the level of formal ideology, Ivory Coast seemed much closer to Ahidjo's *liberalisme planifié*. Especially in the late 1960s and 1970s, its ca-cao boom led to its being heralded as proof that capitalism could work in Africa. President Houphouët-Boigny set the example himself by pos-ing as *le grand planteur*. Yet here again there were considerable differ-ences in the ways in which the regime tried to forge a national citizen-ship. The main one—curiously, almost ignored in the literature about Ivory Coast nation-building when this process was still in full swing[3]—was Houphouët's open door policy, mentioned in chapter 4. This distinctive policy was to become a hot issue during the collapse of his model of na-tional growth in the last few years before his death in 1993. Throughout the 1960s and 1970s, nation-building in Ivory Coast meant the regime's consistent support for migrants. Various factors may have played a role here (see Arnaut 2004 and Chauveau 2000). Initially, a strong factor was the heritage of the Pan-Africanist notions of the early RDA (Rassemble-ment Démocratique Africain), the broad nationalist movement in French West Africa in the 1950s, with Houphouët as one of its main leaders. Di-rect economic considerations must have played a role also: as noted ear-lier, at least for some time the influx of migrants, both from the northern part of the country and from neighboring states, was an important factor in the rapid growth of cacao production in the south.

In the ideological propaganda of Houphouët's regime, African hospi-tality—focused on the role of the *tuteur*, ready to welcome strangers—

became a recurrent theme. People were admonished to accommodate strangers in accordance with these "African" principles. This culminated in Houphouët's audacious 1963 statement "La terre appartient à celui qui la met en valeur" (the land belongs to the one who works it).[4] There is a clear contrast here with Ahidjo's policy of "national equilibrium," which generated stiff competition within each regional group. As noted above (chap. 4), when Houphouët's model came up against a fixed frontier of increasing land scarcity, especially in the southeast, it triggered a powerful xenophobic reaction – first in terms of *Ivoirité* and later expressed in Gbagbo's more diffuse ideas of *autochtonie*. Thus the Ivorian formula for nation-building set the stage for an obsession with purifying the nation of foreign elements. In this context, autochthony acquired quite a different meaning than in Cameroon. In the latter country it imposed a distinction within the citizenry – *les autochtones* claiming to be first-class citizens, thus relegating strangers, even those who were recognized as Cameroonian citizens, to a secondary category. In Ivory Coast, a more drastic version of autochthony prevailed, which implied that citizenship should be restricted to *autochtones* only (cf. President Gbagbo's plan for the Opération Nationale d'Identification—chap. 1). At first autochthony in Ivory Coast was mainly directed against immigrants from neighboring countries, but increasingly it also excluded northerners who came from areas that used to be part and parcel of the Ivorian nation-state. In this conception, rituals of autochthony could be seen to coincide with rituals of nation-building, though a drastically reduced "nation" was now envisioned.

In such a context the appeal to belong to the soil acquired great emotional power. This triggered, for instance, a quite forced intellectual production around the idea of *Ivoirité* as common to all *Ivoiriens* (even though among them one had to distinguish between those with mythological origins and others without such an origin). Mass rallies of the Jeunes Patriotes became festivals of autochthony with so much tension and excitement that they certainly produced a "shared perception of belonging" that overrode other forms of identification. Again, all this excitement arose within a specific politico-economic context. A crucial factor was that the cacao boom, for decades the basis of the country's prosperity, was running up against the limits of its spatial expansion, and this directly increased the locals' resentment of Houphouët's immigration policies. Access to land became an issue with particularly broad political ramifications. In such circumstances belonging to the soil acquired great emotional force—even to the extent of sometimes usurping the idea of the nation. Yet emotionally powerful as the vision of autochthony became in this context, it shows the same limits as in the Cameroonian case: the narrow obsession with the local that it imposes combines badly with protagonists' preoccupation with global circuits (recall what was said in chapter 4 about the Young Patriots' hesitation to return to the village and their tendency to sell local assets so as to purchase a ticket for France or, even better, the United States).

*   *   *

Bayart and Mbembe are certainly right in emphasizing the connivance of the *dominés* in the rituals of nation-building (cf. chap. 6 above). Even though these were highly authoritarian performances, they were taken seriously by many people who were eager to get access to the all-powerful state, one way or another. Yet the swift evaporation of much of this ritual suggests that these more official forms of nation-building had hardly struck root. In all three cases considered here—Cameroon, Guinea, and Ivory Coast—a clear rupture took place in the 1990s. The time-honored rituals of nation-building to which people had become accustomed ever since independence—the well-organized rallies of support for the national leader, controlled with considerable show of force by the gendarmes, the disciplined parades of schoolchildren in their neat uniforms, and the dances of the women of the one party—quite suddenly disappeared. They were replaced with more lively political rituals, more attuned to multipartyism and even more to a celebration of local belonging.

It is worth noting, however, that the rituals of nation-building themselves appeal to the soil, though in a different sense: in all these cases, the national soil and the idea of *la patrie* were central. Why then did these rituals hardly work—in the sense of bringing about an "aesthetic concentration"? A tentative answer might point to the clearly artificial, "made up" character of nation-building rituals. What all three cases above have in common was that this forging of citizenship—like the nation-building process as such—was deeply marked by notions of social engineering, with the regime trying to control the project in most explicit ways. Any open form of dissent was severely punished, and the national rituals were strictly directed and enacted, as in the example of the minister's visit to Makaland. Very much in accordance with the prevailing vision of modernization that at the time dominated not only academia but also the vision of most politicians and, even more important, the world of the "developers," nation-building was a project imposed from above. Was it the strict coordination from above that prevented the "concentration" through which a ritual can induce a feeling of "authentic belonging"?[5] A point that seems to confirm this is the resilience, noted in chapter 6, of soccer as one of the main remnants of nation-building. In most countries this sport remained central in people's nationalistic feelings, but it was also at the margins of all the dirigisme that marked nation-building. Indeed, soccer was about the only aspect of nation-building that allowed for spontaneous participation by the crowd, condensed in most dramatic bodily expressions (cf. the conclusion to chap. 6).

Autochthony and the Search for Ritual in Europe

In the European examples quoted above there is again a direct appeal to the soil as a symbol of a special form of belonging. This is given with the prevalence of the *autochtoon/allochtoon* discourse in the Netherlands and Flanders, but similar references play a role in other countries where the term *autochthony* is less current. In these European contexts the meaning of *soil* as a referent seems to be more diffuse (which does not necessarily mean that it is less powerful). In the case of the Netherlands, people appear to be hardly conscious of the chtonic root implied by the term *autochthony*. After all, here this term was chosen almost by accident. As noted in chapter 5, it became current only as the necessary counterpart to *allochtoon*, and this latter notion was introduced out of a sort of embarrassment, as a potential neutral and scientific term that could serve as a general label for all immigrant groups. As noted, the Dutch needed a novel term: the much more logical notion of *immigrant* remained anathema because up to the 1980s the country refused to consider itself an immigration country.

Yet the term *allochtoon* very rapidly lost this neutrality. It became a highly emotional notion, acquiring a clear pejorative slant. Probably this was further exacerbated by an inherent inconsistency: indeed, as noted earlier, it became more and more the question how people born in the Netherlands (the "second generation," seen by many as the main source of problems) could be labeled as being "from a different soil." By opposition, the Dutch came to identify themselves as *autochtonen*, but in this context this remained an even vaguer notion. Still, this term as well soon acquired emotional impact, although its content remained very diffuse. Chapter 5 noted some determined efforts, especially after 2002, when *inte-*

gration became the buzzword, to try to give more substance to this notion. If more pressure was necessary for these *allochtonen* to "integrate," especially in cultural respects, it was urgent to have a firmer idea of what they were to integrate into. Prime Minister Jan-Peter Balkenende appealed to common values; journalist Paul Scheffer to common stories; Rita Verdonk, minister of integration and immigration, ran into serious difficulties when she had a film made that was intended to serve as the basis for the new *inburgeringstest* (citizen's test—cf. chap. 5). Clearly the quintessence of Dutchness was not that easy to conceive.

Strikingly, in none of these initiatives did the soil serve explicitly as a referent. This was one of the reasons that in the Dutch case the meaning of the term *autochtoon* remained quite loose. In a very general sense the soil reference was there and served to give the term its diffuse emotional charge. But it was not enough to achieve the kind of "aesthetic concentration" that gives some African rituals of belonging such an emotional impact. A final example, Dutch experiments with the naturalization ceremony, will show how difficult it proved to be to give substance to the autochthony notion in a European context.

• • • • • • • • • • • • • • • •

Mid-2006 when Rita Verdonk was still functioning as minister of integration and immigration, the naturalization ceremony finally became a fact in the Netherlands. But it had been preceded by a long and tortuous debate. In a seminal paper—as yet one of the few academic publications available on the new ceremony—anthropologist Oskar Verkaaik highlights the rift that marked the very conception of this idea. It was first introduced in 2000 by Minister Rogier van Boxtel (of the last "Purple" cabinet, which became the main target of Fortuyn's attacks). Van Boxtel was one of the first to insist that people should finally accept that the Netherlands had become an *im*migration rather than *e*migration country. Taking older immigration countries (especially Canada) as an example, van Boxtel saw a naturalization ceremony especially as a welcome to immigrants and a ritual of inclusion into an emphatically cosmopolitan society.

After the government's dramatic shift to the right in 2002, under the impact of Fortuyn's electoral success, the idea was continued by the new minister, Verdonk, albeit after some hesitation and with very different intentions: the ceremony should now become an important instrument of integration. It should remind the new citizens of Dutch national norms

and values and impress on them that "divided loyalties" were not acceptable. As Verkaaik (forthcoming: 3) puts it, it was "no longer part of a proposed open policy towards immigration [as under van Boxtel] but, rather,
about tighter regulation of migration." Some of this duplicity continued
to confuse the realization of the ceremony. In a letter to the municipalities
about the ceremony, Verdonk emphasized that it should have the character of a "party"—yet clearly it was meant as quite a stern kind of party,
since it also was to be a "lesson in manners." In Verdonk's version, the welcoming aspect was relegated to the background; the ceremony rather was
to be a last, disciplinary moment in a long *inburgeringstraject* (integration
trajectory).

However, the plan for the ceremony duly respected municipal autonomy. In practice it was not the minister but each municipality that decided on the content, and at this level a remarkable uncertainty followed.
Verkaaik (forthcoming, 11) gives a most baroque enumeration of the varied
forms the municipalities invented for their ceremony. There were certain
common elements—especially lots of coffee and even more cheese. But
the more substantive elements varied widely: from symbols of Dutch *gezel-
ligheid* (local cookies and such) to soccer or windmills or the Dutch fear of
inundation by the sea. Indeed, the quite stunning variation that Verkaaik
and his students discovered in their study of how municipalities gave shape
to the new naturalization ceremony is a clear sign of considerable uncertainty about how to fill in the notion of Dutch culture.

In many places the uncertainty gave way to downright resistance to
the idea of the ceremony itself. Verkaaik (forthcoming, 12–13) quotes one
municipal official who condemned all the creativity, which for him was "pa-
tronizing"; he just wanted to stick to "empty symbols" like the flag or the
national anthem. Others even went straight against the purport of Verdonk's letter by praising cosmopolitanism in their speeches and warning the
new citizens not to give up their culture of origin. Several informants told
the researchers that the whole idea of a naturalization ceremony was "un-
Dutch." Indeed, for many Dutch *autochtonen* there is not only uncertainty
about what Dutch culture is but also reluctance to accept the very idea of
such a national culture.

• • • • • • • • • • • • • •

Thus the "aesthetic concentration" evoking "shared sensorial perceptions"—explored in previous chapters in relation to African funeral

rituals—did not come about in the Dutch case. For some new citizens, the moment of naturalization must have been an emotional one. Yet the ritual as such—maybe again because it is a blatant example of social engineering—does not condense this emotion in a compelling way. There is hardly any substantive appeal to the soil, and even though there are attempts to involve bodily aspects—special ways of dressing—one can speak of techniques of the body in only the broadest sense of the phrase.

It is important to note that on other occasions, rituals did emerge which vividly illustrate that such "aesthetic concentration" can still induce an "authentic form of belonging" in Dutch society. The most obvious example is of course the resurgence of religion in a supposedly secularizing world. But a strong second is the frenzy around national sport teams—of course first of all soccer, as in Africa, but in the Dutch case also speed skating.

• • • • • • • • • • • • • •

Since the speed-skating championships mostly take place in cold surroundings, the behavior of the "Dutch legion" there takes on especially noticeable forms. People stand in the cold in the strangest outfits, of course all in orange, the national color: men wear Scandinavian warrior's helmets with horns and huge orange wigs, women put orange birds on their heads, the few bare parts of the body are painted in orange or in the colors of the national flag. The crowd is in constant motion, singing and swaying. There is clearly a "concentration" here that evokes, at least for the moment, what is to these supporters apparently an "authentic feeling of belonging." Here again, there is no evident coordination or leadership, and the rituals (the outfits, the songs) are constantly changing; yet people seem to adapt themselves more or less intuitively to such changes. Especially this aspect evokes concepts of subjectivation and techniques of the body: people's roles are shaped by the common ritual in their adornment of the body and their endlessly repetitive movements and singing. Indeed, there is an emotional frenzy that seems to follow a basic but constantly changing scripts, just as in the African funeral rites described earlier.

• • • • • • • • • • • • • •

Similar traits are evident in other ritual moments, such as the spectacular launching of the ashes of popular singer André Hazes in 2005 by a rocket from a pier into the sea near Hoek van Holland. Hazes's songs—a distinctive style of what the Dutch call *smartlappen* (tearjerkers)[6]—raised strong emotions among many. His statue, just around the corner from my house, has quickly become a new pilgrimage site, where people keep putting flowers—often stuck between his arms with clumsy emotionality—and where no one should dare to park his bicycle (as was made emphatically clear to me when I put mine there in a moment of absent-mindedness).[7]

Can we conclude from this that the soil no longer works as referent in societies like the Dutch one, and that the focus that can empower rituals—in the sense of inspiring "aesthetic concentration"—has to be sought elsewhere? That might be too easy a conclusion.[8] Of course, a big difference from the African settings is that in Europe the large majority of the population no longer lives directly from the soil; most people do not need to claim land for a farm or a plot to build a house. Yet even here claiming a special link to the soil appears to stem from an apparently "basic" need, in which direct socioeconomic interests and more symbolic meanings of the land are difficult to separate. Thus, even though the choice of *allochtonen/autochtonen* terminology in the Netherlands was more or less accidental, the terms' reference to the soil soon acquired its own effects. As said, these notions are difficult to reconcile with the strong emphasis on integration. After all, how can an allochthon ever become an autochthon? Indeed, there is a direct link between this terminology and the quite surprising simplicity with which the media in the Netherlands keep opposing autochthons to "Moroccans," "Turks," and others, even though the latter are mostly born in the Netherlands. This suggests that the tension between the notion of *allochtonen* and the idea of integration as a process is not just a question of terminology: labeling immigrants as *allochtonen* seems to correspond to a reluctance among many Dutch—including politicians—to confront the possibility that *allochtonen* will ever "integrate."[9] In the Dutch case, the reference to the soil remains diffuse: it still evokes a certain emotionality but does not clearly focus it. It is very difficult to give the idea of autochthony more substance. Yet the emotional charge that clings to the notion is strong enough to create confusion and uncertainty.

*   *   *

So the soil does *not* speak for itself. This is why it is important to historicize notions like autochthony with their naturalizing implications. The "global conjuncture of belonging" brought a return of highly localized preoccupations, as the flip side of intensifying processes of globalization. This set the context for the emergence of autochthony movements in highly varying corners of the globe, appealing to a primal form of belonging based on a special tie to the soil. Yet in comparative perspective it is clear that, despite its naturalizing appearances, the reference to the soil is historically circumscribed. Only in some contexts and depending on specific politico-economic circumstances do references to the soil permit the kind of condensation that can imbue autochthony rituals with an overriding sensation of an "authentic form of belonging."

The question whether this is good or bad might be a futile one in view of the fact that there *is* some sort of return of the local across the globe. Moreover, it is certainly possible that in some parts of Africa present-day autochthony movements can form a new and firmer basis for the crystallization of citizenship, as some anthropologists have recently suggested (see n. 42 in chap. 2). Indeed, the articulations of autochthony with the nation-state are many and full of surprising turns. All the more reason to take the content of the discourse (whether historically correct or not) most seriously. The challenge is then how to avoid succumbing to its apparent self-evidence and the suggestion that an appeal to the soil is "naturally" the ultimate form of belonging. Both autochthony's naturalizing tendencies and its inner inconsistencies are crucial, since this paradoxical combination can explain why it can lead to so much confusion and uncertainty in practice.

The present-day global conjuncture of belonging seems to go together, all over the globe, with increasing impatience with pluralism and cultural differences between people. As Appadurai (2006) warns us, we live in a time when identities tend to become "predatory." This applies certainly to autochthony with its strict refusal of "divided loyalties" and its insistence on absolute priority for those "born from the soil."[10] However, this self-assured exclusion is in marked contrast with autochthony's uncertainty in practice. Especially its "receding" quality, encountered so often in the cases considered in this book—the uncertainty about who or what is "really" autochthonous and hence the tendency to draw ever closer circles around who/what belongs or does not belong—creates the paradox emphasized above: behind the apparent certainty of its "natural" claims, autochthony hides nagging insecurity because of the preoccupation with "false" autochthons, wolves among the sheep, who have to be unmasked. This is also why Achille Mbembe's characterization of autochthony as inspired by a vision of an "Otherless universe" is so gloomy (Mbembe

2000:25): it evokes a universe in which there can be no place for any other; yet as a consequence—and on top of this—it is marked by an almost paranoiac drive toward purification and a never-ending search for foreign elements hiding inside.

This drastic exclusionary tendency and this quest for purity make autochthony discourse problematic, in Africa as well as in other parts of the globe.[11] Already in the classical Athenian example this implied a view in which staying in place is the norm and migration the exception. All the more important to emphasize that migration is as old as human society and that autochthony's "Otherless universe" is therefore an impossibility. There may be considerable wisdom in Kwame Anthony Appiah's plea for a combination of cosmopolitanism and identity—or, to put it more concretely, in his idea that we need "common stories" in order to live together but that these stories must address diversity and allow for conversation across differences.[12]

Notes

Preface and Acknowledgments

1. This was Gyanendra Pandey. Jean-François Bayart offered me an equally powerful title, *La Terre Ment* (The Land Lies)—a reversal of Marshall Pétain's passionate (or pathetic?) slogan in 1940 *la terre ne ment pas* (the land never lies), with which he tried to persuade the French to join him and his Vichy regime in collaborating with the victorious Germans. My other first-line commentator, Birgit Meyer, did not suggest a title but gave me at least as much to think about (see further the acknowledgments below).

Chapter One

1. Cf. Clifford Geertz (2000:246): "Cosmopolitanism and parochialism are no longer opposed; they are linked and reinforcing. As the one increases, so does the other." One of the aims of this book is to highlight the fact that this applies as much to present-day Europe—marked by a sudden return of identities that were increasingly seen as parochial—as to Africa.

2. From classical Greek *autos* (self) and *chtonos* (soil).

3. This dictionary defines *autochthonous* in the sense of "son of the soil" but also in a geological/botanical sense (as in autochthonous rock formations or plants). For *allochthonous* only the latter sense is mentioned (see *New Shorter Oxford English Dictionary* [Oxford: Clarendon, 1993]). *Autochthonous* is now increasingly used in Anglophone social science texts and also in everyday language in certain areas (for instance in some parts of Anglophone Africa and in the Pacific).

4. I realize that lately colleagues and authorities from this country insist on retaining its French name, Côte d'Ivoire, even in texts in English and other languages. Indeed, in many recent publications, most of my Anglophone colleagues have switched from "Ivory Coast" and "Ivorians" to "Côte d'Ivoire" and "Ivoirians." I

would like to underline that this is a very exceptional step. Would it be so easily accepted from the Dutch if they would insist on "Nederland" rather than "The Netherlands" in English texts? or, to suggest a more sensitive example, for the Germans to insist on "Deutschland" instead of "Germany"? The claim that the French name "Côte d'Ivoire" should be used in English texts seems to be a typical expression of the identity fever that comes across so sharply in the discourse of advocates of *Ivoirité* and autochthony in that country—a preoccupation that this book seeks to relativize. I prefer, therefore, to stick to the terms that used to be current in English publications: Ivory Coast and Ivorians. The fact that, in this case, the quest for authenticity hinges on a French name, clearly of colonial origin, makes the excitement around this issue all the more surprising.

5. In 2004, after having been convicted for racist propaganda, the Vlaams Blok (Flemish Bloc) changed its name to Vlaams Belang (Flemish Interest).

6. Ruth Marshall (2006:12), following Judith Butler, speaks very aptly of the great "performative power" of autochthony discourse in Ivory Coast.

7. Many thanks to Reimar Schefold for this reference.

8. See also Chérif 2006.

9. Indeed, the Athenians went even further by declaring their autochthony to be absolutely unique among all the Greeks: their city was the only place where the citizens—at least the "real" ones—were *autochthonoi*; therefore it could justly claim preeminence over all the Greeks, and certainly over the barbarians.

10. See Euripides 1995; unfortunately only a few fragments of the text have been conserved.

11. Socrates pretends in his dialogue that he has been trained in how to deliver an *epitaphios* (funeral oration) by none other than Aspasia, Pericles' famous spouse (or rather "partner"?). Some (Detienne 2003:21) emphasize the ironical elements in the Menexenes dialogue. However, it seems clear that once Socrates'/Plato's exemplary oration gets going, irony gives way to patriotism (see also Bury 2005:330).

12. Cf. also Pericles' famous *epitaphios* for the Athenians fallen in the first years of the long war against Sparta, and Demosthenes' funeral addresses from a later period (second half of the fourth century) when Athens was threatened again, this time by the Macedonians (Philippos, father of Alexander; Loraux 1996:44). There are, of course, striking parallels with very different times and situations. Cf. Maurice Barrès, champion of French nationalism in the 1880s, and his famous dictum that the main things needed for creating a *conscience nationale* were "a graveyard and the teaching of history" (Barrès 1925:1:25; cf. also Detienne 2003:131).

13. Detienne (2003:42) translates a variant of the king's name, Erichthonios, as "the Très-Terrien."

14. It is indeed clear that the veneration of Erechtheus, the archfather of Athenian autochthony—the king, mentioned before, who was locked inside the earth itself by Poseidon's revenge—cannot be that old. Archaeologists maintain now that the Erechteion, his temple where Athenian autochthony was sanctified, was built

between 430 and 422—that is, at the very same time that Euripides wrote his Ere-chtheus play, in which Athena orders the Athenians to build this temple (Collard, Crop, and Lee 1995:193; Detienne 2003:44). A similar tension between founding and belonging haunts Plato's *Republic*. The founder of his model city—who nec-essarily must have come from elsewhere to found this "new" city—has to acquire a certain aura of autochthony in order to create a myth of belonging: Plato de-scribes this as "a beautiful lie" that will serve as the basis for the civic instruc-tion of its newly settled citizens (Rosivach 1987:303; cf. Loraux 1996:176; Detienne 2003:56).

15. Again the parallels with present-day struggles are striking: for example, Le Pen's halfhearted attempts to reserve the notion of *Français de souche* for those who have four grandparents born in France, a proposition he rapidly had to give up since many of his followers would not meet this criterion (see below chap. 5); or the fierce debates in Ivory Coast over *and* versus *or*—that is, whether father *and* mother had to be Ivorian in order to grant Ivorian citizenship to their offspring or whether father *or* mother would suffice for this.

16. Later, this same Ion is to learn that his "real" mother is the sole inheritor of the city's autochthonous royal line. Greek stories seem to love playing havoc with lines of descent!

17. In his last chapter, Marcel Detienne also focuses on present-day historians and their ongoing contribution to the reproduction of autochthony thinking. His main example—and a quite shocking one—is Fernand Braudel and one of the lat-ter's more recent books, *L'identité de la France* (Paris: Flammarion, 1986). Braudel made his name with *La Mediterranée* (1949), showing in a challenging way how to write a history that surpassed the limits of the nation-state and nationalist thinking. So it is a bit worrying that the same Braudel starts his later book by emphasizing that, after all, a historian is really at home with the history of his own country—a familiarity that leads Braudel to project *notre hexagone* (the favorite national metaphor to indicate France and its territory) back into prehistorical times and to link the Paleolithic drawings of Lascaux to French identity. Detienne (2003:142) cites all this as an illustration of the "extraordinary weight of nationalist thinking" that in the end could constrain the view of even a historian with such a broad vision as Braudel.

18. In adopting the notion of *autochtone*, the French colonizers in the Sudan may have been inspired by earlier French policies in Algeria, where the notion was applied to the Berber culture in order to generate a split between local Arabs and Berbers. I thank Baz Lecocq for pointing out this direction for further research.

19. Recent authors emphasize that all the binary oppositions that have been used to contrast French to British colonial rule are highly tenuous: *politique des races* versus Indirect Rule, as much as *assimilation* versus association. Especially during the first decades of colonial rule, French officers had often a free hand in imposing highly variable arrangements at the local or regional level. As military

men, many of them were as impressed as the British protagonists of Indirect Rule by African chiefs and their often theatrical display of power. Still, it is also true that French governors—maybe more than their British colleagues—learned to be distrustful of the powerful chiefs, like Samory (or earlier Omar Tall), who opposed them so fiercely in the Sahelian region (see Geschiere 1993; also W. Cohen 1971; Lombard 1967; Crowder 1964).

20. In practice, however, the French also soon found themselves obliged to give chiefs—even if these were somewhat condescendingly qualified as *auxiliaires indirects*—a central role in the their colonial administration (see Crowder 1964; Lombard 1967; Geschiere 1993).

21. See Janet Roitman's seminal interpretations of the notion of *la population flottante* that became a true obsession among the first French administrators in the Chad basin (Roitman 2005).

22. See Crowder 1964; Lombard 1967; Suret-Canale 1964.

23. Cf. Malkki 1995 and chap. 4 below on the role this pejorative aspect of the notion plays in the tragic opposition between Hutu and Tutsi in Rwanda and Burundi.

24. Cf. Meyer 1999 on a similar emphasis on territorialization in the work of many missionaries in Africa, which, again, could be contradicted—especially in the first years of missionary work—by a preference for working with migrants.

25. Historians (cf., for instance, Lucassen and Lucassen 1997) may emphasize that, demographically, migration in many parts of the world was more important in earlier centuries. Yet it is clear that the facilitating of mobility by new technology conjures up a vision of a rapid increase of migration, and it is this vision that plays such a central role in much autochthony discourse. Cf. also Appadurai's powerful definition (1996) of globalization as increased mobility of "goods, people and ideas"; in this triplet, ideas are at least as important as the other two.

26. An overview of speeches by World Bank directors and other representatives from 1972 to 1989 (see Geschiere 2008) shows how deep a shift took place in the 1980s.

27. In this respect there is again an interesting difference from the related notion of "indigenous": the latter seems to retain its exoticizing tenor, as it mostly refers to "others"—people of a non-Western background. Autochthons are not necessarily the others; indeed, the term can also be adopted by majority populations in the West (see also end of section on "A Primordial yet Global Form of Belonging" above).

28. Particularly galling is the memory of the French institution of the Indigénat—the lower juridical status of the *indigènes* (in sharp contrast to the *citoyens*)—which, until 1944, gave the harsher forms of French colonial rule (coercive labor, corporal punishment) a formal basis. Cf. also the challenge implied by the quite brutal name—at least in French—of a recent film, *Indigènes*, on the generally neglected role of African soldiers in the French army in World War II.

29. Indeed, the 2007 United Nations Declaration on the Rights of Indigenous Populations has the official French title *Declaration des Droits des Peuples Autochtones.*

30. The term "Washington Consensus" was coined by economist John Williamson in 1989, in order to summarize basic and supposedly novel principles behind IMF and World Bank policies at the time. Apparently he later bitterly deplored having launched this term (see Wikipedia article on "Washington Consensus").

31. I thank Daniel J. Smith for his critical comments on this point. See also Ong 2006.

32. Striking illustrations of this penchant are given in the recent thesis by Juan Obarrio (2007) on Mozambique, which in many respects offers a fascinating view of what the author terms the "Structural Adjustment State." For instance, a senior American UNDP official assured Obarrio that "communities know who they are and know also their boundaries perfectly well"—this to counter warnings by some observers that "the" community in which his organization wants to base its new projects might in practice be highly elusive and volatile. Similarly, a British US-AID consultant insisted that "communities will be like corporations, unified single legal subjects under the new land law" (quoted in Obarrio 2007). Cf. also Lars Buur and Maria Kyed 2007, who similarly note the unexpected comeback of traditional chiefs in a neoliberal context.

33. Mbembe 2000:35; my translation. Cf. also Mbembe 2000:25 on autochthony as "le rêve fou d'un monde sans autrui," powerfully translated by Ruth Marshall as "an otherless universe" (Marshall, personal communication on autochthony in Ivory Coast, Leiden, July 2007).

34. Cf. also Carola Lentz on northern Ghana (2006:247–50).

35. See, for instance, Guyer 1993; Miller 1988. See also older literature on "the stranger" in Africa, which highlighted the various opportunities of giving a stranger a place in society, whether by integrating him or by giving him a separate but clearly institutionalized position (see Fortes 1975). William Shack and Elliot Skinner (1979) emphasized rather the growing exclusion of nonnationals since independence, but their focus was mainly on exclusion from the nation as a whole. The growing emphasis on autochthony in the 1990s made for more localist forms of exclusion, often directed against immigrants who are citizens of the same nation-state and have lived for generations in a certain area (cf. also Dorman, Hammett, and Nugent 2007).

36. That such pressure can have quite dramatic consequences was graphically illustrated by a terrible accident in the Netherlands in 2005: eleven "illegal" immigrants burned alive after the provisionally erected prison near airport Schiphol caught fire. They had been locked up there, some for months already, waiting to be deported. There was a direct link to the 2003 switch in Dutch immigration policies, when the new minister, Rita Verdonk, started an operation to extradite "illegals" on a scale that clearly surpassed the capacity of the Dutch public services to handle things with some decency (see chap. 5 below).

37. See Kymlicka 2004; Isin and Turner 2002; also Taylor 1994a and b; cf. also Saskia Sassen's emphasis (2002) on the emergence of "denationalized" forms of citizenship as at least as important as "post-national citizenship."

38. See Duyvendak, Pels, and Rijkschroeff i.p.; see also Ghorashi 2006.

39. Cf. Nora 1989. Cf. also Gyan Pandey's criticism that Nora's ex cathedra pronouncement seems to be a bit premature in light of developments in Asia, Africa, and Latin America. The more recent developments in Europe suggest that here as well "memory" is alive and kicking (Pandey 2001:9–12).

40. Cf. Arnaut 2004 on Ivory Coast; the danger of characterizing autochthony as "postnational" is of course that this obscures how strongly present-day autochthony discourse remains focused upon the nation-state. Speaking of "postnational" in this context is warranted only to emphasize that in its more recent forms autochthony discourse still remains deeply marked by the history of the nation-state and its deep variations in different regions. Cf. also Pandey 1990 on the close connections between community, colonial history, and nation-building in India.

41. Elsewhere (Geschiere and Nyamnjoh 2000:424) we have discussed autochthony—at least for Africa—as a new, emptier form of ethnicity. Recent debates have highlighted the historical, constructed nature of ethnicity despite its often primordial claims. Still, an ethnic groups needs a name, a special history, and often its own language to prove itself. Autochthony needs none of this, only the claim to have come first. This seems to make it even easier to relate to constant changes in boundary marking in a globalizing world.

42. Cf. Meyer and Geschiere 1999 on globalization as a dialectic of flow *and* closure.

43. Or as Birgit Meyer (2008:719) summarizes Bruno Latour on this: "[If] there is nothing beyond construction, we'd better take constructions seriously" (see also Latour 2002 and 2005:88).

44. Cf. Barrès 1925, and see note 11 above.

45. It would be interesting to further compare it in these respects with other forms of belonging—notably with religion and the varying ways this creates a feeling of belonging. In a religious context—at least in world religions like Christianity and Islam—there seems to be a determined effort to surpass the local and create a broader supralocal form of belonging. For such religious belonging, history must be of central importance. However, it is a rigidly controlled history—so here again belonging seems to sit uneasily with history. Ethnic claims to belong seem to be closer to autochthony discourse. In ethnic discourse, though, references to the soil are often ambiguous, since ethnicity requires, as noted, a common history (see n. 41 above), which nearly always refers to an original migration from elsewhere. In such comparisons, autochthony may stand out as based on a single but very powerful referent, the soil; yet apart from this ultimate referent it seems to be surprisingly empty and malleable.

46. See the ironizing perspective developed by Bayart 1996 and the more murderous debunking of the notion in Brubaker and Cooper 2000 (reprinted in Cooper 2005).

47. Cf. also Burnham 1996 on "the politics of cultural difference" in northern Cameroon.

48. It is striking that in this seminal text Baumann sees violence as an "anti-grammar." This is logical in his approach, since violence is meant to destroy the Other and thus robs the Self of a counterpoint it needs. There might be some confusion here between academic language (in which it is clear that a complete denial of the Other necessarily blurs the profile of one's own identity) and commonsense perceptions, in which violence, unfortunately, seems to be an effective solution. Baumann runs the risk of giving violence an exceptional status by defining it as an antigrammar; this might deny its everyday quality in practice (as emphasized, for instance, by Pandey 2006).

49. Cf. also Baumann 1999:21, where "identification" is proposed as a more dynamic alternative for "identity."

50. Foucault's notion of *techniques de soi* focused on their inscription in the body, thus rejoining Marcel Mauss's older notion of *techniques du corps*.

51. Cf. Taussig 1993:xvii; van de Port 2005:152.

52. See Bayart 1996 and notably 2004/2007, where he gives the following paraphrase of the notion of subjectivation (with reference to Foucault 1984:12, 17): "In other words, the important thing is to understand not what one is, but how one 'recognizes oneself' as a 'subject,' in the twofold meaning of the word; the important thing is this 'hermeneutic of the Self.' . . . To do this, we should not analyse behaviour or ideas, societies or 'ideologies,' but the 'problematics' through which being has to be thought and the practices on the basis of which they are formed" (here quoted from the English translation, 127–78). See also Bertrand 2002, notably pp. 85–112, for a very interesting elaboration on autochthony and subjectivation in Java.

53. Meyer uses *aesthetics* here in the older Aristotelian sense (which risked being superseded by a narrower Kantian version of the notion as the rational appreciation of beauty). Meyer and Jojada Verrips (2008) emphasize that for Aristoteles *aesthesis* rather referred to the human capacity of combining all five senses in one total sensorial experience. In this line of thought, *aesthetics* stands therefore for the capacity to bring about a shared sensorial experience that overcomes the fragmentation that many see as characteristic of the modern world. See also Verrips 2006.

Chapter Two

1. This chapter contains several passages from an article ("Capitalism and Autochthony") that I published with Francis Nyamnjoh in *Public Culture* 12, no. 2

(2000). Many thanks to Francis for his permission to use these passages in this chapter and for all his inspiration while we worked together on this topic.

2. Antoine Socpa, oral communication; see also Bayart, Geschiere, and Nyamnjoh 2001:177.

3. Of course, behind this emphasis on unity, Ahidjo's famous "politics of regional balance" (see below) reaffirmed the existence of regional, or rather ethnic, blocs as the crux of political realities.

4. To give just a rapid example: in 1971, when I started my fieldwork in the East Province, Jean Mabaya, the area's former political champion, who in the early 1960's had even been chairman of Parliament, blamed his abrupt fall (he had even been imprisoned for some time) on his mistake of publicly referring to Bamileke immigrants from West Cameroon as *allogènes*. In his view, this would have called down the wrath of Ahidjo, who would have seen it as an unforgivable sin against the official ideology of unity. Other rumors rather referred to Mabaya's plans to stage a coup. But it is true that in those days *allogène* was a term that politicians did well to avoid in official parlance.

5. See also Konings 2003 for a very incisive analysis of a similar conflict within the church in South-West Province.

6. For academic studies, see Jua 2005b; Konings 2001 and 2003; Konings and Nyamnjoh 2003; Socpa 2002; Geschiere and Nyamnjoh 2000; Nyamnjoh 1999; Yenshu 1999; Nyamnjoh and Rowlands 1998; Zognong and Mouiche 1997; for the debate in Cameroonian newspapers and periodicals, see below.

7. Present-day Cameroon is the product of a complex colonial history. After 1885 this area came under German colonial rule. In 1914 it was divided between the British and the French. At independence (1960–61) the two parts reunited, so the present-day country consists of an Anglophone and a (much larger) Francophone part.

8. *The Herald*, April 16, 1997.

9. The term *rural-urban continuum* is from Dan Aronson in a 1971 article on West Nigeria. See Geschiere and Gugler 1998 for an overview of the relevant literature.

10. See especially Bayart 1979 and Joseph 1977.

11. 1 The UPC was Cameroon's first nationalist movement, which was outmaneuvered when the French installed Ahidjo as a more cooperative partner and granted their part of the colony independence under the latter's authority.

12. Similarly, the name of the largest group among the Francophones in this area, Bamileke, seems to be a colonial invention, a corruption of an expression interpreters from the coast used for "peoples of the mountain"; prior to colonial conquest, the multitude of small chieftaincies in this amalgam had not formed a unity and had no general name.

13. There was, however, a splinter group, SWELA II, that opposed the all-too-close alliance with Biya. However, this group rapidly disintegrated in the face of

SWELA I's successes in promoting southwestern elites in the corridors of power around Biya.

14. For Bakweri marginalization, see Ardener 1962 and Courade 1982; it is noteworthy that Musonge remained prime minister for eight years, exceptionally long in Cameroonian history, and that he was succeeded in 2004 by another Bakweri, Ephraim Inoni.

15. *Cameroon Post*, November 12–18, 1996, 1, quoted in Konings and Nyamnjoh 2003:119; the latter quote also *The Herald*, June 6–8, 1997, 1, for a remarkable statement by South-West governor Oben Peter Ashu (another SWELA/CPDM diehard) during the campaign for 1997 elections: "We are ready to fight to the last man to maintain our son as Prime Minister. This is the time for all South-Westerners to be ready to die or survive.... We have the Prime Minister and what we need now is satisfaction and social amenities."

16. *The Herald*, December 13–14, 1996; my thanks to Francis Nyamnjoh for this citation.

17. Several observers maintain that without such rigging the result would have been just the inverse and Fru Ndi would have been elected.

18. An obvious question is why the major opposition parties did not succeed in following the same strategy by playing on the internal divisions in Cameroon's ethnic regions. After all, other regions are also marked by internal tensions—the "Beti area" of the Centre, South, and East provinces (generally seen as Biya's bastion) as much as the others. One answer is, of course, that it was the control over the state apparatus that enabled the Biya regime to intervene so easily in internal dissension in other areas. Another answer is that the continuing influx of Grassfields immigrants, both Anglophone Bamenda and Francophone Bamileke, forms a highly controversial issue not only in South-West but also elsewhere. Indeed, throughout Cameroon the SDF did draw the votes of these immigrants. But precisely because the rest of the population saw this as a problem, the party had difficulty in enlarging its support beyond its "own people."

19. See, among others, Nyamnjoh and Rowlands 1998.

20. Cf. *Cameroun Tribune*, no. 6037 (February 14, 1996): 1; *The Herald* 288 (February 26–28, 1996): 4; *Impact-Tribune* 7 (April/May/June 1996); Wang Sonne 1997.

21. See Austen and Derrick 1999:44, 184.

22. *The Herald* 288 (February 26–28, 1996): 4; see also *The Herald* 458 (May 14–15, 1997): 2. Of interest is that the demonstrators called themselves Sawa (sea people) and not Douala. The genealogy of the former term is not quite clear. It emerged quite recently (toward the end of the 1970s) to signal the sociocultural and linguistic affinity of people living along the coast (the Douala but also the Batanga near Kribi). However, especially since 1990, the term has come to be used in an ever wider sense. The Bakweri (many of whom, especially high up the slopes of Mount Cameroun, used to describe themselves as mountain people, with deep

fear of the sea) now identify also as Sawa, and even the Banyangi around Mamfe (150 miles into the interior) are sometimes included. No wonder people now speak of the Greater Sawa Movement. Cultural and linguistic affinity seems to have become less important as a criterion to join the "Greater Sawa" than a common fear of Bamileke and Bamenda immigrants from the densely settled highlands farther into the interior.

23. *L'Effort Camerounais*, February 23, 1996.

24. The ruling CPDM party has consistently refused to set up an independent electoral commission.

25. See, for an early example, Ava Jean in *Le Patriote*, January 11, 1993, and also the many articles by Mono Djana, a professor of philosophy at the University of Yaoundé I and a particularly outspoken supporter of the government (for an overview, see Mono Djana 1997).

26. Eboua is former secretary-general at the president's office and former lecturer at the prestigious École Nationale d'Administration. He is also an "autochthon" of the Mungo, an area close to Douala, where the local population has been swamped by Bamileke immigrants to an even greater degree than in the neighboring South-West Province.

27. See also chapter 6 on many parallels elsewhere in Africa, where the strong emphasis on burying in the village similarly turns out to be a neotradition, emerging in the context of the present-day "global conjuncture of belonging."

28. Rudin 1938; Rüger 1960; Mandeng 1973. Again, it may be useful to emphasize how rapidly such stereotypes can change: only a few years earlier, in 1891, when the Bakweri of Buea defeated a panicky German expedition force, a completely different ethnic stereotype of especially the mountain Bakweri prevailed in German writings; for a short period they were depicted as fierce and dangerous barbarians. See Geschiere in press (b).

29. The land issue had a much broader resonance in this region because of the Germans' large-scale expropriations to create their plantation complex. In German times, the Bakweri hardly had any chance to protest against this (though the link with the "apathy" noted by the Germans and their reluctance to work on the plantations—on their own land!—may be clear). But under British rule, there were increasing demands by Bakweri politicians for a return of the land (especially in 1946, when the former German plantations were handed over, despite all Bakweri protests, to a newly founded parastate agency, the CDC [Cameroon Development Cooperation]; see Molua 1985). In this context as well, the political charge of autochthony ideas is clear. Despite the Biya regime's ostentatious support for autochthony movements and its professed intention to protect "minorities," it seems deaf to Bakweri demands that, with privatization approaching, CDC lands should be returned to their rightful Bakweri owners (Konings and Nyamnjoh 2003:173).

30. National Archives Buea, Ag/15a, Minutes of the Bakweri Clan Council Meeting, March 15, 1944. This absolute refusal to have strangers represented in

Native Administration was at the time quite new. In 1927, for instance, the assistant divisional officer proposed appointing a representative of the Hausa community in Buea as a member of the Buea Native Court. The district head (already Chief Mbele Endeley III) and the other court members agreed, apparently without any protest. However, then, the resident (the assistant divisional officer's superior), clearly a purist of indirect rule, blocked this innovation: "How can we appoint a stranger on a Native Court?" (National Archives Buea, Te 1, letter by ADO Buea, February 14, 1927, and answer by Acting Resident Buea, April 1, 1927).

31. In Francophone Cameroon, already by 1962 Ahidjo succeeded in suppressing all opposition parties; either their leaders were locked up or they accepted inclusion in Ahidjo's one party, the Union Camerounaise (UC). In Anglophone Cameroon, Ahidjo's counterpart, Vice President John Ngu Foncha (from the North-West), ensured that his party, the KNDP (Kamerun National Democratic Party), completely dominated politics. In 1966 Ahidjo imposed a merger of his UC with the Anglophone parties into the UNC (Union Nationale Camerounaise), which now also acquired an English name (National Cameroonian Union, or NCU).

32. See, for instance, Ardener 1956 and Matute 1988; however, Ardener (1956: 23) mentions also that mythical ancestors some Bakweri informants mentioned seemed to correspond to Douala ancestors.

33. In 1987, the incumbent at that time of the Bonjongo chieftaincy, Samuel Mbengou Efessoa, asked me whether I spoke German. When I confirmed that I did, he produced a document from 1914 in which the German authorities appointed his father (and predecessor) Lucas Woka as *Hauptmann* (chief) over the villages of the "Lower Bakweri" around Bondjongo. I dutifully translated it for him, and he was clearly very satisfied with the contents. He kept wondering whether "the Buea people had such a document."

34. According to my informants, this was mainly because of serious dissension within the Endeley family; see Geschiere 1993. However, in those days the government chose to leave many chieftaincies vacant, especially in the southern and eastern parts of the country, where chieftaincy was generally seen as a colonial creation without traditional roots. In his 1986 book, President Biya himself had advocated a gradual "weakening of traditional authority" since it was mostly hereditary, while his policy would be to strengthen more democratic local communities (1986:56). The quoted phrase evoked indignant reactions from the western and northern parts of the country, where many people were proud of their traditional chiefs and felt that Biya as a southerner (Bulu) had no understanding of traditional chieftaincy. In this respect again there was a dramatic change around 1990.

35. This happened in November 1991 Again, this date is not accidental. After 1990, with the onset of democratization, the Biya regime made another U-turn in its attitude vis-à-vis chiefs. Suddenly vacant positions were filled all over the country, including the southern areas. Chiefs at the higher echelons now receive a

salary from the government. Like civil servants—who, as mentioned, were encouraged to create regional elite associations—they are therefore hardly in a position to oppose the regime. They also seemed to offer an alternative channel to mobilize votes for the regime, now that the one party had lost its monopoly. In the west and northwest, where chieftaincy was (and is) a strong institution but where many of the subjects wanted to vote for the SDF and against the regime, this put the chiefs in a highly precarious position (see Mouiche 2005).

36. For interesting comments on both Endeley's "coronation" and the "revived" *ngondo* ritual, see *Times and Life: Cameroon's Monthly Magazine* 1, no. 8 (1992). See also Austen 1992.

37. This was indeed quite a change. At the end of the 1980s people's relation to the sea became a topic of lively discussion in Buea for very practical reasons. With the onset of the economic crisis (formally announced by President Biya on TV in 1987), people looked for alternative sources of income. Smuggling to Nigeria became a tempting alternative. However, the best route from Buea was over sea in often highly unreliable canoes. Women in particular expressed a morbid fear of this. "How can I go in a canoe? I belong to the mountain!" as my good friend Charlot from Buea exclaimed.

38. See, for instance, Konings and Nyamnjoh 2003:131.

39. It should be noted, though, that the numbers involved are very different here: in 1990 the Bamileke would still constitute only 20 percent of the city's population.

40. See Socpa 2003:79 and Ava Jean in *Le Patriote*, January 11, 1993.

41. In Yaoundé access to the soil seems to be more important than the funeral, since here the "autochthonous" Beti also bury their dead in villages that are often at considerable distance from the city.

42. That such recurrent tendencies can be of direct practical relevance may be clear from an emerging academic debate on how to evaluate the new role of elite associations and the affirmation of regional belonging in African politics. My emphasis here has been on the divisive impact of the politics of belonging—notably because, at least in the Cameroonian case, the regime tried to use elite associations and the general preoccupation with autochthony to divide the opposition (cf. also Nyamnjoh and Rowlands 1998 and Konings 2001). This view has recently been criticized notably by a group of British anthropologists (Evans in press; Mohan and Hickey 2004; Englund 2004) who see these regional associations rather as valuable building blocks for a new kind of nation-building, less imposed from above—both in Cameroon and elsewhere. These authors stress that there is no necessary contradiction between ethnic identification and national citizenship. It is certainly true that all sorts of articulation between local belonging and the nation-state are possible, depending on the changing politico-economic context. Yet I am wondering whether these authors do not underrate the segmentary implications of current discourses of autochthony and belonging. Even in the South-West,

from which several of the more positive evaluations of new elite associations come, these seem to be in a constant process of splitting up as soon as substantial prizes are to be divided.

Chapter Three

1. This chapter further develops an argument from a contribution I wrote for a volume edited by Harri Englund and Francis Nyamnjoh, *Rights and the Politics of Recognition in Africa*; see Geschiere 2004a.

2. For an overview of the dramatic changes in the World Bank's approach to development, see Geschiere 2008a.

3. There have been some exceptions. In the town of Yokadouma, the UNDP had regular support (this UNDP is generally seen as the party from the north; indeed, some groups in Yokadouma have historic links to the Adamawa); and in 1996 the SDF (seen as the party of the Anglo-Bami) obtained a majority in the municipal council of Bertoua, the province's capital.

4. This was in striking contrast with the bank's insistence on the completion of the pipeline from Chad to the Cameroonian coast, which would cross right through the forest zone and encountered—like the exploitation of the Chadian oil reserves in general—fierce resistance from environmental advocates. It seems that the bank's solid support for groups combating further depletion of the forest is meant to balance its equally firm insistence that Chadian oil reserves be opened up.

5. This highly simplifying overview of the intricacies of the forest issue on the ground are based on my experiences as one of the supervisors of the social science research project for a large-scale, multidisciplinary program organized by Tropenbos (Wageningen, the Netherlands) and Institut de Recherche Agricole pour le Développement, or IRA (Yaoundé, Cameroon) aiming to develop a model for such a sustainable exploitation of the forest. The research for this program took place between 1992 and 2000 in the Kribi area (South Province); I profited from the possibility of comparing with my earlier research in the East Province. Moreover, the program enabled me to undertake a brief stint of fieldwork in the East to check on recent effects of the new forest law in that region. See the overall report on the social science research projects for this program (Van den Berg and Biesbrouck 2000).

6. It concerns law 94/01 of January 20, 1994, *portant sur le régime des forêts, de la faune et de la pêche*. See also its "decree of application" 95/33 of August 23, 1995.

7. Even the new law does not abrogate this principle. However, under the new *plan de zonage*, which was executed as part of the preparation of the law, a limited part—indeed a very limited part—of the state domain is set apart as a special zone within which local communities can create their own forests and get them registered by the state.

8. However, as said, the area available for the creation of community forests is strictly limited by the new *plan de zonage*, which largely respects the state's claims on all uncultivated territory.

9. In the East Province these were, notably, the Dutch SSDL project in the Lomie/Messok area, the Belgian PFC project around Messamena, and the API/ APFT program around Dimako.

10. See notably Millol and Pierre 2000; Nguiffo and Djeukam 2000.

11. However, a British DFID project working within the Ministry of Environment and Forests in Yaoundé produced a manual sketching a detailed outline of the procedure; this certainly contributed to the surprisingly widespread response to this part of the new law. By February 2001, eighty-nine applications for a community forest had already been submitted to the ministry, the large majority coming from Est Province. Of these, thirteen had already been approved, and two had even made a first start with the exploitation of their forest. All thirteen that had been approved were heavily supported by outside projects. Estimates were that about 50 percent of the rest were also advanced by a project, while the others where promoted by external elites from the region.

12. For a trenchant criticism of a development policy that tries to base itself upon "the community," see Bähre 2002 (on African National Congress policies in present-day South Africa). On the notion of community and its pitfalls more generally, see Pandey 1990; Bayart, Geschiere, and Nyamnjoh 2001; Amit 2001 and also Amit's recent collection (2002).

13. Cf. Laburthe-Tolra 1977; Geschiere 1982; Guyer 1985; Burnham 2000.

14. Another nickname of this new weed was (and is) *bokassa*.

15. The SIPs and SAPs were two consecutive experiments by the French after 1900 to impose special taxes on the new cash-crop production by the peasants in order to carry out collective projects—which were seldom to the interest of the peasants themselves. The meanings of these abbreviations—Sociétés Indigènes de Prévoyance and Sociétés Agricoles de Prévoyance—were thus quite ironic. Cf. Suret-Canale 1964:299, who relates the quite peculiar name of the SIPs to the general complaint among the French colonial authoriities about the *imprévoyance* of the *indigènes*. See also Mann and Guyer 1999.

16. See Geschiere 1982. I am referring here to one of Talcott Parsons's famous "pattern variables," "ascription" versus "achievement." In "traditional" societies status would be mainly "ascribed," while in "modern" societies it would more often be "achieved"; and of course "kinship"—often illustrated with examples from Africa—was seen as some sort of primal form of ascription. This all too simplistic contrast of "ascription" as supposedly prevailing in African societies with "achievement" prevailing with "us"—incorrect on both sides—is still omnipresent, though often in more implicit forms than it was in the heyday of "modernization" theory.

17. This fear of "being eaten" directly refers to "witchcraft," which is supposed to thrive in the intimacy of kin, especially when inequality and jealousy play a role.

The urban elites are supposed to be much richer than their kin in the village (indeed, many are); therefore it would be particularly dangerous for them to return for too long into the intimacy of the family in the village (see Geschiere 1997; Geschiere and Nyamnjoh 1998).

18. Earlier there had been little economic incentive for the elites to invest in the village. The main resources in those days—cacao and coffee plantations—required considerable investment of labor. In practice this led to severe problems for the few elites who did try to create larger plantations around their village of birth. The locals mostly prefer to work on their own farms, and elites who tried to recruit labor from elsewhere (some even tried to make Baka ["Pygmies"] work for them) ran into difficulties time and again (see Geschiere 1982).

19. REFID stands for Rassemblement des Fils et des Filles du Haut-Nyong pour le Développement. Kul Bebend means literally "Force of the Bebend" (a subgroup of the Maka). The Mboans are another subgroup.

20. In a 2001 circular of the project, one of the Dutch experts wrote, for instance, with some sarcasm: "Only now we find that these villages do have elites."

21. Interestingly, it concerned a Maka woman from the same area, who had had an affair with a Frenchman. The latter had given her some money when he left the country. According to the villagers, the woman had used her money to obtain an official *vente de coupe* in quite irregular ways; according to my friends, she had also used her funds to influence the *autorités administratives*, who in their authoritarian way helped her to cheat the villagers out of their rights. Various stories about local confrontations with the woman's workers indicate also how much the times have changed: in various locations her workers were chased away, in one village an engine of hers was blocked by the villagers and stood inactive for months without any intervention of the gendarmes—which would have been unthinkable a few years earlier. Indeed, as Alain Karsenty (1999) has shown clearly, the new approaches to the exploitation of the forest, imposed mainly by donors, will deeply affect the state's control over these regions.

22. The example is discussed in a paper by Philip Burnham and Monica Graziani (2004)—still one of the few studies to analyze in detail the vicissitudes of the new law's application at the local level.

23. The Baka are the "Pygmy" group living in this area—see chapter 4 for their particular role in relation to the new opportunities created by the forest law.

24. It is an interesting question why these "strangers" had migrated to this far-out village, from which the road seems to lead to nowhere. There were rumors that they were involved in smuggling through the more inaccessible part of the forest to Gabon and Congo Brazzaville, but I could not verify this.

25. See Geschiere 1982. The impact of the precolonial slave trade from the coast must have been minimal in this part of the forest. In the second half of the nineteenth century, the Maka and other groups in the east were terrorized by warlike bands of the Yebekolo and Mvang, who must have already had access

to firearms from European factories on the coast and who used these to force the groups farther in the interior to "pay" them regular levies of young boys and girls. But slavery within these groups themselves cannot have been that far developed.

26. That is, a man of another Bagonkou segment; apparently the group had become so big that this act of adultery was no longer considered to be a minor affair between "brothers."

27. A complicating factor to the forest area is that everybody agrees that the "real" first-comers are the Baka ("Pygmies"). All other groups tell myths of origin that explain how they came and found the Baka already present. This is also why the latter are supposed to have a really deep knowledge of the forest. Yet for the villagers the term *autochthony* does not seem to apply to these first-comers— apparently since they do not qualify as "citizens." For more on the Baka and this striking equation of autochthony with citizenship, see chapter 4.

Chapter Four

1. See note 4 in chapter 1 for an explanation of why I prefer to retain the English name of this country, rather than giving in to the recent insistence of Ivorian colleagues and authorities that the French name (Côte d'Ivoire) should be used even in English texts.

2. *Notre Voie*, July 28, 2002, quoted in Marshall 2006:28.

3. *Le Patriote*, March 21, 2002, quoted in Marshall 2006:27.

4. About the *donzo*, see Bassett 2003.

5. In the 1980s, Gbagbo—then a professor of history—was, for instance, associated with CODESRIA (Council for the Development of Social Science Research in Africa), a prominent African center for social studies, located in Dakar and certainly then of strongly Marxist inspiration.

6. Moreover, CURDIPHE published a review with a similarly ambitious title: *ETHICS* (*Etudes et théories de l'humanisme ivoirien pour la synthèse culturelle*).

7. CURDIPHE 2000, quoted in *Politique Africaine* 78:66–67, my translation; cf. Arnaut 2004.

8. CURDIPHE 1996:46–50; quoted in *Politique Africaine* 78:67–69, my translation.

9. A typical example of this tension is, for instance, Laurent Gbagbo's startling claim, in his 2002 book on the Bété, that the latter are truly autochthonous to the southwest area of present-day Ivory Coast. Indeed, under Gbagbo's leadership, "his" Bété became the main bearers of the autochthony ideology in Ivory Coast. However, Dozon (1985) shows that this group is a good example of an ethnicity that crystallized in the confrontation with colonial rule (the very name Bété was not in use prior to the colonial conquest). Moreover, the various groups that nowadays constitute "the" Bété have oral traditions on migrations from various sites into their present homelands. The background to Gbagbo's claim will be clear:

the Bété can play their present-day role as the country's autochthons par excel-
lence, leading the struggle against foreign invaders, only if these older historical
narratives about migrations are ignored.

10. *On est ensemble,* broadcast on Channel I, National TV Ivory Coast, February 23, 2003, quoted in Konate 2003:66, my translation.

11. See also Chauveau 2000; Dozon 1997.

12. Cf. Li 2000 and her emphasis (noted in chapter 1) on ecological concerns as
an important factor in the "global conjuncture of belonging" and its xenophobic
implications.

13. Chauveau and Dozon 1985; Chauveau 2000; Dozon 1985; Losch 2000. See
also Ruf 1988; Boas 2005.

14. The saying *Ivoirien aime bureau* seems to apply more to the southern
groups than to the northerners.

15. In 1947 the two colonies were separated again administratively.

16. Demery 1994:73, 115, quoted in Losch 2000:19.

17. Dembélé 2002:166 and 2003:38; Arnaut 2004:236. This idea was also present
in many of the formulations of President Bédié and his intellectuals concerning
l'ivoirité—no wonder that this notion had little appeal among other groups.

18. Cf. also Banégas (2007) on the subsequent proliferation of *parlements, ago-
ras, sénats,* and other *congrès* in the townships of Abidjan as spaces for *débat
démocratique* and political socialization of the young.

19. In earlier years he was president of FESCI; cf. also his quote above that he
could no longer believe that Hitler was bad, since Western media are so unreliable.

20. Initially notably the Dyula were seen as an "avant-garde économique du
progrès" (Dozon 1997:786; see also Delafosse 1912); after cacao cultivation took
off in the 1920s, Baoule migrants were considered to be particularly important for
the *mise en valeur* of the more fertile south.

21. To summarize briefly, the PDCI, Houphouët-Boigny's former national
party, was incapable of nominating a generally acceptable candidate because of the
blatant misrule and unpopularity of Bédié, its former leader; the same Bédié had
effectively blocked the candidacy of the candidate of the north, Ouattara, because
of his supposed foreign origins. Moreover, the predations of the army of General
Gueï had made the latter an equally impossible candidate. Thus Gbagbo was the
only serious candidate left. The turnout was around 36 percent, and Gbagbo accumulated a little over half of the vote. The Ivory Coast drama might have evolved
differently if these elections had offered a more open choice.

22. See Li 2000 and chapter 1 above.

23. Indeed, the European states with their recent obsession for closing their
boundaries are a striking example of this trend. See chapter 5 below and Bayart
2004.

24. In this respect Henry-Michel Yeré's paper (2006) adds interesting elements.
He starts his text on Ivory Coast's autochthony—which he characterizes as "a battle for the soul of the nation"—with the memorable date January 26, 1992. However,

this turns out not to be a high moment of incipient autochthony but rather a cele-beration of national unity after the Ivorian soccer team won the African Cup of Nations. Yere's paper is from 2006, but Ivory Coast's success in making it to the soccer world championship in Germany in 2006 became another high moment of nationalism, with several star players emphatically defending the country's unity. I will come back to the role of soccer as the main remnant of the period of forceful nation-building in Africa and its potential role as an alternative focus of belonging (chap. 6).

25. Marshall borrows the title from a menacing quote from Mamadou Kouli-baly, the number two of Gbagbo's FPI. As his name indicates, he is partly of north-ern origin, which seems to make him all the more vehement in propagating the party's xenophobic ideology. Koulibaly claimed that the war would be salutary for the nation: "at least we'll be able to know who is who" (Marshall 2006:11).

26. Another point highlighted by the Ivorian case is the intertwinement between autochthony and new religious movements. Dozon (1995; 2001) shows that the up-surge of autochthony was preceded in the southwest by a remarkable switch in the tenor of prophetic movements that proliferate in this area. Formerly prophets had often admonished people to work for national development, borrowing all sorts of elements from the Christian churches. But already in the early 1980s a new prophet acquired great popularity in the area with sermons that went in a completely oppo-site direction, preaching a kind of religious version of autochthony for defending people's own cultural heritage and belonging. Mike McGovern (2005) discusses an example of an even more militant *pasteur*—he was indeed heavily armed—invading the southwest in early 2005 from Liberia, with a similar message. The productive interface between autochthony and religion, just like autochthony's precarious relation with the colonial project and with subsequent national citi-zenship, are points of a more general relevance which I will return to later.

27. Maquet (1961) proposed characterizing the Tutsi-Hutu relation in Rwanda as one between castes. The big problem is, of course, that intermarriage between the two groups was far from rare. However, as in Yugoslavia or Ivory Coast, such practices of intermarriage hardly served to limit the violence between these groups.

28. This would be the main intention of the quite enigmatic "Banyamulenge" name by which kiRwanda-speaking groups who had lived much longer in southern Kivu try to differentiate themselves from recent Rwandan immigrants.

29. This is a quote in Jackson 2006:16 from Agathon Rwasa, a Hutu leader from Burundi, who evoked the possibility of an intertwinement of the four re-gional crises (in Burundi, Rwanda, Congo, and Uganda), which would lead to a definitive Tutsi victory throughout the region. Such fantasies show that the no-torious "Hamitic Hypothesis" is still very much alive in the region. This thesis was originally launched by European anthropologists and missionaries to explain internal inequalities in precolonial states in the area as an outcome of the histor-ical subjection of local Bantu agriculturalists by cattle-keeping "Nilotic" invaders

coming from the north (the sons of Ham?). Scarcely any academic would dare to defend this thesis today (the whole idea of a Nilotic invasion is severely contested), but the notion still plays a major role in the political competition between groups throughout this area (see notably Malkki 1995).

30. Cf. Willame 1997:41, who quotes figures that this MIB alone would have moved more than eight-five thousand Rwandan immigrants between 1937 and 1955. Mathieu and Tsongo (1994:392) speak of more than 300,000 Rwandan immigrants into the Kivu between 1920 and 1970; they note for the Massisi—the area on which the MIB focused—that since 1975, Banyarwanda were thought to make up more than 70 percent of the population (elsewhere in the Kivu between 25 and 50 percent).

31. Cf. also Catherine Boone's challenging comparison (2003) of developments in Senegal, Ivory Coast, and Ghana, which shows how easily similar discourses—here also centering on the access to land—cross the borders between Anglophone and Francophone Africa.

32. Cf. the article by Comaroff and Comaroff (2001), cited above, on a popular panic about a huge fire on the Cape Peninsula—destroying South Africa's cherished heritage of fynbos—which easily became articulated with national concerns about the postapartheid invasion of the country by "aliens" from other parts of Africa. See also Lonsdale 2008 for a critical analysis of recent developments in Kenya (the bloody confrontations of Luo and Kikuyu in the beginning of 2008) in terms of autochthony.

33. With many thanks to Robert Moise for his generous comments on this section (see also Moise 2003).

34. In the early 1970s, the villagers in east Cameroon, where I did fieldwork at the time, had on the contrary to pay an extra tax for the Animation des Pygmées, to the great dissatisfaction of my neighbor, who used to protest: "They do not pay any *impôt* themselves, they empty our forest killing all the animals, and then we have to pay for them?"

35. Moise (2003: chap. 6; and oral communication) cites a very interesting example of a young Baka who worked for an international company (which is happening ever more with the growing interest in the exploitation and/or conservation of this part of the forest) but had great trouble in traveling since he had no ID. He solved this by having his teeth filed—an old custom among the Baka, now abandoned by most younger people—in order to "prove" his being a Pygmy and use this as a sort of Baka alternative to an official ID.

36. There is an interesting contrast here with the discourse of indigeneity ("indigenous peoples"), which to a certain extent does work in the Pygmy case (see chap.1 on the quite different genealogies of what seem to be almost similar notions, autochthonous and indigenous).

37. See Leonhardt 1999 and 2006:74; cf. also Turnbull 1961 (notably chap. 1) and Putnam 1948 on the Mbuti "Pygmies" of the Ituri forest in east Congo.

38. Cf. a very interesting contribution by Daniela Pes (forthcoming) on the recent popularity of Baka healers among the political elites, now even in the capital Yaoundé; see also Moise 2003: chap. 4.

39. See also Moise 2003: chap. 7, 389–90; he recounts how soccer has become an important pastime for young men in Baka camps along the road. Sometimes people travel more than fifty miles to play in matches between teams from different camps or simply to attend them. Baka teams also play against Bantu teams. One Baka team even played in Yaoundé with some success.

40. Apparently there are quite different trajectories in this respect. Alec Leonhardt (2006) reports on villages close to the border with the savannah where former Baka are so "integrated" that it is hard to distinguish them from the "Bantu" villagers. But he discusses also examples deeper in the forest where Baka took over the village from their former Bantu patrons (who preferred to go and live along a new road through the forest) and very much continued their own style of life, albeit with the inclusion of all sorts of modern elements (especially guns, cigarettes, and alcoholic drinks). In his view, education will have more permanent effects: the growing gap within the Baka communities between youth with some schooling and uneducated elders means that the former have less and less of the local knowledge necessary to pursue the old way of life. His own research assistant from a settlement close to the town of Yokadouma, who had attended primary school, was shocked to find, on a visit to a group of his cousins deeper in the forest, that they no longer considered him a Baka; he had become a "citizen."

41. This incident was clearly related to the general irritation of the villagers that Bagyeli increasingly sell their bushmeat to new labor camps in the area instead of offering it to their Bantu "patrons" in exchange for gifts like palm wine. Thus, complaints about Bagyeli being thieves seem to become ever more frequent.

42. Bantu villagers reacted in similar ways in the Lomie area when another group of nuns encouraged a group of Baka who had settled around their community in Le Bosquet to submit a request for the recognition of their own community forest under the new law. This met with great indignation among the villagers, who threatened to chase the nuns away if they continued to help the Baka with this initiative. In other parts of the forest as well, villagers considered the very idea that the law would benefit also the Baka to be preposterous. The Baka might be the firstcomers in the forest, but the new law and the possibility of claiming formal ownership of part of the forest were only for them, the villagers. Clearly, it is not enough to be autochthonous for filing claims to the forest under the law. This is only for citizens, and the Baka do not qualify as such.

43. Moise (2003) makes a very interesting comparison with Pygmy groups that have a long history of living together with more centralized social formations. The Baka and the Bagyeli in Cameroon, like most Pygmy groups in the forest, related mainly to village communities that were part of highly segmentary social formations (little central authority). The same applies to the Mbuti groups in the Ituri

forest of east Congo. However, Twa groups in Rwanda have a long history of being deeply involved in the highly centralist organization of the Rwanda kingdom. Yet in this context as well, they seem to hardly qualify as citizens of the polity. They could play a special role at the court of the *mwami* (the Tutsi sovereign, ruling over both Tutsi and Hutu) precisely because they were outside the normal rules.

Chapter Five

1. Special thanks to Frank Bovenkerk, Bambi Ceuppens, Jan Willem Duyvendak, Susan Legêne, Wasif Shadid, and Hans van Amersfoort, who helped me to find my way through the intricacies of discourse and practices of autochthony, immigration, and integration in Europe, especially in the Netherlands and Flanders.

2. But compare the longer history of the notion in France. For instance, it played a central role in political debates in the country between republicans and aristocratic royalists ever since Abbé Sieyès in his famous 1789 address "Qu'est-ce que c'est le tiers état?" indicated that since the aristocrats were so proud of their Frankish descent, they were in fact "strangers" who belonged to the "forests of Germania," rather than to the French soil. The real French stock would come rather from *les Gaulois*—that is, from Celtic origins; they really belonged to the French soil (cf. Noiriel 2007:15; cf. also Détienne 2003:124; Bayart 1996:52; and Barrès 1925, who developed a more conservative interpretation of the link with the soil as the criterion for being a *Français de souche* [lit., of the trunk]).

3. Cf. also Noiriel 2007:140, who shows that in 2007 France's new president, Nicolas Sarkozy (himself of Hungarian descent), succeeded in attracting the Front National vote by emphasizing a distinction between earlier immigrants (for instance, Hungarians, Poles, Spaniards, or Italians) who did integrate and more recent ones (notably Muslims) who refuse to do so and therefore constitute a serious danger.

4. Heidegger 1934–35/1989:214. Rob Garbutt drew my attention to this link (see Garbutt 2006); also many thanks to Kate Crehan and (through her) Johannes Fritsche for helping me out on Heidegger. See further Fritsche 1999 and Bambach 2003:14.

5. Bambach 2003:xxiv, quoted in Garbutt 2006.

6. See, for instance, van Donselaar and Rodriquez 2006.

7. When in 2006, an official report concluded that indeed the situation in the prison had been completely unacceptable, two other ministers (of justice and of public housing and planning) took the responsibility for this and stepped down, but Minister Verdonk (immigration and integration) stayed on. Moreover, elsewhere—especially in the notorious *bajesboten* (prison boats)—"illegals" remained locked up under equally unacceptable circumstances.

8. For a short but sharp portrait of Fortuyn, see Buruma 2006, chap. 2. Buruma emphasizes that precisely this general enthusiasm for Fortuyn's flamboyance in a country "well-known for its Calvinistic restraint and its bourgeois dedain for

excesses" made him a much more interesting figure than other populists like Le Pen in France or Haider in Austria (Buruma 2006:46). Cf. also J. E. Ellemers's view of Fortuyn as "a pure case of charismatic authority" (Ellemers 2002); see also Dick Pels's hesitant comparison with Mussolini (Pels 2002).

9. Only quite recently has the wider public become fully aware of the shocking figures that showed the Netherlands to have had the highest percentage of Jews deported among the Western European countries occupied by the Germans in World War II.

10. See also van der Veer 2006. Fortuyn's performance and even more those of Wilders and Verdonk (the present-day leaders of the New Right in the Netherlands) are strongly reminiscent of the "politics of resentment" that McGovern (2004:11–12) sees as typical for the success of the autochthony movement in Ivory Coast (see the previous chapter). Indeed, McGovern's take on resentment—referring to Weber, he proposes to study it not as a sentiment but as a social idiom allowing for the condensation of a wide array of grievances (he speaks also of the powerful emotion of being "victimized")—suggests seminal starting points for understanding the present-day "conjuncture of belonging" in Europe as well.

11. Rinus Penninx (2006) emphasizes that already in the 1990s official policy stressed integration, albeit mainly socioeconomic integration. According to others, not even Scheffer's emphasis on cultural integration was particularly new. See a 1990 column by Frank Bovenkerk in *De Volkskrant* in which he criticized the new government policies based on the 1989 WRR report *Allochthonenbeleid* (see below in this chapter) as a definitive rupture with the idea of a multicultural society; this report inspired new government policies (already in 1990!) which addressed the problems of ethnic minorities as following from the "incomplete integration" of *allochthonen* as individuals. In this context the culture of immigrants was apparently (already then) seen as a barrier to integration (Bovenkerk 1990). The novelty of Scheffer, Fortuyn, and others may rather be that they deemed considerable pressure necessary in order to achieve cultural integration. See also van der Veer 2006; Vasta 2006; Ghorashi 2006.

12. For 2000, Scheffer cited the following figures: roughly 1.5 million people—a little less than 10 percent of the total population—would come from the "target groups of Dutch minority policy" (that is, mainly Turks, Surinamese, Moroccans, and Antilleans—from the Dutch Antilles). But for 2015 Scheffer quotes a prognosis of two million people from these groups (12 percent of the population). See the section "*Allochtonen*: A New Term on the Dutch Scene," below, for critical comments on the way the official figures are calculated and prognoses are projected; an important issue is how the quaint but crucial notion of *niet-westerse allochtonen* is defined in official statistics.

13. Wasif Shadid characterizes Scheffer's attack as a switch from "blaming the system" to "blaming the victim": whereas in earlier days solutions to the immigrant problem were sought in efforts to ameliorate the system, Scheffer put the blame

to a large extent on the immigrants themselves since the latter supposedly refused to integrate (Shadid, oral communication; see also Shadid 1998 and 2006).

14. See also Shadid and van Koningsveld 1992.

15. In institutional respect there still remain important vestiges of pillarization (cf. Shadid and van Koningsveld 2002).

16. Cf. Buruma's suggestion that Scheffer and Fortuyn had one thing in common, apart from obvious differences: "a certain yearning for something that may never have existed, but whose loss is keenly felt nonetheless...The same culture, a common understanding" (Buruma 2006:127–28).

17. This is also why, in the 1980s, Lijphart could advocate the same model of "pacification democracy" for South Africa, where consensus on common values or common history was conspicuously lacking between the various population segments, (Lijphart 1985). Striking is that in his 2007 book, Scheffer is even more adamant in drawing Lijphart into his own "consensus view." On p. 171, he reproaches his critics for "overlooking the chapter on 'national consensus' in the classical study of Arend Lijphardt." In the English version of Lijphart's book (1986), this is chapter 5 and its title is "The *Narrow* National Consensus" (italics mine). In the Dutch version (1968) it is chapter 6; here the adjective *narrow* is absent from the title, but the tenor of the brief introduction goes in the same direction as the English title: "In the Netherlands, both the degree and the extent of political consensus are very limited, but one vitally important element of consensus is present: the desire to preserve the existing system" (Lijphart 1986:78; cf. 1968:93). This is a far cry from the kind of value consensus Scheffer projects into the past. In the rest of his book Lijphart emphasizes the ideological rifts between the pillars. Often Scheffer's search for consensus seems to imply a quite special reading of the authors he quotes. For instance, Wil Kymlicka, the well-known advocate of multiculturalism in Canada, might be surprised to find he is basically in agreement with Scheffer (Scheffer 2007:269; see also Prins 2007–8). Such confusions are exacerbated by Scheffer's cavalier disdain for current standards for references: in the whole book there is no single reference to a page numbers, so it is difficult to track down his quotes or the opinions he attributes to other authors.

18. Etty 2004. Interestingly, this collection of *De Gids* had as title *Misverstand Nederland* (lit., Misconception the Netherlands—even without a question mark!). The title might reflect the uncertainty that Scheffer's call for a return of a national élan had created.

19. It is quite interesting to note that even Buruma—an international and quite nuanced publicist, who was born in the Netherlands but tries to offer a more distanced outsider's view—cannot resist joining in the search for what is "typically Dutch." Buruma was quoted above (n. 16) as doubting whether the kind of "common understanding" Scheffer and Fortuyn were longing for had ever existed. Yet in the course of his interesting book on the change of course in the Netherlands, the most divergent traits are more or less implicitly related to a Dutch common

core: "bourgeois satisfaction...when smugness is challenged panic sets in" (11, 15); "offensiveness projected as a sign of sincerity" (228); "the Dutch notion that everything must be said" (221); "the venting of moral emotions" (230); "deeply religious" (230–31); "van Gogh liked to call himself the village idiot.... And yet he wanted to be taken seriously too. This wanting it both ways is a common disease in Dutch intellectual discourse" (112). Thus the book, highly sophisticated in its analysis, offers an unintended example of how difficult it is to escape the tendency to look for a national core. Moreover, it graphically illustrates how difficult it is to grasp this core in view of the striking discrepancies between the various aspects which Buruma appears to see as "typically Dutch."

20. Cf. also Duyvendak, Pels, and Rijkschroeff forthcoming.

21. Cf. also Fortuyn's book (2002) with the rhetorical title *The Puinhopen van Paars* (lit., The Dumps of Purple). The two cabinets under Prime Minister Wim Kok were called "purple" since, for the first time in Dutch history, they were based on a coalition between liberals and socialists (respectively right and left in Dutch policies), while the Christian Democrats—in the middle of the Dutch political spectrum and therefore until then always represented in government—were this time obliged to be in the opposition (this was generally seen as a sign that pillarization was a thing of the past). Fortuyn's meteoric rise in Dutch politics was mainly based on his success in attacking the lack of ideological inspiration of these "purple" cabinets.

22. Cf. Irene Bloemraad's 2006 comparison between Canada and the United States in this respect. She characterizes U.S. policies as "laissez-faire immigrant integration." The "melting pot" idea of the early twentieth century has long been superseded by a "salad bowl" model (5, 146). Bloemraad explicitly mentions the recent Dutch switch as an example of a turn toward "a state-directed assimilation reminiscent of Americanization efforts in the early twentieth century" (233). Her main conclusion is that the Canadian persistence with a conscious multicultural approach (it is now about the only country that still defends this principle) had much more positive effects on immigrants' integration—especially because the government's special programmes for immigrants created an institutional infrastructure—than have recent U.S. policies.

23. Cf. a review by Scheffer (*NRC/Handelsblad*, February 9, 2007, 29) of Aristide Zolberg's recent history of immigrants in the United States (2006). Typically, Scheffer dwells especially upon Zolberg's showing that immigration has had a highly tortuous history in the United States as well, but he leaves out Zolberg's emphasis on the central role of economic arguments and political opportunism— constantly overriding issues of cultural integration—in the struggle over immigration policies in that country (see for instance Zolberg 2006:390, 435, 440).

24. On assimilationist tendencies in the new Dutch policies see also Shadid 2006:8, 19 and Leeman and Pels 2006.

25. A telling example of how different the Dutch situation is from the French is the so-called *schoolstrijd* (lit., school struggle) that dominated internal political

relations for a good part of the twentieth century. The issue was the autonomy of education on a Christian basis *and* the right of Christian schools to be fully financed by the state. Religious and political leaders of the Protestant and Catholic pillars saw control over education as vital for the ongoing cohesion of their pillar; for them, this also meant full public recognition and financing of their schools (up to university level). This issue still marks Dutch politics. In the recent concern over the expansion of Islam schools in the country, the Christian Democrats will never permit any doubt concerning the right for schools on a religious basis to exist. And since they are almost always represented in government (the major exception was the "purple" cabinets in the 1990s), an official denial of Muslim parents' right to have their schools subsidized remains impossible. The only solution for adamant opponents of Islamic schools is to try to have public subventions withdrawn on the ground of mismanagement or bad performance. Applying a French ideal of *citoyenneté* as a homogeneous national culture under the aegis of the state might prove to be difficult indeed in such a situation.

26. Luckily, this is one of the more important points where Scheffer's 2007 book is more nuanced and better informed. In this book, he emphasizes that in many respects the U.S. struggle with immigration has been as difficult as the present one in Europe. Moreover, he recognizes the most obvious lesson of the American example: the room that was created there, after considerable struggle and still contested, for "hyphenated citizenship" (Dutch-American, Italian-American, Asian-American)—combining national citizenship with room for difference. Indeed, Scheffer's emphasis (2007:338) on the success of the United States "in overcoming the original religious and racial limitations of the idea of citizenship" and drawing ever wider circles for the inclusion of new waves of immigrants (first the Germans, then the Irish and Italians, then the Asians and so on) suggests that he sees this as an example to be followed for opening up Dutch citizenship. This reflects a general trend in Scheffer's 2007 book: more attention to room for difference within consensus; see further below.

27. See also Tabappsi 2007.

28. The reason for this dramatic decision was that Hirsi Ali declared publicly that she had lied about the circumstances under which she obtained asylum in the Netherlands. Verdonk's argument was that she had to be consequent in the application of her policies (and indeed, her IND—Immigration and Naturalization Service—followed the strict principle that any lie would lead to immediate refusal of an asylum request). However, Parliament—apparently finally awakened to the practical consequences of the draconian treatment of asylum seekers, now that a person from their midst risked becoming a victim—refused to follow the minister in this. Typically, Verdonk refused to step down, so that the whole cabinet fell.

29. Moreover, an overview of the press's reactions to the WRR report *Identificatie met Nederland,* cited above, and Princess Maxima's public relativizing of the notion of "a" Dutch identity shows how controversial such ideas have become. Most columnists—the new guild of opinion leaders in the Netherlands—seem to

equate any nuancing of the idea of "the" Dutch identity to a return to a dated multiculturalism. To those who dominate Dutch media in the present constellation, any suggestion that integration can work only if it allows for difference means that one ignores the anger of the autochthonous majority about past permissiveness to allochthons. In this line of thought, Dutch identity has to be well defined and closed. Any idea of different degrees of identification is leftist or multiculturalist nonsense.

30. H. Verwey-Jonker, ed., *Allochtonen in Nederland* (1971); many thanks to Frank Bovenkerk for showing me this collection.

31. Jan Rath (1991:171) mentions the telling example of a civil servant at the ministry who, still in the 1980s, diligently crossed out the term *migrants* in all reports he had to evaluate and changed this to the "right" term: *ethnic minorities*.

32. Cf. what was said above about the geological/botanical connotations the term has in English (reference to *Oxford English Dictionary*, n. 3 in chap. 1).

33. In the 1970s, the term could apparently still be used with quite different meanings; for instance, in 1974 Lodewijk Brunt used it to refer to possible tensions between villagers and urbanites who had recently come to live in the village he studied (south of Rotterdam); he chose the terms *autochtoon* and *allochtoon* as Dutch translations of the central terms in the classic study by Norbert Elias and John Scotson, *The Established and the Outsiders*. Around 2000, when I regularly supervised students during a fieldwork training in Drenthe—still one of the most rural parts of the Netherlands—I discovered with some surprise that locally the terms were still used in this sense. Clearly, their meaning has been highly variable for quite some time.

34. However, for instance in a 1975 article, Han Entzinger (then a civil servant at the ministry, later professor of migration studies, and as such playing a central role in policy making on immigration issues) used the term *allochthonous minorities* (Entzinger 1975:326, 333; cf. also Rath 1991:174). See also WRR 1979 and *Minderhedennota* 1982–83.

35. Bovenkerk (1989) argued, for instance, that then the Dutch had to be categorized also as an ethnic minority. In general, the term *minority* as such was increasingly seen as condescending and therefore less politically correct.

36. Van Praag 1971:40–41; see also *Regeringsnota inzake Buitenlandse Werknemers* (The Hague), January 14, 1970.

37. It is noteworthy that the board hardly offered any justification for this inclusion of the second and third generation. In the passage concerned, there is only a reference to a publication by J. E. Ellemers and R. E. F. Vaillant (1985), on a quite different topic, which, again, adopts the "third generation" criterion without any further elaboration. The Dutch terminology (*in het derde geslacht*) has strong biblical overtones. Maybe the "third generation" clause should be seen as a leftover of the nation's Protestant past. In any case, it remains a bit disturbing that this board, composed of academics, did not signal the clear *contradictio in terminis* that

it thus created: persons of the second or third generation were born in the Netherlands and can therefore hardly be defined as "having been born from another soil"
(the meaning of the Greek *allochthon*). Equally striking is that the board gives a
highly unorthodox etymology of the root term *chthoon* as "soil" (which is correct)
but also as "world" (which is quite unorthodox). Thus, the report contains indications of a certain struggle with the terminology. In subsequent decades it would
become further apparent that this terminology was not easy to control.

38. However, it remains an open question how the third generation of
immigrants—at present only barely in existence—will be included in official statistics when it starts to manifest itself.

39. Cf. Groenendijk 2007, who warns especially (110) that the adoption by the
CBS of the term *allochtoon* in official statistics meant that the parents' country
of origin became an officially registered item, which made it easier for politicians to use it as a criterion in legislation and policy making. It is, indeed, striking
that the Netherlands was more prepared than any other Western European country to include such data—elsewhere much more quickly interpreted as signs of
discrimination—in official statistics. An explanation might be, again, the pillarized
past which made a differentiated view of the national citizenship quite "normal."
A consequence is that it has remained common, even in the Dutch media, to speak
of "Maroccans" or "Turcs" in reference to persons of the second generation who
were definitely born in the Netherlands—a way of speaking that always surprises
Americans and also people from other European countries.

40. Of course, this is quite surprising in a longer historical perspective. The
Netherlands, like many other Western European countries, has a long tradition
of receiving and integrating immigrants. Apparently, the Dutch view of their
country as decidedly an emigration country is—like in other Western European
countries—linked to the emergence of former settler colonies (United States,
Canada, South Africa, and Australia) as major receivers of European immigrants,
and the celebration of the melting-pot ideology in at least some of these countries.
The more recent Dutch fears over immigration may be linked to the crisis of 1930s
and the perception of massive unemployment as an ever-present threat. It is striking that the self-definition of being an emigration country took root so quickly and
so profoundly.

41. Thus it was only in the 1990s that the role of Islam became a dominant issue
in the Dutch debates about immigration. This was subsequently reinforced by international events (especially 9/11). Within the country, Hirsi Ali's quite simplistic
attacks on Islam as such and her criticisms of what she saw as the "laxity" of Dutch
official policies in containing such dangers served as a catalyst in this respect (for
instance Ali 2006).

42. There is an interesting parallel here with Keith Hart's present-day unhap-
piness with the notion of "informal economy," which he himself launched in 1973.
When working in Ghana, Hart had been struck by the incompleteness of the

official economic statistics used by the World Bank and other established development institutions. He coined the notion of "informal economy" to highlight the importance of various unofficial economic activities taking place in the shadow of the formal economy. In the 1980s, however, the World Bank and the IMF eagerly adopted this notion in order to justify the imposition of draconian structural adjustment schemes on states in Africa and elsewhere. In this view, cuts on the formal economy were acceptable since the "informal economy" could act as a sort of safety net—an interpretation that led Hart to turn against his own term.

43. Cf. Comaroff and Comaroff 2000 on the increasing mobility of people and images as crucial to the volatile character of "millennial capitalism" (cf. also Appadurai 1996).

44. De Beer and Sprangers 1993:13. The authors continue by proposing also a distinct delimitation of the *autochtonen* category: all persons born in the Netherlands with Dutch nationality and from parents born in the Netherlands. Thus they seem to have dropped the "third generation" criterion of the 1989 report *Allochtonenbeleid* by the WRR.

45. Wilders's plea for including Christian education in the school curricula is particularly striking. Wilders still claims to be a liberal—indeed, he feels he represents the *real* liberalism. In the Dutch context, liberals have always been the main opponents to the very idea of confessional schools (remember what was said above about the *schoolstrijd*—the struggle for recognition of Christian schools—as a key theme in recent Dutch history). The image of a liberal pleading for Christian education is therefore quite surprising.

46. Cf. also the Dutch philosopher and Heidegger expert Herman Philips—he is always cited by the Dutch-Somali politician Hirsi Ali as her most important mentor for teaching "how to think"—who sees no problem in opposing " 'the' culture of tribal Islamic societies of Arab countries" from which the immigrants come, to the Dutch secular culture (*NRC/Handelsblad* September 27, 2003, 7). The use of the term *tribal* for societies that for centuries have been deeply involved in state formation, going through long-term processes of differentiation, by a philosopher who frequently chides his colleagues for tendentious uses of terms is quite striking and also symptomatic of the vehemence of the Dutch debate on immigration, especially where culture is concerned. Cf. also Scheffer—still in his more nuanced 2007 book—on "the tribal culture of Africa" (321). In this respect Hirsi Ali herself was more sophisticated, because she did not oppose "cultures" but rather "Islam" to "Enlightenment" (see for instance Ali 2006). However, she did this again in a quite simplistic way: in her confrontational strategies it was apparently necessary to propagate a scarcely nuanced image of "the" Islam (and of "the" Enlightenment).

47. See Scheffer 2007:261–82. The relevance of this old debate for the present situation is not directly clear, especially since there is now general agreement—also among anthropologists—that respect for cultural difference should not exclude ethical judgement.

48. Central in this debate was James Clifford's *The Predicament of Culture* (1988); for a short overview, see Geschiere 2004b.

49. Cf. Geertz's recent plea for a more pluralistic concept of culture ("What we need are ways of thinking that are responsive to particularities...a plurality of ways of belonging and being") and his warnings against what he calls the "cookie-cutter concept of culture" as highly problematic, especially in the present times of increasing cosmopolitanism *and* parochialism, the one reinforcing the other (see Geertz 2000:224, 246, 250). A good example of what the reification of culture can lead to is Sniderman and Hagendoorn's recent study of prejudices in the Netherlands concerning the immigration issue (2007). These authors feel that their survey from the end of the 1990s indicates an absolute failure of multiculturalism. The question is of course whether the Dutch approach until then could, indeed, be characterized as "the most ambitious policy of multiculturalism" (xi). But even more worrying is that for these authors, "culture" is apparently such a closed entity that the answers to their survey permit them to clearly separate cultural identity and economic self-interest (chap. 4). They conclude that "under the present circumstances cultural identity is the dominant factor" (125). Apparently they are hardly worried by doubts whether the people they interviewed make such a separation between culture and economics. Indeed, when "culture" has to be properly delimited so that it can serve as one item in a survey, results can become quite absurd!

50. A striking illustration of Scheffer's rigid notion of culture is his sketch of the village cultures of the Turkish and North African countryside, which seem to come straight from some sort of unreconstructed modernization vision in which "traditional society" is seen as in every respect just the negative counterpoint of the "modern" one (Scheffer 2006:23). Such images based only on contrast are never very helpful. Scheffer still seems to believe that the "community" in these societies blocks each and every expression of individualism and ambition. Anthropological accounts of these societies—in many respects "big man" societies—invariably note the celebration of individual achievement which immigrants often practice in new ways in their new environment. Thinking in the binary oppositions to which Scheffer still wants to stick when culture is at stake makes one overlook the unexpected convergences and articulations between supposedly different cultures that are central in any "integration" process.

51. 1 Cf. Gyan Pandey's critique that this is too narrow a view (Pandey 2001: 11). See also Noiriel 2007:8.

52. Respectively, a soccer player of Moroccan descent and the Dutch queen (Canon van Nederland 2006:24).

53. Interestingly, when the committee's proposal was discussed in Parliament (June 27, 2007), only an MP from Groen Links (the environmental party) warned that history could divide as much as it could unite. All the other parties agreed completely on the importance of history for creating a common basis for citizenship (many thanks to Susan Legêne for drawing my attention to this debate).

54. In comparison the Danish canon, enumerating a fixed number of national cultural monuments, is more fixed and probably also more closed in a nationalist sense (see:www.kulturkanon.kum.dk/).

55. Of course "window" 47—"Multicolored Netherlands after 1945: The multicultural society"—provides an opening for this. Still, the inclusion of this window does not answer the basic question of how to deal with a well-defined historical heritage that stems from elsewhere and is taken along to the Netherlands by specific groups of migrants. An important question for the future effects of this canon might be to what extent window 47 is sufficient for this.

56. In 2005, after it had been condemned for racist propaganda, the party adopted a new name: Vlaams Belang.

57. In many respects the Vlaams Blok can be seen as the successor—and wants to be seen as such (although it is more and more prudent about this ancestry)—to the antidemocratic Flemish nationalist party Vlaams Nationaal Verbond, which sided with the Germans in World War II, exploiting the widespread bitterness among the Flemish population over the continuing political and cultural dominance of the Francophones (however, as Ceuppens [2006] and Huyse [1991] emphasize, this should certainly not imply that collaboration with the Nazi regime was more common among Flemings than among Walloons).

58. See *NRC/Handelsblad* March 22, 2006, 3. Of interest also is the general uneasiness in present-day Germany with the notion of *Leitkultur* (lit., leading culture). The notion was launched by right-wing intellectuals with a CDU (Christian Democrat) background, in order to suggest that certain principles of German culture should be normative for integration policies. However, the very idea of a German culture that would have its own essence is worrying to many Germans, in view of the recent history of the country.

59. Noiriel (2007:53) indicates that in France the notion of "national identity" was quite new—it was borrowed in the 1960s from American debates, to defend the right of regional subcultures; however, the idea as such is older (although for Noriel not older than the nineteenth century), but then different terms (*caractère national* or *personnalité nationale*) were more current.

60. Cf. Sahlins 2004 on the great difficulties in the eighteenth century for *étrangers* in getting themselves recognized as French citizens even if they had already lived for longer periods on French soil.

61. Noiriel 2007:35; cf. also the Barrès maxim quoted earlier (chap. 1) that the main things needed for constructing a nation are "a graveyard and the teaching of history" (Barrès 1925, vol. 1:25, cf. also Detienne 2003:131).

62. An interesting counterexample is present-day South Africa. Recent studies (Pillay, Roberts, and Rule 2006; cf. Mattes 1999) speak of a very high degree of patriotism there, among all layers of the population. Yet the authors also emphasize that it is difficult to link this to shared values or a shared vision of history. Apparently patriotism can be fed by other factors as well; in South Africa, the way

this country presents itself to the outside world as a new nation might be a binding factor.

63. Cf. also Bloemraad's conclusions, cited earlier, that Canadian multiculturalism has better effects for immigrants' integration than does U.S. "laissez-faire immigration integration," since in the first case the government's special programs for immigrants have helped building a congenial institutional infrastructure (Bloemraad 2006).

64. See for a seminal and at the same time pragmatic approach to explore how culture and difference can go together, a recent collection by a number of younger anthropologists, edited by Francio Guadeloupe and Vincent de Rooij (2007).

65. See also Appiah 2006. Cf. also Geertz, who asks for "an intricate, multiply ordered structure of difference within which cultural tensions that are not about to go away…can be placed and negotiated" (2000:257). In the Netherlands, Halleh Ghorashi has recently offered a programmatic statement on the importance of using a conception of culture which leaves scope for difference: "[in this conception]…links are central and not the boundaries between cultures. Not the construction of culture difference is the point of departure but situations where people meet" (Ghorashi 2006:45).

Chapter Six

1. See chapter 1 above and the references there to Bayart 2004 and Foucault 1984. What follows here is especially inspired by stimulating conversations on these issues with Jean-François Bayart, Romain Bertrand, Birgit Meyer, and Mattijs van de Port.

2. See chapter 1 and cf. Meyer 2007 on religious images and authentic belonging; and van de Port 2004 and 2005 on the ongoing quest for "authenticity" in modern contexts; see also Meyer and Verrips 2008.

3. An exception might be the vast literature on the realities of Ujamaa socialism in Tanzania in the 1960s and 1970s. But even there the focus seemed to be much more on a critique of this version of socialism—notably its neglect of the realities of class oppositions at the local level (see Saul 1974)—and hardly on the government's efforts toward nation-building or the forging of Tanzanian citizens. Another exception might be Congo/Zaire, where the more lively aspects of Mobutu's nation-building—notably his use of the splendid Congolese music—received some attention, albeit in a later phase (see White 2008). For Cameroon, there is Bayart's seminal 1979 study, which, although mainly concentrated on struggles at the national level, offers fascinating glimpses of how they were expressed in everyday life at the grassroots level.

4. The rest of this section is based mainly on my data and observations on nation-building in the Maka area (East Province), where I did most of my fieldwork.

This area had (and has) quite distinctive traits (difficult-to-access part of the forest, strongly "segmentary" patterns of organization, no central authority prior to the colonial conquest, and so on), and there are no doubt important differences from the impact of the new postcolonial regime in more "developed" parts of the country (for instance, around the capital, Yaoundé, or the main economic center, Douala). Still, the following may serve to identify certain recurrent and basic aspects of what nation-building meant on the ground. For a broader view, refer to more general studies of the country as a whole, notably to Bayart's seminal work (1979) on the dogged *recherche hégémonique* that characterized the regime of Ahidjo.

5. Cf. Bayart 1979:232: "the ethics of unity is nothing else than the ideological representation of the *recherche hégémonique*, or more precisely its key word, constitutive of its reality" (my translation).

6. See Joseph 1977 and Mbembe 1996.

7. In fact, Ahidjo's entry into politics in 1946 was mainly based on the fact that he was one of the few young men from the north with some education (even though he had obtained only a primary school certificate) and, more important, on the unswerving support of the French administrators, who rightly spotted him as a highly cooperative politician. Their positive impression of the young Ahidjo was confirmed by both his work as a clerk in the post office of Garoua (until into the 1950s) and his humble origins. He did not descend from any of the powerful aristocratic families of the Islamic sultanates of the north; his father was completely unknown, and in the 1970s there were insistent rumors that his mother had had an affair with a white soldier. Such a meteoric career—from clerk to prime minister—was typical for the time around independence, when minimal educational qualifications would suffice for winning a top post in the new national hierarchies. In the Maka area, there were continuing rumors that Mr. Malouma, the MP who had given such an elated and at the same time threatening speech during the minister's visit, had not even obtained his primary school certificate. It was said that in 1970 he tried to register more or less in secret for the exam, but when people noticed his name, it was suddenly withdrawn from the list. But this did not stop him from monopolizing the MP position for the region until 1980; he even ascended to the Comité Central of the Bureau Politique National, the real national center of power.

8. I refer here especially to the Francophone part of Cameroon. In the Anglophone part—that is, the part of the former German colony that was conquered by the British in 1914—the presence of the *grand parti national* remained less pervasive (this part joined Cameroon only later and maintained a special status until 1972; here only in 1966 did Ahidjo succeed in forcing regional political leaders to join his UNC).

9. Cf. Bayart 1979:233: "it was on the basis of the struggle against the most politicized fractions of its population [that is, the UPC, mentioned before—PG] that the Cameroonian state established its authority"; cf. also Joseph 1974.

10. Cf. the brutal disciplining—referred to in chapter 2—of some of the boys in the village where I lived in 1971; when they founded a checkers club, the gendarmes raided the village and took them along to the *commissariat* in town for an *avertissement*. In 1967 the Ahidjo regime imposed ratification of a law that explicitly forbade any association "of an exclusively tribal or clannish character" (see Bayart 1979:251).

11. In the beginning of my research, when I was still quite naive—later on I was told in no uncertain terms by the DO to refrain from any research on politics—I did a little survey among forty villagers asking them what in their opinion were the functions of the party and what were those of the *administration*. All of my respondents emphasized the close collaboration between party and *autorités administratives*; none came up with anything like interest articulation as a function of the party.

12. Cf. Moussa Yaya, one of Ahidjo's most powerful barons: "Voting is not only a right or a function, it is an absolute obligation" ("Le militant et les élections," in Union Nationale Camerounaise, *Ier conseil national de l'Union nationale camerounaise tenu à Yaoundé du 5 au 8 novembre 1967* [Yaounde: Imprimerie Nationale, 1967], 146, quoted in Bayart 1979:239).

13. Cf. Bayart 1979:237 for similar examples of roundups and arbitrary exercise of violence.

14. Bayart 1979:259 highlights important variations between regions and also over time in the sale of party cards. My impression that in the villages where I worked nearly all people had their party cards is based on their emphatic statements that this was so. Probably there was some exaggeration here, since confessing that one had not paid might entail all sorts of difficulties. Unfortunately I did not have the leeway to check this in the party archives (of course there was no chance at all of getting access to the archives of the *section* controlled by the towering figure of Mr. Malouma, the MP himself). Yet it was certainly true that all citizens who could not show their party card at the omnipresent roadblocks would run into serious difficulties. In any case, then, the more mobile people had to have their party card.

15. Cf. also Bayart 1979:253 on the leaders' firm belief in the "pedagogic virtue" of the new institutions as a new but basic element in their *recherche hégémonique*.

16. In the 1970s, some people in the East Province whispered about an overambitious politician from near Abong-Mbang who, by way of exception, had returned from Tchollire; however, he had become completely insane.

17. See Bayart 1979:272–74 on how the party organization, highly disciplined as it was, nevertheless offered openings for putting pressure on the party top.

18. *L'Effort Camerounais* 576 (January 29, 1967), quoted in Bayart 1979:183. Cf. what was said above about the *quadrillage politique* of the country and the strict interdiction of any association outside the framework of the party. Compare

also what was said above in chapter 3 about structural reasons for the eastern elites to keep a certain distance from the village, certainly in Ahidjo's days.

19. No wonder that, as said above, under Ahidjo's regime the kind of elite associations that played such an important role in many other African countries could hardly develop. Again, there is a difference here with other regions, notably Anglophone Cameroon, where such associations existed prior to the one-party period and where they continued to play a role, albeit more or less underground.

20. Cf. Houphouët Boigny in Ivory Coast (see below); yet here the principle was much less formalized than it was under Ahidjo.

21. Characteristically, moreover, it was Ahidjo who decided who could represent which region (see also chap. 2). Only later on, when more political debate was possible, did I discover, for instance, that Charles Ndoumba, who already under Ahidjo held a prestigious post in the party, was supposed to fill one of the positions included in the Maka quota. The people in the area where I worked certainly did not think of Ndoumba as a Maka. They told me that his mother might be from the region but his father was a Douala; so he should be considered a Douala, all the more since he had lived all this life in that city. Yet in those days, Ahidjo's clique could decide who could count as a Maka, and no one dared to protest against this—at least not openly.

22. Maybe the most surprising element in this statement is the suggestion that women could only say yes. This is certainly not in line with the behavior expected from Maka women. In the big village palavers, women are often as vocal as men, and in everyday life a Maka woman is expected to know how to defend her rights. Maybe my spokesman expressed a male ideal (indeed, Maka men—young or old—will invariably complain of women's lack of submissiveness, often for very concrete reasons).

23. However, old men's stories about the coming of the Germans (their first confrontation with whites) still express people's absolute shock at the kinds of obedience demanded by these new authorities (see Geschiere 1982).

24. Probably my own relative youth when I came to Makaland for the first time made people all the more uneasy about my role, which seemed not to fit into the usual categories. Now that I m older and (after thirty years) more familiar to the villagers, the switch is less obvious (even though it still is there).

25. See Geschiere 1997 on the close link between witchcraft and intimacy.

26. In fact, some friends told me that I was on the list of the SEDOC (the feared intelligence service of those days) for asking too many questions about politics. At the time I was convinced that it was Malouma who had mentioned my name to them, since I had been too eager in my efforts to win an interview with him (and then have him tell his life story!). But if I was blacklisted, there were never concrete effects (in the sense that there was never an attempt to confiscate my notes—though it may have made people reluctant to talk to me), and I never had any proof that Malouma was after me. Probably I overrated my own importance to him.

27. In fact, several of my informants—all potential rivals of Malouma—commented that because of all the different positions he accumulated, he was so rich that he could buy the support of the strongest *nganga*; for this reason it was impossible to unseat him (see Geschiere 1997:122).

28. Cf. his comparison in the speech cited earlier between people's joy at Christmas because of the coming of Christ and the excitement in the Eastern Province that the minister had come to visit.

29. For more information on the Maka funeral and its context, see Geschiere 1982, chap. 2.

30. I focus here on the funeral of an older man. The funeral of a woman often entails extra complications, since it may give rise to fierce conflicts about where she should be buried: in the village of her husband and children or in her village of origin with her brothers. Maka kinship reckoning is, at least formally, strongly patrilineal. Men should live in the village of their fathers, and women should move to another village at their marriage. Thus, the position of a woman is somewhat ambivalent: in some respects, certainly if she bears sons, she is included in her husband's *njaw boud*, yet ultimately she is supposed to belong as *mame* (aunt) to the lineage of her brothers and their children.

31. Maka patterns of organization were (and are) highly segmentary. Up till the colonial conquest (1905), no fixed positions of authority existed above the elders who supervised small family hamlets. Nonetheless, local groups that were related through marriage or through a claim of common descent could occasionally work together. But between unrelated hamlets, there was a constant state of *domb*. My informants always translated the latter term as *guerre* (war). However, a better translation might be "hostility": the Maka area was certainly not in a state of permanent war before the "pacification" by the Germans, yet there was always the threat that violence might erupt between unrelated local groups (see Geschiere 1982).

32. This became really dramatic toward the end of the 1980s, when there was a severe shortage of cash throughout this region due to the abrupt collapse of world-market prices for cacao and coffee (the main cash crops). Around 1990, it became completely impossible for the villagers to sell any of their crops; bags with cocoa and coffee were rotting along the road, with no traders coming to buy them. Suddenly the villagers had to do practically without money. Strikingly, the impossibility of making funeral and bride-price payments was seen as the most urgent problem in this context. As one man complained to me in 1991: "What am I supposed to do? I have hardly any money left. My mother is ill and needs to go to the hospital. But my father is dying and I have to bury him properly." Of course, he had to give priority to the funeral payments, but this meant that his mother did not go to the hospital and died only a few months later. This example shows that the process of monetization of "traditional" rituals is to a large extent nonreversible.

33. The Ewondo live around Yaoundé, the country's capital. They are part of the larger ethnic bloc of the Beti, who live in the central part of the same forest

zone as the Maka and whose sociopolitical organization has similar traits (until the colonial conquest organized in autonomous family villages with hardly any central authority above the village level).

34. Once there, I realized that I should never have accepted the invitation to attend this defense. The authorities had insisted that it should go through despite all the unrest, as a manifestation that the university was functioning.

35. See Geschiere 1997. See also Smith 2004 on the continuing preoccupation among Igbo with being buried "at home." In this article Smith similarly emphasizes the flip side of the urbanites' involvement with the village: the funeral is becoming more and more the occasion at which growing tensions between villagers and urbanites come to the fore.

36. How deeply felt this notion is became clear to me when in 1992 there was for three consecutive evenings an item on Cameroon TV news of a young *bandit* who had been killed in Yaoundé and whose body was not claimed by anyone. A picture of the body was shown with the comment that this was new and a sign of general abandonment. The second day the item was complemented by a short interview with a Catholic priest (a European) who had created a small cemetery where people who died in the streets and were not claimed by any relatives could be buried. The images made a deep impression—both the abandoned body and the humble cemetery in the city. People talked for days about it.

37. See Ruel 1969; see also Niger-Thomas 2000.

38. For these groups—the Bamileke must be understood as a conglomerate of smaller chiefdoms that only in colonial times were grouped together as "the" Bamileke—this related to a tradition that the eldest heir receives his father's skull; therefore, the longer one's line of skulls, the more privileged one is as belonging to the eldest line over several generations.

39. Antoine Socpa, oral communication. Cf. also the very interesting data of Sverker Finnström, a Stockholm/Uppsala anthropologist, on changing funeral rituals among Acholi migrants (from the north of Uganda) in Kampala, the country's capital. Since it was becoming too expensive to send the body of a deceased person home for the burial—at quite a distance from Kampala—people began to take home the pole that was used to close the grave in the city. However, suspicious bus drivers began to charge for such a pole as if a person were being transported, or they refused to take a pole that clearly symbolized a body. So people now try to hide these poles in their luggage. Finnström hopes to soon publish on this as part of an extremely interesting broader complex of changing funeral rituals developed since the time when Acholi young men began to serve for the British in the "King's African Rifles"; many thanks to him for allowing me to refer already to this here (see also Finnström 2008).

40. Elsewhere, especially among the Bamileke in the west and the Bamenda in the northwest, elites had already been building houses in the village for a longer time. Yet even there, the new need to prove one's belonging to the village inspired many elites to greater efforts in this direction.

41. A subgroup of the Maka and also the name of the canton where I did my main research.

42. Cf., in chapter 3, the cases where villagers told the elites not to meddle with their projects for starting a *forêt communautaire*. Expressions like "They have their salaries, so why do they come here to profit from our forest?" indicated that the villagers even seemed prepared to deny that the urban elites still belonged to the village.

43. A point made most eloquently by Romain Bertrand (2002:87) for Java when he discusses the apparent return of village autonomy after the fall of Suharto in 1998. There are striking parallels here with developments during the 1990s in Cameroon.

44. Cf. Roitman 2005 and chapter 1 above.

45. Recall also what was said above (chap. 3) about the Young Patriots in Ivory Coast, who, as champions of autochthony, return to the village to claim their part of the ancestral lands, squandered by their elders and appropriated by *allogènes*; however, as soon as they have it, they sell it—again to migrants—in order to be able to buy a ticket to Europe (see also Chauveau and Bobo 2003:16).

46. See, for instance, the special issue of *Afrika Spektrum*—"The Other Game: The Politics of Football in Africa"—that Susan Baller edited (2006).

Chapter Seven

1. See http://www.marechal-petain.com/etat%20_francais.htm. Many thanks to Jean-François Bayart for the references to this striking slogan. It comes from Pétain, but it evokes the ideas of Maurice Barrès, the prominent nineteenth-century French conservative quoted above, who used such slogans to distinguish the *vrais Français* from those who had more recently acquired citizenship (see chap. 5).

2. The Programme de Démystification was applied especially in the beginning of the 1960s but went on much longer.

3. Cf. for instance M. Cohen 1973 and 1973–744; see also Amondji 1984.

4. Chauveau 2000:105; Chauveau adds, however, that in 1966 Houphouët did not succeed in getting his proposal accepted for double nationality for immigrants, which he saw, according to Chauveau, as the "supreme phase of his model for economic and political control."

5. In this respect the example of Senegal is of special interest. Here the formation of the nation-state was strongly supported by Islamic brotherhoods. The rituals of the nation coincided to a large extent with those of the brotherhoods (cf. Villalon 1995). This may have created a setting in which nation-building was more broadly rooted in society and less one-sidedly imposed by the regime. Maybe as a consequence of this, the 1990s brought less of a rupture here. Despite an alteration of the party in power, the close alliance between regime and brotherhoods continued to be central in politics. Autochthony movements remained limited to

the country's periphery (especially to the Casamance, where historically Islamization was more partial). Here, as in Guinea, the regime was not forced to resort to supporting autochthony in order to remain in power (see further Cruise O'Brien and Diouf 2002 on nation-building in Senegal and the special role of the country's peripheral areas in this process).

6. Hazes's speciality was that he wrote nearly all of his songs (both text and music) in such a way that nobody else can sing them: whole parts of the text just do not seem to fit into the cadence of the music, except when he sang them himself.

7. Indeed, Hazes's funeral was reminiscent on a modest scale of several unexpected explosions of ritual activity with great emotional involvement in modern societies, like the "White March" in Belgium in 1996 and, of course the most spectacular of all, the global mourning for Lady Di in 1997.

8. In twentieth-century Dutch nationalism, however, the soil did constitute an important referent. Cf. the numerous songs about the national soil: "O dierbaar plekje grond waar eens mijn wieg op stond" (O dear piece of soil where my cradle stood) and "Waar de blanke top der duinen" (Where the white tops of the dunes...),which were still quite popular in the 1950s. However, for most Netherlanders it is hardly possible to quote these old songs without an ironic smile. Maybe this earlier overextension of the national soil as a referent—already then quite artificial next to the heavily emotional appeal of the pillars (Catholic, Protestant, and so on), which did not invoke the soil—is what makes it so difficult to give the new notion of autochthony any substance in the Netherlands.

9. Cf. the "quality" newspaper *NRC/Handelsblad* (July 31, 2007, 2) publishing an overview of young people from different backgrounds and their *thuisvoelen* (feeling at home) in the Netherlands, in which without further justification *autochtone jongeren* are contrasted with Moroccans, Turks, and Surinamese young men (though all the latter were also born in the Netherlands).

10. Cf. chapter 5 above on the difficulty of placing the integration policy inspired by the autochthony discourse in one of Gerd Baumann's "grammars of identity and alterity," precisely because it seems to imply a complete denial of the Other (Baumann 2004).

11. Mbembe (2000:38) sums up very well this extremely exclusionist tendency that can easily dominate in autochthony discourses: "Each and every identity must be translated into a territorial reference. There is no identity without territoriality" (my translation).

12. Appiah 2005:245, 258 (see also Appiah 2006); confer also Geertz's plea, quoted in chapter 5, for creating "a structure of difference within which cultural tensions that are not about to go away, or even moderate, can be placed and negotiated" (Geertz 2000:257).

Bibliography

Ali, Ayaan Hirsi. 2006. *Mijn Vrijheid: De Autobiografie*. Amsterdam: Augustus.

Amit, V. 2001. A Clash of Vulnerabilities: Citizenship, Labor, and Expatriacy in the Cayman Islands. American Ethnologist 28, no. 3: 574–95.

———., ed. 2002. Realizing Community: Concepts, Social Relationships, and Sentiments. London: Routledge.

Amondji, M. 1984. *Le PDCI et la vie politique en Côte d'Ivoire de 1944 à 1985*. Paris: L'Harmattan.

Appadurai, Arjun. 1996. *Modernity at Large: Cultural Dimensions of Globalization*. Minneapolis: Univ. of Minnesota Press.

———. 2006. *Fear of Small Numbers, An Essay on the Geography of Anger*. Durham, NC: Duke Univ. Press.

Appiah, Kwame Anthony. 2005. *The Ethics of Identity*. Princeton, NJ: Princeton Univ. Press.

———. 2006. *Cosmopolitanism: Ethics in a World of Strangers*. New York: W. W. Norton.

Apter, D. 1965. *The Politics of Modernization*. Chicago: Univ. of Chicago Press.

Ardener, Edwin. 1956. *Coastal Bantu of the Cameroon*. London: International African Institute (IAI).

———. 1958. Bakweri Fertility and Marriage. Paper presented at conference in Ibadan. Published in Edwin Ardener, *Kingdom on Mount Cameroon*, ed. Shirley Ardener, 227–43. Oxford: Berghahn, 1996.

———. 1962. *Divorce and Fertility: An African Study*. Oxford: Oxford Univ. Press.

Arnaut, Karel. 2004. Performing Displacements and Rephrasing Attachments: Ethnographic Explorations of Space, Mobility in Art, Ritual, Media, and Politics. PhD diss., Ghent Univ.

Aronson, D. 1971. Ijebu Yoruba Urban-Rural Relationships and Class Formation. *Canadian Journal of African Sudies* 5:263–79.

Austen, Ralph A. 1992. Tradition, Invention, and History: The Case of the Ngondo (Cameroon). *Cahiers d'Etudes Africaines* 32:285–309.

Austen, Ralph A., and Jonathan Derrick. 1999. *Middlemen of the Cameroon Rivers: The Duala and Their Hinterland, c. 1600–c. 1960*. Cambridge: Cambridge Univ. Press.

Auzel, Ph., and P. N. Nkwi. 2000. La foresterie communautaire dans le Sud du Cameroun: État du processus, acteurs impliqués et perspectives—Mission d'identification dans les Provinces de l'Est, du Sud et du Littoral. Report for Department for International Development (DFID), Yaoundé.

Bähre, E. 2002. Money and Violence: Financial Mutuals among the Xhosa in Cape Town, South Africa. PhD diss., Univ. of Amsterdam.

Baller, Susan, ed. 2006.The Other Game: The Politics of Football in Africa. Special issue, *Afrika-Spektrum* 3.

Bambach, Charles. 2003. *Heidegger's Roots: Nietsche, National Socialism, and the Greeks*. Ithaca, NY: Cornell Univ. Press.

Banégas, Richard. 2007. *Côte d'Ivoire: Les jeunes "se lèvent en hommes"—Anticolonialism et ultranationalisme chez les Jeunes Patriotes d'Abidjan*. Papers of the CERI (Centre d'Études et de Recherches Internationales) 37. Paris: Sciences Po.

Banégas, Richard, and Ruth Marshall. 2003. Côte d'Ivoire, un conflit regional? *Politique Africaine* 89:5–11.

Barrès, Maurice. 1925. *Scènes et doctrines du nationalisme*. Paris: Plon.

Basset, Thomas J. 2003. Dangerous Pursuits: Hunter Associations (*Donzo Ton*) and National Politics in Côte d'Ivoire. *Africa* 73, no. 1: 1–30.

Bauman, Gerd. 1999. *The Multicultural Riddle: Rethinking National, Ethnic, and Religious Identities*. London: Routledge.

———. 2004. Grammars of Identity/Alterity: A Structural Approach. In *Grammars of Identity/Alterity*, ed. Gerd Baumann and Andre Gingrich, 18–50. Oxford: Berghahn.

Bayart, Jean-François. 1979. *L'état au Cameroun*. Paris: Presses de la Fondation Nationale des Sciences Politiques.

———. 1996. *L'illusion identitaire*. Paris: Fayard. Translated as *The Illusion of Cultural Identity* (London: Hurst, 2005).

———. 2004. *Le gouvernement du monde*. Paris: Fayard. Translated as *Global Subjects: A Political Critique of Globalization* (London: Polity, 2007).

Bayart, Jean-François, Peter Geschiere, and Francis Nyamnjoh. 2001. "J'étais là avant": Problématiques de l'autochtonie. Special issue, *Critique Internationale* 10:126–95.

Bayart, Jean-François, Béatrice Hibou, and Stephen Ellis. 1997. *The Criminalization of the State in Africa*. Oxford: Currey.

Beer, Joop de, and Arno Sprangers. 1993. Het Effect van de Buitenlandse Migratie op de Omvang en Samenstelling van de Bevolking. In *Migratie, Bevolking en Politiek: Nederland als Immigeratieland in een Westeuropese Context*, ed. H. van Amersfoort, 11–27. Univ. of Amsterdam: Institute of Social Geography.

Benedict, Ruth. 1934/1953. *Patterns of Culture*. New York: Mentor.

Bertrand, Romain. 2002. *Indonésie, la démocratie invisible: Violence, magie et politique à Java*. Paris: Karthala.

Biesbrouck, Karin. 1999. Agriculture among Equatorial African Hunter-Gatherers and the Process of Sedentarization: The Case of the Bagyeli in Cameroon. In *Central African Hunter-Gatherers in a Multidisciplinary Perspective: Challenging Elusiveness*, ed. K. Biesbrouk, S. Elders, and G. Rossell, 186–206. Leiden: Centre for Non-Western Studies (CNWS).

Biya, Paul, 1986. *Pour le libéralisme communautaire*. Paris: Pierre-Marcel Favre.

Bloemraad, Irene. 2006. *Becoming a Citizen: Incorporating Immigrants and Refugees in the United States and Canada*. Berkeley: Univ. of California Press.

Boas, Morton. 2005. Citizenship, Land, and the Ivorian Crisis: A Crisis of Autochthony? Paper presented at the conference of the Norwegian Association for Development Research, Ås, June 19–21.

Boone, Catherine. 2003. *Political Topographies of the African State: Territorial Authority and Institutional Choice*. Cambridge: Cambridge Univ. Press.

Bovenkerk, Frank. 1989. Treurtonen. *De Volkskrant*, September 13.

———. 1990. Grote Garnalen. *De Volkskrant*, March 28.

———. 2002. Essay over de oorzaken van allochtonen misdaad. In *Nederland Multicultureel en Pluriform?* ed. J. Lucassen and A. de Ruyter, 209–47. Amsterdam: Aksant.

Bovenkerk, Frank, and Yucel Yesilgöz. 2004. Crime, Ethnicity, and the Multicultural Adjustment of Justice. In *Cultural Criminology Unleashed*, ed. Jeff Ferrel, Keith Haywards, Wayne Morrison, and Mike Presdee, 81–97. London: Glasshouse.

Braudel, F. 1949. *La Méditerranée et le monde méditerranéen à l'époque de Philippe II*. Paris: Colin.

———. 1986. *L'identité de la France*. Paris: Flammarion.

Brooks, G. 1993. *Landlords and Strangers: Ecology, Society, and Trade in Western Africa, 1000–1630*. Boulder: Westview.

Brubaker, Rogers, and Frederick Cooper. 2000. Beyond "Identity." *Theory and Society* 29:1–47.

Brunt, Lodewijk N. J. 1974. *Stedeling op het Platteland: Een Antropologisch Onderzoek naar de Verhoudingen tussen Autochtonen en Nieuwkomers in Stroomkerken*. Meppel, Netherlands: Boom.

Burnham, Philip. 1996. *The Politics of Cultural Difference in Northern Cameroon*. Edinburgh: IAI and Edinburgh Univ. Press.

———. 2000. Whose Forest? Whose Myth? Conceptualisations of Community Forests in Cameroon. In *Mythical Land, Legal Boundaries*, ed. A. Abrahamson and D. Theodossopoulos, 31–58. London: Pluto.

Burnham, Philip, and M. Graziani. 2004. Local Pluralism in the Rainforests of Southeastern Cameroon. In *Rural Resources and Local Livelihoods in Africa*, ed. Katherine Homewood, 177–97. Oxford: Currey.

Buruma, Ian. 2006. *The Death of Theo van Gogh and the Limits of Tolerance*. New York: Penguin.

Bury, R. G., ed. 1929/2005. Plato IX. Loeb Classical Library. Cambridge, MA: Harvard College.

Buur, Lars, and Helene M. Kyed, eds. 2007. *State Recognition and Democratization in Sub-Saharan Africa: A New Dawn for Traditional Authorities?* New York: Palgrave Macmillan.

Canon van Nederland. 2006. *Entoen.nu, Rapport van de Commissie Ontwikkeling Nederlandse Canon*. The Hague: Ministry of Education.

Ceuppens, Bambi. 2006. Allochthons, Colonizers, and Scroungers: Exclusionary Populism in Belgium. *African Studies Review* 49, no. 2:147–86.

Ceuppens, Bambi, and Peter Geschiere. 2005. Autochthony: Local or Global? New Modes in the Struggle over Citizenship and Belonging in Africa and Europe. *Annual Review of Anthropology* 34:385–409.

Chauveau, Jean-Pierre. 2000. Question foncière et construction nationale en Côte d'Ivoire. *Politique Africaine* 78:94–125.

———. 2005. Les rapports entre générations ont une histoire: Accès à la terre et gouvernementalité locale en Pays Ghan (Centre-Ouest de la Côte d'Ivoire). *Afrique Contemporaine* 214:1–17.

Chauveau, Jean-Pierre, and Koffi Samuel Bobo. 2003. La situation de guerre dans l'arène villageoise: Un exemple dans le Centre-Ouest ivoirien. *Politique Africaine* 89:34–48.

Chauveau, Jean-Pierre, and Jean-Pierre Dozon. 1985. Colonisation, économie de plantation et société civile en Côte d'Ivoire. *Cahiers ORSTOM* 21, no. 1:63–80.

Chauveau, Jean-Pierre, and Paul Richards. 2007. Rural Youth in Recent Wars: An Agrarian Perspective on Coastal West Africa. Paper presented at AEGIS (Africa-Europe Group for Interdisciplinary Studies) conference, Leiden, July 2007.

Chérif, Mustapha. 2006. *L'Islam et l'Occident: Rencontre avec Jacques Derrida.* Paris: Odile Jacob.

Clifford, James. 1988. *The Predicament of Culture*, Cambridge, MA: Harvard Univ. Press.

Cohen, D. W., and A. S. Atieno Odiambo. 1992. *Burying SM: The Politics of Knowledge and the Sociology of Power in Africa.* London: Currey/Heinemann.

Cohen, Michael A. 1973. The Myth of the Expanding Centre: Politics in the Ivory Coast. *Journal of Modern African Studies* 11, no. 2: 227–46.

———. 1973–74. Urban Policy and the Decline of the Machine: Cross-Ethnic Politics in the Ivory Coast. *Journal of Developing Areas* 8, no. 2: 227–33.

Cohen, William B. 1971. *Rulers of Empire: The French Colonial Service in Africa.* Stanford, CA: Hoover Institution Press.

Comaroff, Jean, and John Comaroff. 2000. Millennial Capitalism: First Thoughts on a Second Coming. In Millennial Capitalism and the Culture of Neoliberalism, special issue, *Public Culture* 12, no. 2: 291–344.

———. 2001. Naturing the Nation: Aliens, Apocalypse, and the Postcolonial State. *Journal of Southern African Studies* 27, no. 3: 627–51.

Contamin, Bernard, and Harris Memel-Fote, ed. 1997. *Le modèle ivoirien en question: Crises, ajustements, recompositions.* Paris: Karthala.

Cooper, Frederick. 2005. *Colonialism in Question.* Berkeley: Univ. of California Press.

Courade, Georges. 1982. Marginalité volontaire ou imposé? Le cas des Bakweri (Kpe) du mont Cameroun. *Cahiers ORSTOM, Sciences humaines* 19, no. 3: 357–89.

Crowder, M. 1964. Indirect Rule, French and British Style. *Africa* 33(4):293–306.

Cruise O'Brien, Donald, and Mamadou Diouf, eds. 2002. *La construction de l'etat au Sénégal.* Paris: Karthala.

CURDIPHE (Cellule Universitaire de Recherche et de Diffusion de Idées et Actions du Président Konan Bédié). 2000. L'Ivoireté, ou l'esprit du nouveau contrat social du Président H. K. Bédié, document. *Politique Africaine* 78:65–69.

Dagevos, J., M. Gijsberts, and C. van Praag. 2003. *Rapportage Minderheden 2003: Onderwijs, Arbeid en Sociaal-culturele Integratie.* The Hague: Sociaal Cultureel Planbureau.

Delafosse M. 1912/1972. *Haut-Sénégal-Niger.* Paris: Maisonneuve.

Dembélé, Ousmane. 2002. La construction économique et politique de la catégorie 'étranger' en Côte d'Ivoire. In *Côte d'Ivoire: L'année terrible, 1999–2000,* ed. Marc Le Pape and Claudine Vidal, 123–71. Paris: Karthala.

———. 2003. Côte d'Ivoire: La fracture communautaire. *Politique Africaine* 89:34–48.

Demery, L. 1994. Ivory Coast: Fettered Adjustment. In *Adjustment in Africa: Lessons from Country Case Studies,* ed. I. Husain and R. Faruqee, 73–115. Washington, DC: World Bank.

Derrida, Jacques. 1997. *The Politics of Friendship.* London: Verso.

Detienne, Marcel. 2003. *Comment être autochtone? Du pur Athénien au Français raciné.* Paris: Seuil.

Deutsch., Karl W., and William J. Foltz, ed. 1963. *Nation-Building.* New York: Atherton.

Dorman, Sara, D. Hammett, and Paul Nugent, eds. 2007. *Making Nations: Creating Strangers, States, and Citizenship in Africa.* Leiden: Brill.

Douglas, Mary. 1963. Techniques of Sorcery Control in Central Africa. In *Witchcraft and Sorcery in East Africa,* ed. John Middleton and E. H. Winter, 123–43. London: Routledge and Kegan Paul.

Dozon, Jean-Pierre. 1985. *La société bété: Histoires d'une "ethnie" de Côte d'Ivoire.* Paris: Karthala/ORSTOM.

———. 1995. Gbahié Koudou Jeannot: Le prophète annonciateur de la crise. *Cahiers d'Etudes Africaines* 138–39, XXXV 2–3: 305–31.

———. 1997. L'étranger et l'allochtone en Côte d'Ivoire. In *Le modèle ivoirien en question: Crises, ajustements, recompositions,* ed. B. Contamin and H. Memel-Fote, 779–98. Paris: Karthala.

———. 2000. La Côte d'Ivoire entre démocratie, nationalisme et ethnonationalisme. *Politique Africaine* 78:45–63.

———. 2001. Post-prophétism and Post-Houphouëtism in Ivory Coast. *Social Compass* 48, no. 3: 369–85.

Duyvendak, Jan Willem, and Menno Hurenkamp. 2004. Kiezen voor de Kudde. In *Kiezen voor de Kudde: Lichte Gemeenschappen en de Nieuwe Meerderheid,* ed. Duyvendak and Hurenkamp, 213–22. Amsterdam: van Gennip.

Duyvendak, Jan Willem, Trees Pels, and Rally Rijkschroeff. Forthcoming. A Multicultural Paradise? The Cultural Factor in Dutch Integration Policy. In *Immigrant Incorporation in the United States and Europe,* ed. J. Mollenkopf and J. Hochschild.

Eckert, Andreas. 1995. Cocoa Farming in Cameroon, c. 1914–c. 1960: Land and Labor. In *Cocoa Pioneer Fronts since 1800: The Role of Smallholders, Planters, and Merchants,* ed. William G. Clarence-Smith, 137–53. London: Basingstoke.

———. 1999. *Grundbesitz, Landkonflikte und kolonialer Wandel, Duala 1880 bis 1960.* Stuttgart: Steiner.

Ellemers, J. E. 2002. Pim Fortuyn: Een Zuiver Geval van Charismatisch Gezag. *Facta* 10, no. 7: 2–5.

Ellemers, J. E., and R. E. F.Vaillant. 1985. *Indische Nederlanders en Gerepatrieerden.* Muiderberg, Netherlands: Coutinho.

Englund, Harri. 2004. Introduction: Recognizing Identities, Imagining Alternatives. In *Rights and the Politics of Recognition in Africa*, ed. H. Englund and F. B. Nyamnjoh, 1–29. London: Zed.

Entzinger, H. B. 1975. Nederland Immigratieland? Enkele Overwgingen bij het Overheidsbeleid Inzake Allochtone Minderheden. *Beleid en Maatschappij* 2, no. 12: 326–36.

Ero, Comfort, and Anne Marshall. 2003. L'Ouest de la Côte d'Ivoire: Un conflict libérien? *Politique Africaine* 89:88–101.

Etty, Elsbeth. 2004. Katholieken Elastieken—Protestanten Olifanten. *De Gids* 167, no. 5/6: 373–77.

Euripides. 1995. *Selected Fragmentary Plays*, vol. 1. Trans. and ed. C. Collard, M. J. Cropp, and K. H. Lee. Warminster, UK: Aris and Philps.

———. 1999. *Euripides IV.* Trans. and ed. D. Kovacs. Loeb. Classical Library. Cambridge, MA: Harvard Univ. Press.

Evans, Martin. i.p. Primary Patriotism and Multiple Identities: Hometown Associations in Manyu Division, South West Cameroon. *Africa.*

Ferguson, James. 2006. *Global Shadows: Africa in the Neoliberal World Order.* Durham, NC: Duke Univ. Press.

Finnström, Sverker. 2008. *Living with Bad Surroundings: War, History, and Everyday Moments in Northern Uganda.* Durham, NC: Duke Univ. Press.

Fisiy, Cyprian. 1999. Discourses of Autochthony: Regimes of Citizenship and the Control of Assets in Côte d'Ivoire. Paper presented at African Studies Association meeting, Philadelphia, November 1999.

Fisiy, Cyprian, and Peter Geschiere. 1991. Judges and Witches, or How Is the State to Deal with Witchcraft? *Cahiers d'Études Africaines* 30, no. 2: 135–56.

Fortes, Meyer. 1975. Strangers. In *Studies in African Social Anthropology*, ed. M. Fortes and S. Patterson, 230–53. London: Academic.

Fortuyn, W. S. P. 2002. *De Puinhopen van Acht Jaar Paars.* Uithoorn, Netherlands: Karakter.

Foucault, Michel. 1984. *Histoire de la sexualité*, vol. 2, *L'usage des plaisirs.* Paris: Gallimard.

Fritsche, J. 1999. *Historical Destiny and National Socialism in Heidegger's "Being and Time."* Berkeley: Univ. of California Press.

Garbutt, Rob. 2006a. White "Autochthony." *Australian Critical Race and Whiteness Studies Journal* 1, no. 2: 1–16, available at http://www.acrawsa.org.au/journal/issues.htm.

Gbagbo, Laurent. 2002. *Sur les traces des Bété.* Abidjan, Côte d'Ivoire: Presses Universitaires de la Côte d'Ivoire (PUCI).

Geertz, Clifford. 2000. *Available Light: Anthropological Reflections on Philosophical Topics.* Princeton, NJ: Princeton Univ. Press.

Geschiere, Peter. 1982. *Village Communities and the State: Changing Relations of Authority among the Maka of Southeastern Cameroon*. London: Kegan Paul International.

———. 1993. Chiefs and Colonial Rule in Cameroon: Inventing Chieftaincy, French and British Style. *Africa* 63, no. 2: 151–76.

———. 1997. *The Modernity of Witchcraft: Politics and the Occult in Postcolonial Africa*. Charlottesville: Univ. of Virginia Press.

———. 2000. Money versus Kinship: Subversion or Consolidation? Contrasting Examples from Africa and the Pacific. *Pacific Journal of Anthropology* 1: 54–78.

———. 2004a. Ecology, Belonging, and Xenophobia: The 1994 Forest Law in Cameroon and the Issue of "Community." In *Rights and the Politics of Recognition in Africa*, ed. H. Englund and F. Nyamnjoh, 237–61. London: Zed.

———. 2004b. The Return of Culture: Anthropology's Temptations. In *Africa and Its Significant Others*, ed. I. Hoving, F.-W. Korsten, and E. van Alphen, 85–95. Amsterdam: Rodopi.

———. 2007. Lord Lugard in the Present: Indirect Rule and Present-day Struggles over Autochthony and Exclusion. IAI Lugard Lecture. AEGIS conference, Leiden, July.

———. i.p.a. The World Bank's Changing Discourse on Development. In *Readings in Modernity in Africa*, ed. P. Geschiere, B. Meyer, and P. Pels. Oxford: Currey/Bloomington: Univ. of Indiana Press.

———. i.p.b. Von Gravenreuth and Buea as a Site of History: Early Colonial Violence on Mount Cameroon. In *Encounter, Transformation, and Identity: Peoples of the Western Cameroon Borderlands, 1981–2000; Essays in Honour of Shirley Ardener*, ed. Ian Fowler. Oxford: Berghahn.

Geschiere, Peter, and J. Gugler, eds. 1998. The Politics of Primary Patriotism: The Urban-Rural Connection; Changing Issues of Belonging and Identification. Special issue, *Africa* 68, no. 3.

Geschiere, Peter, and Stephen Jackson. 2006. Autochthony and the Crisis of Citizenship: Democratization, Decentralization, and the Politics of Belonging. In Autochthony and the Crisis of Citizenship, ed. Peter Geschiere and Stephen Jackson, special issue, *African Studies Review* 49, no. 2: 1–7.

Geschiere, Peter, and Francis.Nyamnjoh. 1998. Witchcraft as an Issue in the "Politics of Belonging": Democratization and Urban Migrants' Involvement with the Home Village. *African Studies Review* 41, no. 3: 69–92.

———. 2000. Capitalism and Autochthony: The Seesaw of Mobility and Belonging. In Millennial Capitalism and the Culture of Neoliberalism, ed. Jean Comaroff and John Comaroff, special issue, *Public Culture* 12, no. 2: 423–53.

Geschiere, Peter, Francis Nyamnjoh, and Antoine Socpa. 2000. Autochthony versus Citizenship: Variable Effects of Political Liberalization in Cameroon. Report for Ministère des Affaires Étrangères, Paris.

Ghorashi, Halleh. 2006. Paradoxen van Culturele Erkenning: Management van Diversiteit in Nieuw Nederland. Inaugural lecture, Free Univ., Amsterdam.

Groenendijk, Kees. 2007. Allochtonen of Burgers: Definitiemacht in Debat en Wetgeving over Immigranten. In *Macht en Verantoowrdelijkheid, Essays voor*

Kees Schuyt, ed. J. W. Duyvendak, G. Engbersen, M. Teeuwen, and I.Verhoeven, 101–11. Amsterdam: Amsterdam Univ. Press.

Gruénais M. E. 1985. Du bon usage de l'autochtonie. *Cahiers ORSTOM: Série Sciences Humaines* 21, no. 1: 19–24.

Guadeloupe, Francio, and Vincent de Rooij, eds. 2007. *Zo Zijn Onze Manieren— Visies op Multiculturaliteit in Nederland.* Amsterdam: Rozenberg.

Guyer, Jane. 1985. *Family and Farm in Southern Cameroon.* Boston: African Studies Center, Boston Univ.

———. 1993. Wealth in People and Self-Realization in Equatorial Africa. *Man* n.s. 28, no. 2: 243–65.

Halbwachs, Maurice. 1950. *La mémoire collective.* Paris: PUF (Presses Universitaires de France).

Hart, Keith. 1973. Informal Income Opportunities and Urban Employment in Ghana. *Journal of Modern African Studies* 11, no. 1: 61–89.

Heidegger, M. 1934–35/1989. *Holderlins Hymnen "Germanien" und "Der Rhein."* Ed. Suzanne Ziegler. Frankfurt: Klosterman.

———. 1966. *Discourse on Thinking.* Trans. John M. Anderson and E. Hans Freund. New York: Harper.

Huyse, Luc. 1991. *Onverwerkt Verleden: Collaboratie en Rrepressie in België, 1942–1952.* Leuven, Belgium: Kritak.

Isin, Engin F., and B. S. Turner, eds. 2002. *Handbook on Citizenship Studies.* London: Sage.

Izard, M. 1985. *Gens du pouvoir, gens de la terre: Les institutions politiques de l'ancien royaume du Yatenga (Bassin de la Volta blanche).* Cambridge: Cambridge Univ. Press.

Jackson, Stephen. 2003. War-Making: Uncertainty, Improvisation, and Involution in the Kivu Provinces, DR Congo, 1997–2002. PhD diss., Princeton Univ.

———. 2006. Sons of Which Soil? The Language and Politics of Autochthony in Eastern D.R. Congo. In Autochthony and the Crisis of Citizenship, ed. Peter Geschiere and Stephen Jackson, special issue, *African Studies Review* 49, no. 2: 95–122.

Joseph, Richard. 1974. Ruben Um Nyobe and the "Kamerun" Rebellion. *African Affairs* 73, no. 293: 428–48.

———. 1977. *Radical Nationalism in Cameroun: Social Origins of the U.P.C. Rebellion.* Oxford: Oxford Univ. Press.

Jua, B. Nantang. 1997. Spatial Politics and Political Stability in Cameroon. Keynote address to "Cameroon, the Biography of a Nation" workshop Amherst College, November 20–23.

———. 2005a. The Mortuary Sphere: Privilege and the Politics of Belonging in Contemporary Cameroon. *Africa* 75, no. 3: 325–55.

———. 2005b. Of Citizenship, Public Spaces, and National Imagining in Cameroon. *African Anthropologist* 12, no. 1: 100–116.

Karsenty, A. 1999. Vers la fin de l'état forestier: Appropriation des espaces de la rente forestière au Cameroun. *Politique Africaine* 75:147–62.

Konate, Yacouba. 2003. Les enfants de la balle: De la FESCI aux mouvements de patriots. *Politique Africaine* 89:49–70.

Konings, Piet. 1993. *Labour Resistance in Cameroon: Managerial Strategies and Labour Resistance in the Agro-industrial Plantations of the Cameroon Development Corporation.* London: Currey/Heinemann.

————. 2001. Mobility and Exclusion: Conflicts between Autochthons and Allochthons during Political Liberalization in Cameroon. In *Mobile Africa: Changing Patterns of Movement in Africa and Beyond,* ed. Miriam de Bruijn, Rijk van Dijk, and Dick Foeken, 169–94. Leiden: Brill.

————. 2003. Religious Revival in the Roman Catholic Church and the Autochthony-Allochthony Conflict in Cameroon. *Africa* 73, no. 1: 31–56.

Konings, Piet, and Francis Nyamnjoh. 2003. *Negotiating an Anglophone Identity: A Study of the Politics of Recognition and Representation in Cameroon.* Leiden: Brill.

Kwayyeb, Enoch. 1967. Rapport entre parti-gouvernement et administration. In *Ier Conseil National de l'Union Nationale Camerounaise,* 107–37. Yaoundé: Imprimerie Nationale.

Kymlicka, Will. 2004. *Contemporary Political Philosophy, An Introduction.* Oxford: Oxford Univ. Press.

Laburthe-Tolra, Philippe. 1977. *Minlaaba: Histoire et société traditionnelle chez les Beti du Sud Cameroun.* Paris: Champion.

Landau, Loren. 2006. Transplants and Transients: Idioms of Belonging and Dislocation in Inner-City Johannesburg. In Autochthony and the Crisis of Citizenship, ed. Peter Geschiere and Stephen Jackson, special issue, *African Studies Review* 49, no. 2: 125–45.

Latour, Bruno. 2002. What Is Iconoclash? Or Is there a World beyond Image Wars? In *Iconoclash: Beyond the Image Wars in Science, Religion, and Art,* ed. Bruno Latour and Peter Weibel, 14–18. Cambridge, MA: MIT Press.

————. 2005. *Reassembling the Social: An Introduction to Actor-Network Theory.* Oxford: Oxford Univ. Press.

Leeman, Yvonne, and Trees Pels. 2006. Citizenship Education in the Dutch Multiethnic Context. *European Education* 38, no. 2: 64–75.

Lentz, Carola. 2003. "Premiers arrivés" et "nouveaux venus": Discours sur l'autochtonie dans la savane ouest-africaine. In *Histoire du peuplement et relations interethniques au Burkina Faso,* ed. R. Kuba, C. Lentz, and C. N. Somda, 113–34. New York: Greenwood.

————. 2006. *Ethnicity and the Making of History in Northern Ghana.* Edinburgh: Edinburgh Univ. Press for IAI.

Leonhardt, Alec. 1999. The Culture of Development in Bakaland: The Apparatus of Development in Relation to Baka Hunters-Gatherers. PhD diss., Princeton Univ.

————. 2006. Baka and the Magic of the State: Between Autochthony and Citizenship. In Autochthony and the Crisis of Citizenship, ed. Peter Geschiere and Stephen Jackson, special issue, *African Studies Review* 49, no. 2: 69–94.

Le Pape, Marc, and Claudine Vidal, eds. 2002. *Côte d'Ivoire: L'année terrible, 1999–2000.* Paris: Karthala.

Lévi-Strauss, Claude. 1958. *Anthropologie structurale.* Paris: Plon.

Li, Tania Murray. 2000. Articulating Indigenous Identity in Indonesia: Resource Politics and the Tribal Slot. *Comparative Studies in Society and History* 42:149–79.

———. 2002. Ethnic Cleansing, Recursive Knowledge, and the Dilemmas of Sedentarism. *International Social Science Journal* 173:361–71.

Lijphart, Arend. 1968. *Verzuiling, Pacificatie en Kentering in de Nederlandse Politiek.* Amsterdam: de Bussy (here quoted from 2nd ed., 1976).

———. 1985. *Power-Sharing in South-Africa.* Berkeley: Institute of International Studies.

———. 1986. *The Politics of Accommodation: Pluralism and Democracy in the Netherlands.* Berkeley: Univ. of California Press.

Lombard, J. 1967. *Autorités traditionnelles et pouvoirs européens en Afrique noire: Le déclin d'une aristocratie sous le régime colonial.* Paris: Colin.

Lonsdale, John. i.p. Soil, Work, Civilisation, and Citizenship in Kenya. *Journal of Eastern African Studies.*

Loraux, Nicole. 1996. *Né de la terre: Mythe et politique à Athènes.* Paris: Le Seuil.

Losch, Bruno. 2000. La Côte d'Ivoire en quête d'un nouveau projet national. *Politique Africaine* 78:5–25.

Lubbers, Ruud, and Carolina Lo Galbo. 2007. *De Vrees Voorbij: Een Hartenkreet.* Amsterdam: De Bezige Bij.

Lucassen, Jan, and Leo Lucassen. 1997. *Migration, Migration History, History: Old Paradigms and New Perspectives,* Bern: Lang.

Luning, S. 1997. Het Binnenhalen van de Oogst: Ritueel en Samenleving in Maane, Burkina Faso. PhD diss., Univ. of Leiden.

Malaquais, Dominique. 2001a. Anatomie d'une arnaque: Feymen et feymania au Cameroun. *Les Études du CERI* 77.

———. 2001b. Arts de feyre au Cameroun. *Politique Africaine* 82:101–18.

Malkki, Liisa H. 1995. *Purity and Exile: Violence, Memory, and National Cosmology among Hutui Refugees in Tanzania.* Chicago: Univ. of Chicago Press.

Mandeng, Patrice. 1973. *Auswirkungen der deutschen Kolonialherrschaft in Kamerun.* Hamburg: H. Buske.

Mann, Gregory, and Jane I. Guyer. 999. Imposing a Guide on the *Indigène*: The Fifty Year Experience with *Sociétés de Prévoyance* in French West and Equatorial Africa. In *Credit, Currencies, and Culture: African Financial Institutions in Historical Perspective,* ed. E. Stiansen and J. I. Guyer, 118–45. Uppsala: Nordiska Afrika Institutet.

Maquet, Jacques. 1961. *The Premise of Inequality in Ruanda: A Study of Political Relations in a Central African Kingdom.* Oxford: Oxford Univ. Press.

Marshall, Ruth. 2006. The War of "Who Is Who?": Autochthony, Nationalism, and Citizenship in the Ivorian Crisis. In Autochthony and the Crisis of Citizenship, ed. Peter Geschiere and Stephen Jackson, special issue, *African Studies Review* 49, no. 2: 9–43.

Mathieu, Paul, and A. Mafikiri Tsongo. 1998. Guerres paysannes au Nord-Kivu (RDC), 1937–1994. *Cahiers d'Études Africaines* 150–52, XXXVIII, nos. 2–4: 385–416.

Mattes, Robert. 1999. Hypotheses on Identity and Democracy: Community, Regime, Institutions, and Citizenship. In *Identity? Theory, Politics, and History,* vol. 1, ed. S. Bekker and R. C. Prinsloo. Pretoria: Human Science Research Council.

Matute, D. L. 1988. *The Social-Cultural Legacies of the Bakweri*. Lagos, Nigeria: Salvation Army School.

Mbembe, Achille. 1992. Provisional Notes on the Postcolony. *Africa* 62, no. 1: 3–38.

———. 1996. *La naissance du maquis dans le Sud-Cameroun, 1920–1960*. Paris: Karthala.

———. 2000. A propos des écritures africaines de soi. *Politique Africaine* 77:16–43.

———. 2001. *On the Post-colony*. Berkeley: Univ. of California Press.

———. 2002. Les nouveaux Africains: Entre nativisme et cosmopolitanisme. *Esprit* 10:1–10.

McGovern, M. 2004. Umasking the State: Developing Modern Political Subjectivities in 20th Century Guinea. PhD diss., Emory Univ.

———. 2005. When Do People Kill over Autochthony? The State, Violence, and the Politics of Resentment in Côte d'Ivoire. Paper presented at Social Science Research Council conference on Autochthony and Citizenship, Gorée, April.

Mebenga, Luc T. 1991. Les funérailles chez les Ewondo: Changements socio-culturels, changements économiques et évaluation de l'esprit de solidarité. Thesis (3rd cycle), Univ. of Yaoundé I.

Meyer, Birgit. 1999. *Translating the Devil: Religion and Modernity among the Ewe in Ghana*. Edinburgh: Edinburgh Univ. Press for IAI.

———. 2006. Modern Mass Media, Religion, and the Dynamics of Distraction and Concentration. Lecture, Amsterdam, June.

———. 2008. Religious Sensations: Why Media, Aesthetics, and Power Matter in the Study of Contemporary Religion. In *Religion: Beyond a Concept*, ed. H. de Vries, 704–23. New York: Fordham Univ. Press.

Meyer, Birgit, and Peter Geschiere, eds. 1999. *Globalization and Identity: Dialectic of Flow and Closure*. Oxford: Blackwell.

Meyer, Birgit, and Jojada Verrips. i.p. Aesthetics. In *Key Words in Religion, Media, and Culture*, ed. David Morgan. London: Routledge.

Miller, Joseph. 1988. *"Way of Death": Merchant Capitalism and the Angolan Slave Trade, 1730–1893*. Madison: Univ. of Wisconsin Press.

Milol, C. A., and J.-M. Pierre. 2000. Impact de la fiscalité décentralisée sur le développement local et les pratiques d'utilisation des ressources forestières au Cameroun: Volet additionnel de l'audit économique et financier du secteur forestier. Manuscript, Yaoundé.

Minderhedennota. 1982–83. Den Haag: Tweede Kamer der Staten-Generaal, 16102, no. 20–21.

Mohan, G., and S. Hickey. 2004. Relocating Participation within a Radical Politics of Development: Critical Modernism and Citizenship. In *Participation: From Tyranny to Transformation*, ed. S. Hickey and G. Mohan, 59–74. London: Zed.

Moise, Robert. 2003. Loved Ones and Strangers: Society, History, and Identity in Equatorial Africa. PhD diss., New York Univ.

Molua, H. 1985. The Bakweri Land Problem, 1884–1961. MA thesis, Univ. of Ibadan.

Monga, Célestin. 1995. Cercueils, orgies et sublimation: Le coût d'une mauvaise gestion de la mort. *Afrique 2000* 21:63–72.

Mono Djana, H. 1997. Anti-Plaidoyer pour les ethnies. In *La démocratie à l'épreuve du tribalisme*, ed. F. Eboussi Boulaga. Yaoundé, Cameroon: Friedrich-Ebert Stiftung.

Mouiche, Ibrahim. 2005. *Autorités traditionnelles et démocratisation au Cameroun: Entre centralité de l'etat et logiques de terroir*. Munster, Germany: Lit Verlag.

Ndjio, Basile. 2006. "Feymania": New Wealth, Magic Money, and Power in Contemporary Cameroon. PhD diss., Univ. of Amsterdam.

Ngayap, Pierre Flambeau. 1983. *Cameroun: Qui gouverne?* Paris: L'Harmattan.

Nguiffo, S.-A., and R. Djeukam. 2000. Le droit contre la foresterie communautaire? Analyse des contraintes jurididque à la mise en oeuvre de la foresterie communautaire au Cameroun. Paper, SNV (Stichting Nederlandse Vrijwilligers/ Netherlands Development Organisation) and WWF (World Wildlife Fund), Yaoundé.

Nicolson, I. F. 1969. *The Administration of Nigeria, 1900–60: Men, Methods, and Myths*. Oxford: Clarendon.

Niger-Thomas, Margaret. 2000. "Buying Futures": The Upsurge of Female Entrepreneurship; Crossing the Formal and Informal Divide in Southwest Cameroon. PhD diss., Leiden Univ.

Noiriel, Gérard. 2007. *A quoi sert l'identité nationale?* Paris: Agone.

Nora, Pierre, 1989. Between Memory and History: "Les lieux de mémoire." *Representations* 26:7–24.

———. ed. 1992. *Les Lieux de Mémoire*. Paris: Gallimard.

Novick, Peter. 1999. *The Holocaust in American Life*. Boston: Houghton Miflin.

Nyamnjoh, Francis. 1999. Cameroon, a Country United by Ethnic Ambition and Difference. *African Affairs* 98, no. 390: 101–18.

———. 2006. *Insiders and Outsiders, Citizenship and Xenophobia in Contemporary Southern Africa*. London: Zed/Dakar: Codesria.

Nyamnjoh, Francis, and Michael Rowlands. 1998. Elite Associations and the Politics of Belonging in Cameroon. *Africa* 68, no. 3: 320–37.

Obarrio, Juan. 2007. The Spirit of the Law in Mozambique. PhD diss., Columbia Univ.

Ong, Aihwa. 2006. *Neoliberalism as Exception: Mutations in Citizenship and Sovereignty*. Durham. NC: Duke Univ. Press.

Oyono, Ferdinand. 1956. *Une vie de boy*. Paris: Julliard.

Oyono, R. 2002. Infrastructure organisationelle et dynamiques de la gestion décentralisée des forêts au Cameroun: Éléments d'anthropologie écologique et leçons intermédiaires. Working paper, World Resources Institute (WRI), Washington, DC.

Pandey, Gyanendra. 1990. *The Construction of Communalism in Colonial North India*. Delhi: Oxford Univ. Press.

———. 2001. *Remembering Partition: Violence, Nationalism, and History in India*. Cambridge: Cambridge Univ. Press.

———. 2006. *Routine Violence: Nations, Fragments, Histories*. Stanford, CA: Stanford Univ. Press.

Pandey, Gyanendra, and Peter Geschiere. 2003. The Forging of Nationhood: The Contest over Citizenship, Ethnicity, and History. In *The Forging of Nationhood*, ed. Gyanendra Pandey and Peter Geschiere, 7–27. Delhi: Manohar.

Pelican, Michaela. 2007. Mbororo Claims to Regional Citizenship and Minority Status (North-West Cameroon). Paper presented at AEGIS conference, Leiden, July.

Pels, Dick. 2002. Fortuyn en het Fascisme. *Facta* 10, no. 7: 6–9.

———. 2003. *De Geest van Pim*. Amsterdam: Anthos.

Penninx, Rinus. 2006. Après les assassinats de Fortuyn et de van Gogh: le modèle d'intégration hollandais en déroute? *Critique Internationale* 33:9–27.

Pes, Daniela. n.d. Recours à l' invisible: Personne et pouvoir chez les Baka du Cameroun. Manuscript, Univ. of Torino.

Pillay, Udesh, Benjamin Roberts, and Stephen Rule, eds. 2006. *South African Social Attitudes: Changing Times, Diverse Voices*. Pretoria: Human Science Research Council.

Pleij, Herman. 2004. *De Herontdekking van Nederland, Over Vaderlandse Mentaliteiten en Rituelen*. Amsterdam: Prometheus.

Prins, Baukje. 2007–8. Bruggenbouwer of Onheilsprofeet? Het "Wij"van Paul Scheffer. *Contrast* 14–15 (December 2007–January 2008): 46–48.

Putnam, Patrick T. L. 1948. The Pygmies of the Ituri Forest. In *A Reader in General Anthropology*, ed. Carleton Coon, 322–41. New York: Henry Holt.

Ramdas, Anil. 2000. Een Multicultureel Feest. *NRC/Handelsblad*, February 7, http://www.nrc.nl/W2/Lab/Multicultureel/ramdas.html.

Rath, Jan. 1991. *Minorisering: De Sociale Constructie van "Etnische Minderheden,"* Amsterdam: SUA.

Robertson, R. 1992. *Globalization: Social Theory and Global Culture*. London: Sage.

Roitman, Janet. 2005. *Fiscal Disobedience, An Anthropology of Economic Regulation in Central Africa*. Princeton, NJ: Princeton Univ. Press.

Rosivach, Vincent. J. 1987. Autochthony and the Athenians. *Classical Quarterly* new ser. 37, no. 2: 294–306.

Rudin, H. R. 1938. *Germans in the Cameroons, 1884–1914*. New Haven, CT: Yale Univ. Press.

Ruell, Malcolm. 1969. *Leopards and Leaders*. London: Tavistock.

Ruf, François. 1988. *Stratification sociale et économie de plantation ivoirienne*. Paris: Université de Paris X.

Rüger, A. 1960. Die Entstehung und Lage der Arbeiterklasse unter dem deutschen Kolonialregime in Kamerun, 1895–1905. In *Kamerun under deutscher Kolonialherrschaft*, ed. H. Stoecker, 1:149–242. Berlin: Deutscher Verlag der Wissenschaften.

Sahlins, Peter. 2004. *Unnatural Frenchmen*. Ithaca, NY: Cornell Univ. Press.

Sassen, Saskia. 2002. Towards Post-national and Denationalized Citizenship. In *Handbook on Citizenship Studies*, ed. E. F. Isin and B. S. Turner, 277–91. London: Sage.

Saul, J. S. 1974. The State in Post-colonial Societies: Tanzania. *Socialist Register* 1974 (ed. R. Milliband and J. Saville), 349–72.

Scheffer, Paul, 2000a. Het Multiculturele Drama. *NRC/Handelsblad*, January 29, http://www.nrc.nl/W2/Lab/Multicultureel/scheffer.html.

———. 2000b. Het Multiculturele Drama: Een Repliek. *NRC/Handelsblad*, March 25, http://www.nrc.nl/W2/Lab/Multicultureel/000325a.html.

———. 2006. *Terug naar de Tuinstad, Binnen en Buiten de Ringweg van Amsterdam*. Inaugural lecture, Univ. of Amsterdam (Vossiuspers).

———. 2007. *Het Land van Aankomst*. Amsterdam: De Bezige Bij.

Schuster, John. 1999. Poortwachters over Immigranten, het Debat over Immigratie in het Naoorlogse Groot-Brittannië en Nederland. PhD diss., Univ. of Utrecht.

Shack, William A., and Elliott P. Skinner, eds. 1979. *Strangers in African Societies*. Berkeley: Univ. of California Press.

Shadid, Wasif. 1998. *Grondslagen van Interculturele Communicatie: Studieveld en Werkterrein*. Houten, Netherlands: Bohn, Stafleu, van Loghum.

———. 2006. Guest Editor's Introduction: Public Debates over Islam and the Awareness of Muslim Identity in the Netherlands. *European Education* 38, no. 2: 4–22.

Shadid, Wasif, and P. S. van Koningsveld. 1992. *De Mythe van het Islamitische Gevaar: Hindernissen bij Integratie*. Kampen: Kok.

———, eds. 2002. *Religious Freedom and the Neutrality of the State: The Position of the Islam in the European Union*. Leuven, Belgium: Peeters.

Shami, Seteney. 1999. Circassian Encounters: The Self as Other and the Production of the Homeland in the North Caucasus. In *Globalization and Identity: Dialectic of Flow and Closure*, ed. Birgit Meyer and Peter Geschiere, 17–47. Oxford: Blackwell.

Simone, AbdelMaliq. 2001. On the Worlding of African Cities. *African Studies Review* 44, no. 20: 15–43.

Siret, M. 1946–49. *Monographie de la région du Haut-Nyong*. Yaoundé, Cameroon: Archives IRCAM (Institutes des Recherches Camerounaises).

Smith, Daniel Jordan. 2004. Burials and Belonging in Nigeria: Rural-Urban Relations and Social Inequality in a Contemporary African Ritual. *American Anthropologist* 106, no. 3: 569–79.

Sniderman, Paul M., and Louk Hagendoorn. 2007. *When Ways of Life Collide*. Princeton, NJ: Princeton Univ. Press.

Socpa, Antoine. 2002. *Démocratisation et autochtonie au Cameroun: Variations régionales divergentes*. Munster, Germany: Lit Verlag.

———. 2006. Bailleurs autochtones et locataires allogènes: Enjeu foncier et participation politique au Cameroun. In Autochthony and the Crisis of Citizenship, ed. Peter Geschiere and Stephen Jackson, special issue, *African Studies Review* 49, no. 2: 45–67.

Suret-Canale, J. 1964. *Afrique noire occidentale et centrale II: L'ère coloniale, 1900–1945*. Paris: Éditions Sociales.

Tabappsi, Timothée. 2007. La riposte des exclus: Les migrants africains sans-papiers d'Europe face aux tentatives d'endiguement des flux migratoires extracommunautaires. Manuscript, Niamey.

Takougang, J., and M. Krieger. 1998. *African State and Society in the 1990s: Cameroon's Political Crossroads*. Boulder: Westview.

Tatah Mentan, E. 1996. Constitutionalism, Press, and Factional Politics: Coverage of SAWA Minority Agitatons in Cameroon. In *La réforme consitutionnelle du 18 janvier 1996 au Cameroun: Aspects juridiques et politiques*, ed. S. Melone, A. Minkoa She, and L. Sindjoun, 182–93. Yaoundé, Cameroon: Friedrich-Ebert Stiftung.

Taussig, Michael. 1993. *Mimesis and Alterity: A Particular History of the Senses.* London: Routledge.

Taylor, Charles. 1994a. *Multiculturalism: Examining the Politics of Recognition.* Ed. A. Gutman. Princeton, NJ: Princeton Univ. Press.

———. 1994b. The Politics of Recognition. In Taylor, *Multiculturalism: Examining the Politics of Recognition*, ed. A. Gutman, 25–73. Princeton, NJ: Princeton Univ. Press.

Triaud, J. L. 1998. "Haut-Sénégal-Niger," un modèle positiviste? De la coutume à l'histoire: Maurice Delafosse et l'invention de l'histoire africaine. In *Maurice Delafosse: Entre orientalisme et ethnographie; Itinéraire d'un africaniste (1870–1926)*, ed. J.-L. Amselle and E. Sibeud, 210–33. Paris: Maisonneuve.

Tsing, Anna. 2007. Indigenous Voice. In *Indigenous Experience Today*, ed. Marisol de la Cadena and Orin Starn, 35–68. Oxford: Berg.

Turnbull, Colin. 1961. *The Forest People.* New York: Simon and Schuster.

Van Amersfoort, Hans, ed. 1993. *Migratie, Bevolking en Politiek: Nederland als Immigratieland in een Westeuropese Context.* Amsterdam: Univ. of Amsterdam, Institute for Social Geography.

Van den Berg, J., and K. Biesbrouck. 2000. *The Social Dimension of Rainforest Management in Cameroon: Issues for Co-management.* Wageningen, Netherlands: Tropenbos-Cameroon Programme.

Van den Brink, Gabriël. 2006. *Culturele Contrasten, Het Verhaal van de Migranten in Rotterdam.* Amsterdam: Bert Bakker.

Van de Port, Mattijs. 2004. Registers of Incontestability: The Quest for Authenticity in Academia and Beyond. *Etnofoor* 17, nos. 1/2: 7–23.

———. 2005. Circling around the *Really Real*: Spirit Possesion Ceremonies and the Search for Authenticity in Bahian Candomblé. *Ethos* 33, no. 2: 149–79.

———. 2006. Visualizing the Sacred: Video Technology, "Televisual" Style, and the Religious Imagination in Bahian Candomblé. *American Ethnologist* 33, no. 3: 444–61.

Van der Veer, Peter. 2006. Pim Fortuyn, Theo van Gogh, and the Politics of Tolerance in the Netherlands. *Public Culture* 18, no. 1: 111–24.

Van Donselaar, Jaap, and Peter Rodriquez. 2006. *Monitor racisme en extreemrechts.* Amsterdam: Anne Frank Stichting.

Van Praag, C. S. 1971. Het Overheidsbeleid Inzake Allochtone Groepen. In *Allochtonen in Nederland*, ed. Hilda Verwey-Jonker, 19–45. The Hague: Ministry of Culture.

Vasta, Ellie. 2006. From Ethnic Minorities to Ethnic Majority Policy: Changing Identities and the Shift to Assimilationism in the Netherlands. Working Paper 26, Centre on Migration, Policy and Society, Oxford Univ.

Verkaaik, Oskar. Forthcoming. Painless Conversion: The Curious Absence of the "Decisive Act" in Dutch Naturalization Ceremonies.

Verrips, Jojada. 2006. Aisthesis and An-easthesia. *Ethnologia Europea* 35, nos. 1/2: 27–33.

Verwey-Jonker, Hilda, ed. 1971. *Allochtonen in Nederland.* The Hague: Ministry of Culture, Recreation and Social Work.

Vidal, Claudine. 2002. Du conflit politique aux menaces entre voisins: Deux témoignages abidjanais. In *Côte d' Ivoire: L' année terrible, 1999–2000*, ed. Marc Le Pape and Claudine Vidal, 215–51. Paris: Karthala.

Villalon, Leonardo. 1995. *Islamic Society and State Power in Senegal: Disciples and Citizens in Fatick*. Cambridge: Cambridge Univ. Press.

Von Oppen, Achim. 2003. *Bounding Villages: The Enclosure of Locality in Central Africa, 1890s to 1990s*. Habilitation treatise, Humboldt Univ., Berlin.

Vuijsje, Herman, and Jos van der Lans. 1999. *Typisch Nederlands, Vademecum van de Nederlandse Identiteit*. Amsterdam: Contact.

Warnier, Jean-Pierre. 1993. *L'esprit d'entreprise au Cameroun*. Paris: Karthala.

White, Bob W. i.p. *Rumba Rules: The Politics of Popular Dance Music in Mobutu's Zaire*. Durham, NC: Duke Univ. Press.

Wienia, M. 2003. *The Stranger Owns the Land, but the Land Is for Us: The Politics of Religious Landscape in Nanun, N. Ghana*. Leiden: Instituut voor Sociaal-Culturele Studies.

Willame, Jean-Claude. 1997. *Banyarwanda et Banyamulenge: Violences ethniques et gestion de l'identitaire au Kivu*. Brussels: CEDAF (Centre d'Étude de Documentation Africaines).

WRR (Wetenschappelijk Raad voor het Regeringsbeleid). 1979. *Etnische Minderheden* (Rapport aan de Regering). The Hague: Staatsuitgeverij.

———. 1989. *Allochtonenbeleid* (Rapport aan de Regering). The Hague: SDU.

———. 2007. *Identificatie met Nederland*. Amsterdam: Amsterdam Univ. Press.

Yenshu, E. 1999. The Discourse and Politics of Indigenous/Minority Peoples Rights in Some Metropolitan Areas of Cameroon. *Journal of Applied Sciences* 1, no. 1: 59–76.

Yéré, Henri-Michel. 2006. "La Côte d'Ivoire, c'est la Côte d'Ivoire!" A Reflection on the Idea of the Nation in Côte d'Ivoire. Manuscript, Basel.

Zahan, D. 1961. Pour une histoire des Mossi du Yatenga. *L'Homme* 1, no. 2: 5–22.

Zognong, D. 1997. La question bamiléké pendant l'ouverture démocratique au Cameroun. In *Démocratisation et rivalités ethniques au Cameroun*, ed. D. Zougnon and I. Mouiche, 123–55. Yaoundé, Cameroon: CIRIPE.

Zognong, D., and I. Mouiche. 1997. Introduction to *Démocratisation et rivalités ethniques au Cameroun*, ed. Zognong and Mouiche. Yaoundé, Cameroon: CIRIPE.

Zolberg, Aristide. 2006. *A Nation by Design: Immigration Policy in the Fashioning of America*. Cambridge, MA: Harvard Univ. Press.

Index